Dolly

published by

REED BOOKS
Los Angeles

This Hardback original is published by Reed Books, a division of Addison House Inc. Publishing Office: Reed Books, 9155 West Sunset Boulevard, Los Angeles, California 90069. Marketing and Sales Office: c/o Addison House, Morgan's Run, Danbury, New Hampshire 03230.

First edition: September 1978
Designed by Bernard Schleifer
ISBN 0-89169-523-0
Library of Congress Number: 78-53981

Manufactured in the United States of America

The author gratefully acknowledges permission to quote material from the following sources:

For lyrics and the following songs: "In the Good Old Days," copyright © 1968; "Coat of Many Colors," copyright © 1969; "Down From Dover," copyright © 1969; "My Blue Ridge Mountain Boy," copyright © 1969; "He's A Go-Getter," copyright © 1969; "Touch Your Woman," copyright © 1971; "Daddy Was An Old-Time Preacher Man," copyright © 1970; "Down On Music Row," copyright © 1972; "The Greatest Days of All," copyright © 1972; "My Tennessee Mountain Home," copyright © 1972; "Jolene," copyright © 1973; "Love Is Like A Butterfly," copyright © 1974; "Sixteen Years," copyright © 1974; "Two," copyright © 1974; "You Are," copyright © 1975; "The Bargain Store," copyright © 1975; "The Seeker," copyright © 1975; "He Would Know," copyright © 1975; All copyright by Owepar Publishing Co. International copyright secured. All rights reserved. Used by permission.

For lyrics and the following songs: "Light of a Clear Blue Morning," copyright © 1977; "Two Doors Down," copyright © 1977; "Where Beauty Lives in Memory," copyright © 1977; "I Wanna Fall in Love," copyright © 1978; All copyright by Velvet Apple Music. International copyright secured. All rights reserved. Used by permission.

"Something Fishy," copyright Combine Music Corp., 1966. International Copyright Secured. All rights reserved.

"It's Sure Gonna Hurt," copyright 1962; "Dumb Blonde," copyright 1966; by Tree Publishing Company, Inc., International Copyright Secured. All rights reserved. Used by permission.

"Puppy Love," copyright TEK Publishing. All rights reserved. Used by permission. "Girl Left Alone," copyright Fort Knox Music and TEK Publishing. All rights reserved. Used by permission.

"Holding On to Nothin'," copyright by Passkey Music Inc. © 1968

Quoted material from "Dolly Parton is Such Sweet Sorrow," April 23, 1976; copyright The Village Voice Inc., 1976; reprinted by permission of The Village Voice.

For my parents,
the other pride of Tennessee.

Acknowledgments

TO EVERYONE WHO GAVE so unselfishly of his memories and his time for this project, I am deeply grateful, especially to the following:

In Sevierville and Knoxville: Bud Brewster, Bobby Denton, Ruth Green, Harold E. Harlow and the Knoxville News-Sentinel, Ruby Hatcher Maples, Archie Ray McMahan, Jack McMahan, the Reverend Jake Owens, T.A. Robertson, Bob and Barbara Taggart, Cas Walker and Estelle Watson.

In Nashville: Lucy Adams, Bob Allen, Charlene Bray, Mrs. Henry Cannon (Minnie Pearl), Joan Dew, Mary Fielder, Jerry Flowers and the publicity staff of RCA, Fred Foster, Judy Hunt, Buddy Killen, Bill Littleton, Joan McGriff, Stella Parton, Richard A. Peterson, Don Roth, Tom Rutledge and LaWayne Satterfield.

In New York: Dave Hershey, Martha Hume, and Mark Liff.

A very special thanks to the journalists who shared transcripts of their interviews with me: Bob Allen, Barry Bernson, Mark Liff, John Morthland, and LaWayne Satterfield.

Love and Kisses to the following who helped way beyond the call of friendship, and without whom this book might not have been possible: Tom and Dorothy Barrett, Tom Casassa, Jim Chapman, Nancy Dunne, Steve Estes, Dan Fleming, Joe Glass, Steve Greil, Betty Harrington, Karen Johnson, Gene King and King's Record Shop, Betsy Kronish, Brenda Lee, Carolyn Lee, Mr. and Mrs. Allan Nash, Stella Parton, Don Roth, LaWayne Satterfield, Clarence Selman, Ronnie Shacklett, and Elizabeth Thiels. Thanks also to everyone who volunteered information off the record.

Finally, the Patience and Understanding Award goes to my publishers, Don Ackland and Russell Barnard, and to my editor, Gypsy DaSilva and designer/production man, Bernard Schleifer.

Most of all, thanks to Martha Hume, for suggesting the idea years ago, to Michael Bane for suggesting me, and to Dolly, for being herself.

Contents

Dolly

Hello, Dolly!

"LOVE IS LIKE A BUTTERFLY," Dolly Parton has written in one of her most popular songs. In many ways, the lady herself is like a butterfly, something she recognized innately years ago as a towheaded child playing in the fields near her East Tennessee home, when nature provided the only things bright and pretty she could afford. With the imagination that would in time earn her worldwide recognition and acclaim, little Dolly saw the colorful creatures as "fancy dressed-up girls going to a party." If the Partons' economic state held little promise that Dolly would grow up with parties and fancy clothes, Dolly knew somehow that all the riches and finery in life would come to her, just as soon as people saw her unique and original talent.

"Butterflies are colorful and bright and gentle and have no way to harm you," Dolly has often said. "They go about their business and bring others pleasure while doing it, because just seeing one flying around makes people happy. I'd like to think of myself as bringing people happiness while I do my business, which is my music. I'm content with what I am, and butterflies seem to be content to be just what they are, too. They're gentle, but determined."

Perhaps only those who failed to realize just *how* determined Dolly Parton is doubted that she would be able to enjoy a successful solo career after leaving the Porter Wagoner show in 1974. Or maybe even then it was a mixture of jealousy, the desire to pigeonhole and the inability to perceive the whole of Dolly's talents—certainly the main factors behind Nashville's early resentment of Dolly's crossover plans—that caused so many in Music City to say it was only a matter of time before Dolly fell on her face.

The criticism has mostly subsided now (oddly enough, with the rapid acceleration of Dolly's career), but through it all, Dolly rarely has lost patience with her critics, explaining over and over that she wasn't leaving country but merely taking it with her wherever she went, ending with, "There's nothing I can say right now. It's at a critical time in my career. People are just waiting to see what it is I'm doing. But they'll see. They'll know."

As Dolly nears superstar status, surely even the Nashville diehards are beginning to understand what Dolly was talking about all along. She is still one of America's most popular country entertainers, but she is also on the verge of establishing herself with the pop audience, as well, as evidenced by the platinum success of her *Here You Come Again* album and the double-sided hit, "Two Doors Down"/"It's All Wrong, But It's All Right," which dominated both the pop and country charts; the latter song held the number one position in country for several weeks.

More important is that Dolly is well on her way to becoming a fixture of American culture, a woman whose name evokes much more than country music, or *any* music, for that matter, a woman whose name is starting to be a household word. Johnny Carson fell head over heels in love with her the first time she appeared on *The Tonight Show* in January of 1977 and has many a night since mentioned her in his monologue. Barbara Walters found her no less intriguing, and when she interviewed Dolly for one of her TV specials, it seemed that Barbara had met her match and that it was Dolly who controlled the interview. Suddenly Dolly was a national star, with a look-alike doll on the market, pictures and interviews in publications from *Rolling Stone* to *Time* and *Vogue* and *Playboy*, and female impersonators adding her to their acts. More than that, though, people who had seen so many entertainers come and go that almost nothing would impress them sensed that Dolly Parton was indeed something special.

In short, there is a national fascination with her, one built on something more complex than the silky mane and the sensuous smile of Farrah Fawcett-Majors, or the fresh-faced girl-next-door quality of Cheryl Tiegs. It's not just her X-rated figure that has captivated everybody, nor her outrageous costumes and hairstyles, nor the funny things she says that combine to make her a Character. Nor is it only her mesmerizing voice, her inimitable vocal style and the power of the lyrics she pens, because it's a safe bet to say that half of her fans couldn't name one of her songs or even know that she writes. Probably it's a combination of it all, topped off by the fact that Dolly comes across as being for real, the genuine article, despite the deliberate and obvious falseness of much of her exterior. Her ambivalences and contradictions seem somehow natural, normal, and almost totally uncontrived. She's a sex symbol who didn't set out to be one (and who exudes vibrations that she finds sex a great source of amusement), a person made up of many childlike qualities (a child's innocence, vulnerability and curiosity, a child's sense of loyalty and devotion, not to mention a childlike name, voice and giggle) housed in an undeniably womanly body and packaged with a first-rate mind.

All of this works to make her instantly likeable and to bring out a protectiveness in people, men and women alike, who don't even know her. My landlord, who has never laid eyes on Dolly Parton in person, and who bears no fondness for country singers, informed me, "If you say anything bad about Dolly in that book, I won't like you." A similar warning came from Jo Coulter, Nashville's famed make-up artist, who worked on both

Porter's and Dolly's TV series, among others, and who considers Dolly a dear friend. "You want to protect Dolly and keep her safe," she says. "And I'll fight anyone who says anything bad about her."

Dolly is no saint, of course, and she, like everyone else in the world, has done a few things that have disappointed people through the years. But I have not met one who was unable to forgive her; they go on loving her just the same, content to sit back and take pleasure in Dolly's irrepressible, infectious *joie de vivre,* honestly hoping she succeeds at whatever she tries.

And there is really little chance that she will not. Not only does Dolly seem to have no limits to her talents—whether for songwriting, singing, or performing, or for her new frontiers of prose writing and acting for television and movies—but also she has a high-powered Los Angeles management firm, Katz-Gallin (formerly Katz-Gallin-Cleary), behind her to help put her where she wants to go and to help her decide which projects are most advantageous to her career. Though it may be premature to declare Dolly a superstar, "It's a sure thing," as she sings on her *Heartbreaker* album, with both Katz-Gallin and Dolly putting their all into making her one.

It is not superstar status that some of those diehard Nashville critics object to, they say. In fact, they add, no one is more deserving or talented than Dolly. But they are no less adamant in questioning the ways in which Katz-Gallin and Dolly are going about it. The criticisms range from hurt feelings because Dolly no longer employs the people she did and that she is no longer as accessible as she once was (not even to friends), to genuine fears and concerns, not only about country music but about what larger success might mean. She is becoming a Professional Personality, they say, showing up in places that have nothing to do with music, such as on *Hollywood Squares.* That, in itself, can't be harmful. It may dwell on the trivial and, by the nature of the show, prohibit Dolly from displaying some of her best talents, but it does get her face and name before a segment of the public that might not otherwise know her. Certainly more disconcerting than that is the commercialization of Dolly, or Dolly's allowing herself to be presented to the public in ways that are demeaning to the image she has always projected, and which Nashville has always held of her, such as in posing for the cover of *Playboy* magazine in a bunny suit and showing up on a poster as Daisy Mae in the hay, complete with bare legs, thighs and shoulders. Many of Dolly's friends find that shocking, if only for the fact that Dolly has always been very modest about her body. Others say it's all in good fun, but worry that the public is apt to pay more attention to Dolly's abundant physical attributes than they are to her music and will eventually treat her with less respect than she deserves, or, even worse, decide she's not to be taken seriously.

Just as strong are the fears of some in Nashville about what Dolly's crossover says about the way the industry is changing. There are those who understand and readily accept the fact that Dolly wants to appeal to a broader audience and applaud her pop effort but who fear that she (and so many others, including Kenny Rogers, Crystal Gayle, Dottie West) is weakening the boundaries that separate country from pop and rock, contributing to the dissolution of an American tradition. While that is indeed something to ponder, if the truth were known, some in Nashville may also fear that the quest for the crossover sound will lure more and more artists to Los Angeles (where *Here You Come Again* and *Heartbreaker* were recorded mostly with West Coast musicians) and that in time Music City may no longer be quite the recording mecca it has been.

Which is hardly Dolly Parton's fault. She was not the first country giant to pursue a crossover career, sign with L.A. management and record in California, nor will she be the last. (She *was* the first established female country star to do it, however, which may account for a lot of flack from closet chauvinists who object to Dolly's larger career because they want "their" women to stay where they've always been.) Nevertheless, she's gotten a lot of "blame" in the last few years, something she can't understand.

"I want to do everything I possibly can," she told me in early 1977. "I just want to see what I can do. Why not? Ain't that what life is about? Why can't I expand? Why shouldn't I try? I really feel like I'm fighting a battle when I didn't start a war. I'm not going to limit myself just because people won't accept the fact that I can do something else. I'm gonna do whatever I feel is necessary to express myself. I'm just trying to make progress."

As tame and as reassuring as those words sound, Dolly's "progress" is still a combustible subject in some Nashville circles. Nashville is a gossipy town—far more gossipy than Hollywood, for example, but no one says anything bad about anyone in public here and especially not in print. Some refrain out of fear of losing a job, others out of fear of jeopardizing Dolly's friendship. Porter Wagoner, who promised me an interview for a month and then finally changed his mind, refrained apparently from fear of "injuring Dolly's career," as he put it to John Morthland of *Country Music* magazine, explaining why he wouldn't talk about his breakup with Dolly. When first told I wanted to interview him, Porter remarked to his secretary, Joan McGriff, "She might not want to hear what I have to say." After a month's deliberation, he decided against telling his side of the story, sending along the message, "I just don't believe I have anything to say for Dolly's book."

Then there was the opposite problem. Many of the people who love Dolly are totally oblivious to any faults she might have. To them, there is no one more beautiful, or talented, no one smarter or nicer, kinder or down to earth. In short, she is all things good and wonderful, and any thought slightly to the contrary would be heresy.

That's a problem (and it is certain to have its negative counterpart) every biographer encounters. But one problem I was not prepared for was the Parton family's reaction to writers and the idea of a biography being written at all. My first glimpse of that came when I knocked on the door of the battered red trailer behind the House of Prayer in the Boogertown community of Sevierville. Jake Owens, pastor of the church and Dolly's seventy-nine-year-old maternal grandfather, fixed a stare on me that seemed anything but Christian. (I may have awakened him from his Saturday afternoon nap.) When I told him my purpose in coming, Reverend Owens, the inspiration for "The Old Time Preacher Man," proceeded to tell me in no uncertain terms to go ahead and write my book, but that I'd get no information from him. Then, surprisingly, he invited me inside, where he alternated being suspicious and grandfatherly and warm. In our two-hour visit that day and in our talk after his sermon on Sunday, we discussed every subject that came into our minds, from dogs and cats to premarital sex. Every subject, that is, except Dolly. Reverend Owens had firm ideas and opinions about everything, but one was stronger than the rest: *No interviews.*

This is odd behavior, indeed, for Brother Jake, who has always loved publicity, has appeared on the Grand Ole Opry with Dolly, and has gotten up from a summer's nap, changed clothes and gone to the church to join with a group of reporters granddaughter Stella has brought to meet him and hear him play the fiddle and piano. His daughter, Dolly's mother, Avie Lee Parton, has usually been known to be cooperative with the press, too. I had no idea she would be otherwise as I waited one Sunday afternoon for the family pick-up to pull up outside their modest house in the working-class Antioch section of Nashville. But when I told her my name and intention, Mrs. Parton, who was standing in the living room taking a roll of blue toilet paper out of the wrapper when I knocked on the door, flew into a rage, shouting "No interviews" at the top of her lungs. Dressed in red stretch pants and a black and red flower-print overblouse, she flung her arms above her head in animated emphasis, holding the toilet paper like a deadly missile, primed and aimed to hurl through space at the sound of my first negative word. Although the toilet roll never became airborne (I may have been spared only by Mr. Parton's frequent and embarrassed requests of his wife not to be rude), Dolly's mother made it perfectly clear I was not welcome in her home. The reason lies squarely between the covers of a small paperback biography of Dolly that appeared in October 1977, a book the family finds so inaccurate and distasteful that they now brand all writers poison and refuse to meet with any reporter, even to set the record straight!

Dolly is only thirty-two, yet this is a wonderful time to be looking at Dolly Parton's life, as she stands on the brink of all that she has worked and planned for. And what an incredible life it has been so far! More than just a quintessential rags-to-riches story or testament to the Protestant ethic,

Dolly's life is proof that childhood fantasies and daydreams *can* indeed come true—if you spend every waking moment of your life seeing to it that they do.

Dolly would probably like to say that a good measure of her life was predestined, that she had little control over the direction she has taken, little say-so in becoming a star. Although I know that Dolly has worked hard to get from the two-room shack on the bank of the Little Pigeon River to the twenty-three-room Brentwood mansion she lives in today, I, too, am a great believer in Fate, and think that certain things—Dolly's success for one—were just *meant* to happen.

In several ways, Dolly's butterfly analogy doesn't quite fit. She may be as beautiful and alluring as the butterfly, but she is nowhere as fragile and defenseless. Where a butterfly may wither and die if its wings are battered, Dolly only strengthens under attack, so steely is her determination, so strong is her sense of self-preservation. If she has bent and made concessions to several of her co-workers in the past, she has always rallied to her own cause in the end, determined to get on with the plan she set for her life years ago as a child playing near her Tennessee mountain home, chasing butterflies, chasing dreams.

Although she's always felt an affinity with the butterfly, Dolly didn't visibly adopt it as her symbol—wearing its likeness on her clothing and using it as her logo—until the early '70s. Perhaps even then it was premature. Because it is really only now that the cocoon has started to open, and the magnificent multitude of colors that is Dolly Parton has begun to appear.

ALANNA NASH
Nashville, May 1978

1. *Sevierville*

Even before spring has officially arrived and all the buds have yet to make their seasonal debut, the trip south on I-75 from the Bluegrass region of Kentucky down through East Tennessee to Knoxville is a late-afternoon driver's paradise. Once over the Tennessee border from the Old South gentility and respectability of the small Kentucky college towns of Berea and Williamsburg, the highway juts sharply off course from its flat, straight, monotonous predictability. Even if one has not felt particularly confined by the restful if unexciting layout of the Kentucky topography, the steep inclines and dips of the Cumberland Mountains produce an undeniable feeling of freedom and exhilaration, a gentle, lilting sensation of being rocked in nature's cradle. Each bend and valley brings a visual treat more spectacular than the last—from the sight of the late-day sun filtering through scattered clouds in tones of butterscotch and honey, painting the farm houses and animals in impressionistic glow, to the way the heavy metal jaws of progress took the highway out of rock with uncustomary daintiness, leaving the banks and cliffs looking like three-tiered limestone wedding cakes.

Just as the interstate runs up along a narrow bridge, the countryside below comes into view. A little white frame church, tidy and spotless and picture perfect, nestles into the side of the pines, and down along the old road, long the only way south to Knoxville and the Great Smoky Mountains, a lone Black Angus highsteps his way home, swishing his tail behind him, silhouetted against lush green fields in the last glorious moments of sunset.

Many of Dolly Parton's best songs have celebrated the simple beauty of just such bucolic scenes, and it is with eager anticipation of discovering the setting of "My Tennessee Mountain Home" that one picks up Highway 441 leading south from Knoxville to Sevier County, filled with visions of june bugs and honeysuckle vines that wait but thirty miles down the road in the foothills of the Smokies.

Perhaps that is why what lies ahead on 441 comes as such a shock: Long before the Sevierville city limits sign, the merchants of the area engage in silent battle for the dollar of the passing motorist, each Day-Glo billboard

("Porpoise Island/Hawaiian Show/Now Open") bigger, gaudier and more visually assaulting than its predecessor. Soon it's apparent that a tourist mecca of the first order beckons ahead, and that someone has realized that there is indeed gold in them thar hills. It starts in earnest just beyond downtown Sevierville with the highly commercialized area of Pigeon Forge, boasting the Silver Dollar City amusement park where Dolly's uncle Robert sings under the name of John Henry III, a string of motels, including a Ramada Inn where Dolly's older sister, the published poet Willadeene, waitressed before moving to Nashville not long ago, and every fast food restaurant from Long John Silver's to Wendy's Hamburgers. That is only a taste of what is to come, however. It all culminates in Gatlinburg, long the vacation spot for the middle-income families in T-shirts and Bermuda shorts who crowd into Ripley's Believe It or Not and Forbidden Caverns, and long the playland of the wealthy jet setters who fill the ski chalets and slopes by day and lounge away the nights drinking and listening to the big-name entertainment booked into the main rooms of the fancier motel chains. "Only the rich folks went to Gatlinburg," Dolly's sister Stella remembers. "Folks like us just worked there."

Although the sight of all this gives immediate rise to the thought that Dolly Parton's backwoods upbringing might be the figment of a press agent's imagination, half a mile off 441, once past the opulent Gatlinburg Country Club and several good-size expensive homes, one finds another world co-existing in peaceful incongruity. If the tacky souvenir stands of Pigeon Forge offer up all that is plastic and phony and trivial in America, beyond Country Club Lane lies that which is most basic and real. Tucked away in the narrow, winding roads are the hollows populated by the descendants of the European immigrants who came here centuries ago, who brought with them a strong hand and sturdy back for farming, a love for storytelling and singing, and a fierce, rigid code of morality and humanity, the latter gleaned from fundamentalist religion, beliefs which in some instances embraced snake-handling and always promised eternal damnation for sinners.

Progress is slow to affect these pocket communities with names such as Caton's Chapel and Richardson Cove—electricity came to the area in about 1950, and the county finally got around to paving most of the roads some time later. People here live pretty much as they always have, close to the land and to their beliefs. You might be hard-pressed to find snake handling practiced in the little cinderblock and frame churches there now, but the art has not died out ("Rattle Snake Kingdom/See our 200/Snake Milking" reads a sign on 441), and religion is still a dominant part of life. Many of the communities have no "town," per se, and if they center on anything, it is the church, be it Church of God, United Methodist or Baptist. Here the church is not only the house of worship, but also a place to gather to sing and play music (some of the ancient hymns are still learned by the shape note method), a place, in years past at least, where you were likely to meet your life's partner.

As seventeen-year-old Robert Lee Parton looked through the church window at the group gathered for the revival in White Pine, Tennessee, he felt his heart stop. There, sitting with her sister and cousin, listening to her father preach against the evils of sin, was the prettiest fifteen-year-old girl he had ever seen. One-quarter Cherokee Indian, Avie Lee Owens, with her brown eyes, her high Indian cheekbones and black hair down to her waist, was almost the exact physical opposite of the young blond boy of Scotch-Irish heritage. Standing there looking in the window, Lee Parton decided he'd found the girl he wanted. "They tried to elope, but it didn't work out because they were so young," one of their children relates today. "Finally Grandpa married them two days later, and their puppy-love romance has lasted thirty-eight years."

Avie Lee grew up with her children. "When she got married, it was a frightening thing, and she started having babies right away, 'cause she didn't know how to prevent it," Dolly has said. "Nobody'd ever talked to her about it." Willadeene, their first-born, came along within the year. Shortly after followed David and Denver.

The family remembers the birth of the next child, Dolly Rebecca, in the wee hours of January 19, 1946, as an unusual occasion. "It snowed the night she was born, then the sky turned bright blue the next day," Willadeene told journalist Joan Dew. "All the neighbors came from miles to see the new baby. She was the most beautiful baby I'd ever seen, the first in our family with blond hair and fair, ivory skin." Dr. Robert F. Thomas, whom Dolly was to immortalize in her song bearing his name, delivered the baby at home, a log cabin known as the Ken and Martha Williams place, on Pittman Center Road. Lee Parton had no money to pay him. "He was paid with a sack of corn meal," Dolly tells with a twinkle in her eye. "We used to grow our own corn. We'd shell it, and Daddy would take it to the mill. So that's what I cost—a sack of meal. Too bad it couldn't have been flour," she continues. "He'd'a had more dough!"

Although Dolly often jokes about her family's poverty ("Most people have three rooms and a bath. We had four rooms and a path. Sure we had runnin' water. When we'd run and get it!"), Lee and Avie Lee's existence was always a struggle. In the young children's early years, Lee sharecropped wherever he could, and the family moved often. The Partons had moved at least once, to a house on Middle Creek Road, by the time Stella was born in the spring of 1949. Bobby's arrival preceded hers. (Dolly would be the last Parton child to be born at home, with the others delivered at a local clinic or a Knoxville hospital. "My momma could get pregnant just by Daddy explaining the advantages of the pill to her," Dolly would joke on national TV.) Despite the hardships, each of the Parton children speak of their childhood with pride.

"As far as hard times, you know, we had some rough ones," Dolly remembers. "But I was a happy person, born with a happy heart and a happy nature. I had a good momma and a good daddy, and you know when you have that you're gonna manage some way. There were times we didn't have it as good as we should've, but that's part of life. My daddy hit some rough spots in life, but you can imagine how it would be with that big responsibility of so many children and having to just live here and there trying to get roots enough to say you were settled. We moved so often, but it was good for my nature, because I like to move. It was always excitin' to me. In a way, I always thought I wanted to have a home that was always there, but then we would no sooner get moved in one place, seemed like, then we were moving to another. But there was an excitement about it, 'cause living way back in the mountains like we did, there was nothin' else to do."

By the time Dolly was five (or three, depending on the source), Lee had managed to save enough money to buy a farm of several hundred acres on Locust Ridge. That was to be a big move, indeed, and it is to that house and farm that Dolly's memory drifts when she recalls her childhood. The Locust Ridge house was Dolly's Tennessee Mountain Home, the house pictured on the album cover and celebrated in song.

If ever Dolly's house becomes a national shrine (and that is not too far-fetched an idea, considering Dolly's growing legion of fans and the near-mythical, mystical aura Dolly has deliberately created for her native region), Sevier County will have not only to issue maps of the area but also to hire tour guides, so remote is the location and so harrowing the trip. It is literally impossible to find if you are not a Sevier County native (and two of those got lost with me, trying to find it), even if you have two hand-drawn maps supplied by well-wishing residents of the area. Then if you do manage to find the right road and hollow and take just the right forks, there is the problem of the roads. They are too narrow in most places for two cars to pass, and in several spots, only the holding of breath and saying of prayers keeps you from falling into a precipice or stream. Not to mention the hairpin turns, or the fact that the roads are unpaved gravel. Suddenly, only because Dolly's first grade teacher, Mrs. Archie Ray McMahan, has been kind enough to get in the car and guide you there, you stand before the little four-room shack between Locust Ridge and Webb's Mountain at the absolute end of the road and depths of the hollow. It is a place so isolated that the Partons' nearest neighbors were two miles away, and news of births and deaths was communicated by the ringing of the church bell at the top of the mountain.

No matter how many pictures you have seen or how much you have fantasized about it, you are not prepared. It is the most extreme rural poverty imaginable—direr even than Dolly has painted it—and as you stand there gazing at the ancient washing machine on the porch and the inoperative still off to the side of the house in front of the rusted automobile parts and the scraggly chickens, you feel guilty for having wondered if Dolly has exaggerated her humble origins. With that, Hazel Williams, sister of the current owner, comes out on the front porch. A large mountain woman who has not quite yet gotten used to strangers stopping at her house to gawk and take pictures, she hurries out to the hen house and returns moments later with half-a-dozen brown eggs gathered in the apron of her orange dress. Then she disappears back into the house and blushes self-consciously when you knock on her door to thank her. If the house and scene appear bleak and depressing to a visitor, Mrs. McMahan insists that when the Partons lived there, "It was just like the others around it. Hasn't changed much since then."

Yet, when Dolly returned in 1973 to shoot the album jacket photo, she was surprised at the improvements made on the house "over in the holler," as she calls it. "It's really been updated since we lived there," she said in '75. "Looks good now compared to how it looked then. We never had a tin roof so nice. They've added that. They've got some grass now, too. We used to sweep the yard; we never had grass, there were so many of us kids. When somebody was coming to visit us," Dolly told Toby Thompson for the *Village Voice*, "Momma'd say, 'Get the broom and we'll clean up the yard.' So we'd sweep the yard, you know. It was just beat down dirt. And boy, in a place or two it would really shine!"

Luckily the children were not so rough on the tobacco crop, the family's main source of income. Out back of the house, they kept their pumpkin patch and grew their corn, beans, potatoes and turnips for their own larder. "We didn't have things we wanted, but we didn't starve," Dolly recalls. "Really we ate fine. We were hungry for a variety of things, but as far as going hungry with our bellies empty, we never had to do that. We had just simple things. Like for breakfast we always had just gravy and biscuits. For dinner and supper we had beans and potatoes, which is something that so many people have. We were lucky to have it. And we made our own soap, ground our own meal. About all we had to buy was coffee, sugar and flour."

The Partons also made their own moonshine, Dolly remembers. "My family often made home brew, moonshine . . . Now it is pure, raw, hard—it'll burn you up—it'll set your feet on fire. I tasted it but the times I've tasted it, I'd never had anything to drink, and anything like that tastes terrible. In the mountains that's another way of makin' a livin'. They do it for money but, then, they really enjoy their work."

If the family lacked for all it needed or wanted, it was not because Lee Parton didn't work hard. By the time Dolly was eight, her father began working several outside jobs in addition to his farm chores, digging ditches to lay the pipes for a textile mill being built in Sevierville and then signing on as a concrete finisher. While on the latter job, Lee partially disabled a leg, "scooting around on the cement in the winter and summer finishing concrete," remembers Stella, who, like Dolly, considers her father "the next thing to God," and calls him the hardest-working person she knows.

"The Partons are very independent people," she says. "They're a very proud family. They never ask for anything. If they can't get it for themselves, then they do without it. They may not have good educations, but they're always very hard-working. We may have gotten favors, where people would send us used clothes, but we never got charity. Daddy always paid for everything we got."

And Lee Parton knew how to stretch his dollar. He'd take his family to Bush's Canning Factory, where bent cans of food went for a fraction of their usual cost. Sometimes the labels were torn off the cans, but the Partons soon learned to read the codes on the bottoms, differentiating green beans from hominy. "Daddy may have only gone to the second grade, or something, but he's a real smart manager," says one of his children.

"He always made sure we had a Christmas treat and that Christmas was always fun. I don't remember ever having a really bad Christmas. Daddy would buy a bushel of oranges, a bushel of apples, bananas or grapefruit, things that we didn't have every day like everybody else does. And we always had candy and a present and a Christmas tree. We used to wear boots in the winter time, and since we didn't have a fireplace, Momma had us line our little cowboy boots up at the front door so Santa Claus could fill them up. She always thought that where there's a will, there's a way."

Avie Lee was no less adept at taking care of her family, from seeing to it that they were clean and properly clothed, to making sure they ate the food provided. Sometimes that took a little doing, and when it did, Avie Lee called upon her imagination. "If she made baked beans and we didn't like 'em, she called 'em cowboy beans," Stella remembers. "She'd say that's what cowboys ate out on the prairie. Of course, kids are gonna eat if they hear a big tall tale." But a far more ingenious trick was Avie Lee's stone soup. Although neighbors recall the Partons always had "two fine hogs to butcher at the end of the year," there was not always meat enough for soup. Avie would add a freshly scrubbed rock to her potatoes, onions and tomatoes, psychologically canceling any feeling of deprivation her children might feel, and bringing a touch of excitement to an otherwise drab meal, all the while telling her children how much more fortunate they were than some children who had nothing to eat. "Avie Lee always had imagination," says her sister, Estelle Watson. "I guess that's where Dolly gets that. Avie's a great mother and a fine person. She kept everything going in those rough times."

Aside from telling stories, Avie Lee Parton had one other special talent, that of singing old folk songs she'd learned from her harmonica-playing grandmother Owens, born a Messer (or Messar), descended from the

Cherokee Indians who populated the Carolinas. Often Lee would join in on the singing, accompanying the group on banjo and guitar. Perhaps because the musical tradition is so strong on the Owens side of the family, there is a notion that Lee and Avie Lee's children inherited their musical prowess solely from her side of the family. "That's very unfair," Stella claims. "I think the Parton side of the family is equally talented. And more handsome, too," she adds. "They all sing, they all like songs. They're really more bluegrass and gospel than they are country, but they're really musicians."

The family sing-alongs stand out in each Parton child's memory as some of the happiest hours of their lives, and out of the twelve Parton children, seven are now working or at one time worked as professional musicians. The influence of the gatherings seems to have been especially strong on Dolly, who had begun singing at the tender age of eighteen months. Before she was old enough to start school, she was hearing melodies of her own invention in her mind. Soon she began hearing the words, too, and fashioning them together with the few chords she deciphered on the "guitar" she made at age six and a half from an old mandolin and two bass guitar strings. "The first song Dolly ever made she was seven years old," Mrs. Parton has often said. (Dolly fixes her writing debut at age five.) "She came in one day and said, 'Will you write it down for me?' I've still got it, but I won't let her have it. She has a copy of it, but I've got the one that was written down at the time she made that song."

"I've got thousands of songs, *boxes* of songs," Dolly says. I never forget a melody and I seldom forget the words if I've sung it more'n three times." Then, as if for proof, she breaks into "Little Tiny Tasseltop," one of her first efforts, a song she wrote for the corncob dolly her father made her: "Little tiny tasseltop/You're the only friend I got/Big brown eyes and corn silk hair/How you make me smile./Little tiny tasseltop/I love you an awful lot/Hope you never go away/'Cause I want you to always stay." The childish nature of the song was atypical of those years, Dolly has told reporters. Most of her songs centered around tragedies, such as loved ones dying in the wars, or at least concerned subjects far too heavy for most seven-year-olds. "I had a gift of rhyme," she says. "I'd listen to the conversations the grownups was having, and I'd make up songs about them."

Despite the seriousness of those thoughts, Dolly's early involvement in music appears to have been motivated more by escapism than by the need for creative expression. If reality meant sleeping four and five to a bed, a fantasy world was infinitely preferable. There, in her own private little fairyland, Dolly was more than just a poor farmer's daughter. There, she would have the money to buy the pretty things she had yearned for. And if her fantasy world offered only temporary escape, if, when the music stopped, she was still a poor little girl in a hand-me-down dress, even then she began figuring a way that the music would go on forever, carrying her to a place where millions of people would know and love her, and she would make them happy, just by being herself. There, little Dolly Parton figured, she would be a Star. Late Saturday nights, when she was supposed to be asleep, Dolly would lie awake in bed and listen to the Grand Ole Opry beamed from Nashville, 200 miles across the state. Electricity had not yet come to Locust Ridge, and Dolly had to strain her ears to hear the high-pitched moans of the singers over the whistle and crackle of her daddy's battery radio. But when her fantasies took over, she heard it loud and clear, and she was up on the WSM stage with Hank Williams and Patsy Cline. "Someday I'm gonna be on the Grand Ole Opry," she told her daddy the next day before church.

The thin, white-haired preacher man does not look at all pleased to see the young visitor standing outside his trailer door. I smile anyway, and ask if he is Reverend Owens. He frowns, and makes a noise to tell me he has not understood. "Are you Reverend Owens?" I ask again in a louder voice. "Yes," he answers suspiciously. I tell him my name and say I am writing a book about his granddaughter, Dolly. The preacher man shakes his head, smiles a guarded smile and rolls his eyes. An awkward silence follows. "You want to know about me or about Dolly?" he asks. "Well," I say, laughing self-consciously, "about both." There is a mistrust in his voice as he says everything about Dolly has already "been wrote up." I say yes, but that I want to get it firsthand, that Dolly has talked about him so much I've wanted to meet him. We stand there eyeing each other, both unsure of what to say or do. Finally he goes on: "What is it you want to know?" I tell him I'm particularly interested in the music Dolly sang in church as a child. This does not register. I repeat the key words. Twice. Reverend Owens asks me to spell it. I reach for my reporter's notebook, and he shakes his head and smiles as if he has just caught me stealing from the collection plate. "You're not gonna write anything down," he says, his voice suddenly surly. And then the reason comes out. Another girl had been to see him, he says. Real nice young lady. But she had gone back to Nashville and written things about him and his family that didn't set too well. Not only that, she had made errors, he says, gotten names wrong. I tell him I'd like to correct them, set the record straight. He shakes his head again. It wouldn't be right to make another writer look bad, he tells me, but she sure had made a lot of folks around there upset. "Called me 'a banty rooster' in that book. Lots of people around there didn't like that." But it wasn't just her. Writers are always doing things like that, writing things that make people look bad, getting facts wrong. "They should have come to me," he says. I point out the obvious fact that I have done just that. Reverend Owens shakes his head slowly and closes his eyes for an instant. "I'd like to help you . . .," he begins, in a tone that tells me he is not about to, and then his voice trails off. I smile my pre-goodbye smile, and just as I am ready to admit defeat and thank him for his time, he invites me inside.

The little red trailer is old and cramped, but it seems to have everything a seventy-nine-year-old widower might need. We sit together at the front of the trailer on a built-in couch. A kitchen and small breakfast table and chairs separate us from the hallway leading back to Reverend Owens's sleeping quarters. I apparently let in some flies when I opened the door, and they buzz against the screens on the windows behind us as we begin to get acquainted. I have ceased to be an interviewer for the moment, only a visitor, and an uncomfortable one at that.

We get the pleasantries out of the way—where I'm from and the fact that my grandfather lived in the area all his life. Reverend Owens, dressed in a pink-striped shirt, multicolored checked pants and house slippers, asks if I'm a reporter. I tell him yes. "I'm a teacher," he says, smiling broadly, his brown eyes shining. "I've got one of the nine gifts. Do you know what that means?" We look it up. First Corinthians, 12:28. Despite a problem with a nerve on the left side of his face, Reverend Owens has wonderful sight for a man his age. He pulls the *Bible* right up in front of his face and moves his finger along the page. This is the fifth *Bible* he's worn out, he tells me with pride, and shows me the handsome leather binder around it. A present. "I'm also a poet and a writer," he says. I say I knew he wrote songs because Dolly recorded his "Book of Life" on her album of sacred songs, *Golden Streets of Glory*. You wrote the liner notes for it, too," I add. The smile freezes on Reverend Owens's face, and for a moment I am sure I've said the wrong thing. I sit in terrified silence as my host stands up. "Would you like to see some pictures of Dolly?" he asks. I tell him yes, and try not to act overeager as he walks to the back of the trailer to get what I imagine will be the family album.

But when he returns, he is carrying a stack of phonograph records. Records made by various members of his family. Everyone in his family who plays and sings. Except Dolly. "Couldn't find any of Dolly's pictures," he says, and slips an album by John Henry III on his old General Electric hi-fi. John Henry (Robert Owens) is one of Reverend Owens's five sons. If he has changed his name to obscure the family connection, he undoes it on the back of his album jacket, where he is pictured smiling with his famous niece, who gives him a written plug as well. His music is a pleasant mixture of country and blues, befitting the burly, bearded man pictured on the cover. "The Owenses have black hair," Robert's father tells me, pointing to his smiling son. "Dolly takes after her daddy."

When Robert finishes his first side, Reverend Owens takes the record off and puts on a recording of his daughter, Dorothy Jo Hope. A minister like her father, Dorothy Jo shares writing credit with Dolly on several of Dolly's well-known songs, including the tribute to Reverend Owens, "Daddy Was an Old Time Preacher Man." "Dorothy Jo," he says as her high, piercing voice comes through the speakers, "she wrote the 'Preacher Man.' " Then he shows me a picture of her daughter, Debra. In case I have not yet begun to understand that Reverend Owens feels Dolly's fame has overshadowed the rest of his talented family, he then plays a few cuts from *The Parton Family Sings in the Garden*, an inspirational album Avie Lee, Willadeene, Stella and Cassie cut several years ago.

But he has saved the best for last. Down at the bottom of the stack is an album called *Songs of the Smoky Mountains* put together by Reverend Owens's son Bill a decade ago, featuring Dorothy Jo on banjo, Jake on fiddle and Bill on guitar. "Bill and Dolly, oh, they had a tough time when they started out," he says, handing me the album jacket as he puts the record on. Then he points out that he wrote some of the liner notes himself:

> This is a true story. This the story of my old fiddle. The reason I say old is because I've owned it for 48 years. I was visiting my Grandpa Issac Messar in Cherokee Falls, S.C., when I was 19 years old, and he was telling me the history of the fiddle as he knew it himself. He lived to be 93 years old. He bought it for my uncle, Frank Messar, for building a small frame house. I bought it from my uncle Frank. Grandpa bought this fiddle from a cousin of mine and he says he's sure it once belonged to my Great Grandfather Solomon Grooms in Tennessee. My father's grandfather on his mother's side, his daughter married a Sutton, in North Carolina. Well, the story goes that one of the Sutton boys was visiting Grandpa Grooms in Tennessee, and Grandpa Grooms decided to go home with the Sutton boy. He took his fiddle with him. As they came to the top of Chestnut Mountain, they met some men who claimed to be the White Caps. [Note: The White Caps of those days were a group of people somewhat similar to the Ku Klux Klan of today.] Grandpa Grooms was a Union man, and they did not like him, so they told him to play his favorite tune on the fiddle. He played "Morgan's Retreat." As he played, they killed him. It is said that the Sutton boy took the fiddle home, and it was passed from one to another. Finally, I got it for keeps. It most likely has been in the related families for over 100 years.—Jake Owens

While I have been reading the notes, Reverend Owens has slipped into the back of the trailer. When I look up, he has his fiddle case in his hand. He walks over to the scratchy hi-fi and puts the needle on "An Uncloudy Day." Then he takes out the historic red and yellow fiddle and tucks it under his chin. He picks up the tune in mid-stanza, playing and singing along to the record, holding the fiddle like a real mountain musician, his palm resting on the underside of the neck, the whole length of the first joints lying flat on the fingerboard, the fingers of his right hand reaching high up on the bow. Rosin is caked a good two inches on the bottom of the fingerboard. "Heh-HEH!" he chortles when the song's done, his delighted smile reaching clear across his face. "Did'ja know that one? Not many people can sing and play fiddle at the same time. See there, you got somthin' no one else did. The old man played his fiddle for you." We exchange a smile. "My uncle Frank asked me for five dollars one time back in 1920. I knew what he wanted it for—to buy his marriage license. I told him if he didn't give the five dollars back, I'd just keep the fiddle. So I paid five dollars for it!" He claps his hands together with glee.

"I guess the music comes through me," he says, putting the old fiddle back in its case. "My mother was a singer. I mean, a *real singer*. How she could sing! Dolly comes closer to her than anybody." He takes another record from the stack. Kitty Wells. I know what is to come. "See here," he says, pointing out a song. " 'Singing His Praises.' I wrote that when I was thirty-six years old. Over forty years ago. Dorothy Jo was seven when I wrote that song, and now she's forty-nine. I still write, you know. Songs and poems. And letters. I might just write you a letter if you write me first. When you come back—I enjoy talking to people with wisdom—I might show you some of my poems. Now, Willadeene," he continues, "she's good. She's extra good."

"You a Christian?" Reverend Owens suddenly asks. I tell him yes, although I don't attend church as much as I should. "How much do you weigh?" he wants to know. "A hundred and eighteen." Reverend Owens slaps his hands together again. "Heh-HEH! That's what me and my wife weighed together the day we were married!" We share a laugh. "I was twenty. We were married for forty-nine years." He pauses. "You married and got kids?" I tell him no, and then he asks how old I am. "You know," he tells me in a low tone, as if someone might overhear. "A woman's got to be careful about goin' all the way, about how much of herself she gives a man before he takes her to the altar." "Oh, I know," I confide solemnly. A girl can't guard that too closely. Reverend Owens feels some consolation is in order. "You'll find that fella you're looking for," he says. "Don't lose hope."

I am feeling more at ease now, and since he has mentioned his famous granddaughter more than once, I gather the courage to try one more time. "About Dolly . . . ," I begin. The Preacher Man shakes his head. "I'd like to help," he says. "But get it from other reports. As sure as I tell you something, one of my children will say, 'Daddy, did you say *that?*' " But the other reports are wrong, I point out. "You've told me that yourself, but you won't correct them." The Preacher Man stands firm. Perhaps it is the tension of the moment. Perhaps it is the heat. Whatever, I begin to cry. Reverend Owens doesn't quite know what to do. "A man with any heart . . . ," he says, and stops. "Dolly would cry right along with you." That makes me cry all the more. "I'd like to help you, but I just don't take the chance," he says, and then his voice turns meek. "Don't tell people the Preacher Man didn't treat you right," he asks, almost pleading. I know now that I have put him in a bad position, and I tell him I understand. "Come to the church service tomorrow if you can," he says. I tell him I'd like that. "You know," he says, bending his knees a little so that he is looking up into my face and smiling tenderly, "Sometimes people get saved!"

If the songs Dolly made up as a child offered her escape, the songs she sang in her grandfather's church offered another kind of freedom. "Our services would be mostly music," Dolly told Toby Thompson of the *Village Voice* in 1976; "different families, different individuals gettin' up to sing. The old hymns. Above that they was just about the biggest thing we did recreation-wise. House I lived in when I was little, we had to walk four miles to the mailbox. So church was a social event. More than just Sunday; we'd have revivals, prayer meetings, service different evenings of the week. Nothin' fancy; didn't have to wear shoes if you didn't own any. A lot of people walked; some, their husbands would bring them, drop 'em off, the wives and kids. Husbands would sit outside in their cars and wait, those who didn't want to attend. Younger boys would sneak around to the window and try to get the young girls to come out. Then we'd call the service to order. We'd pray beforehand, and Preacher would say, 'Does anybody have any special songs?' 'Course everybody did, so we took turns. People'd bring tambourines, guitars, banjos, fiddles. And we would *sing*."

They are singing a hymn I don't recognize the following morning when I arrive late at the little white House of Prayer that Reverend Owens and his kinfolk built in the early 1950s. Reverend Owens is seated at the old piano the church bought from his sister "when her hands got all crooked up and she couldn't play." The hymn over, Reverend Owens, dressed in his favorite red shirt, maroon pants and maroon print tie, and wearing his hearing aid and black-framed glasses this morning, gets up and walks to the pulpit. The congregation—nine women, one man and seven children, all well-dressed—sits down in front in the first of the fourteen pews. According to the board on the wall, attendance was higher—up to thirty-five—the previous week, perhaps because it was Easter.

The House of Prayer ("For All People, ISA, 56:7," reads the sign out front) is laid out simply and functionally. The bathrooms, located at the very front of the church, open out onto the street. But Reverend Owens has tried to make it all as attractive as possible. There's gold carpet on the floor, matching the tassels on the wine velvet drapes. The windows are covered with self-stick paper in stained-glass design. And on the wall directly behind Reverend Owens is a large color mural of Jesus and Mary.

"Grandpa's church is like the Southern Baptist, only a little more charismatic, a little more spiritualistic, like a Southern Negro church," Stella says. There is no snake handling in Reverend Owens' church. And no one is rolling in the aisles in need of saving, either. But then this is just Sunday School. The service is at 7 P.M. Reverend Owens, a preacher since he was seventeen, follows no real doctrine other than the scripture, Dolly has said, and after the saying of the Lord's Prayer, Reverend Owens asks the congregation to turn to Psalms 149–150. He walks down and stands in front of the first pew.

" 'Praise ye Jehovah,' " he reads, holding the Bible only inches from his face. 'Sing unto Jehovah a new song, And his praise in the assembly of the saints. Let Israel rejoice in him that made Him: Let the children of Zion be joyful in their King. Let them praise his name in the dance.' "

"Now, I never could dance a lick, but I sure could play the music!" Reverend Owens says, interrupting himself, bringing the *Bible* down. "Have you ever noticed," he continues, a big smile gracing his face, "how people would dance at home or anywhere but in the church?"

" ' . . . Praise him with trumpet sound: Praise him with psaltery and harp. Praise him with timbrel and dance: Praise him with stringed instruments and pipe. Praise him with loud cymbals: Praise him with high sounding cymbals. Let everything that hath breath praise Jehovah. Praise Jehovah.' "

With all that talk about music, the congregation stands for another song. Then it's time to pass the collection plate. Reverend Owens takes a dollar out of his own wallet and drops it in and then hands another dollar to a red-haired woman in the second row. She puts it in the plate as it comes around. Total offering: $17. "Dolly will support us with contributions from time to time, but things remain simple," Reverend Owens has said.

The offering in, Reverend Owens sends the children off for their lesson, and instructs the adults to turn to The Song of Solomon. Brother Charles Headrick sees I have no *Bible,* and brings one over. Reverend Owens reminds his flock that when the *Bible* speaks of the Bride and the Bridegroom, the bride refers to the church, and the groom to Jesus Christ. "Now here, the bride speaks with the daughters of Jerusalem," he tells them.

" 'Let him kiss me with the kisses of his mouth; For thy love is better than wine,' " he reads. Again the *Bible* comes down. "They say a little wine is good for the stomach, but I don't believe in takin' a dram of it myself," he says. "But," his voice gets excited, "I want to tell you, I'd rather have the wine of Jesus then all the beer that Billy Carter can make! That man is a disgrace! He's a disgrace to the Presidency! I'd like to get a chance to tell him, but I guess I won't."

The *Bible* goes back up. " 'Thine oils have a goodly fragrance; Thy name is as oil poured forth; Therefore do the virgins love thee. Draw me; we will run after thee: The king hath brought me into his chambers; We will be glad and rejoice in thee; We will make mention of thy love more than of wine: Right do they love thee.' "

"Now here we're talkin' about the loving conversation of the Bride with the Bridegroom," Jakes says.

" 'I have compared thee, O my love, To a steed in Pharaoh's chariots.

Thy cheeks are comely with plaits of hair, Thy neck with strings of jewels. We will make thee plaits of gold With studs of silver. . . . My beloved is unto me as a bundle of myrrh, That lieth betwixt my breasts.' "

The *Bible* comes down. Reverend Owens smiles. The congregation titters. " 'That lieth betwixt my breasts,' " he repeats. "Isn't that a wonderful thing to think of!" "Ummmmm, yeah," Brother Headrick says, and the women giggle. "It means Jesus will stay there with her all night long!" Jake says. "Now everybody needs to have that knowledge."

"You know, talkin' about the Bride and Bridgroom," Owens continues, putting the *Bible* aside for a minute. "I've married a lot of couples. And I don't know if this is true, but I heard tell of a couple that when they married and supposed to say, 'I do,' the man said, 'I will if she will!' " The congregation convulses.

Brother Headrick pipes up. "You ever kiss the bride, Jake?" The women giggle and smile. Jakes loves it. "Why, no, Charles!" Jakes says. "You think a man wants the whole community kissin' his wife before he gets home and goes to bed?" He gets a charge out of himself, smiling broadly and adjusting his glasses on his head. "I'm a natural person, Charles," he continues, "but I don't believe in *that!*"

"My religious beliefs are very, very strong," Dolly says. 'Course, we were so involved in church. That's about the only thing we ever did was go to church. We knew the *Bible* so well, I knew the *Bible* like a book!" She stops and laughs at herself. "I read it a lot myself, 'cause it was fascinatin' to me. My Momma always read to us and told us stories and everything.

"Still, I know that the *Bible* says you must believe and be baptized—and I do believe in God and I have been baptized—but I don't consider myself a Christian. I would like to think that I have a Christian outlook on life as far as the way I treat people. I feel like that one wrong thing you do to somebody else is a sin. But for me to say that I am a good Christian, I would have to be devotin' the same kind of time to God and givin' him all my efforts the way that I am with this business. To me, that's the only way that I can appreciate a Christian, a person that I see is doin' all that they possibly can. Then you can say you are truly a Christian if you feel it in your heart. And it's selfish to say that I am when I am not.

"It bothers me a lot. It don't bother me, like if I think about it in a sensible way, because I have this direct contact with God, you know. I feel like God and me have always been good friends. I'm just totally aware of Him. I talk to Him just like I talk to anyone. If something's goin' wrong, I'll talk to Him about it. I feel that God protects me; I feel he's with me even though he knows what I am. And I feel that he appreciates me bein' honest about it, because he's gonna know anyway. I feel he helps me even though I am a sinner. I know that he's never left me. I know that I count on him, and I know I depend on him. I feel like I owe my success so much to that, because nothin' good ever happens to me that I don't remember to thank God for that happenin' to me. Nothin' bad ever happens to me that I don't remember to ask God to help me out of it.

"But still I don't claim to be a Christian, because I am always honest with God. I always say, 'I know I can't fool you,' and I know I can't fool myself, either. I can fool other people if I feel there's a need to, but I don't like to. I don't tell nobody that I'm a Christian. In fact, a lot of people condemn me for sayin' this. They say, 'Well, I wouldn't go around tellin' people I'm not a Christian.' I say, 'Well, I'm not a hypocrite. If anything, I'm just a sinner. I'm a strong person in ways, but I'm talkin' about weak as far as me bein' able to be strong enough to say, 'Yes! I will not stray from this. I am definitely a Christian!' There will be a lot of people that will say, 'Well, I am very disappointed to hear you say this in that particular way.' But that's how I feel. God forgive me if I've said it wrong. I could care less about what people think about it as long as me and God are straight. I'm not serving people, anyway."

It was not only that recognition of weakness that motivated Dolly to write "The Seeker," but a feeling that some people around her had misplaced their faith, turning often to Dolly when they should have turned to God.

"I had tried to get back close to God," she remembers of the writing of the song. "It's such a big part of me that I had it on my mind. I had tried to live right, and there were so many people countin' on me, that I was settin' an example for, and I was seein' that I was failin'. I thought, 'These people are not followin' God. They're tryin' to follow *me!* They're not lettin' God set their example. They're lettin' *me* set it. I can't do that for these people.' These were family, friends, people who care about me. I got it on my mind that there were too many people bein' led astray by tryin' to do as I do. I felt like people were lookin' at me all the time, and I was afraid I was goin' to fail them. Religion is such a touchy thing to me. I take it so serious. It's a precious thing to me. It's so sacred to me that I won't mess with it to try to present a big image for myself. I *am* God-loving, and I'm also God-fearing."

Several of Dolly's relatives and friends believe that at some point in her life, Dolly will devote her life to Christ and make a public commitment to serving Him, either through gospel music or oratory. Dolly herself didn't discount that possibility.

"I've never been able to allow God to use me the way I've always used Him, but I know that someday that will come," she says. "I don't know when, and I don't know how, but I will know it in my heart that it's time for it. That's what religion means to me. God is such a part of my life. I also think that when I do take that step, the people that have always counted on me and looked up to me and depended on me will know that I'm sincere about it. They will know that I am truly doin' my very best. I'm not sayin' I'm gonna do all I can in music and then I'm gonna serve God. If it got on my heart and my mind heavy enough, I'd have to drop it right now. I would have to drop everything else and follow Him, but, as of now I feel like He is allowin' me to touch people, to reach out, in my own way."

Reverend Owens has dismissed Sunday School early this morning, making an excuse to the congregation that he has to go to Knoxville because he wants me to hear a tape of a radio broadcast he made with his daughter Dorothy Jo Hope. Dorothy Jo has had some miracles revealed to her in her lifetime, Jake says proudly, and Dorothy Jo seems no less proud of her father as she introduces him on the tape:

"He's The Old Time Preacher Man," she tells the listening audience, "and he's been telling us some wonderful things, how that God has dealt with his life, and the way God has used him in so many ways, and told us many good things and miracles and many things. He has a message on his heart today, and he'll talk to us some on the New Heaven and the New Earth. And I know it's gonna be great. So just tune in, sit down and listen, relax, and listen to what God has got to say to us through this sermon and His annointed minister. We bring to you right now, Reverend Jake Owens. God bless you right now, Jake Owens."

Reverend Owens has based his sermon on Chapters 21 and 22 of Revelation.

"What we want to do now is show you some things that's gonna take place in this New Heaven and New Earth," he begins. "Now the heaven that Jesus is a-talkin' about, and the earth He's talkin' about, is a heaven you can see now, and the earth you live on. That's a-gonna pass away, and the scientists who say that God is a-gonna renew this earth and make it NEW [his voice rises in drama and excitement] had better get on another book and start writin' some other kind of a lie!" He pauses a moment. "Excuse me, I didn't know I was gettin' that rough. Now listen. I'll tell you one thing, you'd better believe what the word says!

"There'll be no more anything like in this world we live in now. If you overcome the sin in your life, and the sin in this world and fall out with the Devil and quit workin' for the Devil and go to workin' for God, you can drink in that fountain of life. But if you don't change your way of doin', you'll pass away with the world and go to the lake that burned the fire and brimstone, in another place, you know.

"Now, we see here, the book describes a big city there. You can all read that. I see here in the twenty-second verse, 'and I saw no temple therein for the Lord Almighty and the lamb, or the temple of it.' God, and the lamb, which is Jesus Christ, was both there, and the city had no need of the sun, they didn't need the sun, neither the moon, to shine in it, for the glory of God did lighten it. And the lamb is the light thereof." He gives a joyous little chuckle. "Praise God forever! Ain't that wonderful to be in a place like that?"

"UM-hum!" Dorothy Jo says.

"Now, you can be in a place like that if you live like you ought to down here," Jake continues. "But you'd better live that life. It's up to you to live that life. Praise God, hallelujah! I thank the Lord for this wonderful scripture. I hope you're gettin' somethin' out of it. *I* am. Praise God, if I couldn't enjoy the work of God, I'd quit." He reads: " 'And the gates of it shall not be shut at all by day, for there shall be no light there.' Now, how about *that!* Ain't that *wonderful?!*"

"Yeah, it is," Dorothy Jo intones.

"You won't have to have no electricity. You won't have to cook none. You don't have to get more wood, you don't have to go to the store. You can lose every bit of your natural, flashy, lucky pleasure in this life, and you'd better lose it, and get that breath that will lead you and guide you on, and praise God when this ol' earth passes away. Then you will land right into the brand new one! Praise God! [Joyous chuckle.] You won't have to take no furniture, either."

"Amen!" shouts Dorothy Jo.

"You don't have to have your furniture! You won't have to have no musical instruments! You won't even have to have a light!"

"They're all furnished!" prompts Dorothy Jo.

"It's all furnished! And it's paid for!"

"Amen! All bills paid for."

"And hallelujah, who pays for it?" Jake asks.

"All bills paid!"

"The bills are paid and everything's clear, there ain't no debt!"

"That's gonna be better than the Garden of Eden, won't it?" asks Dorothy Jo.

"Praise God, I'm a-tellin' you," Jake says, bursting with enthusiasm. "I hope you're a-gettin' somethin' out of this!"

"Praise God," shouts Dorothy Jo. "Thank you, Jesus. Amen!"

It is undoubtedly this kind of fire-and-brimstone-go-to-Hell-on-a-poker-right-quick sermon that Dolly Parton grew up hearing, sermons in which her granddaddy "preached hell so hot that you could feel the heat." This particular sermon has not been without its effect on Reverend Owens either. He has stared transfixed at the tape recorder the entire thirty minutes it took to play the tape, and now he is beaming.

"Had you ever heard anybody preach on the twenty-first chapter before?" he asks. "They don't. People *ought* to preach on things like that. They misunderstand Revelation. They get it crossed up and some take some spiritual part of it and maybe let on like it might be the carnal part. Like our lesson this morning was on both sides of the question: the natural and the spiritual side. Now, that Solomon was a lover of women, don't you see," he says, taking my elbow and leaning in. "He *loved* pretty women. And he really was, no doubt, a great mixer with women, because he married a thousand of 'em. And I say they killed him! I guess he died satisfied!" He lets out with a big laugh, his brown eyes dancing as he slaps his leg. "Oh," he adds then, "I'd better hush my mouth!"

Brother Headrick, who is the street cleaner in Gatlinburg, has stayed behind to hear the sermon, too, and he laughs along. As we walk outside, he shows me the bumper sticker on his car: "If your God is dead, try mine. He lives." Then he reaches for his wallet in the pocket of his worn pants. He pulls out a dog-eared card that certifies him as a Church of God minister and hands it to me. I congratulate him and tell him it's very nice and hand it back. "No," he says shyly, looking at the ground. "You keep that. Somethin' to remember me by."

"Well, I hope you got a lot out of that," Reverend Owens says, locking up the door. I ask if I might get a picture of him inside. He gladly unlocks the door and walks up to the pulpit to pose. The shutter clicks. As I pack up my camera equipment, Reverend Owens slides onto the piano bench. "I'll play you one verse," he says, and launches into a robust rendition of "Singing His Praises." His voice is strong and hearty, and it does not matter that he hits an occasional stray note or misses a few altogether as he pounds forthrightly along. Because it is simply delightful, and most of all, authentic and unadorned.

"That was great!" I tell him as he jumps off the bench. Owens claps his hands together with joy. "You sweet thing," he says, and I hug him. Brother Headrick moves in for a hug, too.

"Are you glad you came?" Owens asks me. I surely am. "We're glad you're here, ain't we, Charlie?" Charlie blushes and stares a hole in the ground. I hug them both again. "Bless your heart," Owens says, grinning, standing in the door of his little church. "You come back when you can. Come back and stay a whole week with us sometime! We'll show you the whole mountain. And don't forget!" he calls out as I get in my car, "It costs just fifteen cents to mail a letter!"

2. *The Magic of Believing*

Of all the passages Dolly Parton read in the *Bible* as a child, one, Matthew 17:20, impressed her young mind above all others: "For truly as I say to you, if you have faith as a grain of mustard seed, you will say to this mountain, 'Move hence to yonder place,' and it will move; and nothing will be impossible to you."

"People are teachin' positive thinking and the magic of believing," Dolly says today, "but somebody had to feel and know that sort of thing naturally in order to start the program. I just happen to be one of those people born with that gift of believing, of having all the faith in the world. A lot of it comes from my religious background, but it's really just my true nature to be a positive person. I have no negative sides. I've read those books about havin' a positive attitude, but they just told me things I already believed. In fact, readin' 'em was just like I was sayin' it myself. But it all stems from faith in God, knowin' that there is a higher power than ours. You have to have a child's faith, pure, innocent faith. I *believe* a thing will happen. I see no reason why it cannot. The *Bible* doesn't say *some* things are possible. It says *all* things are possible. And when I read that years ago, out of a child's faith at the time, I'm sure, I just thought, 'Well, I can have whatever I want, and I can do whatever I need to do.'

"I'm a dreamer, but I'm a doer, too. All of my life, there has been this strange thing about me. A thing that I can feel; it's almost as if it's something within me that says, 'Do this and that.' The part of my career that looks like plannin' is the part that's already planned out for me. It's just like it's there. I don't try to outstep or outdo it; I wait until I feel it. It's not an actual voice, or an actual thing that I can see. But even as a very small, young child, I knew when I should walk in a room. I knew when I should exit. I knew when I should be somewhere when I was wanted; I knew when I was not. I knew the right things to say and do to get out. See, I don't know what it is. That's why I say it's a God-given thing."

If, as Dolly told Barbara Walters in a television interview in December 1977, she never felt she belonged as a kid, that she always felt "different," certainly it was not every child in the hollows outside Sevierville who instinctively knew how to conduct her young life. And it was not every child who by the time she entered the first grade, began thinking of ways to, in Dolly's words, "put legs and wings" on her prayers. And on her songs.

To be a star, Dolly realized, it was important that she let everyone know just how well she could sing. Although it frightened her so that her heart raced, every morning during chapel services in the one-room Mountain View school, Dolly would get up in front of twenty-six students—ranging all the way up to the seventh grade in 1951–52—and sing the hymns she had learned in church. "It was just a carry-over from Sunday to Monday," Archie Ray McMahan remembers.

Occasionally, however, Dolly would sing some of the old songs her mother had sung to her, the old folk songs Great-grandmother Messer had known, some with more verses than even most adults could remember. "But Dolly had a fantastic memory," her teacher recalls, sitting in her lovely old antique-furnished farmhouse in Richardson Cove. "She would remember all the verses and sing them."

Dolly's close friends today point with pride to the fact that Dolly seldom forgets anything. But Mrs. McMahan says that Dolly's gift of memory worked a hardship on her teacher. "If Dolly heard a lesson read, she wouldn't study, because she knew it without learning. She'd memorize it. I didn't realize what was happening until one day she was reading—just flying along—and I noticed she wasn't even looking at her book. She was looking around the room, but saying all her words. I got to work with my flash cards then. But I would notice where she could do a song in her mind and remember to put it down on paper when she got somewhere."

School records show that Dolly missed thirty-one days of school her first year. The way Mrs. McMahan describes Mountain View, built new that year and named by a student for its proximity to Webb's Mountain, it's a wonder Mrs. McMahan's young charges attended as often as they did. Today, the site of the schoolhouse is hard enough for visitors to find. But when Dolly attended, the location was even more remote, two-and-a-half miles off a dirt road that rutted out frequently in winter, making it difficult for anyone to get in. "Everyone walked to school, as I did," remembers Mrs. McMahan. "I rode a school bus up the road about three miles, got off and walked up the mountain two miles. Then when I got through in the afternoon, I walked back down two miles to catch the bus. I was in the best physical shape that year I'd ever been." Such a long walk in the winter months was often hard on the children, who huddled as best they could around the stove in the back left corner, never really getting warm until well up in the day. Often Dolly arrived at school with half-frozen feet from her walk up the mountain. As Mrs. McMahan held her on her lap and rubbed the red, aching toes, Dolly, exhausted from her journey, drifted off to sleep.

If the idea of facing the walk did not encourage the Parton children to stay home, they often missed school when their father needed help bringing in the crops. Dolly followed along behind the others, picking up the potatoes as Lee plowed them up. Occasionally, she would spy a brightly colored stone or a piece of tinted bottle in the new-turned earth, and while her brothers and sister passed it by, Dolly, fascinated by anything that sparkled or gleamed or contrasted with the gray/brown/green of her surroundings, quickly put the treasure in her pocket. Later in the day, she would use it as a prop in the stage plays of her fantasies.

"Dolly was always outgoing and full of life as a child," her aunt Estelle Watson remembers. "She was just real happy. I guess you could say she was a tomboy. She growed up there with them two older boys, and she'd play and climb trees and try to do everything they could. She was active at sport's, too. Dolly just enjoyed life."

As much as Dolly talks about her family's poverty in those early years ("Dolly's the one that promoted that image of how far back in the hills they lived, and about the outhouses and no running water," says a friend who knew her when she was in high school), Mrs. McMahan never thought about the Partons being poorer than any of the other families in the community. "They might have been, but I don't know that they were," she says, giving the matter some thought. "I do know that Lee always brought a good tobacco crop, which was the main money crop in this area. And they always had a good cow to milk, they had milk and butter, and he grew lots of potatoes. They had a good garden, and they always had plenty of pork. I do know that for a fact, because the children would tell that they'd butchered hogs or that they'd stayed home to dig potatoes and say how many bushels they had. Some of the stories out make it look like Lee didn't provide for his children. But we all know he did work and provide for his family, even though he sometimes had to go into Knoxville on construction jobs. I know they didn't have a surplus of worldly goods, but I thought they had a good life. And I know they had a lot of love in their family."

With all those children to care for—twelve in all, counting Larry, who died shortly after birth—Avie Lee often neglected herself, making sure her family got along. Sometimes she worked herself into sickness. And then there were the miscarriages, two or three.

Yet, whatever hardships or troubles Dolly encountered at home, Mrs. McMahan recalls, like Dolly's aunt, that Dolly was always a happy little girl. "What I remember best about Dolly from that first year is her friendliness and how that little face always beamed. She smiled all the time, and regardless of how much fussing and fuming went on, she didn't get in fusses. She just smiled and let everybody fight their own battles. I remember her little ol' bright eyes and that smile. I can still see her just like she was then, and the smile is still the same."

The ever-pleasant, ever-smiling exterior is characteristic of the grown-up Dolly, too, unless someone offends her or interferes with her plans. Apparently, she'd learned to take care of herself by the time she entered school. "Sometimes if she thought she ought to have her say, she said it," Mrs.

McMahan says. "If she wanted to talk or tell something, she did, or if the other children said anything to her, she always had an answer for them. I don't remember anyone ever trying to run over Dolly, so I guess she had spirit from the beginning."

Still, neither Mrs. McMahan nor T. A. Robertson, the other one of Dolly's grade school teachers I spoke to, had the slightest inkling that Dolly would be famous one day.

"We didn't think that about anybody," Mrs. McMahan says. "We just wanted them to do well. At that time, very few children from that community went to high school. In fact, I don't think there had been *any*. The children that were in the sixth grade that year had more potential for going to high school than any of that particular group. But they didn't go out to school too much because they would have had to walk quite a little ways to catch the school bus; two or three years later, the county put a bus on closer to their homes, and that made it possible for more to go all the time."

But the county had done nothing about the roads on Locust Ridge the following year when Tillman (T. A.) Robertson took over as teacher. Sitting in his Pittman Center home, Robertson, now retired, remembered that he kept his small tractor at the foot of the mountain for the days when the snow and mud made it almost impossible to climb. Several years after he signed on as teacher, Robertson complained to the superintendent so often that the county made a new road and gravelled it. "That place has really developed since I started teaching there," he says in his deep, slow way of talking. "When we went up there, you couldn't get up at all without chains in the wintertime. Other things have changed wonderfully up there, too. People used to have the little coal oil lamps, 'cause electricity didn't come in there until about ten years ago. And everywhere people'd go, they'd have to walk. Now they have good roads, they all have better jobs, workin', makin' money, have nice homes. They've really come out. But I'll tell you," he adds, shaking his head, "for Dolly to have come out of there, well, that girl should be commended. Not enough credit's been given her, and she made it hard. The family had the necessities of life, but that was all. Had nice clothing, and the mother kept 'em clean, and they had plenty to eat. They were not paupers, just good poor people like the rest of the people lived up there. Just exceptionally good, nice people."

Robertson and his wife love Dolly Parton. So much so that Robertson named one of his prize fox hounds after her. The trophies Dolly, the dog, has won adorn his handsome old upright piano.

Dolly was still just six when she entered Robertson's class, since Archie Ray McMahan had mistakenly enrolled her a year early. "She just always impressed me as a personality," Robertson says. "Every time you'd look at Dolly, she'd smile. I don't know as I ever saw her grouchy or sulled up. But that's just a characteristic of the whole family. All those kids are that way. I spanked ol' Denver one time, and he just smiled up at me, and that was it. But Dolly was a fine kid. Don't know as I had to get after her about anything at all."

And little Dolly knew just how to keep Robertson fond of her. Early every morning, Robertson would send all the children in the early grades to the blackboard to practice their printing and cursive writing, starting Dolly off with the form, "My name is Dolly Parton," and then switching to "Dolly Parton is my name." As Dolly completed each sentence, she'd turn around to seek the approval of her teacher. Each time she did, Robertson winked at her. And Dolly would wink right back. "Boy, she could wink the keenest of any kid I ever saw," Robertson says. "She'd pop right back at you and wink. Always had a little knack of wit, of humor. You could never get anything on her."

Robertson says Dolly was never a show-off or loudmouth in his class, but she did nonetheless do things that distinguished her from her classmates. Such as the times she took the red crayons from her pack and applied them, lipstick-like, to her mouth and cheeks, an early sign of her fascination with color and makeup which was to figure so prominently in her '70s look. "It was comical to me," Robertson recalls, smiling, "but I didn't say anything about it, except maybe to brag on it a little."

He did not find Dolly's singing comical, however. "I didn't think of her as a special child, but I knew she had an exceptional voice, a different voice," he says. "Her mother told me her tonsils bealed [swelled] and bursted and affected her voice. I don't know if that had anything to do with it, but she was a good singer. I'd take my old guitar up there, and we'd sing. Dolly didn't sing any more than the rest of the kids did, but every time you wanted a group to sing, she was ready."

Robertson didn't intend to stay long at the Mountain View school, but he realized he had a smart group of kids, children with potential who really needed someone to work with them, to take them places and show them things. And he set out to help them. Every other year, he took the eighth grade 200 miles to Nashville to see the Grand Ole Opry. And he started a school softball team. Willadeene, whom Robertson remembers as "an exceptional kid, who at twelve, thirteen, fourteen years old was like a grown woman, just ladylike," played second base. Denver and David played, too, and the team won thirty-five out of thirty-six games, losing the one by a single run. A letter to a dog food company brought the children team caps, and by encouraging his class to write people around the world, Robertson enabled his children to receive money and clothes in the mail. They also had visitors from Alaska. And when the children needed eyeglasses or operations to have their tonsils removed, Robertson figured out a way to get them through government assistance. Since the children seemed to enjoy music and singing so much, Robertson often took them down to the *Mid-Day Merry-Go-Round* radio program in Knoxville. Local grocer and politician Cas Walker broadcast a show from the same place every day, and Robertson soon had his kids singing on Walker's program. At Christmas and the end of the school year, Robertson would take the gang down to appear on Walker's TV show. To Dolly, it was the beginning of a dream come true.

Robertson had taught one full year in the Mountain View school when it burned to the ground. Before the school was built, the members of the Evans Chapel Church had allowed school to be held at the church, and classes were once again taught there after the fire. School records show that Dolly enrolled in the third grade at Caton's Chapel School in August of 1954, apparently having stayed out of school a year.

Although Dolly writes in the liner notes for *My Tennessee Mountain Home* that she lived in the Locust Ridge house "from the time I was five years old until I was ten," Jack Hurst in his book, *The Grand Ole Opry*, fixes her years on Locust Ridge from ages three until eight. That is probably the more correct chronology, judging from the school record and incidents in Stella's memory. True to their nature, the Partons moved several times in the next short while: first, eight miles to a home on the Pittman Center Road, where Randy was born (and slept in a banana box because the family had no bassinet); second, twelve or fifteen miles to Bird's Creek; and then another five miles or so into the Caton's Chapel community. "The moving was excitin' to me," Dolly says today. "I still love to move; I can't stand to be idle. In fact, I like to always be idlin'! I'm always goin'. I guess I'm like a gypsy, a country gypsy."

Stella recalls that the move to Caton's Chapel almost ended in tragedy. "I was about five when we lived on Bird's Creek, and I remember that on the move, they had a wreck on the truck with all the furniture. Destroyed everything we had. But we were fortunate, because Denver had just been begging—he was probably about ten years old—to ride on the back of the truck and get in the dresser drawer. But they wouldn't let him, and it was lucky they didn't, because he would have been in the dresser when everything toppled over the hill."

The drive into Caton's Chapel from Pigeon Forge tells the story of Dolly Parton's childhood. The breathtaking rhododendron and forsythia compete for space with the pines and laurels on the winding mountainside, suggesting the most poetic of Dolly Parton's lyrics. But then the poverty and the heartbreaking aspects of her youth are represented, too: the rusted refrigerators and washing machines on the front porches of the houses, the automobile graveyard on a hill around the bend from where the Partons settled, the hubcaps and hood ornaments reflecting an eerie hue in the moonlight . . . Granted, the homes on this road are far superior to many of those deep in the hollows around Locust Ridge; up at the top of the road, near the Gatlinburg Country Club, the homes must run high into the thousands of dollars.

Several miles away on that same road stands the Caton's Chapel School, a modern brick building built in 1956–57. Dolly attended its predecessor for a year or two while the new school was being erected, and it was at the old two-room school, heated by a potbellied stove, that the famous Coat of Many Colors incident occurred, when Dolly was nine. Everyone who has heard Dolly's song knows the story of how Avie Lee sewed scraps of cloth together to fashion Dolly a coat in which to have her first school picture taken, all the while telling her little girl the *Bible* story of Joseph and his coat of many colors. The next morning as she dressed for school, "I felt so proud, thinkin' I looked exactly like Joseph in my coat," Dolly recalls today. But when she got to school, her classmates taunted her and laughed at her neediness. The shutter snapped, freezing the tears Dolly cried through her smile. Apparently, from what Dolly told Chet Flippo of *Rolling Stone*, the incident was far more traumatic than the song lets on. "That was a very sad and cutting memory that I long kept deep within myself. I remembered all the pain of it and the mockery. How the kids had tried to take my little coat off and I was just sprouting . . . boobs, you know, and I didn't have a blouse on under it because I done *well* just to have a little jacket to wear. So when the kids kept sayin' I didn't have a shirt on under it, I said I *did* because I was embarrassed. So they broke the buttons off my coat. They locked me in the coat closet that day and held the door closed and it was black dark in there and I just went into a screaming fit. I remembered all that and I was ashamed to even mention it and for *years* I held it in my mind." Today Dolly calls "Coat of Many Colors" her favorite of her own songs, and often dedicates it "to all the Mommas" at her concerts. "I wouldn't worry about it," Avie Lee had told little Dolly when she got home. "They're only looking with their eyes, and you're looking with your heart." Years later, Dolly would still remember her Momma's words. "That's the way I've always tried to see things," she said on an RCA album, *Great Moments at the Grand Ole Opry*. As usual, Avie Lee had turned a painful experience into a learning situation.

The Partons lived in three houses in Caton's Chapel, all in a one-mile area directly behind the school, before moving into the house there that is most often associated with them, situated on a forty- or fifty-acre farm on Caton's Chapel Road. The last property the Partons owned in the area, Lee bought with the money he made selling a cinderblock house he and his family built on a hill just up the road. "I remember that little block house," Dolly says. "It was the first home we built. I think it cost like $3,000 to build. 'Course, at that time, that sounded like a million to us. We'd hear Daddy say, 'It's gonna cost $3,000!' But it was strictly just block, and it had a cement floor. Real rough. We didn't even have a ceiling inside the house. I remember we had rafters. Then I remember we put wallpaper up over the rafters to hide the bare tin roof. But it was home to us." Years later, the Partons would buy back the house, and live there until they moved to the seventeen-acre farm Dolly bought for them in Lebanon, Tennessee. (A farm they eventually sold.) Dolly's older sister, Willadeene Blalock, and her son, Mitch, lived in the block house, now bricked over, until they, too, moved to Nashville. (The house was unoccupied in the spring of 1978.)

On down the road, the little farmhouse the family owned has been remodeled into a half brick, half frame dwelling, used until recently as the office of a land development corporation. But when the Partons lived there, the house was a white colonial, according to Stella, and pieces of the original boards are visible under neath the current exterior.

The young couple who now own it, Bob and Barbara Taggart, paid $27,000 for the house and two acres of land. "Around here, that's good," they say. The Taggarts lament the fact that the house was not left in its original style and hope to restore it. "It's nice that they modernized it," says Mrs. Taggart, gesturing toward the improvements made in the kitchen, "but they took away the charm. There were two fireplaces downstairs, one on each side. It's a shame they didn't leave it the way it was." Mrs. Taggart guesses that when Dolly lived there, the children slept upstairs in one of the two small bedrooms, where the door is only five feet, eight inches tall. The Taggarts and the Partons have one thing in common—each family filled the little house with children, and Mrs. Taggart, who had an Acuff-Rose *100 All-Country Hits* songbook on her shelf, hopes the musical Partons left good vibrations behind. "This child just loves gospel," she says, patting one on the head. "I'm gonna have one playin' fiddle, one banjo and another guitar. And I'm expecting one more, so it'll have to sing."

Avie Lee was expecting one more when she lived in Caton's Chapel, too. Five months into her pregnancy, she contracted spinal meningitis and lost her hearing in one ear; like many others with impaired hearing, Avie Lee now talks louder than normal. But the illness took a greater toll. Her son Larry died when he was only a few hours old. The family buried him in a nearby cemetery. Today, they still speak of the Parton children as numbering twelve, always including Larry, because as one of them put it, "Just because I have ten more brothers and sisters doesn't mean I don't miss him. We're a very close family." The doctors didn't expect Avie Lee to live. "But she's a very strong-willed person," Stella says. "She was in the hospital for weeks and weeks. Daddy was digging ditches during that time, but he paid the hospital bills. It took him three years. And the payments were so big that they garnisheed his check. Still he didn't quit his job. What he had left over, we lived on."

"Momma was so often sick," Dolly told Toby Thompson in 1976, " 'cause there were twelve of us kids. . . . We like to tease Momma, say she always had one on her and one in her. Looked forward to each child, though . . . some kinfolks would say, 'That's all Avie Lee and Lee need is another kid,' poor as we were. Well, Momma took sick so often that us older ones got to claim the next kid, that is, to take care of it within the family. Then we had one little brother to die. And he was supposed to have been mine. Oh, that really hurt me deep, 'cause I was at that age where I took things so hard . . . ten years old, just tryin' to grow up and be a child at the same time . . . I remember how we cried and grieved over that child. Then at the funeral, we had some relatives who said, 'You'd think that people with eleven wouldn't miss one . . . It's a good thing the poor little baby died.' "

Poetic license aside, there were not yet eleven children in the Parton family at the time Larry died. The twins, Floyd and Frieda, had not been born, nor had Rachel, the baby of the family. "When the twins were born, I was nine, and I got to pick which one I wanted, the boy or the girl," Stella recalls. "Of course, I didn't want a girl; I wanted a boy. Momma had said, 'Stella, you get the next one, and if it's twins, Cassie, you can have one of them.' Cassie was a year younger than me, and that's how it turned out. I got Floyd, and she got Frieda. They were six-month babies, so they weighed only three pounds apiece. When Floyd was an hour old, he had a collapsed lung, so he stayed in the incubator for six weeks. Almost didn't make it. Frieda stayed in for five weeks. She got to come home before Floyd did, and when they brought her, I thought, 'She's kinda cute.' They circumcised Floyd the day they brought him home, and I thought he was so ugly! Bless his heart, that was the ugliest kid I ever saw that day, because his hair was about that long, straight black Indian hair, from Momma, and it stuck out all over his head like a porcupine. His eyes were swollen shut from crying from the circumcision, and his cheeks were all chapped and raw. I thought, 'Gosh, what an ugly kid!' and I tried to talk Cassie into trading babies with me. But she wouldn't. In a couple of days, Floyd got cute, so I thought, 'I'm glad I didn't trade my baby.' He's still real close to me. He kinda considers me his second mom. But we all have a second mom in the family."

As traumatic as Larry's death was to Dolly, a wonderful thing happened to take her mind off the tragedy. She had been progressing with her music, and when she was eight, her uncle Bill Owens had replaced her two-stringed mandolin with a real baby Martin guitar. As she practiced the chords her uncle taught her, she felt stardom could not be far off.

And she was right.

Local stardom, at least. At eight, she had gone to the Pines Theater in Sevierville with her mother and brothers and sisters, and, according to a man who was there, summoned up the courage to ask if she might sing a religious number on the show. The crowd responded with wild enthusiasm, and Cas Walker, the Knoxville grocer and politician who sponsored the show (and on whose TV show Dolly had appeared with Robertson's class), asked Dolly to come on his radio program every now and then. Dolly had been appearing on the show sporadically for the last two years, but now that she was ten, Walker asked her to be a regular. And for a salary! Twenty dollars a week to start with; eventually, in the eight years she was to stay with the show, up to thirty dollars per week, with additional payment, usually twenty-five dollars a night, for the live shows the group performed out of town.

Twenty dollars a week meant more in 1956 that it does now, of course, but Dolly earned every cent of it. At 5:30 every morning Walker had a radio program, *The Farm and Home Hour,* on which he peddled groceries, badmouthed competitors and politicked in between gospel and cornball country tunes sung live in the studio by the local entertainers. Then every day from 11:30 to 12:30, he had another live radio show. On Wednesday and Thursday nights, he had thirty-minute television shows. Although Walker says "there was many a time" Dolly didn't come to the early show, she seems to have made every performance she possibly could, which was no easy matter. "This Dolly, she's a hustler," Walker says, meaning his words to be complimentary. "She'd come forty miles from Sevierville and be on that show and then go back to school every day. Then she'd get off and come back and be on the noon day show most of the time."

Dolly couldn't have done all this, of course, unless someone drove her. Sometimes it was her uncle Bill Owens. Most of the time, though, it was her aunt, Estelle Watson, Avie Lee's sister, who lived in Knoxville. "I didn't pay much attention to Dolly's singing when she was little, 'cause that was just part of our family," Mrs. Watson says. "But when she was ten or eleven, I saw she was just determined to be a singer. I figure if you want to do anything bad enough, you can do it, and she was good, even then. 'Course, she couldn't have gone if I hadn't lived in Knoxville, 'cause the family wouldn't have let her come as young as she was. But I didn't mind driving her 'cause she wanted to do it, and of course, I've always been ready to help anyone, especially my family, if they needed it." Dolly stayed with her aunt in Knoxville in the summers between high school, and during this time, Dolly was appearing on Walker's shows three times a day, three days a week. By now, Walker had both an early morning and a nightly television show, and Dolly would work those, along with the midday radio program. Estelle drove her each time, and after the noon show on Saturday, she'd drive Dolly back over to Sevierville and pick her up again on Sunday. During the school year, Mrs. Watson says, Dolly worked only holidays, Wednesday nights and the weekends, including Friday, when her aunt would pick her up in Caton's Chapel and bring her into Knoxville to do the shows, then drive her back on Sunday night. Apparently, Dolly was indefatigable. "I've seen Dolly play five shows at Bryson City, North Carolina, from 2:00 in the afternoon until 12:00 o'clock at night, and she'd be right in there," says her old boss.

Cas Walker must surely be among the last of a dying breed. Now in his late seventies, he is a walking legend in East Tennessee. Three times mayor of Knoxville, he is the only mayor in the city's history to be recalled, when a group of voters figured out a way to call a new election and booted him right out the City Hall door. You're liable to hear anything said about Cas Walker in Knoxville, because he's the town's most colorful and controversial citizen. Politics aside (and some say he still runs the city council), Walker made his fortune in the discount grocery business, courting mainly the farmers in the country and the blacks in the city. His stores appear to be everywhere in the region, spilling over into Kentucky and Virginia and other neighboring states. They're everywhere in Knoxville, too, the giant green neon shears cutting through dollar signs at every turn, and the bubbly, bouncy jingle ("Cas Walker shears are cutting away/Back to lower prices every day") assaulting you with every turn of the radio or TV dial. Walker is said to be a self-made multimillionaire (who had no shoes until he was eight)—and to be as tight as paper on the wall. He also loves to see how much he can get away with, one Knoxvillian tells me. "I'll tell you something else," the woman says. "He's got a bigger fence pen for his huntin' dogs than his house is big." She drives me by his modest house for proof, and then takes me to one of his stores so that I might pick up a copy of his newspaper, *The Watchdog*, distributed free at each of his stores. Outside, on the front wall, is a picture of a bull with "we have the lowest prices in town, and this is no bull," written by it, and a crude painting of Walker punching a ghost-like body labeled "Inflation—Enemy #1" in the stomach. Inside, homemade signs dangle from the ceiling and carts full of cheap tennis shoes stand near the front next to the newspapers. This particular store is in a black neighborhood. Today it's full of welfare mothers, each with three or four children hanging on her arm, begging for soda and candy.

Although *The Watchdog* ("The All-American Paper for All Americans") carries no masthead listing editor and publisher, the paper is Cas Walker through and through. The "ears" of Walker's front page feature a picture of a German shepherd on one side, and a bulldog on the other. A box under the shepherd reads: "The Watchdog Publishes The Unvarnished, Naked Truth That Can Be Backed Up In Court." And under the bulldog: "Facts Are Brought Out in The Watchdog That The Other Papers Don't Mention." That's for sure. Sample headlines: "Nine-Year Old Girl Raped—Mother Can't Get Warrant Served"; "The 18-Month City Tax Grab"; "County And City Voters Definitely Don't Want A Hitler Type County Government"; "Derogatory Remarks Against Any Group Should Not Be Made"; "Power Hungry Crowd Trying To Destroy Our Present Form of County, City Government"; "Never Again—Would Anyone Want To See As Disgraceful A Sheriff's Race As Our Last One Was"; and my favorite, "Cas Walker Butcher Beaten Up By Three Cars of Policemen." The accompanying story: "If this butcher was even drunk, he wasn't told it until after he was harassed and beaten up for working for Cas Walker and for what had been written in the 'Damn Watchdog' about the policemen hanging out at Drive-Ins and Honky Tonks. The girls working at this place of business dare not say anything about this incident for fear of losing their jobs." On the back of the eight-page paper, Walker has printed the pictures of everyone who has given him a bad check in the least little while, with their names and addresses, under the heading "Very Important." To the right of that is an advertisement for Walker's own arthritis pain reliever: "The arthritis pain reliever is also a reliever for any kind of a pain that a human body might have ... The capsules are made from an old German doctor's recipe. It has been checked out by Federal inspections and state inspections ... Thirty capsules cost three dollars. This is ten days of relief that you have never known before. Heart patients don't have to worry about taking this arthritis pain reliever. Diabetics don't have to worry about it. In fact, this has been approved for relief of all people."

Walker is almost impossible to track down, since he visits each of his Knoxville stores every day, and is constantly on the go or off coon-hunting or checking out issues for *The Watchdog*. Today, however, he is in his office, the Tennessee Valley Advertising Agency, a small, run-down building that resembles a barbecue stand, set back off Knoxville's Chapman Highway behind a tire store and a hamburger joint. The office will soon fill up with good, common everyday people who have an injustice to report or a favor to ask, and Walker will see each of them, look them square in the face and tell them as sincerely as a man can that he'll do something about it. Chances are he will. "Cas has got that straight-in-the-eye, unhurried, farmer-way of talking that can make you feel like he's putting it to you plumb out the way it happened, even if he's saying it's the God-given truth his old hen laid a purple egg with a *Bible* verse on it," one writer reported after visiting him. And it's true. But you mustn't miss the twinkle in his eye, either.

"Always try to have a reporter at a fire or any big event," he is saying to an employee as I open the door. He calls out for me to have a seat in the anteroom, on absolutely the cheapest, oldest, most worn-out furniture I have seen this side of a junkheap. Five bowling trophies are on a table in the corner, and taking up the entire opposite wall is a bigger-than-lifesize painting of Walker in his younger days. Soon the man himself stands in the door, a marvelous composite of old-time politician and farmer, in a blue-striped suit, blue shirt, green-and-yellow striped tie (with a Cas Walker shears tie-tac), glasses, and red suspenders. He never removes his hat, and I notice when we sit down at his cluttered desk in the back room that his shoe laces are untied. He points out a raccoon that one of his dogs caught; he's had the raccoon stuffed and set on a table next to a sidesaddle his mother owned. A handsome grandfather clock chimes as we begin our chat. Cas loves to talk about Dolly Parton, and he takes the phone off the hook so we won't be interrupted.

"I always looked at Dolly more or less like she was my own," Walker rasps in a voice that is painful to hear. "She's the most unusual person I ever met. In just every way. Now musically, she can play a guitar fine, or she can sing and don't have to have a guitar. She can join in a whole band a-playin', or she can sing in a quartet, or sing a country/western song—she's a natural country singer—and turn right back next and sing 'The Old Rugged Cross' and you'd think she's just reachin' right over into heaven. She's actually a miracle singer. There's just a few of 'em, you know. I haven't seen many people just like Dolly. I mean, everywhere you turn her, she's right, you know. Anything you assign her to do, she'll work at it and be the best at it in a few days. I've seen her come an hour before the show to do a number she was gonna do, and she'd just keep doing it over and over. She's got a lot of determination. But I'll tell you," Walker says, leaning in close, "I believe if Dolly hadn't a-made it as a singer, she would have always had good character, 'cause she stood up against all odds. If there was ever anything wrong, it was way down the line, and I just want to think there wasn't."

What Walker means about Dolly standing up "against all odds," is that little Dolly Parton matured physically just about the time she joined Walker's show as a regular, at age ten or eleven, according to one of the show's musicians, although Walker puts it a little later than that. "She growed up pretty fast," he says. "When she was thirteen, fourteen, she was as big as she is now. That was kind of a hard thing to accept. I still wanted to call her 'Little Dolly,' but she got to be big Dolly, you know." And while Walker fought to keep her in pigtails and little checked gingham dresses, Dolly was experimenting with makeup (Aunt Estelle gave Dolly her first tube of lipstick) and with wearing wigs, according to Bud Brewster, who played banjo on the show, and is now a member of the Pinnacle Boys, a bluegrass band. "She was always hep on wigs," Brewster, a handsome, easy-going man, says. "She wore wigs—I mean, she *loved* 'em. Especially after she got about twelve or thirteen years old. She was just *real* hep on 'em. With her real hair, it was always teased into a bouffant, after she got about twelve or thirteen. And then sometimes she'd put a big long fall back there and let it hang down her back. She liked them high heels, too," Brewster continues. "And, of course, tight dresses. Real short. She was like fifteen years old, then, but I've got pictures of her from that time, and you'd swear she was twenty-five. I'll tell you something else. She could do the Twist back then as good as anybody in the world. She was great! Oh, could she dance! And she enjoyed it, too. She just had a good time. That's all she seemed to worry about."

Naturally, any girl with all that going for her was bound to attract a large segment of the opposite sex. And that's what worried Cas Walker, who'd already had one girl singer on his show get pregnant and rush into a wedding, romancing herself right out of a job. ("I just eased out of it real quick, you know, so they couldn't say it happened on our show.") Walker had no time for women of loose reputation, and he knew Dolly didn't appreciate that kind of person, either. In fact, he recalls Dolly never wanted to follow an act in which someone told an off-color joke. Not only that,

"Dolly never did want you to use a 'bat' or any of those crazy women singers on the show," Walker says. "She was a pretty shrewd operator, and she'd find out things you didn't think she'd find out. If I had a woman on the show who turned out to be no 'count, first thing you'd know, Dolly would slip around and tell me who she was and what she was, and I'd ease her on out."

While Dolly was noticing what the women were up to, the men were noticing Dolly. "I went on a lot of show dates I wouldn't have went on, but she was fourteen or so, and I went to keep her from bein' out there with a bunch of tush-hogs," Walker says. "Those tush-hogs—and there are a lot of 'em in country music—weren't safe to be around women. Just couldn't behave themselves, and I never would let Dolly get out with those kind of people. She might not appreciate that, but it's the truth. Her mother knew it, and her aunt knew about it. Dolly rode with me all the time up in the front seat. And she rode with her head in my lap many a night and slept on the way back. Still, even though she's pretty, men don't advance on Dolly like they would most young girls that's that pretty. I think it's because she kinda holds herself up by usin' the Lord's name a right smart. It's kind of a byword with her, but I think it helps sell . . . well, she does it in a way that you almost know she's religious, you know. 'Course, Dolly's got a lot of good traits, but she's got one real good one. She just never did let nobody start mullin' over her. No one could feel around on Dolly. She stood her own—kept her hands to herself and made everybody do likewise. There just wasn't no such thing as walkin' up and layin' your arm around Dolly. She was just unusual that-a-way and was from the time she was just small. People might cuss her, but they appreciated her, you know."

Not that Dolly really needed Walker to protect her on those long rides home. From what the show's musicians say, Dolly has always known how to take care of herself—and how to get what she wants. "We had twelve or fifteen men and boys on the show," says Bud Brewster, "and you know there's always somebody smartin' off. But she'd always take it good. You could tease her and she'd always laugh about it. And she knew how to handle 'em. She asked one of the boys to play something with her one time, and he said somethin' smart to her, and she turned right around and throwed it back at him real heavy." She said, according to Walker, "You'll pick for me, and you'll be glad to pick for me when I get through with what I'm gonna do. I'm goin' straight to Cas Walker." Brewster says the dialogue went "something like that. But," and he blushes a little in remembering, "it was a little more, well, it was a little stronger than that!" Actions such as that today prompt Walker to recall that Dolly "was as independent as a hog on ice. She stood her ground and didn't let nobody push her around. She's amazing how she gets along with people. She's actually got no bad enemies. She don't want to hurt nobody, but yet she don't want nobody to hurt her. She'll stand up—I mean, she'll stand up like a bantam, if she has to. Couple of times I wanted to say somethin' to her about those short dresses, but she's the kind of person that you're a little hesitant to say anything to, you know, 'cause she's got a temper. I don't believe she ever got real mad at me, but she has at someone else, and she would have at me if I hadn't taken sides with her. Still, I've seen her when I knowed that she could shoot me, but she'd just look a hole through me. I'm confident that her independent ways plus her unusual voice put her over."

With those words, the door opens and Walker's secretary appears. "Did you call the dentist's office to see if my teeth's got back yet?" Walker asks. "I've got my own upper teeth," he says to me, "but these lower ones . . . I had an old woman come in on my television show one morning and knock three of my teeth out. That ruined my plate, you know." I ask why anyone would do such a thing. "Well, I loaned her a hundred dollars on a church bond, and she wanted me to give it back to her so she could show it to her husband, and then bring it back and give it to me. Well, I didn't want her to do that. I was afraid the husband might think, if he found out about it, that I shouldn't be doing that, you know. And she just lost her temper over it. She threatened me three or four days. That morning she came in and wanted to go on television. I told her we hadn't made any previous arrangements and I didn't know what she wanted to talk about. She said she wanted to tell about what a rascal I was, and I said, 'Well, enough people know that already.' Well, she just kept on insisting and finally, we couldn't get rid of her. We was on the air, but we was doin' a tape number, and I made the mistake of sayin', 'Now get out and get over there and let me talk to you after the show.' She just kept on, and I said, 'Get on out of here, you damn big ol' cow, you!' " He pauses for dramatic effect. "That's when she mashed my mouth."

"With what," I ask. "Her fist?"

"Her fist. I was sittin' down, you know. She knocked three of my teeth out, and I got up and opened me up a boot shop in her hind-end then. And I got wrote up all over the whole country about it. I sent her to the hospital 'cause she let on like she fainted. And I went and called my lawyer and he told me just to go on over there and make bond. So I did, and when I come out of the jail, they had television cameras all there, and radio. Mikes ever' place, you know. They said, "Mrs. Tindell's in the hospital. She says you broke three of her ribs." I was supposed to say 'No comment,' but I said, 'Where I kicked Mrs. Tindell, her ribs wasn't near.' Damn thing carried all over the country. Didn't hurt, though. I beat it when it finally went to court."

The secretary reappears. "Mrs. Walker has your dentures. The doctor brought them to the house." "Oh, sure enough?" Walker says, delighted. "Yes," she tells him, "but we need to get him a check. Do we make that out to him or to cash?"

"How much was it?" he asks.

"Three hundred dollars."

"No, no," Walker says, looking shocked. "I don't think I'll pay that. I'm gonna give him the teeth! I ain't gonna pay no such'a price as that. He's crazy! That's just havin' 'em lined! Hell!"

"Well, Mrs. Walker said to get a check for three hundred dollars."

"No, you tell him he'll be longer gettin' three hundred dollars for lining my teeth than he was gettin' grown! That's crazy!" Walker is dumbfounded. "You know," he says, turning back to me, "people will rob you if they think you've got somethin'. I never paid over twenty dollars to line my teeth! That's terrible! When ol' Mary popped the others out, they didn't cost but two hundred and seventy dollars, first ones I had." He breaks into a grin. "I call 'em 'Mary's dentures.' "

All through his retelling of the Dolly story, Walker has talked about Dolly's Aunt Estelle, mentioning her uncle, Bill Owens, only once. "What about Bill Owens?" I ask. "Isn't he the one who's responsible for Dolly being on your show? I've always read about how much he helped her in the early days, moving to Nashville and getting set up there so Dolly would have some place to live when she came after graduation."

Walker is uncharacteristically silent. Finally he says what he can't hold back. "Bill Owens never helped Dolly no more than Khrushchev has helped you. That stuff is all tommyrot. Her aunt's the only person ever actually tried to help Dolly. Everything Bill Owens ever had done for him, Dolly done it. And he's hung on Dolly's strings, but Dolly never hung on his. I don't believe that first person has asked me to help Dolly Parton. Mrs. Parton, for example, never had any idea that Dolly was goin' the places she was. Now, Bill has brought her to the show a few times and took her back, but most of the times her aunt brought her. Bill Owens may be an uncle, but he was just kind of a tush-hog, actually. Later on in life, I think he and his brother got so's they could write some songs. [Bill and Dolly established Owepar Publishing Co., after they'd been in Nashville several years.]But there's no more truth in all that than there is in I jumped across the moon. 'Course, now Dolly liked to build him up, but the truth is the truth. The Owens Brothers [Bill and Louis] sang on my show lots, but I never did pay 'em. And Dolly never did sing with 'em. You know, you've always got individuals that aren't hardly good enough to go anyplace, but aren't hardly bad enough to kick out, either."

Bud Brewster recalls Bill Owens bringing Dolly down from Sevierville so she could appear on the show, and he remembers that both Bill and Louis used to take Dolly over to WIVK in Knoxville and use the studio at night to make demo tapes. Claude Tomlinson remembers it, too. Master of Ceremonies on Walker's live noonday show, Tomlinson engineered those sessions for Dolly and the Owens brothers.

"Even at that age, Dolly's voice was very powerful," Tomlinson says, sitting in WIVK's lower level, a few feet from where he sat with Bill and

Louis Owens back in the early '60s. "In fact, she sounded a lot like she does today, except she's a little more refined now, of course. And then she talked like she was from way back in the hills.* Her uncles would come down here and record demos of songs they had written and that Dolly had written, plus a few songs that were already hits, all for the usual bit of taking them to Nashville to make a presentation and a pitch about Dolly and her capabilities. Later I recognized some of the stuff on her albums. Over a period of years, we'd work three to four hours a night here putting demos on tape, with instruments and so forth. Dolly's sisters would come down and sing harmony. I would master the sessions. Of course, I never charged them a dime for this. Because Bill said we were all in this together, and of course, I was trying to get them started. Bill would say, 'Claude, one of these days we're gonna get something going, and we'll really remember you then.' Well," Tomlinson says, "they must have so much going these days . . ." He lets the sentence finish itself. He says the Owens brothers will come by occasionally when they're up that way.

As for any thoughts that Dolly might have ridden into show business on Bill's coattails, Tomlinson remembers that there was no problem in recording Dolly. She usually got everything on one take. The problem was with Bill. "I always had trouble with Bill, mainly on rhythm. He'd always get messed up, and we'd have to do more retakes." Tomlinson says Bill and Louis pushed Dolly hard. "They recognized talent and they knew if she ever got to be big time, they'd be involved. But I think Dolly did a lot more for her cause than Bill did. I wasn't on top of the scene all the time, but that's what I hear. I know what Bill has said he has done. Of course, it's an ego thing with some people if they've been involved with someone who makes it really big. They might forget just how much they did, but Bill worked hard."

One thing Bill did was drive thirteen-year-old Dolly 200 miles over to Nashville so she could appear on the Grand Ole Opry. Walker says he and Dolly's aunt set the whole thing up with several of the big-name Opry stars, but when asked about it recently, none of the stars could remember having done so.† In fact, no one at the Opry except Dolly remembers the appearance, not Ott Devine, then the Opry manager, nor Jimmy C. Newman, without whom, Dolly says, she never would have gotten on. "My Uncle Bill had an old car with the side caved in," Dolly laughs today. "We'd save up enough money to go back and forth to Nashville, trying to get somethin' goin', because he believed I was gonna be a star, and I was

* Mrs. Watson denies Cas Walker's claim that she hired a woman to teach Dolly speech and charm. "Ain't nobody had to teach her nothin'," she says. "She may have been timid with strangers, but she was always friendly and had a smile for everybody."

† Walker also claims to have given Jimmy Martin, June Carter, The Louvin Brothers, Tennessee Ernie Ford, Loretta Lynn, and Carl and Pearl Butler their start in show business. "I made a terrible mistake with Loretta," he says, wincing. "I told her she had too many children to go anyplace in radio. Ninety days later, she was on the Grand Ole Opry."

fool enough to believe him. So we'd take out every time we'd get a chance. We'd sleep in the car and clean up in fillin' stations. First time I was on the Opry, I went with the intentions of bein' on. Nobody ever told me that you couldn't do anything you wanted to do. I just always thought, 'Well, all you gotta do is just go there and if you sing well, you can be on the Grand Ole Opry.' Gettin' the nerve was probably the hardest part, but we were always blessed with more nerve than sense anyway. But we came to Nashville and went backstage and tried to talk to everybody. Ott Devine said that I was too young, but now I know it was just rules—you can't just walk in and be on the Grand Ole Opry. But I didn't give up that easy. And my uncle and me kept talkin' to everybody backstage, worryin' 'em to death, I'm sure. But finally, Jimmy C. Newman gave me his spot. He had done one spot and he had a second comin' up. I don't know why he did it—out of the goodness of his heart, I suppose, but it's somethin' I'll always remember and thank him for because I feel like he played a part in my career to some degree. So he let me go on, and I sang a George Jones song and got an encore. I thought, 'Boy, this is just great!' Then I got another encore. I thought that was even greater! It was just more than I could really believe."

Although Newman believes he let Dolly take his second spot because "her name must have been on the list and we were running out of time," Ott Devine says Dolly must have gotten to perform for the very reason she remembers—because Newman let her. "Her name was not on the list," Devine says. "I turned her down because we had a policy against using children that age. You had to be eighteen years old, an adult. She just sneaked in there with Jimmy."

If appearing on the Grand Ole Opry fulfilled one of Dolly's dreams, she realized another when she took the bus down to Lake Charles, Louisiana, where her Uncle Robert was in the service, to cut a single for Goldband Records, an obscure local blues-oriented label. Dolly was so small she had to sit on the studio's tallest stool "so the microphone could fit and we could get the fullest capabilities of the song she was recording," remembers Goldband's Eddie Shuler. The A side featured a tune Dolly had written called "Puppy Love" ("I'm old enough now to kiss and hug/And I like it! It's puppy love!"), a teen tune with a rockabilly beat, very much in the style of young Brenda Lee. Dolly sang it with all the passion a thirteen-year-old (she was eleven by some accounts) can muster. The B side had a hillbilly tune that "Parton/Owens" wrote called "Girl Left Alone," in which Dolly feels very sorry for herself—she's a young girl who owes society a debt for her sinful behavior: "I'm a girl left alone, there's no hope for me/I'm tossed to and fro like a ship on the sea/There was a mistake and now I will pay/For those who still love me, I must go on this way." Young Dolly moaned the lyrics all the way through, sounding as if all that tossing to and fro had made her seasick. The slim instrumentation nearly overshadowed Dolly on this one, but not enough to hide the fact that the range is a little beyond Dolly's grasp. Still, it's a charming effort, especially in hindsight. (The two sides were recently reissued on a collector's album. But while "Puppy Love" is generally thought to be Dolly's first record, Skip Trotter of WSEV in Sevierville says that "prior to 1960, when Dolly was just a little girl—eight or ten, maybe—the first record she ever made was right here. She had a little squeaky child's voice, and we made the thing with one microphone on an Ampex 601. It was a poor pressing at that. She's threatened to kill us if we ever play it. We've got it under lock and key." Trotter recalls Dolly's fee at that time for the performances she gave "out in the little country schools" was three dollars. "They dragged her around to all those school houses," he says. "I saw her so sleepy the next day she couldn't hold her head up, where she said they'd had car trouble and she'd gotten out and pushed the car in the mud. She was a determined little girl. Worked at it from the time she was five years old.")

Dolly often sang songs of her own composition, or songs she wrote with Louis and Bill and her Aunt Dorothy Jo, when she appeared on Cas Walker's programs. Brewster says Dolly's songs were ahead of their time. In fact, "she probably wrote a lot of the things she's doin' now back then in the very beginning. That type of stuff wasn't goin' over all that much back then. Dolly's songs had so much down-to-earth meaning to 'em, and the music that was goin' over then was light-hearted stuff. Dolly wrote about basic home-type situations."

Brewster also recalls that Dolly was quite a versatile performer and that even then she demonstrated a fondness for the music she has adopted of late. "We played show dates at schools and things back then, and she would go and sing and be in comedy routines with us. She was always a show person. She knew what it was about. Her personality just seemed to come out on stage. Even though she was bashful, you wouldn't know it when she was on the stage, because she was just so vibrant that it just covered the shyness right up. She sang a song called 'I Love a Tall Man' a lot. That was one of the first songs she sang on the show. And she sang a lot of hymns, done 'em just terrific. Between shows, we'd rehearse songs that she'd written, or she'd play the piano and sing. Back then rock and roll was big. I think if she'd had her druthers then, she'd have been in rock and roll. She was a real great fan of rock and roll. And she could sing it. Believe me, she could sing it! Brenda Lee was definitely one of her favorites, naturally, and she was a big fan of Connie Francis. We sang 'Everybody's Somebody's Fool' a lot. She liked songs you could bounce along with a little bit. Dolly was just a natural," Brewster says. "Everybody knew it. It was no secret. It was just a matter of waiting until she grew up and could do it. Larry Mathis and myself tried to steal her away from Nashville right before she left. In fact, I've still got the demonstration tapes we made. Everybody knew Dolly was gonna make it big."

Including Cas Walker, who has kept tapes he made of Dolly through the years. The day we talked, Walker promised to air a video tape of Dolly singing "Something Fishy" for me the next morning. When I drag myself over to the set at 5:30 in the morning, Walker is sitting in a chair, wearing the same suit he had on the day before, and eyeballing the camera. He's got his new store to plug, one over in Dryden, Virginia, and mentions that he's planning to put a discount drugstore in near it. Another discount drugs is already operating in Dryden, he tells the good folks, "But they're foolin' a lot of people. Like, seventy-five or a hundred people think they're gettin' a job, but as soon as the openin' is over, those people will be let go. We're sure glad to have 'em, over in Dryden, and they're good people, but they'll have to operate just like any other business, for a profit, and they can't with no seventy-five or a hundred people a-workin' for 'em, I'll gar-un-tee you that! If they wind up with anymore 'n fifteen, they'll surprise me! Say, we have pretty Dan up to tell us our next good number," he says with only a minuscule pause, and a four-piece bluegrass band comes on. Dan talks for probably a whole minute before someone remembers to flip his microphone on. He has a hymn for us this morning. "I have a cousin over in St. Mary's Hospital in room three-sixty-three who's a very sick lady," Dan says, "and we'd like to send this over to her this morning, for her family and folks up around Rutledge; we'd like to tell 'em that she's not doin' too well. Her name is Laura Bloomer, of course, and I'd like to send this number over that way and to all the nurses and folks that are so kind and good to her. That's a real fine hospital." A lone open G chord fills the airwaves, and Dan and the boys are into "Pray for Me," in close, high harmony.

From there, the station sells a couple of tractors and some ice cream, and then Cas is back. "Here's something I don't know whether anyone else has had the experience I've had or not, but every now and then you get a-hold of a dentist," he says, staring straight into the camera. "Most all dentists are honest people. I know that. And maybe the one I got a-hold of is honest, but time or two I've got a-hold of people that actually, Jesse James wouldn't be any worse. Now, my lower teeth is a plate, and I paid an ungodly price to get a plate made. I've had several plates. There ain't no such thing as havin' a denture that's completely satisfactory. I know that. But anyhow, he charged me, just to make a denture, six hundred dollars! See, all this happened over this bloomin' trouble I had on television here one morning with that poor old sister. And my top teeth are all mine. Now, I've had dentures relined. And I never paid—one time I paid twenty dollars. Most times dentists have never charged me anything for relinin' my teeth. But I had my teeth relined yesterday, and Lord, have Mercy! I want you to listen to the bill that fella said he wanted me to send him—three hundred dollars! For relinin' my teeth! I'd say five would be excessive. Wanted three hundred dollars! Now, all dentists is not like this. But that's the nearest robbery I've ever been took yet. Anyhow, we know about it now. Let's have some music."

A gospel group is up next, singing "I Had a Vision of Jesus." Then there's a tiller to sell, and some cottage cheese. Then Cas comes back, standing up with huge placards with food prices written on them. "Let me remind you," he begins, "you know these big chains, they have different deals they come out with, like their price cutters, and all this, but I gar-un-tee you, there is not a big national chain where you could begin to buy . . ." At this point he starts shuffling his product cards, rubbing them against his lavaliere mike, muffling whatever he's saying. Finally, he gets it all straight, and pitches his sweet peas and dairy topping, ending with orange and pineapple soda, sixty-four ounces, "or half a gallon," just eighty-eight cents. Just as I begin to wonder if he's forgotten the Dolly tape, Cas says, "Wonder if we couldn't have a real treat up this mornin'. You know, we used to refer to Dolly as 'Little Dolly,' and then she kept growin' up and gettin' bigger and bigger, and we just called her Dolly Parton. Here's one of the numbers she used to do on the show just before she left us here. Dolly Parton up next."

Bud Brewster remembers Dolly actually made the tape on a return visit from Nashville. "Something Fishy" was one of her first country hits for Monument Records, but here she sings it with a grind and a roll in her voice, very Brenda Lee. Still, her essential style is there, along with the beginnings of the Dolly look. Her hair, a white blond shade that contrasts sharply with her black eyebrows, is teased high into a bouffant, set off by silver hooped earrings. She wears heavy black eyeliner and a very traditional, conservative blue date dress. The most striking thing about her appearance is that she's thinner here than she's been at any other time in her professional career.

The song over, it's time to sell another tractor and to plug an antique auction, and when Cas comes back on, he pitches his own brand of rug cleaner, "arth-a-ri-tis" tablets and "superderm salve." "This'll relieve the seven year itch within seven seconds, the ath-a-lete's foot, or any kind of an itchy condition," he promises, and then has a few words to say to the construction crew putting up his building in Harlan, Kentucky. "Let's put two crews on this, and let's get it *done,* for goodness sake. But don't take time to have no dentures relined," he adds. "I gar-un-tee, he'll shore be sorry of this deal. Three hundred dollars to reline just a lower denture! Ain't that somethin'? Poor ol' Jesse James. We orta build him a monument, 'stead-a sayin' he was a bad man. Say, we got the news up next . . ."

3. High School

THE NEW SEVIER COUNTY HIGH SCHOOL, a handsome brick building set out on the Newport Highway outside Sevierville, looks rather much like every other modern high school. Aside from a sign at the entrance that boasts "Sevier County High School, Home of the Smoky Bears," there is nothing noticeable about the school that identifies it with any particular region, and it would fit in comfortably in Coffeyville, Kansas, or in Paramus, New Jersey. Late in the afternoon, the students milling about the hallways look like high school students everywhere. Boys wear KISS belt buckles at the top of their Levi's, and the girls, several as buxom as Dolly in the early stages of her career ("Must be the mountain air," my mother says), wear anything from novelty T-shirts to Gant blouses with their tight-fitting skirts and pants. When the last bell rings, they file out into the parking lot and get into their Volkswagens and Cadillacs.

But down the main hallway toward the gymnasium, Sevier County High School has something which sets it apart from every other high school in the nation—a Dolly Parton commemorative showcase. In it, on the left, is an 8 × 10 glossy of Dolly in a typical publicity pose. And next to it stands the display's prize: Dolly's band uniform, number 39, a cumbersome, white double-breasted affair with big, sturdy impressive buttons, purple braid around the high stand-up collar and cuffs, frayed from wear, and a bear ensignia on the sleeve. "This uniform was retired by the Sevier County High School Marching Band on Oct. 13, 1977, to honor Dolly Parton and her many contributions to the Band," reads an accompanying sign. The sign is very carefully worded. Number 39 is not the actual Dolly Parton band uniform at all. Seems the band department had trouble finding Dolly's personal uniform, and just retired this one symbolically. How the legend grows. Sigh. Still, hard as I try, I simply cannot envision her wearing this or any other band uniform, although a picture, printed in the souvenir books sold at Dolly's concerts last year, exists for proof. There, a smiling young Dolly stands in her uniform—complete with belt, tassels and high-plumed hat with chin strap—and poses with her instrument.

The snare drum.

Further up the hall, next to the pay telephone, a bronze plaque is mounted on the wall: "Dolly Parton: Founder of Dolly Parton Scholarship Foundation, Established April 1970."

At the time Dolly attended the school, then held in the old building, only she could have possibly dreamed that one day this would be here. For if there was any average, ordinary student in the senior class of 1964, it was Dolly Rebecca Parton.

Or so it seemed. "If you had walked in my class then," says Mrs. James Householder, Dolly's American history teacher, "she would have looked just like everybody else. She just did her thing. She was a very normal, giggly little girl with a tremendous sense of humor."

Of course, Dolly was not ordinary or average. She may not have been voted anything in high school, but she'd been a local radio and TV star since she was ten, she'd appeared on the Grand Ole Opry (albeit a Friday night show) and she'd cut a record. Not only that, she was going to be a real Star, and her first year of high school, she let anyone who was interested know that one day she was going to be an Opry regular.

And that did not sit so well with a good portion of the students and teachers of Sevier County High School. For a number of reasons. One former student remembers that then, probably as now, Sevier County High School was attended by city students and by country students, each with their own cliques. Many of the country kids thought Dolly was something special. They'd seen her on Cas Walker's programs, and they crowded around her when she brought her guitar to school and sang her own tunes, some based on actual happenings in the area, others culled from her imagination. "She could just look at something—nature or something happening on the street—and make a song out of it," one classmate recalls. "And she always sang from the heart." Still, some of them made fun of her behind her back, probably out of jealousy. And many of the city kids wouldn't have been caught dead listening to country music. It was, after all, the early '60s, and rock and roll was the going thing, with country at a low ebb. In 1964, when Dolly was still getting up at four o'clock in the morning and going over to Knoxville to appear on Cas Walker's show, the Beatles had taken America by storm, and any kid who was cool at all preferred that music to anything else. Anyone who sang corny country songs on as hick a show as the Cas Walker *Farm and Home Hour,* where three weeks before Easter, a man sat on a "nest" full of "eggs," hatching them into chickens for all the children in the audience, was hardly to be taken seriously as a musician. Or, actually, to have her music shown any respect at all. Especially anyone as backwoodsy as Dolly Parton. "She'd sing just pure country," remembers Ruth Rolen Green, at whose sixteenth birthday surprise slumber party Dolly played and sang. "Back then, where she came from was considered *real* country, because the roads weren't paved and not as many people had cars. I'm sure glad she made good, 'cause she was a great person and she had it rough. The first time I met her, our freshman year, she said she was gonna be on the Grand Ole Opry. Told me that was her dream. I believed she was gonna make it, 'cause I knew she had determination. But most people just laughed at her." So, after that first year, and for the next two, Dolly kept quiet about her plans for the future and about appearing on TV over in Knoxville. If she kept a low profile at Sevier County High School, maintaining a low B, high C average while working toward a general degree with an emphasis on home economics, science and business, she may have done so because she was devoting most of her energies to her own private projects away from school; she was just biding her time until the day all those kids who ignored her, who laughed at her homemade lunches of cornbread and pork, realized that she was something special, after all.

And the more they laughed, the more determined she became. Each day when Dolly came home from school, she worked on her songs. And she and her Uncle Bill continued to send demo tapes to Nashville publishers and record companies. She was not much past fourteen when Buddy Killen of Nashville's Tree International Publishing Co., now one of the best-known and most respected firms in the business, invited her over and signed her to the company as a writer.

"Dolly was a beautiful, sweet girl," Killen remembers today, sitting behind his large desk in Tree's Spanish-style offices. "She was very country and very raw, not pretentious at all. She was just Dolly, and she said what she thought in the way she felt it. She'd talk in her East Tennessee whatever-it-is, and many times you'd have to listen a little close to hear what she was saying. I remember she was very happy and jovial, but she also wanted to talk business. She would laugh a lot, and she was very sincere and warm, but she could be very serious, and she showed a lot of maturity. I really thought she had potential. She sparkled even at that young age. Her voice sounded the same then as it does now, maybe a little stronger today. I knew she was an outstanding, unique talent."

Killen realized that Dolly's uncle was not an outstanding talent, that he would never be a star or even a great songwriter, but he signed him anyway. "Bill was very intense," Killen recalls. "He was sort of a driver, really wanting to get something done. I don't mean he was obnoxious, but he pushed all the time, trying to achieve."

Dolly wanted to be a singer as well as a writer, of course, and by the time she was fifteen, Killen had landed her a recording contract with Mercury Records. In March of '62, two months after Dolly's sixteenth birthday, Mercury released her single, "It's Sure Gonna Hurt," a tune she had written with Bill, and backed it with "The Love You Gave," written by a couple of Tree writers. Listed on the label as "artist" was "Dolly Parton with the Merry Melody Singers," who were actually just a group of people gathered in the studio at the time, including three members of the Jordanaires, Gordon Stoker, Ray Walker and Neal Matthews. "It's Sure Gonna Hurt" bears all the earmarks of the music Bud Brewster remembers Dolly enjoying at the time. Pure pop (except for Dolly's country accent), the tune is highly reminiscent of Connie Francis' "Lipstick on Your Collar," and Dolly sings it up in her best Brenda Lee voice. Still, she sounds younger than she actually was, far too young to be singing about the heartache of love: "Since my baby left me/I don't know what to do/Just couldn't believe my eyes/When I saw him with you./He left me for you, oh/He's treatin' me like dirt/It may not kill me/But it's sure gonna hurt." Produced by Jerry Kennedy, who in time would become known for his work with Tom T. Hall, Johnny Rodriguez and others, "It's Sure Gonna Hurt" went nowhere.

Still, it got some airplay, particularly in Knoxville, where Bill and Dolly hand carried it to the radio stations. At WSKT, they met Bobby Denton, now operations director at WIVK. The two hit it off well, and since he knew what a thrill it was for Dolly to hear herself over the radio, Denton would call her and tell her what time her record would be played. Later, when he moved over to WIVK, Denton frequently saw Dolly and her uncle at station sponsored events. "I remember one time we did a swimming party and show at Whittle Springs," Denton says, "and Dolly and Bill came out. When they did 'What'd I Say,' Dolly hit the high notes fine, but Bill sang flatter than a pancake." He laughs in remembering. "After that I got to be friends with her, and we had a few dates."

Dolly's Aunt Estelle says Dolly didn't date much, and Mr. and Mrs. Parton told a national tabloid that Dolly had time for dates when she wanted them, but she just "didn't want them very often. It wasn't that the boys weren't after her. Dolly just wouldn't take time away from her music. She'd break a date in a minute if a singing job came along."

Denton takes a lot of kidding today about the fact that he used to date a woman who is fast becoming one of the nation's foremost sex symbols, and he blushes when asked what those dates were like. "One time," he says, and breaks into a laugh, "Sevier County was playing Holston and I went with Dolly to the game. She was playing in the band. It was pretty funny, because people had seen her on TV and she had gotten some air-play on her records, and then they saw her in the band uniform with one of those crazy hats on that they wore. They would just freak out, you know, and say, 'Is that Dolly?' I went with her one night to tape a TV show, and then we went to the drive-in. You couldn't watch a movie with her, because she just laughed and talked and giggled all the time. Just talked all the time, non-stop. She's got the craziest laugh in the world, and at that time, she was doing a lot of homespun humor—clichés, you know, like Tennessee Ernie Ford, stuff you don't hear much anymore, like, 'Don't that beat the bugs a bitin'?' She'd just do this in normal conversation. She was always happy. I don't believe I've ever seen her mad. And she was basically very mature. Lived the music business, you know, because she knew what she wanted to do. I'd say that she knew from the first day she went in the business where she was going. I think she's had this whole course charted, even this recent image change, which was a big gamble. She used to say, 'I've got to try to make it. That's what I'm living for.' It really bothered her if she heard someone say they didn't like her record, or if people didn't like her. She went out of her way to be liked."

"I think everybody liked Dolly," says Jack McMahan, Dolly's homeroom teacher and current principal of Sevier County High School. "Even the people who didn't like her music liked her personally. Maybe a few of the girls didn't, but of course, that's high school age. She was always full of life and had a good personality, was easy to talk to, and I think the rank and file liked her whether they liked her music or not." (Some may have been jealous that Dolly's musical activities often allowed her to be excused early from school. She missed on the average twenty days a year her last three years of high school.) Dolly herself remembers she was popular—but "not in the right way. I think a lot of it had to do with the fact I was different," she told a reporter. "I was daring even then . . . I'd tell dirty jokes."

Some of the girls may have felt a little uneasy around Dolly because of the way she looked and dressed. "She had a nice build for a high school girl, she *really* did," Bobby Denton remembers. But Dolly's friends are in conflict when recalling how her look of the early '60s compares with her current vogue. Ruth Green says Dolly "hasn't changed at all, as far as personal appearance. Looked just like she does now." Bobby Denton, on the other hand, says, "I don't think she's changed a lot, except for her dress. She kept a pretty low profile then," he adds when asked if her clothes accentuated her figure.* "People used to say, 'Well, she's got such a small waist. [One student remembers Dolly measuring her waist at seventeen or eighteen inches.] She used to wear a lot of jeans and blouses. I remember one time, she wore a lot of ruffles, but most of the time it was jeans and blouses. And her senior year, she started wearing a lot of makeup. But she was very, very beautiful. Got a tremendous complexion."

As Denton and Dolly's four yearbook pictures point out, Dolly had begun to develop her current look by her junior year. In her freshman picture, the shy, reticent Dolly who was ridiculed because she wanted to join the Grand Ole Opry, wears a tailored white blouse, the collar opened and laid back in a V-shape on her neck. Her blond hair is short and raised on top, the spitcurls around her ears and across her forehead giving her already pudgy face an added chubby look. She has changed her look drastically by

* Shortly after the 1977 Dolly Parton Day, Ken Mink of the Knoxville *News-Sentinel* interviewed one of Dolly's old classmates. "Dolly has always been big in that department," the woman told Mink, referring to Dolly's bust. "Although she now jokes about it, she used to be pretty proud of her anatomy. In high school she never really flaunted it, but she was always wearing clothes that fit tightly around the waist—which emphasized her upper body." Dolly's former school chum also told Mink that she and Dolly spent a lot of their teenage hours discussing the opposite sex. "Dolly wasn't a prude," she said, "but she was conservative around boys. She once told me she felt like getting into a giant bag and zipping it up all the way over her head before going out on a date."

Life may have been "as peaceful as a baby's sigh" at the Partons' Tennessee Mountain Home on Locust Ridge, but the existence the family eked out was one of numbing poverty. (ALANNA NASH) Left, Archie Ray McMahan, Dolly's first grade teacher. (ALANNA NASH)

Above left, Dolly, standing next to Cas Walker, and her grade school classmates perform on Walker's show—her first appearance there. (T. A. ROBERTSON) Above right, Tillman Robertson today, with the trophies his fox hounds—including one named Dolly Parton—have won. (ALANNA NASH) Below, Tillman Robertson's class at Mountain View School, about 1952. Dolly, in a striped shirt, is at center. Four other Parton children appear: Bobby (front row, fourth from left), David (second row, at Dolly's right), Denver (first row, at Dolly's left), and Willadeene (last row, fifth from right). (T. A. ROBERTSON)

Above, the Reverend Jake Owens's House of Prayer; Owens's trailer home is visible at right. (ALANNA NASH) Below left, Reverend Owens outside his church with Brother Charles Headrick after a Sunday School class. (ALANNA NASH) Right, Cas Walker—grocer, politician, TV pitchman, talent scout extraordinaire. (ALANNA NASH)

Above left, Dolly's first publicity photo, for her Goldband single "Puppy Love." Right, before Dolly left home for Nashville, she, Larry Mathis (L) and Bud Brewster (R), musicians on Cas Walker's show, formed a short-lived musical trio. (PHOTO COURTESY BUD BREWSTER) Below, Dolly and her parents, Lee and Avie Lee Parton, in October 1977, when Dolly returned to Sevierville for Dolly Parton Day. (KNOXVILLE NEWS-SENTINEL)

the next year, looking far older and more like a good-time girl than the innocent Dolly of the year before, despite the presence of a circle pin on the band of her shirt. Even more surprising is that Dolly looks decidedly unkempt, and that her unruly hair, a mass of loose curls on top, trailing in a big wave down her back, is a much darker brown than it appears to be in any of her other pictures. The fact that the color matches her eyebrows seems to rule out the possibility that she wore a wig to school that day. (Bobby Denton believes she did not wear wigs in this period, despite Bud Brewster's insistence that she had worn them since she was a child.) But by junior year, the real metamorphosis has taken place. Here, Dolly, who has learned to apply her makeup by now, looks like a real lady. She wears pearls around her neck and hanging down the front of her grown-up dress, and stares away from the camera with a tight-lipped smile, a look reminiscent of her mother. Her hair, while still long in back, shows signs of the teased bouffant look to come, and it is by now a far lighter shade of blond than it was in her freshman picture. With the senior year picture, however, Dolly has finally come into her own. Dressed in a low cowl (probably a drape supplied by the photographer), she looks confident and radiantly happy—and sexy. The baby fat is gone, and Dolly could easily pass for twenty-three or more. Her hair is now bleached a white blond and styled in a short bouffant coif.

Apparently, Dolly has always been a little sensitive and self-conscious about her hair. Archie Ray McMahan, Dolly's first grade teacher and the mother of Sevier County principal Jack McMahan, recalls substitute teaching for her son during Dolly's first high school years. "One day in homeroom period, I said something to Dolly about the way she wore her hair as a child," Mrs. McMahan remembers. "She said, 'Oh, yes, Miss Archie Ray. I just had about seven or eight hairs back then.' She thought it was thin, I guess because her hair was straight and Willadeene's was curly. I've wondered if she had a complex about it, if that's why she wears all those wigs."

Dolly was downright touchy about her hair by her senior year, when Archie Ray and her husband accompanied the class to Washington, D.C. She recalls Dolly looked so glamorous at this point that the bus driver called her "Marilyn" the whole trip. "This was the first or second year they were wearing the bouffant hairdos," says Mrs. McMahan. "Dolly liked that look from the beginning, maybe because it gave her a little height.* She didn't have too much bouffant, though. Her hair looked real nice. I remember we started through a door in the White House, and one of the guides kinda patted her hair and said, 'Is that yours?' And she said, 'Yes, sir-ee, I'll have you know that's mine.' " Mrs. McMahan lets out a laugh. "We got such a kick out of it," she says. "But she always had an answer for everybody. You didn't get one on her."

* Dolly is five feet, no inches, and usually wears five- and six-inch heels to make herself look taller.

If Dolly was overly defensive about her hair with the White House guide, it was probably a carry-over from the times the girls at school had criticized her clothes. Dolly may have kept quiet about intending to become a star, but she had never stopped thinking about it for a second, and her dress reflected her inner thoughts. Too poor to afford the clothes she thought would befit a star, Dolly, probably with her mother's help, set about creating the clothes that matched her dreams. Besides, the people who watched Cas Walker's show already considered her a star, and she had that image to maintain for them. In a classic example of how far ahead Dolly was thinking, one of her classmates recalls that among the clothes Dolly's mother made her was a pair of tight-fitting pants that flared broadly at the knees. Mrs. Parton had put a pleat in each leg, and sewn a different color material in each one. Although they must have looked outrageous to the students of Sevier County High School, especially since Dolly wore an ordinary blouse with them, those pants prefigured the look Dolly was to adopt more than twelve years later, when she designed the costumes Lucy Adams made for her syndicated TV show, *Dolly!* Of the general reaction, Dolly has said, "I wore tight skirts and tight clothes and that didn't go over too good. Other people thought I was a bad influence on their kids."

Still, Dolly was determined none of this was going to get her down. And, now that she had cut a record for Mercury, even one that didn't go anywhere, and had begun to feel more and more confident about herself, by senior year she once again began to talk about her plans for the future. She had talked it over with her uncle, she told her classmates, and as soon as she graduated, she and Bill Owens were moving to Nashville to become songwriters and artists. And she, of course, was going to become a member of the Grand Ole Opry. The reaction this time?

"I have heard two different thoughts," says principal Jack McMahan. "One is that a lot of people made fun of her. But on the other hand, there were many, many who didn't. I truthfully wasn't sure of all her goals, but as far as making the Grand Ole Opry, I thought she would, because she was doing too well for her age. Almost every weekend, she was on a television show in Knoxville. I didn't have much doubt about her making it and going that route. As far as becoming a star, well, that's kinda like saying, 'How big is big?' In my opinion, when she made the Grand Ole Opry, she was a star. When Dolly came on the Grand Ole Opry or on her television show, it didn't really surprise anybody who was in school with her." Bobby Denton shares that thought. "Most people believed her, I think, because she'd had that record out when she was a kid and had gotten a lot of exposure. And then she was determined, and of course, she had a lot of talent."

Dolly had ample opportunities to display that talent at school her junior and senior years. Ruth Green recalls that "back then we had chapel, where all the kids would gather in. Dolly often sang religious songs at that; I know she always liked 'How Great Thou Art.' She said she felt God had helped her through her trials. I can remember her singing at Christmas chapel service, and how the radiance just bounced off her." And Jack McMahan remembers that Dolly sang in a number of assembly programs and talent shows. For a special variety program called *Gay Times,* she even dressed up like Annie Oakley in a red cowgirl outfit, complete with hat, boots and six-shooters, and sang spirited renditions of "Don't Fence Me In" and her old Cas Walker standard, "I Love a Tall Man." Mrs. McMahan remembers she was just "real cute" in it, and others say the enthusiastic applause gave Dolly added confidence and some small measure of peer acceptance.

But there were occasional setbacks to Dolly's blossoming. "Different teachers would be in charge of different assemblies," Jack McMahan says. "Sometimes they would use talent from their own homeroom or talent from other parts of the school. Dolly worked for different teachers scattered through a period of time." But not all the teachers in Sevier County High School loved Dolly's voice or thought she really had enough talent to be presented to the entire school. Tillman Robertson, Dolly's second grade teacher, also taught one of her senior courses. He recalls that Dolly was set to appear on one school program when several of the teachers objected, saying she couldn't sing well enough. "I get tickled at 'em now," he says. "We'll be talking about it, and I'll say, 'You folks down here made your remarks about Dolly, said, "She'll never amount to anything; just runs around here with that ol' guitar tied around her neck." ' I'll say, 'Yeah, and she drives a Cadillac now. I notice you folks still drive these ol' beat-up Chevrolets, Fords and Plymouths.' "

Being told she wasn't good enough was doubtless a painful experience for teenage Dolly, and whether or not she actually ever told any of her teachers or classmates that one day they'd eat their words (there are reports that she did, on occasion, tell the girls, "Some day I'll show *you* how to dress"), she must have thought it and fantasized about the day those very people would scramble for seats to her concerts. She told them that, in essence, and in a polite way, when she returned to the Sevier County High School gymnasium in 1970 and gave a concert to establish the Dolly Parton Scholarship Foundation. This comment off "A Real Live Dolly," a recording made of the show: "Thank you so much, and welcome to the show tonight. I'm gonna have to say that this is the greatest thrill of my life, because I always dreamed about the day when I'd be successful at the business that I love so much and get to come back and do a live show for the people that I love." She went on to recognize Cas Walker, at whose show so many in the audience had laughed, and sang the two songs she performed most on his program through the years, "You Gotta Be My Baby" and "I Love a Tall Man." Shortly before Porter Wagoner came out to join her, Dolly was presented with a certificate of appreciation, signed by the governor of the state. She was then twenty-four years old.

Actually, those teachers and students who had scorned Dolly got their comeuppance a mere three years after Dolly was graduated, when in 1967, County Judge Ray L. Reagan proclaimed October 7 Dolly Parton Day, and 7,000 Sevier Countians gathered in front of the courthouse to hear Dolly put on a show. Skip Trotter of station WSEV had originated the idea of Dolly Parton Day, thinking it would be a small-scale thing, with Dolly coming home to receive the key to the city and a few small but heartfelt accolades. Then he got a call telling him that joining Dolly on her day would be Porter Wagoner, of whose show Dolly had just become a member, Mel Tillis, and Bob Ferguson of RCA. Ferguson had a special presentation to make—Dolly had just been given a long-term RCA recording contract! The crowd cheered at the news. Dolly had already been under contract to one Nashville record company, Monument, but it was a small, independent label, certainly nothing of the stature of RCA. It could easily have been one of the happiest days of Dolly's life. Several months afterward, Dolly called the school to tell them she'd like to give something back for all that Sevier County High School had given her. She planned to establish a scholarship fund, she said, so that each year, three or four Sevier County seniors, usually members of the band, would receive scholarships of several hundred dollars to put toward a college education. Not only that, she said. She intended to donate half the proceeds from each Dolly Parton Day concert to the scholarship fund and half to the band fund, or the operational fund, so that the school might buy new uniforms and instruments or whatever modern teaching equipment it might need.

In 1971, a year after Dolly's concert in the school gymnasium to establish the scholarship, she brought not only Porter and his road show, including Spec Rhodes, but David "Stringbean" Akeman, and the Blackwood Brothers Quartet. Porter, all sequined up and threatening to outdazzle the sun, had a special treat for Dolly's hometown folks. Reporter Jack Hurst was there:

"For a few minutes he seemed almost to ignore that this was a Dolly Parton Day," Hurst wrote. "He made some jokes about the laxative, the rubbing ointment, and the 'temporary weight gain women's pills' whose manufacturers sponsor his highly successful TV program. 'Mel Tillis took two of those Cardui tablets and hasn't stuttered since,' Wagoner said to applause. But within a few moments he was announcing, in his sincerest tones, that time had come for 'something special'—a poem he had written earlier in the day and dedicated to Dolly Parton. He began to read it in the tones in which, for two decades, he has recited profitable spiritual and gospel monologues. Entitled 'One Small Phase of Dolly,' it was vintage Wagoner:

> She was born over in the holler
> Not too far from here
> On January 19, 1946, was the year . . .

There's been lots of stories
About a love affair between Dolly and me,
And I'd be lying to say
That I don't love her in many, many ways.
But not the way the gossiping tongues
Will lead you to believe.
To me, she's like a sister
Or a daughter I love so well.
When they say things about me,
I don't mind;
But when they speak bad of her,
I get hot and feel the fires of hell."

Porter said Miss Dolly returned "almost eighty percent of her earnings to God, to the needy, and to her loved ones."

The poem went over real well with the folks of Sevierville. Until Porter got to the "love affair" part. "I think it would have been better if he hadn't done that," says Cas Walker through tight lips. "I don't particularly like Porter, myself. I never did like nobody that done anything to tear Dolly down. Maybe it was just his silly thinkin', but I felt like people would get the wrong idea, you know. I always felt she was above that kind of thing. She was workin' for him and couldn't tell him not to do it, of course, but still, you know, that's just sayin', 'Well, if you think there's somethin' wrong . . .' I just think it's better not to try to make excuses if you can. I've been elected mayor three times, and if you're charged with somethin', it's better to admit it."

The next few Dolly Parton Days apparently came off without a hitch. The following year, a beauty pageant was held to select a queen to reign over the year's festivities. Contestants were limited to Sevier County High School students, and the winner was treated to an all-expenses paid week's stay in Nashville as Dolly's guest and to a modeling course from Jo Coulter, makeup artist on Porter's TV show. In 1973, the school realized a profit of about $5,000, according to one reporter, and used half of it to buy a videotape machine.

At a press conference held before Dolly's concert in Huntsville, Alabama, in May of 1978, a reporter asked Dolly if she missed the easy life of East Tennessee. "*Easy* life?" Dolly asked incredulously. "Sometimes I miss the slow part, but it was never easy. I miss the mountains. But usually when I get to missin' 'em too bad, I'll go back and restore and get all my old memories back in first gear." But as Dolly's popularity increases, it becomes harder for her to get back to Sevierville, even for Dolly Parton Day. In 1976, just before Dolly officially went with Katz-Gallin-Cleary, she was booked for a concert in nearby Knoxville around the time she was supposed to be home for her annual day. Everyone connected with Dolly Parton Day was terribly upset. A concert in Knoxville would detract from the Sevierville festivities.

Fewer people were likely to come to another Dolly concert so soon, and the school would realize only a fraction of its usual proceeds. The result was that Dolly Parton Day, 1976, was cancelled, but Dolly saw to it that $1,500 ended up in the scholarship and band funds anyhow.

One reason Dolly doesn't make it back to Sevierville so much anymore is because several of the relatives she used to visit there—her parents and her sister Willadeene Blalock—recently moved to Nashville. (Her parents moved to a farm in Lebanon, Tennessee, in 1977, but now live in the Antioch section of Nashville. They are looking for another farm.) Apparently Mr. and Mrs. Parton have not yet adjusted to city living. "They hate it where they're at now," says Stella, " 'cause they don't like to live in an area that close." (In 1974, Dolly told a reporter that for years she'd been trying to buy her folks a house with indoor plumbing, but that her father got antsy if he was "anywhere around where he can even hear automobiles. He says the sounds of nature are sweet as a lullaby.") And adds Stella, "When you're raised in the country and you're a hard worker like my daddy is, you'd just as soon be left alone. Daddy doesn't even like to go out and eat in restaurants. It's kind of a strain on you for people to come up to the house and knock on the door if you're havin' supper and you might be drinkin' buttermilk out of a pint jar instead of a glass. But that's the way you are, and you don't like to have to go around constantly makin' excuses because of what your kids do. It's not fair to them. I can understand it." Mrs. Parton's final words to me: "We just want to be left alone to live a quiet life. You get your story from Stella and Dolly."

Other of Dolly's relatives who still live in Sevierville include two brothers, David, a construction foreman, and Denver, a heavy machinery operator, and Dolly's Aunt Estelle Watson. And there are fifty-two Partons listed in the Sevier County phone directory. "That's just the ones that've got phones!" Dolly told reporter Bob Allen.

When Dolly cancelled her annual celebration in 1976, there were a lot of disappointed people in Sevierville, where today, it seems, someone in each little shop and store on the square has a Dolly story to tell. In Knoxville, too, most people seem to be proud of Dolly, feeling that in "always boosting her home, family and what this area has meant to her, she reflects a good image and is a good representative of East Tennessee," says Harry J. Morgan, owner of WSKT radio. But there are some in Knoxville who think that by Dolly "playing up her humble beginnings, there's been some misunderstanding about East Tennessee. A lot of people think we're all hillbillies here," as one newspaper editor puts it. Still others in Knoxville share Bobby Denton's feeling, that Knoxville can't really claim her anymore. "People even forget she's from here," says Denton. "I mean, you have a tendency to think of Dolly Parton as being one of the biggest stars in the business today. You don't think of Dolly Parton as being from Sevier County." They do thirty and forty miles away in Sevierville and the outlying communities in the foothills of the Smokies. And they're nothing but proud, now, no matter what they might have thought of her when she was in high school.

"Dolly used to ride the school bus with my children, and gosh, we all love Dolly," says a woman in the checkout line at Stewart's Discount Drugs, where Ruth Rolen Green is a pharmacist's assistant. "Yeah, I remember Dolly," the woman continues. "She'd get on that bus with her long pony-tail swingin' and have that old guitar and pencil and paper, writin' songs. She was about sixteen, I reckon, and just sang all the while."

That reminds cashier Eula Watson of when she was a cook at Sevier County High. "I worked next to the band room [where Dolly often wrote songs in between practice on the snare], and I could hear her singin'. Oh, she was good! I said to the other ladies, 'I wish they'd let Dolly sing all the time instead of playin' the band music.' I go to see her every time she comes to the high school."

In October of 1977, when Dolly returned to Sevierville for the first Dolly Parton Day in two years, it seems everybody in town saw her at the high school. In fact, more than everybody in town, since the 5,000 in attendance at the concert exceeded the population of Sevierville by about 1,300. The town knocked itself out paying homage: "Welcome Home, Dolly" banners flew across the highway leading into town, and bank clocks flashed "Hello, Dolly! It's So Good to Have You Back Where You Belong!" in between the current time, temperature and rate of interest. Once the concert got underway, the Sevier County High School Band treated the audience to renditions of "Rocky Top," "Rollin' on the River," and the theme from *Rocky*. Then they launched into a rousing version of "Hello, Dolly," and the lady herself strode on stage, dressed in a hot pink pants outfit and a platinum wig with a yellow rose behind one ear. In the opening ceremony, Dolly was presented with what must be her tenth handmade key to the city ("You all better lock your doors. I can get into any of your houses now!" she told the crowd), and was even made an honorary citizen of Sevierville, since the city officials realized that while Sevierville might be the closest thing Dolly has to a hometown, she was actually raised on Locust Ridge and in Caton's Chapel.

In years past, Dolly would arrive at the school early, dressed in jeans and a simple shirt, and pitch in with the work, setting up folding chairs and tending to whatever chores needed to be done. This year, she stopped at the sound check to chat with old friends and classmates ("Remember me? I was in your English class"), never forgetting to ask about everyone's sister or brother or wife and always remembering their names. But there was something missing, something wrong about this year's Dolly Parton Day, despite Dolly's folksy greeting to the audience: "I've seen all kinda people I know here tonight. And don't forget, I'm just one of you."

The main problem was that Dolly's words didn't match her actions. She had been polite and seemingly glad to see everybody, even introducing the man who delivered her, Dr. Robert F. Thomas, to the audience, and cracking jokes about her bust and her wigs. But she had not really mingled with the folks of Sevierville the way she always had in the past, and a lot of people noticed that security seemed tighter around Dolly than ever before. Now she even had guards protecting her. Immediately after the show, she climbed aboard her customized touring bus and left for Dothan, Alabama, an early stop on a six-week tour her management firm had set up to promote her then new album, *Here You Come Again.* Dolly's friends couldn't help feeling that she was no longer one of them, that she had, in effect, shunned them. They tried hard to believe that Dolly's new management was behind this kind of behavior. But in the backs of their minds, some wondered if success hadn't changed their old friend.

"I think by far there were more comments about it this time than ever before," says Jack McMahan. "I'm sure they have to follow their ordinary routine, but on the other hand, no one is going to hurt Dolly around here. I don't know whether the new management puts more pressure on scheduling and things like that, or whether that's just their basic setup. And I realize Dolly has to have her rest. But I could tell a lot more of an enclosed setup around Dolly this time. Actually, they just kept her closed in. She came in on the bus and they kept her there until a few minutes before rehearsal, when the boys herded her down the hall, ran through a rehearsal and then got her back on the bus. Of course, I realize that more people wanted to see her than she would have time to talk to, but even her mother only got to see her a few minutes. Mrs. Parton said, 'Well, I gave her to the public three or four years ago, and that's the way it's been ever since. I hardly ever get a chance to really see or talk to her.' "

Mrs. Parton was not the only member of the family to have trouble seeing Dolly. When her Aunt Estelle went out to the bus, the woman who had spent years driving Dolly to and from Knoxville for the Cas Walker shows found she couldn't get through the hordes of fans. "I know she's busy, and I don't push my way around when she's got fans to see," Mrs. Watson told me. "I said, 'Well, I'll let the other people see her. I'll see her in Nashville or something.' She's got a lot of folks besides family and friends in Sevierville. When she saw us in the audience, she dedicated a song to us, and I guess that was enough. We take her for granted sometimes. She's like all my other nieces and nephews. We're proud of her, but we don't get real excited, I guess 'cause it's been goin' on so long."

"Dolly's grandfather was in here the other day," Ruth Green says. "He asked how I liked Dolly's last show, and I said I liked it fine, except I didn't get a chance to reminisce like we used to. He said he didn't either. The minute she left the stage, she was gone. They had the bus parked where nobody could get at her. Mrs. Parton said nobody got to see Dolly, not even her. But I'm sure that wasn't Dolly. She just wouldn't allow it. Until she went with this new management, she'd stop and talk, show me through her bus and say she was proud to see you. I don't know about this management," she adds with a worried look. "When you lose a personal relationship with your friends . . . But, you know, people will still love her. Dolly's just that kind of person."

Late that night, after the last note of Dolly's native mountain music and new pop-rock songs had resounded through the school gymnasium, she appeared shimmering and smiling on the TV news in a pre-concert talk. The interviewer asked about the obvious changes in her music. Dolly explained with her irrepressible giggle that she was trying some new things, but keeping the old as well: "I'm really just a little country girl goin' to town."

Thirteen years before, the little country girl had taken a different bus to town, a big, dirty Greyhound with "Nashville" rolled up on the destination window. "I tell you, there's not many high school seniors that would just pack up and move and leave all their friends, leave the family immediately after graduating," says Bobby Denton. "Most of the kids that age, they want to knock around the summer and kill time." But not Dolly. On graduation day, she had gone over to the Sevierville radio station to tell her friends goodbye and had announced in firm, clear tones that "I'm going to Nashville tomorrow, and I'm never coming back 'til I make it." That night, she became the only member of her family to ever be graduated from high school, quite an accomplishment for a girl who came out of an area where anyone who had gone through the eighth grade was thought to be "highly educated."

Dolly was as excited and eager as she could be to get to Nashville, where her Uncle Bill and his family had moved two weeks earlier. But as she climbed aboard that Greyhound with her cardboard suitcase full of dirty clothes (no time to wash them in the haste to get gone) and her folder of songs, her thoughts probably revolved as much around her family as they did her future. They were, after all, the best family in the world. There was Momma, of course, who had worked so hard on that little coat all the kids had laughed at, and who had tried to teach her children—the last being Rachel, born when Dolly was fourteen the difference between right and wrong. And there was Daddy, who had worn out pair after pair of work boots seeing to it that his family had enough to eat. And, of course, there were all her brothers and sisters, starting with Willadeene, who, when she was no more than a child herself, had worked in the school cafeteria for twenty cents a day or a hot lunch, always taking the change and spending it on candy for the little ones at home. Dolly may have thought also of the nights she and the other kids spent listening to their mother tell ghost stories, about ol' raw-headed Bloody Bones who was waiting outside to get any of the children who cried. They slept four and five to a bed then, and at least one of them would get so scared that he'd wet the mattress. But still not one dared to get up, for fear that the Boogerman was hiding under the bed. The younger kids had been irritating sometimes and had often made so much noise that Dolly couldn't concentrate on her songs. But they were just doing what kids do, and though they'd often "fight and scratch," they'd never leave each other without saying, "Well, I love you."

Suddenly, the big, chugging motor of the Greyhound fired up, and Dolly gazed out the window for a final look. There on the pavement stood her whole family, crying and waving goodbye. As Dolly felt the tears welling up in her eyes and streaming down her face, she thought that her heart would surely break. Still, the long coach snaked its way out of the station and crawled onto the highway toward Nashville. Every other mile, it seemed, Dolly wondered if maybe she hadn't made a mistake and wished that she could turn the bus around and go home to the people who loved her. But she knew also that she wouldn't be happy once she got there. She had a job to do, a destiny to fulfill. There really was no choice.

"It's almost been like my life has been planned for me," she told journalist LaWayne Satterfield years later. "I'm a hard worker and a positive, firm believer. As a kid, I knew I would have this, that I would be here. All I ever asked of anybody and of life, is a chance."

Dolly hoped she'd find it in Nashville.

4. "Down on Music Row"

Dolly closed the door on the automatic washer, put a quarter in the slot, and shoved the changer forward. She had never been in a laundromat before, but it hadn't been hard to figure out how everything worked. As the washer filled with water, Dolly got an RC cola out of the machine and stepped out on the sidewalk for her first real look at Nashville. Soon she found herself wandering around the block, thinking about Momma and Daddy and how the whole family had cried the night before as the bus pulled out of sight. The thought made her feel a little lonesome and a whole lot homesick. She hadn't realized just how much she loved them all until she'd gotten on board that bus, and all the way to Nashville, she'd cried herself nearly sick. Dolly let out a sigh. Life was hard sometimes. But this was what she'd always wanted for herself, and as much as she missed everybody at home, she still believed that if she tried long and hard enough, she'd make it in Nashville. From what she'd seen so far, though, Music City was not exactly what she'd thought it would be. Still, every little thing held a real excitement and fascination for her, not only because it was Nashville, where people became stars, but because she'd never been in a town that big before. Momma had cautioned her that there were a lot of people in the Big City who knew every way in the world to trick a young girl hoping to make a name for herself in the music business and that they might try to take whatever money she might make and get her to promise all sorts of things in return for a break. Dolly had already known all of that, of course, but she told Momma she'd be cautious, and she'd be good and not get into any trouble.

She had barely gotten the memory out of her mind when the best-looking boy she'd ever seen in her life passed by in a late-model white Chevrolet. Twenty-one year-old Carl Dean thought the girl on the sidewalk looked pretty sensational, too, and he honked and waved as he went by. "In the country, you speak to everybody, you know, or you're just an ol' stick-in-the-mud if you don't," Dolly was to recall years later. "Me bein' straight from the country, I didn't want him to think I was stuck up or nothin', and besides I was just so proud to *be* here, that I waved back." Then she gets a funny little grin on her face. "Well, I guess kinda in the back of my mind I was maybe flirtin' a little too," she says, and lets out a big giggle that has to tickle everybody who hears it. "But *mainly*," she adds, trying to look serious again, "I was just bein' *friendly*."

Carl Dean got the message, made a circle and came back around. "I thought, 'Uh-oh, I done it this time,' " Dolly remembers. The white Chevy pulled to the curb. "Hello, there," Carl yelled. "You're gonna get sunburned!" "Oh, I don't think so," Dolly yelled back. "How you doin'?" The two started to talk, and Carl suggested they go somewhere and get acquainted. "I wouldn't get in the car with him," Dolly says. "We're not *that* friendly in the country." So Carl parked the Chevy and walked back to the Wishy Washy with Dolly to get her clothes. ("We met at the Wishy Washy and it's been wishy-washy ever since!" Dolly loves to joke.) Dolly switched her clothes to the dryer, and as she and Carl continued to talk, she thought she liked him a great deal. "Where you from?" he asked her. Dolly told him she was from Knoxville, figuring Carl had never heard of Sevierville. Besides, she *was* from Knoxville, kind of, if you considered that's where she'd spent her summers during high school. Carl was impressed. Not so much with Knoxville, not even half the size of Nashville, but with the way Dolly had said the name of the town: "Knox-ville," kind of highfalutin'. Apparently he thought he'd like to hear more. Couldn't they have a date? Gosh, Dolly didn't know. She really liked this Carl Dean. Her best friends in high school had been boys, but a lot of them had been interested in her because half the fun of going to Sevier County High School was seeing how tight Dolly's skirt or sweater was that day. She knew that a lot of them had started lies about her, but at least the boys hadn't faulted her the way the girls had. She'd even gone out with a few of them, but they seemed so immature that she felt like their mother, or something. But Carl was different. Something inside her just seemed to click when she first saw him. Tall, and dark and shy, he seemed to be the kind of boy she'd always looked for. And he reminded her some of her daddy, the way he seemed so strong and independent. She got up and took her clothes out of the dryer, hoping Carl wouldn't notice the unmentionables. "How about it?" Carl asked again in his slow drawl. He'd been pretty much of a loner in high school, and he'd never loved a girl in his whole life. Now that he'd found somebody who really interested him, he wasn't about to let her get away so easily. Dolly came up with a compromise. She didn't think she knew Carl well enough to go on a date with him, but he was welcome to come calling at her Uncle Bill and Aunt Cathy's apartment near the State Fairgrounds in South Nashville. Carl knew the address. They weren't far away from it right then. And Carl didn't live but a little ways away himself. He'd come over and help her babysit her aunt and uncle's little boy. Each afternoon when he came, Dolly sat outside with him on the fire escape while she watched her little cousin, wanting to ask Carl inside but not daring to, since Bill was on the road and Cathy was waitressing at Shoney's. Finally, Cathy had a day off, and when Carl came over to pick Dolly up, he took her right over to his house to meet his parents. This Carl Dean was surely special.

But she had to cut out some of this romancing. She hadn't come to Nashville to get married, for goodness sake. She'd come to be a star. But first there was the little matter of letting people know she had the talent to be one. Each morning, she and Bill would set out to make the rounds of the places that had anything to do with fame and fortune, including the Ernest Tubb Record Shop, where they thought they might catch some of the artists and pitch them their songs. The Dolly mythology—helped out by Dolly herself in her song, "Down on Music Row"—has it that she arrived in Nashville "sleepy, hungry, tired and dirty," and sat all alone on the steps of RCA, where she ate a stale sweet roll before walking over to the Hall of Fame. There, the songs says, she washed her face in the fountain, out front, and stared with awe at the names in the walkway of stars, the line, "I could feel that change a-comin'," implying that Dolly knew it was only a matter of time before her name would be there, too. Dolly did indeed know that one day she would be bestowed with such an honor, but the mention of the Hall of Fame was simply a poetic addition, since the Hall of Fame was not yet built in 1964. Yet just as the song contains an addition or two, it omits certain people and circumstances that figured heavily in Dolly's first years in Nashville.

In her first letter home to Momma and Daddy, dated June 2, 1964, Dolly told her parents not to worry about sending her money, "because I've got a job singing on an early morning television show here called *The Eddie Hill Show,* and a couple of folks already told me that they might record a couple of my songs." Although she doesn't say it, that probably came about through her association with Tree Publishing. Dolly has always given the impression that she arrived in Nashville broke and without a friend in the world, with only her dreams to sustain her. "I didn't know nobody in this big city," she said in 1975. In actuality, she was still signed to Tree. Bud Brewster remembers that before Dolly left for Nashville, he had asked her if she would cut a record with him and another Cas Walker regular; he had already set it up with King Records in Cincinnati. "I don't think she really understood it, but she was already signed with some agency in Nashville at that time," Brewster says. "She really wanted to do it, but she was afraid to, because they'd already signed those papers." (Dolly probably was uncertain whether Mercury Records planned to try again with her after "It's Sure Gonna Hurt.") Whatever the situation, she was not totally unknown on Music Row. "She had slowly made contacts, and she'd come down and spend a lot of time around the office and get to know people," Tree's Buddy Killen says. "She knew many of the writers and people in the business by the time she got here. Nothing was really happening for her yet. I think she'd had a few songs recorded, but she just hadn't quite developed enough to be a popular writer at that time. Still, she had a place to go if she wanted, because when she came to town she was still signed with us. She and Bill had it very rough, I remember," Killen adds. "I'm not sure if I advanced her money or not. I probably did. There weren't many that I didn't."

But Dolly was not only ambitious, she was impatient. And after a short time, when it looked as if nothing was ever going to happen for her at Tree, she went to Killen and told him she wanted out of her contract. "I let her go," he says. "I still had years on her contract, but I work like that. I don't want to hold somebody to a contract who doesn't want to be here." (Killen, knowing you can't force creativity, had never put pressure on his writers to come up with so many songs a year.) "And she was right," he continues. "Nothing was happening for her. But it took her a few more years before anything at all started to happen. We were trying. I would do demos with her all the time, and I was always working with her, trying to get something done. But wanting to do it and getting it done is sometimes different, you know. And truthfully, she just wasn't ready. It was premature on my part to sign her when I did. She needed the seasoning to finally break through."

In leaving Buddy Killen, the first man in Nashville to give her any kind of real professional break, Dolly was to set a pattern she would follow throughout her career. Dolly knew that no matter how much she cared for a person, and no matter what their personal relationship, if she had to choose between friendship and advancement in her career, the career would always win out. Just as it was hard to leave home that morning after graduation, it was hard for Dolly to leave Buddy Killen. Later, it would be difficult for her to leave Porter Wagoner and even harder for her to break up her Traveling Family Band. Today, no matter how attached she becomes to her musicians, if she finds a better picker, or if one of the band in any way jostles the group's compatibility, he soon finds himself looking for another job. Though this sort of strength, drive and ambition may in time earn Dolly a reputation for being "hard-nosed," survival is the name of the game, especially in the fast-paced world of pop music, where Dolly now hopes to triumph.

A much more serious omission in "Down on Music Row" was the name of Fred Foster, the man who (with the exception of Porter Wagoner) did more for Dolly Parton's career than anybody else and who first pointed Dolly in the pop direction more than twelve years ago. Dolly's song says "Chet [Atkins] and Bob [Ferguson] at RCA, well, they listened to my songs that day, and they both told me that I was on my way." But when Dolly first came to town, every record company in Nashville—including RCA—turned her down. Every record company except Monument, that is, the brainchild of Fred Foster. Now the most successful independent label in Nashville, Monument was in 1964 known primarily for turning out Roy Orbison's big hits, including his gold, million-seller, "Pretty Woman." Foster remembers receiving a phone call one day from a friend in the production department at Capitol Records. Capitol had just turned down "a great girl singer," the friend said, and asked if Foster would see her. "What's her name?" Foster asked. "Dolly Parton."

Foster remembers the fateful call while sitting at a table in his elegant office. "She came out and sang me three or four songs, and I said, 'Is your writing free?' and she said yes, and I said, 'OK, we'll work out a deal.' Then I told her I liked her," he adds, "and I'll never forget the look on her face. She said, 'Everybody has turned me down.' "

Foster, a kind, congenial man, couldn't understand why. She epitomized everything a record man looks for in an artist. She wrote her own material, and she had a readily identifiable sound. "The instant you heard her you would never forget that was Dolly Parton. Obviously, there are people who can't stand to hear her sing," Foster says, echoing Dolly's own frequent statement: "My voice is strange. You have to acquire a taste for it. You either learn to like it a lot or you learn never to like it any." "But that's true of every superstar that has ever been," he continues. "If you are pleasing a lot of people, you are displeasing a lot of people. I felt Dolly was very gifted musically, and she sang perfectly in tune." Plus, she had looks and innate charm. Foster knew it could all be developed into what Dolly is today. "It could be developed even *further* than you see today," he says. "I thought she had an unlimited career to be a number one recording star, a movie star—whatever she wanted to be. I still think so."

And Foster just plain-out liked Dolly Parton. "She reminded me of some of my relatives," says Foster, who grew up on a farm in Rutherford County, North Carolina. "She was shy, obviously intelligent but green in the ways of the world, particularly the city. She was very quiet and reluctant to talk to you at first, but when she did start talking, you could see a fire burning away underneath—she was determined."

The months after that were some of the roughest Dolly had ever known. She still played some occasional jobs with her uncles, but she had moved out of Bill and Cathy's apartment after five or six months and gotten a small place of her own on Music Row. Her finances dwindled to nothing. "For two weeks once, I lived on mustard and relish. Things you have in the refrigerator to eat alongside of somethin' else?" she says with a question, making sure you understand. "Thought I was goin' to starve to death; I still can't eat a bite of relish." About the only time Dolly got a regular meal was when she went on a date, which wasn't often, since Carl was now off in the Army. Too, "I didn't date anybody in the music business much because I didn't want to get a reputation. Not that I would have done anything to get one, but you don't have to really." She recalls that the first time she returned to Sevierville, her parents took one look at her and nearly had a joint heart attack. She'd gotten down to ninety pounds, skinny even for a girl no taller than five feet. (It might have been on this visit that she dropped in on Cas Walker and recorded "Something Fishy" on videotape.) Other than that, Dolly looked no different from any other eighteen-year-old, in that the final move to a flamboyant appearance was still in the offing.

Singer Brenda Lee remembers seeing Dolly frequently at the Church of Christ in Radnor about this time. Brenda's manager, the late Dub Albritten, booked Dolly a few singing jobs through his One-Niters agency, and when Brenda met her, she thought Dolly was "awfully nice, and awfully sweet. She struck me as being intellectually aware of what was going on, but she was still able to maintain a very refreshing sort of innocence about everything."

Half because he took such a strong liking to Dolly and half because he knew she needed it to become the star he knew she could, Foster "suggested certain things to her." He pointed out, politely and tactfully, that she didn't know how to dress or how to coordinate colors. She could use some guidelines on how to do her hair and makeup, too; he hired a woman active in children's theater to teach Dolly not only those basic things but also how to enunciate a little better, since she had a tendency to lose syllables at the end of her phrases and to run certain words together. "Dolly spoke almost in colloquialisms, and of course, that's a regional thing, but it still wasn't classy enough for the plans Fred had for her," says someone who knew them both at the time. "She had to effect a lot of the changes herself, but after the tutelage, the changes were very vivid."

Dolly played Eliza Doolittle to Foster's Professor Higgins, and the figure Foster spent on her development is rumored to be $20,000 or $25,000, a sizable sum in '64 and '65. But Foster didn't worry. That was nothing compared to Dolly's money-making potential, and he knew he could make his investment back on her records. Much of his outlay went for sessions, and while Foster loved Dolly's voice and "could listen to it all day," he worked with her long and hard to control her quick vibrato.

The upshot was that Dolly thought Foster hated her voice. Not only was he encouraging her to sing differently, but also he was recording her pop! Why would he stick all those instruments behind her voice if he weren't trying to cover it up? Dolly made it plain to Foster that she was a 100 percent country artist and wanted to cut country records. She had no desire to go pop. If she had, she would never have put up with all that teasing in high school. Eleven years later, in an interview with Mary Campbell of the Associated Press, Dolly would have bitter memories of her Monument days. "My voice is so small and high-pitched and sounded like a kid, so they had me sing rockabilly," she told Campbell. "I was so country myself I didn't fit in. I knew they thought I was dumb. I wrote the same as I do now, country, but they arranged it different. They laughed at the way I talked. I took it personal; it bothered me."

"You've got to keep in mind," Foster explains, "that this was in late '64. What was selling country then was a very hard, heavy sort of music. This was way before the Crystal Gayles and the Emmylou Harrises. Purity was sort of in the back somewhere. I think Loretta had hit by this time." (Loretta won the first of her countless awards in 1962.) "It was very forceful singers who were hitting then. And it just seemed to me that Dolly had too much talent to be confined to any one field of music. If it had been pop, I probably would have been trying to get her to cut country, as well. I thought she could go across the board, and the best way to break her and to get the biggest rewards seemed to be in the teen market because she was young and had that light, thin sort of voice. Ray Stevens [the same Ray Stevens of "Ahab, the Arab" fame] produced some of her pop things, like 'Happy Birthday, Baby,' which made the top one hundred. She might not like to admit that, but it did." Foster stops and gets a faraway look on his face. "I think it's sort of strange that she came back to that [pop sound] after all this time, but maybe we were premature."

What is stranger is that Dolly protested as much as she did. "It's Sure Gonna Hurt" had been as pop as it could be, and as Bud Brewster remembers, Dolly had loved singing Brenda Lee and Connie Francis tunes in between performances on Cas Walker's program, even doing a few of them in her live shows. So why all the fuss?

Bob Beckham, the cowboy president of Combine Music, thinks he knows. Beckham was Dolly and Bill's boss when they were writing for Combine, Monument's publishing arm. "Dolly would write contemporary material, and we would demo it," he says, "so she wasn't really that closed-minded to it. It was just, well, I think if anything else at the time, the pop end of it scared her a little bit." I ask why. "Oh, hell, honey," Beckham says, sitting in front of a stained-glass window in his office. "Dolly came from an extremely poor background. The transition even from that to the realization that she could possibly be a country star was enough of a step. To think any further than that was bound to have been frightful to her at the time." I point out that she began singing on the radio at ten and had been determined enough to work her way onto the Grand Ole Opry at age thirteen. "Oh, yeah, she was a very determined little girl, and she never lacked confidence in herself," he continues, "but I'm sure the ramifications of the business scared her a lot. And I'm sure she became disillusioned a lot, that it was frustrating for her. See," Beckham says, hitting on the point, "Dolly was never cool. She'd always blurt out things that a lot of people trying to be cool would never do. She was refreshing as hell. She had no secrets, and she just couldn't be cool or laid back. That was Dolly. And still is. She ain't puttin' nobody on. What you see is what you get."

It could be, then, that Dolly felt she simply wasn't ready for all that success in the pop market means. "It's a different lifestyle and a different pace in the pop world than in the country world," says Brenda Lee, who's certainly spent a lot of time on both sides of the country/pop divide. "It's a broader spectrum to work within, and you meet a lot of different people." For someone who was just learning how to dress, talk, and make herself up, the idea of mixing with a faster crowd could indeed have been frightening.

On that point, Bekham is certainly correct. But from what other people say, he was not so correct when he said, "She ain't puttin' nobody on. What you see is what you get." Dolly's Combine job was a $50 a week draw, out of which she was expected to eat, pay rent, and send money home. When it became obvious that the money simply would not stretch, Dolly took several part-time jobs. One was as a receptionist at a neon sign company. Another opportunity came when she and Bill visited Moss Rose publishing company, trying to sell their songs. There a man hired her to pose in a bathing suit (or, by another account, wrapped in a beach towel) for a publicity photo used in conjunction with the Del Reeves hit of 1965, "Girl on the Billboard." ("I don't think she'd want to remember that," the man says. "Somebody told me she was trying to find the negatives. I don't know who has them, but I don't think the picture ever got circulated, because we kinda put a stop to it. But Dolly could look good in a grass sack, you know?") Still another of Dolly's fill-in jobs was as a waitress at a Dobb's House restaurant on Murfreesboro Road. According to a co-worker there, Mrs. Ella Shaw, now of Jacksonville, Florida, the Dolly of that time (about 1966, or just before, since the Bill Phillips rendition of Dolly and Bill Owens' "Put It Off Until Tomorrow," on which Dolly sang harmony, appeared while Dolly was still table-hopping) looked quite unlike the Dolly we've come to know today. Her husband, Don, who says he's had his songs recorded by such artists as Ernest Tubb and Happy Goodman, agrees. "No, no, no, she definitely doesn't look the same today as she did then," he says. "Her hair was shorter than it is now, and it seems to me it was a little bit darker. 'Course, when you get into the field that she's in, you do whatever's necessary to make yourself more presentable." Mrs. Shaw remembers Dolly's hair being darker then, too. "It wasn't a light brown or a dark brown. It'd be betwixt and between," she says. "And she wasn't large, either."

Mrs. Shaw's memory appears to have failed her here, because Dolly's high school pictures clearly show that she was well-endowed even then. She was not, however, as big as she is today, but as Dolly points out, she was smaller all over then. Dolly told me, "I've always wore tight clothes, and I've always had big . . . Say I've always been 'well-developed.' " That's true. But through the years, Dolly's bust has seemed to some to have grown disproportionately larger to her ever-fluctuating figure. "Of course, that will always be a controversy," says Charlene Bray of Celebrity Management, Inc. Bray says that in old publicity pictures, Dolly "was just an ordinarily developed girl. So if you develop like that later in life, there's still hope for me. I'm just keeping my fingers crossed . . ."

There are unsubstantiated rumors that Dolly had surgery to increase her breasts, with the usual versions of how and why she did. But while Dolly thrives on the gossip, she won't say whether the rumors are true or not. Even Barbara Walters had no success when she tried to get Dolly to comment on what Dolly would rather keep a mystery. "I always say," Dolly told her, "that if I hadn't of had it on my own, I'm just the kind of person that would've had me some made, if I'd needed it."

Both Foster and Bob Beckham maintain that Dolly was the architect of her own design. "I don't think anybody molded Dolly's sex symbol image except Dolly," says Beckham, who warned me before the interview that he wouldn't answer certain questions. "I think she knew what she had and she knew what the hell she was gonna do with it, and she did it. And I'm sure that Porter must have given her some pointers along the way."

"I don't know what people mean about Porter creatin' my sex image," Dolly told me. "All he did for me was put me on television, and I just showed it off. He didn't try to mold me into any kind of image. He just happened to like me as a person and the way I was. Plus he happened to know I was stubborn, and I dressed as I wanted to. But anyway, I guess because of him, I got to makin' enough money where I could buy the things."

"I don't think anybody molded Dolly's image any more than Dolly did, 'cause she is a very smart little gal," Beckham continues. "*Damn* smart. And she knew the more controversy and the more talk that went on about Dolly at one point, the better it was for Dolly. Not only was Dolly smart, she was "a damn good songwriter," turning out about 120 songs in her three years at Combine, getting three-fourths of them recorded. "I thought she was a great, refreshing talent, with a very, very unique, original voice and a fresh approach to songwriting," says her old publisher, who also remembers that not all her tunes made the grade. But apparently more did than did not. "She used to break meter a lot, and that used to drive me up a wall, and she still does it, and she's successful. So that shows you how much I know. But that was the uniqueness of the whole thing. She was unspoiled and unschooled as a writer. She just did what she thought and felt." Although Bill Owens was often on the road in this early period, playing guitar for such performers as Carl and Pearl Butler, he, too, was signed to Combine as a writer, and he and Dolly wrote several good songs, collaborating on the total effort, rather than one writing the words and the other the music. (The best of their songs, including "Fuel to the Flame," which should have become a standard, can be found on a recent Monument re-release of Dolly's early sides, *In the Beginning.*) "Uncle Bill was a good writer," says Beckham, "but he wanted to be a singer, too, and he just couldn't hack it. Man, he was awful! And, of course, she was so great."

In 1966, singer Bill Phillips recorded one of Dolly and Bill's songs, "Put It Off Until Tomorrow," with Dolly singing harmony. The record made it into the Top 10 on the country charts, mainly, some say, on the strength of Dolly's voice. "Everybody knew Bill's record wouldn't have hit without Dolly Parton on it," says one observer, even though Dolly's name didn't appear on the label. Disc jockeys, mesmerized by Dolly's mystery voice, played the record over and over, and asked everyone who might know just who she was. "That was really the catalyst for Dolly and the thing that brought her to everybody's attention," remembers Beckham.

Shortly afterward, Dolly got her wish to cut country records. A common belief in Nashville (which Beckham shares) is that Foster gave in when he saw how well Dolly's voice had gone over with the country audience. "No," he says. "She convinced me to cut her country. I was strictly going along with her obviously heartfelt wishes. Now there was momentum picking up for her somewhat, because she sang on 'Put It Off Until Tomorrow.' Grandpa Jones said one time you could put Dolly in the Mormon Tabernacle Choir and she would come through. So there wasn't any hiding. You knew who that was if you knew Dolly's voice. That may have been a consideration," he concedes, "but I did it because she asked me to. She really wanted to do it. And I felt we would be stifling her if we forced her to go a way she couldn't really feel. If she didn't get her way one way," Foster remembers, smiling at the thought, "she would come at you the next day with it all dressed up in different language, but it meant the same, you know? That used to amuse me some. But she never stopped until she knew you had her point. Finally, she came to me and she was so unhappy about it. She said, 'If I have to cut that pop music I just want to quit. Now if you'll produce me country, I want to keep going.' So, I said I'd do it."

What Foster didn't tell Dolly was that his definition of country and hers might differ. He had her sing him a lot of her tunes, which were mostly ballads, and then told her they needed something "really up and bouncy," since they'd have to hit a new audience hard. What they decided on was "Dumb Blonde," a Curly Putnam song from over at Dolly's old home at Tree Publishing. Aside from the obvious play on the title, "Dumb Blonde" was perfect for Dolly in every way. It suited her voice well (although she goes a little flat on the first stanza), and she gave it a rared-back, spirited delivery, sounding properly put out with every line: "Don't try to pry your way out of this/Don't try to lie or I'll catch you in it/Don't try to make me feel sorry for you/Just because I'm blonde don't think I'm dumb/'Cause this Dumb Blonde ain't nobody's fool." By itself, the song was a corny, cliché-ridden novelty tune typical of the era ("You know if there's one thing this blonde has learned—blondes have more fun"), but Foster still had his heart set on Dolly crossing over, so while he included the mandatory whining steel guitar, he also sneaked in a harpsichord to set the rhythm and give the record a little more uptown flavor than Dolly might have wanted. But she surprised him and thought the harpsichord added a nice touch. So did everybody else. "Dumb Blonde," released in 1967, was Dolly's first real hit. The day Foster let her know, Dolly looked him right in the eye and gave him her slow smile. "See," she said. "I told you."

The follow-up to "Dumb Blonde" was Dolly's own "Something Fishy," another novelty tune in the same vein as its predecessor—only dumber. Here she suspects that her sportsman husband is up to no good, using his frequent fishing expeditions as a chance to play around: "I guess some large-mouthed bass left that lipstick on your shirt/I don't think you're a fisherman, honey, I think you're a flirt/Well, if you're goin' fishin' then why don't you bring them home?/I think there's Something Fishy goin' on."

When it became obvious that "Something Fishy" was also going to do well on the charts, fan magazines began giving Dolly Parton the big build-up, spurred on, no doubt, by Fred Foster's press release stating Monument expected big things from her. But journalist Bill Littleton, now of *Performance* Magazine, recalls that Dolly had generated genuine excitement on the Nashville music scene. "Dolly was already on Monument when I moved to town, and one of the very first realizations I had when I got here was whatever was going to happen concerning this girl was going to be big," he says. "The vibes were *so* strong. I'm trying to think if there's been anybody else that it was that evident about, and I'm not sure there has been. *Everybody* you ran into was talking about Dolly Parton. *Everybody.* They all had a Dolly Parton story, they all knew her, and everybody had been to lunch with her. It was like the town had adopted her, and she was the fair-haired child. Every time you'd turn around. There was *no way* to stop her. It was going to happen."

Porter Wagoner was hardly oblivious to all this commotion about Dolly Parton, but one of his former employees recalls that six months before Dolly went with his show, Porter made a derogatory remark about Dolly "not being country enough." "Someone had brought up her name to him as a singer, and he just wasn't gonna have *anything* to do with Dolly," she says, his feeling being that Dolly had denied her heritage by singing pop. That was, of course, before she came out with "Dumb Blonde" and "Something Fishy." "It was also before he met her," says the old employee with a laugh in her voice.

Wagoner was, at this point, up a creek. His girl singer, Norma Jean, had gone home to Oklahoma to get married and settle down. He'd tried out a couple of girls for his road show, but none of them, Jeannie Seely included (who, ironically, ended up leaving Wagoner's show only to sign with Monument Records), had really worked out, and here it was time to begin production on his nationally syndicated television show. He'd been auditioning a lot of girls when he called Bob Beckham at Combine. "He said he'd seen Dolly and had been watching her and really liked her," Beckham remembers, "and wondered if she might be interested in taking Norma Jean's place. Well, at that time, Lord, that was a *real* break," Beckham adds, almost reliving the drama. "I tried to be cool about it, and I probably blew it. I said [here he goes into a deep voice], 'Well, I don't know . . .' "

One version of the story has it that Dolly wasn't told why Wagoner wanted to see her (and another has it that Wagoner called her himself at home) but assumed he'd taken interest in a couple of the songs Bill had dropped off at his office. In truth, Porter probably wanted to check out Dolly's authenticity. More than half of his appeal was the way he stood up there in his spangled suits and stared a sincere hole in the camera, tellin' his good friends and neighbors about the miracle powers of Black Draught. Whoever took Norma Jean's place was going to have to sell Cardui tablets with the same sincerity—and believability. Then, too, he had to make sure they complemented each other physically. Would they look good together?

More importantly, would they sing well together? Porter liked duets. They'd boosted his career in the past, and "Satisfied Mind," which he'd sung with his back-up men had been the Song of the Year in 1955. He and Norma Jean hadn't really been a "team"; she'd just been the girl singer on his show. It would be good to have a team, he thought, especially with a girl, a girl who looked and sounded good—but not too good, because he, of course, would remain the star.

Porter also liked the fact that Dolly could write. The day she came over to his office, he was especially taken by a song she sang him that she'd written one day on the riverbank while Carl was fishing, a tune about everything being beautiful. "This song told me so much about her," Porter would later say. "I knew that if a person could sit down and write a song like that, they'd have to have a real soul inside them." Porter thought she'd be fine. "There was a lot that sold me on Dolly," he was to observe, "but I think the deciding factor was Dolly's personality—her warmth, her sincerity, her bein' a real person. She's the kind of girl you can take anywhere under any conditions to meet anyone, and they'd like her . . . She has the type of personality I could sell to people on television and in person." Without much deliberation at all, he asked her to join his show.

"You can imagine how fast I said yes," Dolly was to tell Toby Thompson years later. "I was goin' from horse relish to hot dogs about then." In May of 1967, Dolly was back in Knoxville performing at the dedication of the Skymart. Tex Ritter was also scheduled to appear, and the *News-Sentinel* put him in the lead of its story. The second to the last paragraph included, "Dolly Parton, accompanied by Tiny Day and his troupe, will perform at 8 P.M. Saturday. She has written and sung many songs."

No one could have been more pleased with Wagoner's offer than Fred Foster. Dolly's exposure to millions of viewers weekly could only result in increased record sales and Dolly setting out on the road to the kind of stardom Foster envisioned for her. He'd make back his $25,000 in no time, but he wanted to make sure Dolly got a big piece of the pie, too. Her contracts with both Monument and Combine were up about this time, and shortly after Dolly received the new one, with all her raises and increased benefits clearly outlined, she called Foster and thanked him. Soon Porter visited Foster to talk about how they could mutually promote Dolly, since it was understood she was staying on Monument, and Dolly had just cut another session. Some say that Foster learned Dolly was going on RCA when Porter visited him again and offered him "any amount of money" for Dolly's contract. Here, Foster was supposed to have said that wasn't necessary, that they were all friends, and he wanted to see Dolly do anything that would be good for her career. Foster doesn't tell it exactly that way. Beckham says, "It should have been obvious at the time that the eventual conclusion on that story was she would go with RCA." It was not obvious to Fred Foster.

"I don't know what happened, whether RCA told Porter he and Dolly needed to be together or what," Foster says. "I just don't know." Foster pauses, and the rest of the story seems difficult for him to tell. "She called and asked me if she could have lunch, and I said yes, so she and Bill Owens came down and we went to the Downtowner, or the Pancake House, whatever it was called. And she told me that she was really sorry and she didn't know how to say it, but she would have to go to RCA, that Porter had said that she would have to do that. She was very emotional. And I said, 'Well . . .' " Foster gives a heavy sigh. "Really," he continues, "it hurt me, because I had sort of looked at Dolly as a kid sister. She was part of the family, you know. And I thought I had tried to do everything I could to make it easy for her; I thought we were really good friends. And after all the dialogue with Porter about continuing on and how we could promote together and so on, I just kind of felt deceived. Not necessarily that *she* had deceived me, but that I had *been* deceived. I didn't know quite by whom or what. This really hurt. So, I said, 'Well, Dolly, I'm really sorry to hear that. I wish you the best, and I'll see you later.' And I got up and left. She followed me, and said, 'I wish you wouldn't take it that way. I don't mean it that way.' And I said, 'Well, that's the way it is, you know? There's no easy way to say goodbye, is there?' And she said, 'I want to be your friend.' I said, 'Good. I want to be yours, too.' And then that may have been the only little altercation I had with Uncle Bill, because he was wanting to stop me so we could talk some out on the street, and I told him I didn't think I wanted to talk anymore, and it would be best for him not to bother me. So I went on back to the studio. It was a disappointing time. But she called and came to see me not long after that, and we had a good visit then in the office. She was very emotional about that, though, for quite some time. And I will admit I was, too, because I thought, well, I don't know. In my head, we were just going on and I could see all these great things opening up for her. It's so exciting to be involved in a career that's breaking."

Although Foster says he has "no great quarrel or running feud" with Bill Owens, both he and Bob Beckham say that Dolly's closeness to her family may have hindered her career. That belief is common in Nashville, and while almost everyone lauds the way Dolly has always aided her family through the years, seeing to it that every relative who wanted a job had one, many people say she often hired people who were not qualified. Dolly was not to realize this until way into the '70s, and Foster says she would have done well to have seen it earlier and to have known that they were holding her back. "Bill Owens is a talented man," Foster concedes. "How talented, I don't know, but he is certainly talented. There were so many of us, including Bill, protecting Dolly, it was a wonder that she ever met her husband, you know what I mean? I didn't feel that Dolly needed anyone, really, to write with or sing with or anything else. It wasn't just Bill. Let's not single him out and be unkind to Bill Owens. But Dolly was such a unique talent and a free spirit, that you didn't want to see her confined by any sort of family situation. I told her she was certainly strong enough to fly, that she didn't need extra wings," he adds. "I felt she would have matured much faster, just out on her own, doing her thing."

Owens is now something of a mystery figure. After he ended his association with Owepar Publishing Co., the songwriting concern he and Dolly set up when she went with Porter, he moved to a farm in College Grove, Tennessee, and was occasionally heard from by Nashville song publishers. But no one has heard from Owens in quite some time now, and his brother, Louis, says he has returned to Sevierville.

When Dolly ended her professional relationship with her family, she implemented one of the many suggestions Fred Foster says he made to her about her career. The others included "cutting some pop records with some really contemporary-type pickers, cutting material as of today, and not yesterday," and finding management outside of Nashville, preferably in Los Angeles. "I mentioned two or three firms to her," Foster says, "including the one she's with today." Above all, Foster kept asking Dolly, "Why are you confining yourself to that country road? Why not go all over the place? The country people will still love you."

Foster told her most of that twelve years ago. Today, of course, she is doing just that. While several people in the music business have commented they thought Dolly always knew where she was going, they've added they thought she probably wasn't sure of how to get there. Fred Foster just may have been the one who mapped out her route. The last time Foster talked with her was just after she cut *Here You Come Again,* her first platinum album. "You know," she told him, "you were the one person who always believed in me, believed that I could do all these things. I believe it myself now."

Whatever the reason Dolly left Monument, by 1967 she had a new mentor. Porter Wagoner had a lot to offer Dolly Parton then: a major recording contract, exposure on the number one syndicated television show in the country, and a place on one of the most popular road shows going. "See, aren't you glad you're not married, or you couldn't go," people said when the opportunity came along. "And I said, 'Well, I am married and I am going!' " Dolly told journalist Joan Dew, remembering.

A year earlier, she had slipped down to Georgia and secretly tied the knot with the shy, slow-talking boy in the white Chevy: Carl Dean.

5. *Best Friends*

Dr. L. Don Duvall didn't care much for quicky marriages. Each month, about 300 couples crossed over the Tennessee state line into Catoosa County, Georgia, and got married in Ringgold, the county seat, some ten miles southeast of Chattanooga. Georgia had many such marriage mills on its borders and corners, since state law made it possible for couples to get their blood tests and license and be married in no time, provided they were of age (twenty-one for males, eighteen for females) or had parental consent (at seventeen for males, fourteen for females). That, plus Ringgold's geographic location, made the little town an elopement haven. A lot of people came and got good, legitimate marriages, Dr. Duvall points out today, adding that the laws have since been changed, but even though he got only about one or two couples a month, he still turned away a good number who knocked on the door of the First Baptist Church of Ringgold, wanting a Christian wedding. Mostly, he says, he went on intuition.

Dolly R. Parton, twenty, and Carl I. Dean, twenty-three, as the marriage license reads, were not underage, and there was no legal reason for them not to be married in Tennessee—by Dolly's grandfather, perhaps. But someone at Monument Records had made it clear to Dolly that they didn't think it a good idea for her to be married, since she'd be out on the road often, playing concerts and promoting her records. "But Carl and I had already worked all that out," Dolly told journalist Joan Dew. "I explained to him exactly how I felt about my music—that it wasn't something I did, it was *me*. I told him I had to do it, no matter what. And he knew that my music was what had brought me to Nashville in the first place and that I wasn't going to let anyone or anything stand in my way. I told him he had to be willing to accept this and that I had to know in my heart he could live with it, or we'd end up hurting one another, and I couldn't stand that. He said, 'If that's what you want and that's what makes you happy, then that's what I want you to have.' I had to make sure that he understood that it was really going to happen, because I didn't want him thinking he was marrying a girl who would give up after a few years of trying to make it. I said, 'It may be hard for you to visualize all of this now, but we won't have the kind of marriage other people have because my music is going to take me away from home a lot, and the bigger I get the more demands will be made on my time.' Any other man would probably have thought I was crazy—a kid from the hills talking about all these big plans as though they had already happened—but Carl accepted it. I told him I always dream big, but the difference is I *believe* it will come true." So, on May 30, 1966, Dolly and Carl and Avie Lee drove down to Georgia, and when they returned, nobody said anything about the marriage outside the family for at least a year.

Dr. Duvall had a good feeling about the three people who walked into his church. "She was just a pretty girl, a young, friendly, outgoing mountain girl," he says of Dolly. "I remember I really liked her as a person. I liked him, too. He seemed to be a nice young man. And I liked her mother. She was just a very unaffected person, looked like she had had a hard time but was genuinely interested in her children and was there because she wanted to be a support to her daughter." Dr. Duvall gave Carl and Dolly the usual printed material to read and went over a few things with them before they went into the sanctuary for the ten-minute ceremony.

"She said she had just made her first record," remembers Dr. Duvall. "I asked her to send me one, and she did. I really didn't think she would be much different from so many that try to make good in that field, and in years to come, I was surprised." He was to be surprised, too, in years to come, to see how Dolly's looks had changed. "She was a nice, happy-looking and acting person, and she was a lot better-looking then. Not as affected-looking. She had a really natural beauty. Her hair was sort of blondish, but it wasn't like the wigs that I see today."

When Carl and Dolly first walked into the church, it was Dolly who said, "We want to get married," Dr. Duvall recalls. "The young man was rather nervous. I remember he wanted to take some pictures and went down to the drugstore and got some film. But I think he got the wrong size, or something, and had to go back." A year later, on their anniversary, Carl and Dolly stopped in to say hello. Dr. Duvall thought of them from time to time, and three years ago, he wrote Dolly to ask if everything was all right, if they were still married. He got a handwritten letter back, saying they'd been married nine years. "She said, 'I love him more now than I did then,' " Dr. Duvall quotes. " 'He's my best friend, too.' "

When Dolly finally announced the news, Nashville did a double-back flip. "Tex Ritter and Ralph Emery were doing the late night show on WSM radio, and they talked about that for three weeks," Bill Littleton remembers. *Everybody* wanted a glimpse of Carl Dean. But there were few opportunities to catch one. Carl Dean's public appearances have been rare. One, according to the Knoxville *News-Sentinel*, was the 1970 Dolly Parton Day in Sevierville. And several people in Nashville remember the time Dolly brought Carl to the BMI Awards Dinner not long after they married. Dolly and Bill were to receive an award. "I was very excited, because I'd never been to [an awards dinner] before," Dolly told Joan Dew. "Carl said he'd go with me. That was the first time he'd been to any industry function with me, and it was the last. I was really nervous, but Carl was worse off than I was. He didn't know anybody or anything about the business, and he's a loner anyway, not a socializer at all. He really felt out of place that night. So after we got home, he said, 'Now I know this is what you want for your life, and I'm proud for you because I want you to have it if it makes you happy. But it doesn't make me happy, and I don't want to be part of it. I'm just too uncomfortable. It's not *me*, and I can't get involved in it.' He said, 'If anything ever comes up in your business that I want to go to I'll tell you, but otherwise, don't ask me to go because I don't want to be obligated, and I don't want to feel I'm going to disappoint you when I say no.' Well, that was eleven years ago, and he hasn't asked to go to anything since, and I haven't asked him, so it's worked out fine."

Someone else who was there remembers the night. "Carl made himself very, very scarce after he brought Dolly, and I can see why," says the observer. "The man was completely uncomfortable . . . I don't think she wanted him hanging around and meeting a bunch of music people that he had nothing in common with. I wouldn't say it was embarrassing to her, but he was like a fish out of water. She could have been very proud for you to meet her husband, but I didn't get that impression. I kind of got the idea that she had other things to do, and didn't want him underfoot . . . And, in fairness to the man, we have to assume that . . . it's a drag to him."

In the years since, only a few people on the Nashville music scene have ever met Carl Dean. Not Tandy Rice, president of Top Billing, Inc., the agency that handled Dolly's bookings from the time she went with Porter until she began dealing with the West Coast in 1976. "I wouldn't know Carl Dean if he walked in this office and sat down in that chair," Rice told the Nashville *Banner*. "Never saw the man." Not Dolores Smiley, formerly of the same agency. "I never met him, and never saw him," she told me, "but Dolly was always talking about how great he was, how handsome he was, and what a nice relationship they had." Not Hal Durham, manager of the Grand Ole Opry. Nor Minnie Pearl nor Brenda Lee. "Never seen him in my whole life," says Brenda, whose husband, Ronnie Shacklett, knew Carl in high school. "I've never even talked to him, as a matter of fact, and I'd say Dolly and I are friends."

The fact that one of country music's most dazzling and magnetic stars (and its foremost sex symbol) was married to an almost total recluse was of enough interest that one of the Nashville newspapers ran a non-story about him on page one. Non-story since Carl Dean had practically nothing to say; he didn't want to be interviewed, he explained, but would gladly go sit down with the reporter and have a beer. Several other publications followed suit, all arriving at about the same conclusion—Carl Dean was as tall, thin and dark as his famous wife was short, voluptuous and fair, and as withdrawn as she was outgoing. Nobody knew him, the stories said, adding that he didn't even have a best friend, an erroneous statement. Carl has been best friends since high school with a man who runs a service station on Nashville's Nolensville Road.

When the stories appeared, the family was anything but overjoyed. "Did you see that thing in *The Banner* about Carl?" Avie Lee Parton asked me, so red hot she couldn't keep still. "It's hardest on Carl and us."

Dolly's friend and designer Lucy Adams says, "Carl only talks to people he likes. He'll talk to you if you go out there, but if he doesn't have to, he won't." Despite Adams' view, the tabloid *Star* managed to pry a few quotes out of him. "I have a good business," he told the weekly. "Dolly has her work and I have mine. We didn't plan our lives to come out this way. It just snowballed. If I run for president one day, then I'll talk about me. But Dolly is the one in the public eye, not me. If I went out looking for publicity, it would only detract from what she's doing. And I'm not going to take anything away from her. She's earned it."

At the time Carl and Dolly married twelve years ago, he was a partner in his father's business, The Dean and Dean Asphalt Paving Co. But the company ceased operation about six years ago, some say due to rising labor and production costs, others say because of the elder Dean's personal problems. Whatever, Dolly continues to tell people her husband is an asphalt contractor. Carl is still seen occasionally around town by those who knew him when, and he is always dressed in work clothes and driving a truck. And he can often be seen working on the eighty-acre grounds (220 acres, by some accounts) of the twenty-three room home he and Dolly's uncle Dot Watson built near Brentwood. "He still works in construction, and he takes care of the farm," Dolly says. "He's not a farmer by trade, but he's learned more farmin' than most of us. Because he can't stand to be idle or to have to stay inside. He's up every morning at dawn. This morning he got up gripin' 'cause it was rainin', and he couldn't go finish a patch job he had over at the churchyard in Radnor. When I left, I saw him up at the shed we have up in the woods, where he has all his tools and some old junkers. He buys all kinds of old trucks and cars. Loves to work with mechanics. Him and the two ducks we have were runnin' around the place. They've become very good friends." Carl reportedly also dabbles in real estate.

Because Carl is such a mystery man—steadfastly refusing to be interviewed or let his picture be taken up until just recently—a lot of people in Nashville surmised that Dolly invented him. The idea of saying he existed when he did not, they figure, is that she would have the protection of the image of marriage, without having to be bothered by the curtailments a real marriage involves. According to them, Carl Dean is nothing but a figure in Dolly's Parton's fantasy world.

I am here to tell you that he is real.

In the winter of 1976–77, *Country Music* Magazine assigned me to do a cover story on Dolly for the May 1977 issue. A few weeks after I flew to Waco, Texas, to catch the first night of her tour with Willie Nelson, Dolly was to visit me in a Nashville hotel suite for our interview. I had been told that Dolly was a guard dog about her privacy, that she had never and would not "commercialize" her home by allowing a reporter there. I was flabbergasted, then, when Sim Myers of RCA phoned to tell me that Dolly had changed her mind and would see me at her home. "I hope you realize what a rare treat you have in store," Myers said.

On the day we scheduled to meet, Dolly had just returned to Nashville from five weeks on the road. While she was gone, her family had moved into a lovely English Tudor home on Woodmont Blvd., one of Nashville's better addresses. She and Carl had seen the house before she went on tour. Dolly had told a lot of people—including her Aunt Estelle (whose husband built the Brentwood house with Carl's help in 1973)—that she moved into town because she believed something in the soil or the well-water supply on the farm was making her ill. "Really, I just never did like that house," Dolly told me as she handed me a glass of orange juice. "We're just renting this one till we buy another. We'll probably just stay here, though." To the British music paper, *Melody Maker*, Dolly said, "The farm is just too big for me. I'm not a fool, and when I can see that something is not working I let it go. We thought it would be our dream house, but the rooms were too big, the ceilings too high. The rooms never did surround and cuddle us the way a home should." Dolly let me know although she had said, "Once you walk in the house, you're part of the family," that she really did not like the idea of doing the interview at home, and she especially didn't like the photographer Leonard Kamsler making a studio out of her living room, pushing all the furniture to one side and leaving his equipment there overnight. She had suggested it only because she had a lot of work to do, getting the new house in shape, and didn't want to spare the time it took to go out and meet me. (When we left she said, "Come back anytime, as long as it's not business!")

The interview took place in her living room, a large, beamed-ceiling room filled with red velvet Victorian loveseats and sofas, red oriental rugs, white marble-topped tables, a beautiful old piano and gold-framed pictures. It's a room in which Lillian Russell could have entertained Diamond Jim Brady with ease. In one corner there was a bric-a-brac cabinet containing a $2 bill with Dolly's picture on it, a ceramic sea captain, a china figurine of two angels kissing, a tiny gold slipper, a guitar pin, a glass piano with a raised lid and matching harp, and a couple of glass dalmatians. A large, ornate *Bible* lay nearby, and an old photo of Avie Lee was displayed on a table. On one wall hung a portrait done from the famous "Coat of Many Colors" photograph of Dolly at nine, complete with flowing tears. Next to it hung an oil painting of Carl at about the same age. There were butterflies everywhere: ceramic butterflies with music notes and "Love Is Like a Butterfly" carved on their bases, real butterflies mounted and hung on the wall, and downstairs, where Dolly had many of her writing awards on display, there was even a special chair in the shape of a guitar with a butterfly on the back. Dolly had had it made for the stage. Most of the butterfly mementoes are gifts from fans. She gets literally thousands every year, yet her former guitarist Tom Rutledge says she keeps them all.

"You can't ask me nothin' I ain't been asked before," Dolly said, setting a cup of hot chocolate before me. But before I switched on my tape recorder, she asked if I'd care to hear *New Harvest . . . First Gathering,* which had not yet been released. With that, Dolly got up from one of the rugs, took off an album by the Ozark Mountain Daredevils and replaced it on the turntable with a test pressing of her own. As we sat together listening, Dolly sang along on the first cut, "Light of a Clear Blue Morning," slapping her thigh to the beat, her foot popping up reflexively on the offbeat. Before I knew it, the tone arm had made its way through five wonderful songs, the likes of which I had never heard from Dolly Parton. "You want to hear the second side?" she asked. I did. "Well, before that," she said, "Carl is here—he's workin' outside—and I want him to come in and fix the fire. But he doesn't want to hear my record, so we'll have to wait."

Dolly went outside to get Carl, and I waited eagerly for their footsteps. "I don't want to be interviewed," I heard him say in a rural accent as Dolly brought him in through the side porch. She told him he wouldn't be—as much a warning to me as assurance to him. In a moment he stood in the living room, looking shy and uncomfortable in the presence of a stranger. Still, he was friendly and polite and after a little hesitation took my outstretched hand. Tall and thin, bordering on gaunt, he was dressed in blue jeans, a flannel shirt, an old Army jacket, work boots, gloves and a blue wool cap. But he was still ruggedly handsome, and as he tore apart boxes to feed the fire, he turned and looked at his wife as if she were the only woman in the world. It was February, the dead of winter. Carl had a cold and the sniffles and gave that as the reason he wouldn't be eating at the table with us when Dolly told him she'd invited me to stay for some of her famous spaghetti. "I'll just tell him you're a friend," she had said, since the Deans rarely socialize and never entertain. I wondered if he didn't just feel funny having me in the house or if he were afraid I might try to question him.

As Carl continued to fix the fire, nobody said much of anything, and I sensed a strain; Dolly seemed a little nervous and tense. "Here, Daddy, you want my chocolate?" she said, handing him her cup. I thought she might be trying to pacify him—here it was her first full night at home in more than a month. At that time he almost never traveled with her and had yet to attend one of her concerts. And here she'd agreed to let a stranger encroach on the little time they had together.

If I felt I were trespassing, the feeling faded as Carl reappeared several times, usually to bring Dolly and me something to drink as we taped late into the evening. "Y'all growing roots?" he asked at midnight. With each successive visit, he was more at ease, more likeable and charming.

On that first encounter, however, Carl disappeared all too soon, and when he was out of earshot, Dolly got up and flipped *New Harvest . . . First Gathering* to side two. "He's good as gold, really," she said as the music began. "He just doesn't want to hear the record, 'cause we're both so emotional. He'll put it on and listen to it sometime when he's here by himself, and if he likes it, he'll tell me it's pretty good. I bought him a video tape recorder, and he tapes me every time I'm on TV, but he won't watch it unless he hears I done good. You know," she added with a little girl's smile and giggle, "he loves me good and all, but I'm really not his favorite singer. We have a great relationship and he's a wonderful person, but he's not my biggest fan. He likes bluegrass and hard rock music."

I tell Dolly I'm especially glad to have met Carl, since some people think she made him up. "I know that's a big rumor," she says with a small self-satisfied grin, lending some credence to a statement that a friend of hers has made to the effect that Dolly loves to be mysterious. "He's a real mystery person to the public. That's good, though." She decides she shouldn't have put it like that. "I mean, that's fine with us, and fine with him. He loves me good, and my career bein' separate from my marriage is perfectly natural for us. We like it that way. It's too right and too natural and too comfortable and too secure for it to ever be anything else."

Shortly before our interview, a magazine had printed a short item that indicated the reason Dolly and Carl were so certain their marriage would work out was because they lived together first for two years. "Oh, I didn't *live* with him!" Dolly gasps when I bring it up. "I made the mistake of sayin' that out of country innocence. What I said was, 'We've been together twelve years, married for ten.' I meant we *went* together. Now, I especially don't like things like that, because my marriage and our relationship are sacred things to me. He's just the most precious thing in the world. He's the only thing that remains untarnished in this business. And then people will take what little information you're willing to give . . ." She looks genuinely hurt and disappointed. "Maybe I made it sound like that," she adds, "but if I did, I didn't mean to. If I cared enough about somebody to live with 'em, I would care enough about 'em to marry. But, I can't say. We married young. I don't know what I would have done had I not married when I did. Not that it would matter whether we did or not, because we loved each other. But we didn't, and I don't like that, sayin' I lived with my husband two years. I'm just a bit old-fashioned in my beliefs about things like that. It almost embarrasses me to think that somebody would think I did that."

But so widespread is the curiosity about Dolly and Carl in Nashville that you can find somebody to say almost anything about them. Another of the prevalent rumors is that they have a "business arrangement marriage," with Dolly giving Carl half of her earnings in exchange for his name, supposedly to counteract Porter's possessiveness. "Umm, these stories are fun," Dolly said when I asked her about it. "Now that doesn't bother me," she added, with forced nonchalance, "but it's certainly interesting. That one's weird, too, because I was married for a year before I even knew Porter. And it's certainly not a business arrangement. Or if it is," she says, her tone turning bitter, "it's smart business."

While Dolly's life-style suggests she might champion the women's movement, she in many ways fits the stereotypical country girl mold. Rock singer Linda Ronstadt, a friend of Dolly's, said recently, "[Dolly] taught me that you don't have to sacrifice your femininity in order to have equal status. The only thing that gives you equal status with other musicians is your musicianship. Period." Yet, when Dolly is asked by another interviewer how she feels about the Equal Rights Amendment, she says, "I don't make comments. I feel I'm a lucky person to be able to do what I want to do. I'm not doin' it to spite anybody or to say that I'm doin' it because I'm a woman. I'm just glad that I can do what makes me happy. I don't voice my political beliefs."

Much of the talk about Dolly and Porter probably started because for years, Dolly was on the road 120 to 200 days of the year and saw Carl infrequently. Barbara Walters, for one, couldn't seem to understand how or why Dolly would stay in a marriage under those conditions. "The man gives me freedom," Dolly responded resolutely. "So why get married?" Barbara asked. "Well, why not?" Dolly countered. "I mean, if what you want most is freedom," Barbara said, "why have a husband . . . tucked away someplace that you see six weeks a year?" "He has the same freedom," Dolly told her. "See, the thing of it is, you don't find a person that you can be happy with and can accept you the way you are and can share the things and the plans for the future and enjoy your home. We have our foundation, we have our roots, we have all the things that everybody's lookin' for, and that's happiness in the marriage."

"Well, what about when you're on the road?" Barbara continued. "Weeks at a time. No temptations?" "Well, I didn't say that we've never had temptations," Dolly said, using her mysterious tone. "When you have these temptations," Barbara pressed, and Dolly laughed, "does anything happen that he could be jealous of?" "No, not really," she answered. . . . I'm just sayin' I wouldn't want to pry in it. I've got better things to do than to sit around in my room thinkin', 'Oh, what's Carl doin' tonight? I wonder if he's with somebody and this and that."

On one occasion when Dolly was gone, Carl had a "date"—with Archie Ray McMahan. "I go to Nashville about twice a year," Mrs. McMahan says, "and Dolly's folks were always saying I should call her when I came down. She and Carl had been married a year or two then, and she was with Porter. So, I called, and Carl answered, and after I told him who I was, he said Dolly was in Chicago. I said I was hoping we could get together, that I wanted to take them out to dinner. And he just sort of teasingly said, 'Well, now, it's just me here by myself.' So I said, 'Well, *you* come, and I'll take *you* out.' And he did. I enjoyed him so much. He would ask me things about Dolly back when she was little. That night, when Dolly called, he said, 'I've been out on a date tonight.' And after he'd teased her and gone on awhile, he told her who it was, and I think she got a kick out of the fact that her husband had been out to supper with her first grade teacher. I like Carl a lot. I think he's real nice. I haven't been around him anymore, though, except at Cassie's wedding. He gave her away, and then they had the reception down at the American Legion building in Sevierville."

Of course, Carl Dean must have the same thoughts as his wife. "I've heard he's insanely jealous," says someone who's known Carl for years. But what man wouldn't be, knowing the effect his wife has on the opposite sex?

Ed Enoch of the Stamps Quartet remembers all too well. "I met Carl in about 1967 or so when I was in the 401st MP unit here in Nashville in the Army Reserve, and we went to summer camp together down in Georgia," Enoch says. "We just kinda fooled around some together. He was always a real nice, polite, mild-mannered person, a real likeable guy. He talked about his paving business, and we talked music some—I think he played a banjo or guitar, and Dolly had just joined Porter about then. He was happy for her to have her career, and we used to talk about his wife traveling on the road. He said it didn't matter to him, that he wanted her to have her place, and he was proud of her. He really loved her. I remember she came down to see him at Fort Stewart, Georgia, and we took the weekend off and went to the Holiday Inn. We just sat around the pool and talked. And I will never forger her pink bikini bathing suit if I live to be 495 years old. . . . She was beautiful. Her chest wasn't like it is now, but it was very, very nice. Me and a bunch of my buddies were sitting on the side of the pool and I said to my big buddy, Porter Maxwell, 'Boy, that's a star. Now, *that's* a woman!' *Goodness*, I wish I could tell you how she looked in that pink bathing suit!

"They was just typical married people, you know," Enoch says of Mr. and Mrs. Dean. "They seemed very, very happy. I was very much impressed with that, 'cause they seemed so much in love. But it was a respect of one for the other. I could tell how much she tried to make him feel loved. It wasn't overtly sexual. You don't have to throw somebody to the ground, you know. I could just tell that she really admired and really cared for him. It was in her eyes and on her face. She didn't have to say a word. I've since worked shows with her, and Dolly's been quite a beautiful lady. Carl is bound to know that she loves him and is a lady with him and without him. . . . Men respect that, you know. And there's nobody got any more respect around town than Dolly Parton."

Despite Dolly's considerable powers of arousal, she claims she is rarely propositioned. "This is the honest truth, but I have had very few people ever proposition me," she says. "I've been standin' with girl friends when people just say everything to them or just come up and pretty well ask 'em. You know, I have been well thought of, and I have shared conversations with many people. I know that there have been people who have wanted to share more with me, and I would have probably wanted to share more with them, but I was already, well . . . I just wasn't the kind that would go on and do that, because of my own principles and my own morals, and because of my own marriage and my family. To me, sex is a part of life, but it's also a part of love, and in order to share sex would mean that I would have to share love as well. Occasionally, you know, you meet somebody that you really feel something for, but because of obligations and circumstances and all, you just let it go and leave it alone. But that doesn't mean you don't really feel it, just the same. That's why I wrote 'I Will Always Love You.' A lot of people thought, since it came out when me'n Porter split, that it was about him. I wrote another song about that same kind of thing, 'He Would Know': 'In my mind I've made love to you often/But only in my mind can it be so/Because there is someone home that's countin' on me/And if I did, I'm sure that he would know.' But sometimes I wonder about it. You'd think I would get more propositions, because people are always askin' me about it. I think that people know I'm not out for anything. I'm super friendly. I love everybody, you know, and I'm such an emotional person. I think people can read through all of my conversations and my personality that I'm not tryin' to play up to nobody as far as in that sort of way. I think I could handle it, though, because the way I've always been able to get in or out of anything is to joke in a playful way. If somebody asked me that, I would pretend it was a joke and that they were kidding. I'd say, 'Oh, sure, I'll meet you out back!' in a playful way. But I think they always know. Now, be careful how you word all that, please."

Says Dolly's former guitarist, Tom Rutledge: "I've never seen a man get physical with her, but I've seen men get very suggestive after one too many drinks. I know it really, really tees her off, but you'd never know it until afterwards, when she says, 'That son of a bitch.' But she handles it well. She'll put him down to where he'll lose his passion pretty quick. She's good at making her feelings known to someone."

Still, many in Nashville steadfastly refuse to believe Dolly and Carl have the sort of marriage Enoch describes. Rumors that they are separating or divorcing are perennial. One journalist points to the fact that Dolly says she never *discusses* her plans with Carl, but simply *tells* him about them after she's made a decision, and asks, "What possibly would they have in common to talk about . . . ?" Dolly herself says she and Carl have never had a disagreement over her music and get along so well because they're not together enough to pick each other apart.

Favorite grist for the Nashville gossip mill for years has been the "fact" that Carl refused to watch his wife perform. It is hard to know for sure when Carl has been in Dolly's audience. Jo Coulter remembers he came to the first couple of tapings of Porter's TV show after Dolly became a regular. But Dolly explained that he didn't continue to come because it would make him nervous, and he'd be afraid she'd make a mistake.

In 1975, Dolly told Mary Campbell of the Associated Press, "[Carl] is not a show person. He's a quiet and home-loving person. If he comes to a show, he likes to go on his own. Most of the time I don't know when he's coming. It's good that way." Two years later Dolly said that Carl had never attended one of her performances until 1977. Perhaps she was distinguishing between taped and live shows.

On May 5, 1977, Carl drove up to Louisville to see Dolly's Kentucky Derby Festival show in Freedom Hall. Dolly was particularly flamboyant and outgoing that night. She seemed to be totally on top of her better-than-usual performance. "I was a nervous wreck," she told Mike Douglas on the air soon after. "And it was very emotional for him." Another reporter asked Dolly later what Carl had said about her performance. "He thought that if I really kept at it, I might be somebody someday," Dolly replied, dimpling.

After the show, Carl was nowhere to be seen, neither backstage while Dolly signed autographs nor at the reception given for her later on. Nor did any of the concert promoters see him with her at any time during the day, "and we pretty much surrounded her the whole time she was here," says one. That would not have been Carl's style. Mary Fielder, Dolly's back-up singer at the time, recalls Carl came to several of Dolly's concerts in that period, but "You'd never see Carl. He'd drive up and see her, and usually stay backstage or in the audience. Carl's really in the background. He doesn't interfere or include himself in any way."

By August, though, Carl decided he liked his little taste of show business. So much so, that when Dolly took the stage at the Indiana State Fair, she found Carl between back-up singers Anita Ball and Richard Dennison, singing "Higher and Higher"! "Carl's a great practical joker," says Tom Rutledge. "He'll do anything. Here's a guy who never ever came out to the show for six years, and now he's up on stage singing!" Rutledge remembers the band carried a volleyball net under the bus and challenged the musicians in the other bands on Dolly's shows, and that Carl "got right in there and played with 'em. Everybody got to like him real well. He's a fun guy to be around. And he's witty, too."

Why did Carl break his long-standing rule and begin showing up at Dolly's concerts? "He just got tired of people buggin' him about it," Dolly told *Newsday*'s Jerry Parker. "And then he knew I didn't until just lately have my show the way I wanted it to be." Others speculate it was out of curiosity as to exactly what his wife did on the road, both professionally and privately, or that he simply wanted to spend more time with her. Still others say Carl might have wanted to stifle the rumors that his and Dolly's invisible marriage might not be what she said it was, perhaps at the request of Dolly's then-new management, Katz-Gallin-Cleary. Or if L.A. wasn't behind it, some figure, certainly they provoked Carl's latest surprise: posing for pictures with Dolly for general release. Then there's one other school of thought: "Maybe Carl isn't as aloof as he's made out to be," someone at

RCA offers. Indeed. Perhaps it has all been a well-planned publicity stunt. Or maybe just one of Carl Dean's jokes on the world.

Ronnie Shacklett was a year behind Carl at Nashville's Central High School in 1961. The two ran around with the same crowd, though, and had a lot in common. Both grew up in the middle-class section of Radnor, or Woodbine, the Nolensville Road area. Their fathers were friends; Carl's father was in the paving business, and Ronnie's dad was a general contractor. "We were both mechanical people, so to speak," Shacklett says. "We ran equipment, drove trucks and worked weekends for our daddies in the contracting business. We were just neighborhood guys who went to the same school and knew one another." In time, they would share another similarity: they would both marry singing stars.

"Carl was always quiet, a hard-working guy," recalls Shacklett, who now owns several Nashville businesses including the mill. "As far as bein' much of a student, I think he was probably pretty much like myself, just average. At that particular school, it wasn't the thing in those days to be an outstanding student if you were a boy. It was like playin' in the band. Nobody played in the band, 'cause everybody thought you were a sissy if you did that. You played football, or something, and if you made C's, that was fine. We went through school without studying. We were out to have a good time and keep up to date with the times as they were then. Carl and I were in the same bunch that was always together at the ball games and such, and he was considered a pretty sharp guy, a neat guy. We didn't have money, but in those days, Levi's and penny loafers were your dress. You really starched your Levi's then, and you wanted to get 'em white. Yeah, he was neat. It seems to me he played basketball, but he wasn't real athletic. He was sorta into cars. I don't think he went steady, or anything, because he sorta kept to himself. How do you describe somebody who is quiet and not too talkative, sort of a loner, but is a cut-up with the group of guys that he runs with? I don't mean to say he was a bad guy. He wasn't too mischievous. Wasn't a thief or a hubcap stealer, or anything. Carl was just sort of witty. He was quiet, but he was witty. And he would kinda put you on. Just like he does now."

That reminds Shacklett of one of the last times he saw Carl, last winter. "He came in our liquor store, and he had on just an old T-shirt, you know, and it was *cold.* Carl's a right good-lookin' guy," says Shacklett, "but he's gotten a lot thinner than he was in high school. He's sort of gaunt now, just *too* thin. But he came in smilin'—he's always smilin' when I see him—and we were real busy. He said [and here Shacklett goes into a mock-country accent], 'Ronnie, I need ten dollars. You got ten dollars, Ronnie?' I said, 'Well, sure, Carl.' I gave it to him, and he walked around the store for awhile, and then came back and laid the ten dollars back on the counter. I said, 'Well, Carl, do you want it?' He kept sayin' how much he appreciated it, over and over. I don't know whether he meant it or not. He said, 'Well, I might be able to do without it today.' Then he grinned and laughed, and he walked out. I really didn't know what to say to him when he brought it back, 'cause I didn't know what his motive was. I guess he was just seein' if he could do it, if I'd give it to him. I don't think I've ever seen Carl serious. He just puts you on all the time. Seems to me he may be playin' a part, or acting out a role of some sort. Carl was never *that* 'country' in high school."

Another high school acquaintance has the same impression. "The last times I've seen Carl in the past couple years, it seemed like he'd regressed," says the friend, who asked that his name not be used. "He's just not with it. Not long ago, he was driving down the street and saw me, and stopped. Had a T-shirt on, a not-with-it T-shirt, but an undershirt. Solid white. He hung his arm and head out the window and said, 'Hey, there, boy; I ain't seen you in the longest!' But he said this in a real strong country accent. I said, 'Carl, quit that shit,' because he's just not *that* damn 'country.' . . . You know how guys in high school will put each other on all the time? Well, Carl's still jivin'. . . . He's just constantly putting you on."

When Carl's not out on a paving job or stopping to say hello to old friends, he's usually home at Willow Creek Plantation in Williamson County, where the Deans returned after living only a few months in the house on Woodmont Boulevard. In many ways, the area is reminiscent of where Dolly grew up. The Cumberland foothills are in view, and up the road stands the Edmondson Chapel Baptist Church, a small, simple structure reminiscent of Reverend Owens' Church of God. Across the small wooden bridge, the road leads farther out into the country. Grapevines gnarl around the massive tree trunks, and at the beginning of Crockett Road stand two overgrown Crockett family graveyards with stones dating from 1880. Situated nearly at the end of Crockett Road, the Parton-Dean house is easily identifiable, even though there is no name on the mailbox. A two-story white Southern colonial (Dolly calls it a plantation house) with what appears to be white aluminum siding and six apparently handmade Doric columns across the front, the 23-room house ("countin' bathrooms and closets," Dolly says) is balanced on each end by two large rooms. ("I don't have many rooms, but the rooms I have are real big.") A white post and rail fence surrounds the property and lines the blacktop driveway, which is usually blocked to traffic by a matching rail gate. Out on the front acreage, grazing Herefords share space with numerous poplar, beech and dogwood trees and a few buttercups. (When the Deans moved there in 1973, they also had horses, chickens, hunting dogs and male and female spitzes named Mark Spitz and Lickety Spitz.)

It's not too unusual to get a glimpse of Carl working with his equipment and tools out by the shed behind the side gate with the "No Trespassing" sign on it. "He probably spends most of his time just digging holes out there at the farm and fillin' 'em back in," says guitarist Tom Rutledge. "I've always been afraid to ask him what he does, because I think that's really it—

he digs holes and fills 'em back up. He's into machinery, obviously. Maybe he's waiting for a job, or something. I don't know. But he's a real nice guy. I've sat and shot the breeze with him several times." Rutledge laughs and shakes his head. "Don't know Carl at all," he adds. "Nobody does, really."

Certainly not the driver of the Homes of the Stars tour bus.

"I never thought I was that much of a star, but the tour bus comes out there, anyway," Dolly told Johnny Carson. "People will start to take pictures of Carl, and he'll say, 'No, no, no, you've got the wrong one. I just work here.' And, you know, he does a lot of grade work and construction and looks *just like* a gardener or somebody just workin' there." She gets tickled at the thought. "So then they'll start askin' him questions about me—'What's she like? What's she like?' And he'll say, 'Oh, she's really nice. I just love her, but her husband . . . I don't know about him. He's kinda weird!' He's always puttin' 'em on. And once the bus was turnin' around in the driveway and tore down the fence. They said, 'Well, just don't mention that it was the tour bus when they come home.' And Carl said, 'I won't, 'cause I wouldn't *dare* mention it to him, but y'all be careful, ya hear?' " The fans occasionally get to be a pain in the neck, too. "Once in awhile, we'll step out on a porch half-naked on a Saturday mornin', and somebody'll be there ready with a camera," Dolly lamented to Toby Thompson.

While Carl's usually outside, Dolly generally spends her time at home indoors. No matter how she feels today about the house, when she and Carl first moved in, she was terribly excited about it, detailing the floor plan ("Me and Carl drew it up") to every journalist who asked. (Dolly refused to allow her home to be photographed for publication, however, as did several country music stars at the time, perhaps recalling the then recent Stringbean murders.) She had a full basement with bedrooms, recreation room and one of four fireplaces in the house, she said. The other fireplaces were in the den, her music room, and the master bedroom. On the first level, she had not only a modern kitchen, but an old-country kitchen, filled with antiques, including a country cupboard, an old wood-burning stove, the likes of which Avie Lee had used when Dolly was a child, and the table her father had made long ago. The table was originally ten feet long, she remembered, but her father had cut it down as the children grew up and left home, eventually reducing its size to six feet. She had "a big ol' den" on the first floor, too, as well as her own large music room, complete with stage and studio. And she seemed especially thrilled to tell that both the lower and upper part of the fireplace in the music room were made out of rocks and logs from the cabin in which she was born.

One whole side of the upstairs was devoted to Dolly and Carl's "quarters," Dolly said, and was furnished entirely with antiques. She kept all her clothes and shoes in a wing above the den, where she could "hang my clothes in the floor and just pull the door to, when people come." From what her mother told the Knoxville *News-Sentinel*, Dolly *needs* an entire wing for that. "I tell you, she used to change clothes so fast I couldn't rub the scrubboard fast enough to keep up with her. Now, the last time I was at Dolly's home I counted over a thousand pairs of shoes she had. I wouldn't even go to the closet to count her clothes. [Dolly says there are about twelve closets full.] I told her she could retire right now and spend the rest of her life trying on her shoes and clothes." Dolly went on to tell journalist LaWayne Satterfield that she had converted a closet into a make-up room, and that "Me and Carl have a big bathroom with a sunken tub and all the fancy things I'd always dreamed of." Aside from the master bedroom, the second level housed two other bedrooms, two guest bedrooms and two baths.

The first color scheme for the living room was baby pink and red ("I like red to decorate"), with faint touches of blue, set off by red draperies with baby pink valances and tiebacks. "It sounds like it'd be gaudy, but it's real pretty," Dolly said in 1973. Her dining room was red and pink. "I just use a mix-up," she said. "I don't know what goes together. I just know what I like." Three years later, she bought a dining room suite done in antique white and turquoise for a reported $8,000.

"When Dolly's home, she's just like any other housewife," Mrs. Parton told the Knoxville reporter, Ken Mink. "I'm not a very good housekeeper," Dolly admitted to the Fayetteville *Observer*. "I'm sloppy, Carl's neat." Dolly does do her own cooking, however, which is limited mostly to country fixin's and her specialty—spaghetti. I can vouch that the spaghetti Dolly fed me is unlike any spaghetti you've ever had. She makes the sauce from scratch, and it's chock-full of every succulent spice and vegetable that belongs in Italian cooking, ending up more like a thick topping than anything else. As for Dolly's country cooking, her Aunt Estelle says that in the days Dolly lived with her, "She was a good cook. She didn't learn to make spaghetti at this house, but she could fry sausage and make gravy and cornbread and potatoes. She never could make biscuits, though." Dolly says she can't follow a recipe and being creative, likes to concoct her own.

Sometimes, however, all that good food catches up with her. "I've been on a diet for three days," Dolly told me during a photo session last year. "I'm fatter than I've ever been in my life. I gained ten pounds on that Texas tour, 'cause there's nothin' I like better than Mexican food. What do I weigh? I always just say a hundred and a plenty! And I've been workin' on an album, and I always eat like a pig when I do that. I guess I'm too fat in some people's minds [she reads Adele Davis and has lately tried liquid protein in an effort to keep her weight at 110], but I've always looked a certain way." Or, as Dolly told her friend and sometime designer, Lucy Adams, "I've never dieted enough to hurt me!" Aside from performing, the only exercise Dolly gets is when she plays a little golf, horseshoes or tennis (on her own court) or goes for a walk in the woods, where she occasionally cuts some firewood with the chain saw she got for Christmas one year. Wandering in the woods is one of her favorite recreations, except, "I never can get the weeds out of my hair afterwards," she told me once, pulling a twig from her cascading wig. "Takes me forever to get 'em out of all this." Last summer she got determined to do something about her added poundage, and bought a trampoline she saw out on the sidewalk at Zayre's. "I thought it would be great exercise," she says. "When I was little, trampolines were really hot items. I used to pay fifty cents to jump on 'em for thirty minutes. Now that I've got one, I'll be spendin' a lot of time bouncin'. I've never exercised in my life, but I think I could get over my husband easier that I could lose ten pounds." (She laughs, and then has second thoughts about what she's just said, adding, "Be sure and say that was a joke if you say it at all.") "Really," she says, "I've been tryin' to lose ten pounds for ten years. But I don't do anything to stay in shape, except all the natural runnin' that I do. What shape I've got is beginnin' to spread out a little." She shrugs her ample shoulders and grins. "Just one of them things, I guess."

But because Dolly doesn't have much time for recreation does not mean she doesn't have fun. "Everything I do is fun!" she says, sitting on her living room rug. "I enjoy my work. I enjoy my home, I enjoy walkin' in the woods. I've got dogs and cows and stuff, and I enjoy them. And I love to write. I mean, I *love* to write," she adds, her large blue eyes growing wide with emphasis. "Ummmmm . . . what else do I do for fun? People watch. I love to sit and watch people. And, of course," she adds, "I love to travel."

A lot of people, I tell her, think it's terrible that she obviously has more interest in travel and in her career than she has in children. "I've had many babies," she shoots back, tired of hearing about the subject, since she is asked about it in almost every interview. "There's eight children younger than me, and I've raised five of 'em pretty much as my own. You met my sister, Rachel, this morning. She lives here with us." (Rachel, 18, married Dolly's back-up singer, Richard Dennison, in the spring of 1978.) "Dolly's been able to help the younger kids more than anybody else because she had her house, and that's good," says her sister Stella. "But as far as raising anybody, I don't consider anybody raised anybody. We all helped each other get raised, let's say." "Besides," Dolly adds, "I think everybody has a purpose. I give birth every time I write a song." In 1975 Dolly told Associated Press writer Matt Yancey, "You can look at songwriting as a mother-type thing. You first conceive it, and then it develops. You labor with it to get it out, but afterwards it's sort of on its own, and you no longer have that much control over what becomes of it." Or, as she told me, "I don't miss havin' children, let's put it that way." (She has always said she could adopt them if she changes her mind past her childbearing years.) "Someday I may want to have children of my own, but it'll only be when I feel that I am ready to give up part of my career," she told Yancey. "I have children everywhere," she said to me. "Nieces and nephews and brothers and sisters and cousins and friends. I love kids."

"Dolly really does have a love for children," says her former guitarist

Don Roth. "I've seen her watch the six o'clock news and her eyes fill up with tears when they show a child abuse story. She'll say, 'That's just terrible. How could anybody do that to a child?' I think she may have chosen not to have them because she loves them so much. What kind of mother would Dolly Parton be for a child? She's gone six to eight weeks at a time." (Carl has left the decision of having children up to Dolly, but he is said to be fond of children also. "He'd play baseball with my sister's two boys and my boy," says Carl Reagan, the brother of Dolly's Aunt Colleen Owens. "I remember him showin' 'em how to use their gloves one time, and when they got to fussin' and fightin', he'd whup 'em, like they were his own.")

Doesn't this sometime produce just a twinge of guilt? "Never," Dolly says firmly. She never feels guilty about not staying home and taking care of her husband? "No," she says again, shaking her head. "I don't wanna stay home. I like to *come* home, and I like to *be* home when I'm home, but I don't wanna *stay* home. That may sound cruel or silly, but like I told you, I love to travel. That's one of the great things about me and Carl. Now, he likes to be at home, and he likes to do the things he enjoys doin'. He likes to be alone a lot. But me, I like to travel. And he's always welcome to come, even though he don't want to often. But he does sometimes. But at least it's a thing that if we want to see each other, it's just a matter of a phone call to say, 'Why don'tcha come up here?' Simple as that. We're together just enough to keep it excitin'. And Carl and me always take a long vacation. We go to some part of the country he's always wanted to see and I've never really had a chance to see, although I've been there."

On the other hand, Dolly told journalist Joan Dew in 1976 that she and Carl had just returned from two weeks in Wyoming and Colorado, and "in all truth, that's the first real vacation we've ever had that was not distorted by somethin' else, or where we didn't have to hurry back. We go all the time on weekends or somethin', maybe just ride to Mississippi, but this was the first big-time vacation we ever had, and we had the time of our lives. We had a station wagon and camped and cooked out. We really got a chance to get to know each other like we used to before things got so hectic. Not that we didn't already, but it was nice to just be alone. Because I'm so close to my family and there's so many of us, that there's always somebody at our house. It's like a depot, in fact. We love our people. But just as a joke, because there's so much traffic at our house, we were gonna get a registration book and stand and a Coke machine, and put up a sign sayin', 'We accept all major credit cards.' "

In any case, it seems as soon as they get home, Dolly is itching to go again, the gypsy in her aching to feel the rhythm of the wheels beneath her feet. "You grow more restless as the years go on, and you want to get out," Dolly says. "If I'm home more than two weeks straight, I get restless and bored, and I wanna get back on the bus and go." Or, as Don Roth sums up, "Dolly just gets antsy with too much leisure. She doesn't know what to do with it. The road is her life. And she knows how to deal with that."

Whether Dolly loves Carl in both the passionate and the affectionate sense, or simply in the latter, as has been suggested by others, she seems to care more for the love of the audience; that love seems more rewarding to her than the love of one person. "Here is a song a lot of people think I wrote for a lover, but I wrote it for the fans," Dolly told the audience at New York's Bottom Line in 1977, and then she began one of her most effusive of love songs, "You Are": "You are my inspiration, you are the song I sing/You are what makes me happy, you are my everything . . ." When she finished the song, the last of the evening, she blew the audience a kiss. "Thank you for making my dreams come true," she told us. "I love you."

Although the marriage may appear in many ways to be unconventional, with Dolly out on the road working and Carl home taking care of domestic affairs, it seems not only to work for them but also to provide each of them what they need from wedlock. And from all accounts of people who have worked closely with Dolly through the years and seen the two of them together, Dolly and Carl are devoted to one another. "A lot of people can't see how she and her husband get along, but I think I can understand because he's a lot like my husband," says Lucy Adams. "He lets her do what she wants to do and then he's happy. When she's home, which isn't often, it's like a honeymoon. They're just two completely different people, but they're always together, even when they're apart."

"A lot of people don't understand it, and no one who doesn't have a marriage like ours *could* understand it," Dolly admits. "I hadn't intended to marry. All I had ever known was housework and kids and workin' in the fields. But I didn't want to be domestic; I wanted to be *free*. I had my songs to sing, I had an ambition, and it *burned* inside me. It was something I knew would take me out of the mountains. I knew I could see worlds beyond the Smoky Mountains. I hadn't intended to find anybody, but you know how love goes, and I've always felt God has had His hand in my life. The day I met Carl, I felt I found something I'd looked for all my life. And he felt the same way. But he understood that I had to do what I had come to Nashville to do. It was in my blood from a child; I would do it under any circumstances. If he was ill and needed me, then I would quit. I would miss it, but I wouldn't blame him for it. But nobody could ever *make* me quit. And he's never tried that. He'd probably be happier if I *did* quit. But he don't want me to, because he knows I don't want to. He knows it's my life, or it's a *way* of life. He knows he is just a *part* of my life, just like I am *part* of his. I guess we really both have two first loves, our job and each other. We have a great understanding. And I believed it could happen. I thought you were supposed to be happy when you married, and I am. It's a good marriage," she adds in a tone only a hard-core cynic could doubt. "It's solid, and it's firm. We've both only been married once, and that's to each other. But it'll be the only time I'm ever married, unless my husband should die.

Because we're that sure of each other and what we have. I'm sure it will last forever."

Aside from Carl Dean, the person closest to Dolly, she said in early 1977, was her lifelong best friend, Judy Ogle. Or, as Dolly puts it, "I have other friends that are very dear and close to me, but there's nobody like Judy. She knows everything that it's humanly possible to know about me."

The two met, according to Archie Ray McMahan, when Dolly transferred to the Caton's Chapel School. Dolly puts their age at about seven. "The day I walked into the school room," she says, "our eyes just kinda *interlocked.* We were just ugly, poor little trashy kids, but that thing within me said, 'This will be your lifelong friend. This is the one.' She felt it, too." Years later, a journalist would ask Dolly what she looked for in a friend. "Loyalty, honesty and devotion, exactly what I'm willing to give myself," Dolly replied. "A person willing to accept my moods, a person I can relate to." She found it in Judy Ogle. Not only were their personalities compatible, but they shared a common background. They lived but a few miles from each other, and both came from large, poor families. More importantly, as they played in the fields and dangled their feet in the creeks, Judy, shy, red-haired and freckled, sat mesmerized at the tales and dreams her friend spun of the future. "She believed it, too, just like I did," Dolly would say later. "And the *Bible* says that if any two agree upon a certain thing with total faith, it shall be done." In an action that was as much a declaration that they would both devote their lives to finding that dream as it was testimonial to their friendship, Judy and Dolly cut their fingers and let the blood run together. "Really, we never even had to cut our fingers," Dolly says. "Our blood just kinda ran together anyway."

By the time they got to high school, the bond had solidified to the extent that they registered at the same time to make sure they had all their classes together—including band, where Judy played snare drum, too. "We were assigned to a kind of practice period in the band room before regular band practice," Judy once wrote. "We were supposed to use the time to learn how to read music and all that, but we never did. Dolly always went to the piano and wrote songs during the practice period." Whether Judy had much interest in music outside of school is open for debate. Cas Walker says he remembers that "Judy was a right good entertainer, but she wasn't anything to compare with Dolly. She can sing, but she don't have many numbers she can do, and she has to have somebody else pick for her." Jo Coulter says she doesn't believe Judy "is a musician at all, although she knows and appreciates music." And according to Tom Rutledge, who says he's "really close to Judy," Dolly's friend "never had a lot of interest in the creative aspects, in art or that sort of thing."

Judy's relationship to Dolly, then, seems always to have been that of devoted friend, rather than that of someone who hoped to ride into a career on Dolly's coattails. In fact, after graduation from high school, Judy joined the Air Force. Apparently, Judy never meant to make a career of military life, because Dolly says "as soon as I had a place for Judy, she came to Nashville, too." Carla Scarborough, general manager of Owepar, says that Judy took care of the song publishing company for the last part of 1967 and most of '68, "when there weren't many songs in it."

From that time on, Judy was always in Dolly's company, both as her companion, living there at the house with Dolly and Carl and traveling with her on the road, and as her employee, serving as her secretary, shielding her from over-zealous fans and reporters, making phone calls for her, taking care of her clothes, brushing her hair, keeping her songs in order, and even writing the liner notes for Dolly's album, *The Fairest of Them All.* And Judy got a mention in the ad-lib ending of Porter and Dolly's duet, "We'd Have to Be Crazy" as well as a "special thanks for creative ideas and inspiration" on Dolly's *New Harvest . . . First Gathering.* "Oh, she was everything," remembers Jo Coulter from the days Judy came with Dolly to the set of Porter's television show. "Mainly, best friend. And Judy would help her dress or do anything she needed done. But she was there mostly for companionship. I mean, Dolly needed somebody with her, and Judy always had an eagle eye. She always spoke up if she didn't like a shot they were getting, or if something was wrong with Dolly's costume. That was good, because directors are so busy that they don't notice those things. That can make a difference, particularly on a television show, and Judy always kept her eye open to make sure everything was fine with Dolly. She was a good friend."

Not everyone appreciated Judy's efficiency, however. "In 1976, when they were doing Dolly's TV show, man, you couldn't get *close* to Dolly that Judy wasn't there," says someone who was handling Dolly's publicity at the time. "You couldn't get in the dressing room, you couldn't get on the bus, you couldn't do *anything* that Judy wasn't there, and a lot of times when I'd call and want to talk to Dolly, I had to go through Judy. And what I needed to talk about, I needed to talk to Dolly, not to Judy. Judy knew nothing about what I was talking about. She had to go to Dolly and ask her about it anyway. And, really, I didn't feel Judy was qualified to speak for Dolly, or to make the kind of decisions she was given the responsibility to make. A lot of times, she didn't realize the importance of doing an interview, say, for *Esquire*. Dolly had to make these decisions, but she used Judy as a buffer, as a go-between."

The day I visited Dolly's home, Judy acted as another sort of go-between, transporting clothes and belongings from the Brentwood house to Woodmont Boulevard. Dolly told me she and Judy sometimes play a little golf and tennis, but Judy got all the exercise she needed that day, making several trips between the two houses, coming in occasionally to inquire if

Dolly would be needing Lois Ray, the woman who does her porcelain nails, or what she should do toward dinner. At midnight, on Dolly's request, she drove me back to my motel.* (Dolly is said to be frightened to go out much by herself especially at night, since she has had repeated threats on her life.) In contrast to Dolly's curvaciousness, Judy is slight of build; whereas Dolly's hairstyles are bouffant, Judy fixes hers simply. While Dolly dresses in elaborate get-ups, Judy wears jeans and shirts. And as Dolly is vivacious, Judy is quiet. Dolly and Judy appear a good balance, if almost opposites, and while Judy sends out silent messages that she is not about to talk about Dolly to the press, she is polite and pleasing and nice, with a ready smile, the sort of person one would like to have for a friend. To a visitor, Dolly and Judy's relationship seems to change from minute to minute. At one time, their interaction appears to be that of employer and employee, then it's older and younger sister (although they are the same age), then star and doting admirer/friend, with Judy eager to do anything to make Dolly's way easier.

"When you're on the road the way Dolly is, you need somebody to help you carry your bags and stuff and just be a companion," says Tom Rutledge. "Dolly didn't have anybody else but Judy. Out at the house, she'd get stuff together for a trip because Dolly never had time to do it. She acted like a valet for her, but she was more than that. She did all kinds of stuff, but because she *enjoyed* doing it. She enjoyed being with Dolly when she was writing, too, because that's Dolly's special time. Very few people have ever had the opportunity to be with Dolly when she writes. Judy was there a lot. They wrote together, sort of. She'd sing Judy a song and get comments on it, and they'd stay up late into the night." (After I left that night, Dolly stayed up until 4 A.M. writing a song called "Nothing Here Worth Saving Anymore.") "If I think I know Dolly well," Rutledge continues, "Judy knows her a thousand percent better. They grew up together, played softball together, drag raced together, done it all, together."

Where Dolly and Carl's personal life was totally separate from their business, Dolly and Judy had long ago built their relationship on realizing Dolly's career. To many people, it seemed that Judy had no life other than Dolly. "Dolly has been Judy's world," says Carla Scarborough. "She's been her constant companion." And the feeling of a journalist who saw them together several times was that Judy lived vicariously through Dolly. But friends of Judy's react sharply to that, bristling at the idea that Judy Ogle lived her whole life just to serve Dolly Parton, or that she allows Dolly to use her as a psychological crutch. "Judy and I spent a pretty good amount of time together on the bus when I was with Dolly," says Mary Fielder, Dolly's

* I had been there virtually all day. "You're incredible," I told her as I started to leave. "I wouldn't have given a reporter this much time." Dolly gave me a hug. "Yeah," she said, "but you ain't me!"

former back-up singer. "I like Judy a lot. She's a little character. She was real close to Dolly, but she's a very independent girl. She was like a handy-woman for Dolly, but that was her job. She *had* to gear herself that way." Tom Rutledge agrees. "Judy's got a mind of her own," he says. "She doesn't need Dolly."

What everybody seemed to forget—or never knew—was that Carl flat-out refused to go many places in public with Dolly, and as Tom Rutledge pointed out, Dolly had nobody else but Judy to travel with her. They forget, too, that "Dolly couldn't run down to the pharmacy like you and I could, so Judy had to do those things for and with her," Charlene Bray says. "Since they had been childhood friends and shared confidences through the years, Judy was probably the one person Dolly felt she could really trust, and talk to about anything." Then, of course, Dolly was devoted to Judy because Judy was devoted to Dolly's music, and to her dreams, having been there with Dolly as she realized them one by one. "I'm sure Dolly was dependent on Judy, if only for support," says Joan Dew. "There was never any doubt in Judy's mind that Dolly could do anything she wanted. If Dolly said, 'I want to be president of the United States,' Judy would say, 'Let's talk about what we'll do first.' "

Apparently many people in Nashville can't stand to think that Dolly Parton could be beautiful, famous, wealthy, talented, happy *and* well-adjusted, too. And Dolly is not oblivious to it. "Some of the hurtful things people say," observed Joan Dew, "concern her close relationship with Judy." When I ask Dolly about this, she gasps. "That's not the first time I've heard that," she says, looking shocked, hurt and angry, all at the same time. "The reason I gasped is that I didn't think about it bein' in print." She pauses a long while before she begins. "Mine and Judy's relationship is a relationship of its own kind," she finally says with a sigh. "It's hard to explain. I have many relationships of that nature. Because if I love you, I'm always there. If I've loved you once, I'll always love you. But with me'n Judy, it's a rare thing to see people care that much about each other. I can certainly see where that would be misunderstood. Judy and me have been together since we were little children. We saw more sorrow and more hard times and hard work in our growin' up days than you could ever put down on paper. She had a real hard life, things too personal to put down, but her folks were just real poor, there were so many in the family. And I had a hard time, too. We grew up in the country, and Judy and me worked the fields together and played in the creek together, talked about our dreams together. We were friends together because we were a lot alike. We helped each other escape a lot of hard times by the joyous times we had, and she was like a quieter side of me, and I was like a more outgoin' side of her. We went all through school together as best friends. We were just two very compatible people with a deep love for our family, for life in general. We had so much in common as friends—the way we are about people and our values in life, the things we hold sacred, that sort of thing. We always had freedom of speech with each other, freedom of thought, freedom of laughter, and because we were children together, we used to play games together. We used to laugh and joke and run and play together.

"You grow up like that, you never forget the fact that you *were* children together. So now, I'm sure it's real hard for most people to understand two grown women bein' playful and joyful, and to laugh and hug and be excited about things—jumpin' up and down when somethin' good is happenin', knowin' the thrill of excitement, or to hug each other when you've been gone on a long trip. But I hug my sisters, and I hug my mother and my daddy, and Judy is like a part of my family. She's like another part of me. And there is nothin' but beauty in my relationship with Judy. I'm sure that a lot of people who are less than they should be could make somethin' vulgar out of it. Livin' in this day and age, knowin' all the things that I know, I can certainly see [how they'd think that], as close as Judy and I are. A lot of people distort the fact that we're such good friends because it's such a unique thing in its way. They think you have to be sick. But it's like she's devoted to my music and to me. And I'm devoted to her because of it. And we have so much to relate to. We know all the same people. We know all the heartaches of the whole thing. We know all the ups and downs. She's seen me at my best and at my worst. She accepts me both ways. And I do her. She's almost like my shadow. I'm always there, and she's always there. It's like Mutt and Jeff. Or Laurel and Hardy. You don't think of me without thinkin' of Judy, if you know the both of us. There's nothin' sick about it. She lives here with us, along with my sisters, she has her own room here, and she works for me. She takes care of my clothes. That's how she makes her living. She works on my songs, keeps 'em in order. It makes little sense for her to live somewhere else, since she's so involved in my work, and we're good friends. We never have arguments. She is the only person in this world that I could be with twenty-four hours a day, seven days a week, three hundred sixty-five days a year, and never even be aware of the fact that there was any sort of clash. And we never get bored. Sometimes we go for hours in the same room when I'm thinkin' or she's thinkin'—she thinks very deep—without speakin' a word. And it's never taken personally. She knows what I'm thinkin'. She knows the way I look, the way I move. I know the way she looks and the way she moves, too, and I know if she's hurt over somethin'. Not nothin' I do, but I mean her family's so large and there's many personal problems and things like that. Friendship is a true gift from God, and that's the way I accept it. That's the way she accepts it.

"Really, I could talk all day, but that's another thing people are gonna believe what they want to about. But that's all right. Why shouldn't you love all people? I mean, it don't make no difference if you're a man or a woman. You're a human bein'. If you don't experience the love of life and the love of nature . . . well, like I say," she says, sighing heavily again, "it's too beautiful a friendship for me to be able to hear those kinds of things and it not make me wish that everybody could have a friend like Judy. It makes me feel sorry for them, really, and it makes me feel very fortunate. I just hope Judy feels the same about me, and I think she does. In fact, I'm sure she does. It's the greatest friendship of the world."

Left, a rare photo of Carl Dean, clad as usual in work clothes. (MICHAEL A. NORCIA) Below, one of Dolly's prized Herefords grazes on the grounds of Willow Lake Plantation. (MICHAEL BANE)

In the seven years Dolly was part of *The Porter Wagoner Show,* she and Porter became a veritable country music institution. Fiddler Mack Magaha, a member of Porter's band, The Wagonmasters, was important to the duo's sound. (LES LEVERETT, JERRY BAILEY, MICHAEL G. BORUM, BILL PRESTON, MARSHALL FALWELL, JR.)

WSM

Above, Dolly at home in her music room underneath some of her more than 100 citations and awards. (SLICK LAWSON/CAMERA 5)

Left, Dolly and her lifelong friend Judy Ogle. (HOPE POWELL)

6. "Hey, Porter!"

PORTER WAYNE WAGONER had been like any other twelve-year-old tourist visiting Nashville for the first time. Straight off the farm, he stared up at the big, tall buildings so long, the way he tells it, that the roof of his mouth got sunburned. No building had impressed him as much as the home of the Grand Ole Opry, however, and he carried the memory back to West Plains, Missouri, where he dropped out of school before the seventh grade to help his family after his father's illness. The first inkling of the stardom that lay ahead came in his late teens, when the owner of a grocery store where he clerked put him on a fifteen-minute early morning radio show, singing and picking and advertising the specials of the day. That soon led to a weekly series on KWTO in Springfield, where not long after Porter's arrival in 1951, Red Foley put together *The Ozark Jubilee* for television, making Porter a featured performer. Foley taught young Porter a lot. Not only about music and the development of style, but also about conveying honesty and sincerity. In time, Porter would tell Dolly that Foley—one of Dolly's favorite performers (along with Wagoner) when she was a child—had taught him almost everything he knew. He signed a recording contract with RCA in 1955. And in 1957, when the long, lanky farm boy went back to Nashville to join the Opry and stay for good, "I was as much a fan as artist," Porter told John Morthland of *Country Music* magazine. "It was exciting to me to get to know people like Roy Acuff, Ernest Tubb and Webb Pierce. There was a lot of excitement and glamour, and it was just sorta like a dream."

By the time Porter met Dolly, he was a certified star. He'd had numerous top five and top ten hits, and in 1966 and '67, along with the Blackwood Brothers, he won two Grammy awards, for Best Sacred Recording (*Grand Old Gospel*) and Best Gospel Performance (*More Grand Old Gospel*). His syndicated TV show, which started out in 1960 with eighteen stations, was on eighty-six stations in all parts of the U.S. and in Canada. On top of that, out on the road, the sequined wagon wheels rolling along his shoulders, the straw-yellow pompadour, and the friendly, down-home prattle drew crowds every night, 230 days a year. Stardom would pay off so handsomely for Porter Wagoner that in 1978 he would detail his business investments as "a couple publishing companies, a little stock in the Downtowner motel chain, a business and professional man's loan association, land, several duplex houses, and half a million dollars to start Jimmy Dean's Pure Pork Sausage."

The story goes that despite the clout Porter had in the industry, when it actually came down to signing Dolly to RCA, Chet Atkins, head of the Nashville operation, listened to Dolly's tape and told Porter he respected his business sense, and he knew Porter had always had good judgment in the past, but he was sorry. RCA would have to pass on his Dolly Parton, because, as Dolly loves to tell, " 'This girl just can't sing. I don't think she'd sell, because she just *cannot* sing!' " But Porter was sure he could prove Atkins wrong. "Well, I'll tell you what," he supposedly said. "You take out of my royalties what she loses this year, because I believe she *can* sing, and that she'll make it." Dolly's mouth breaks into a wide grin when she relates the story. "I kid Chet a lot," she told freelance writer Sally Duncan. "Every time I go in to sing something for him, I'll say, 'Now I know I can't sing, Chet, but I've got something I want you to hear.' Just joking with him. Of course, now Chet is the biggest fan I have in Nashville. I just didn't catch his ear" that first time. (RCA signed her in October of 1967. Scuttlebutt has it Dolly got her contract only on the strength of her duet potential with Porter.)

Porter's royalties were never in jeopardy. "Just Because I'm a Woman," Dolly's first RCA single, sold a healthy 150,000 copies, reaching number one on the charts. "Porter's a man I have great respect for," Dolly said in 1975. "He gave me a chance. He believed in me, when a lot of people didn't, because of my unique sound. He believed that I had a lot of potential, that it could be almost like a gimmick. That I could catch on."

But with some audiences, it took a little time. Don Howser, who announced Porter's television show for thirteen years, went out on the road some when Dolly first joined Porter's group. "I don't think people mean to be unkind or rude," Howser says, "but there's always some guy out there who'll say something. I remember hearing them yell, 'Hey, where's Norma Jean?' while Dolly was performing. I remember seeing her coming off stage crying, too." Or, as Don Warden, now Dolly's road manager, told Chris Chase of *The New York Times* about that time, "People was rough. I felt sorry for her. I mean, that was for six or eight months that went on. Dolly had a totally different sound. It took some gettin' used to."

One way of getting the audiences accustomed to Dolly's voice was through the duets she did with Porter. A former employee of theirs asserts that the idea for the duets was born out of the uneasiness Dolly felt on stage. Knowing how insecure Dolly must have been standing before thousands of people who wanted Norma Jean instead, Porter is said to have suggested they try a few songs together. They'd had ample time to work them up, since they spent the miles between dates singing and playing on the bus, learning the styles, similarities and limitations of each other's musicianship. While publicist Paul W. Soelberg claims in the liner notes for *The Best of Porter Wagoner and Dolly Parton* that Porter had never thought about doing duets with Dolly before, that's hard to imagine. "Maybe somewhere way back there it might have been done to get Dolly over some stage fright," says Don Howser, "but I think the duets were set up primarily for a commercial purpose. Because they certainly made another feature for the show, as well as another sales tool."

They also at times made some very lovely listening. Usually, Dolly would take the melody, or lead, and Porter would sing tenor harmony, although with Porter's voice being naturally lower, the effect often sounded the reverse. Sometimes they would merely alternate stanzas, harmonizing on the chorus, or Dolly would sing and Porter recite. Occasionally, too, when they traded off parts at the end of a phrase, they gave the impression that four parts were being sung. Whatever parts they sang, though, Dolly's Appalachian purity and Porter's Ozark simplicity blended perfectly. "Our harmony is so close it's almost like blood kin," Porter told Toby Thompson. "Brother and sister, you know, can harmonize better than a great tenor and a great lead singer gettin' together. Oh, that's so true. Dolly and her sisters, for instance [who had sung background on Dolly's records from as early as the Monument days], can sing closer harmony than any professional singers in Nashville. Something about the relationship makes it tighter and blend more natural. Dolly and I sound nearly like brother and sister." Still, it took some planning to get it all to sound as effortless as it did, particularly when it came to phrasing. "We can just glance at each other and know how we're going to say it," Dolly said at the time. "But Porter has different pronunciations on certain words, so we have to figure out whose way we'll use. And another thing—many people think we end together. Well, sometimes it's impossible to end at exactly the same moment, so then I let him put the last sound on the word, particularly with the 's' sound. That way the listener won't get two s's hissed at the same time. So it sounds like there's just one person instead of two. Besides, Porter has enough on his mind during these sessions, so anything I can do to help . . ." By their second duet record, Jerry Chesnut's "Holding On to Nothin'," which really established them as a duet team, Porter and Dolly had also made good use of another phrasing skill—the emphasis of key words, pulled up short and followed by a dramatic pause: "We're holding *on* (pause)/With nothin' *left* (pause)/To hold on to."

"Holding On to Nothin'," recorded January 31, 1968, did so well, in fact, that in May, two months after the duet's release, RCA put out Dolly's solo single, "Just Because I'm a Woman." Its tremendous success proved that Porter's strategy—let 'em warm up to Dolly with the duets, then hit 'em with her solo—worked right down to the letter. But the duets spawned something else, too. Porter and Dolly sounded so convincing in their songs of love's trials and tribulations that a large number of their fans thought they were married. Those in the industry who knew better wondered if they weren't lovers.

Most of their duets through the years concerned love, of course, the number one theme of all contemporary music, and Porter and Dolly did sound indeed as if they meant it, especially in the ad-lib endings of their "funny fight" songs, mandatory in almost every album following the success of "Run That by Me One More Time" in 1970. The duets inspired Porter so that he began writing again after an eighteen-year hiatus. The majority of his and Dolly's duets they wrote themselves. Hal Durham recalls that when other performers ran around backstage visiting before and after their spots on the Opry, Porter and Dolly used every spare moment to write and work on their songs. "When I write funny songs I include some possible ad-libs to use as a starting point," Dolly said in 1971. "But most of what we say on record are on-the-spot ad-libs at the session. I'll throw in something, and Porter will really get me back! We can always make a comeback no matter what gets said first. And it'll usually be funny, because it'll be natural, just like somebody really fighting!" It wasn't just the ad-libs that put the idea of real-life romance in their listeners' minds, though. It was the way they hugged each other (in matching costumes, yet!) and gazed into each other's eyes on the covers of their albums, records with such titles as *Together Always, We Found It, Love and Music, Just the Two of Us,* and *Say Forever You'll Be Mine.* And it was the way they sang so tenderly of the birth, growth and death of "their" children, in "Sweet Rachel Ann," "Christina," "Jeannie's Afraid of the Dark," "Mendy Never Sleeps," "Malena" and "Silver Sandals," to name a few. All these songs were written by Dolly and included formula-like in albums after "Jeannie's Afraid of the Dark" found its way off the B side of "We'll Get Ahead Someday" and became the duo's most requested song. (Archie Ray McMahan believes the song was inspired by an accident that occurred in front of Reverend Owens' House of Prayer, when the young daughter of one of Dolly's cousins was run over and killed. "The fella went on further up the road and had a wreck and killed himself, too," she says. "They were both in the same funeral home. You had a weird feeling being in there, seeing them like that.")

When they weren't "fighting" or "mourning" over their "children," Porter and Dolly worried in song that one loved the other more, or that they'd fallen out of love but couldn't bring themselves to talk about it, felt guilty about extramarital affairs or thoughts, and all-out celebrated and declared their love for each other, in and out of wedded bliss. For a change of pace, they slipped in a tearjerker or two about catastrophes and derelict fathers, a tribute to Reverend Owens and all the backwoods preachers like him—"Daddy Was an Old Time Preacher Man," written by Dolly and her minister aunt, Dorothy Jo Hope, and nominated for a Grammy in 1970—and a few novelty tunes apart from the "funny fight" songs, such as "Her and the Car and the Mobile Home." Much of the material contained some of the corniest and most cliché-ridden lyrics imaginable. They were awful—and wonderful. "We're hauling sixteen years of love in cardboard boxes," Porter and recording engineer Tom Pick wrote in one song, creating the mythical "Love City—Population Two" in another. Dolly added her own brand of hogwash humor by closing out a tune in which the husband and wife have a fight via citizen's band radio with, "I'll C.B.'in' ya." The Porter-Dolly duets were aimed for a very specific audience, an audience Porter knew like the lines in his well-worn, hangdog face.

Interestingly enough, though, the duets did not fit any one musical tradition. Roughly, they were a combination of traditional and contemporary country, the folk structures of some of Dolly's tunes resting comfortably next to one of her blues-tinged numbers, or even next to one of Porter's hokey story songs. What held the divergent styles together were the singers' personalities and the basic instrumentation, sometimes blatantly hillbilly, with the background filled with dancing fiddles and whiny steel guitars, later subtly experimental, while still retaining a country feel. Little by little, the instrumentation got more sophisticated but not so much that it would alienate the duo's mainstream following. In 1969, with the Jack Clement gem, "Just Someone I Used to Know," Porter and (probably nominal) producer Bob Ferguson began bringing up the bass line, allowing it to play a more important role in setting the rhythm and movement of the song, rather than just filling in the bottom. On the same song, they overdubbed a brass choir; the use of brass grew more prominent by Porter and Dolly's next single, Ray Griff's "Better Move It On Home."

By the time the two recorded their last released duet album, *Say Forever You'll Be Mine,* in 1975, seven years after their first, *Just Between You and Me,* their work had taken on a striking maturity. Some of the early duet albums, with their pandering to the blue-collar assembly line worker and trucker mentality, were downright insulting to those listeners with only a passing interest in country music or Porter and Dolly. Arguably, the records were not meant for them. But missing from *Say Forever You'll Be Mine,* fortunately, is the canned corn of the novelty and "funny fight" songs, and the predictability of the little-child-who's-gone-to-heaven stories. Missing too, is the silliness and the breaking of meter that lent an atmosphere of amateurishness to the other duet albums and the underriding light-heartedness that suggested that neither of them really took a lot of their songs seriously. Dolly had gotten a great deal of the childish quality out of her voice by this time, too. All in all, Porter and Dolly sound like level-headed adults here, no longer singing trite, bubble-headed songs about new love. Side one contains two of their loveliest and touching duets ever, both written by Dolly. On the first, the title song, they both give totally believable performances as a couple promising that while life together may not always be pleasant or easy, their love is strong enough that they will never part. Despite the fiddle intro, the subtle steel, the Floyd Cramer-style piano and the recitation bridge, "Say Forever You'll Be Mine" could pass for easy listening, the background singers, prominent and lush throughout the song, joining Porter and Dolly at the finish in what is almost a hallelujah chorus. "Say Forever You'll Be Mine" has all the makings of a standard.

Though not as far-reaching in its appeal nor as lavish in its production, "The Beginning," which finishes up the first side, is a sensitive portrayal of a couple who decide they no longer love each other and plan to divorce, only to find they are expecting a child, discovering on its arrival that they love each other far more than before. Profoundly moving, "The Beginning," performed with just enough restraint and sparse instrumentation to underscore the song's quiet intensity, is undoubtedly one of Dolly's best and most overlooked works. Not only does it point up how much Dolly's writing improved in the years she was with Porter, but it shows the direction in which they were headed in their last days of recording. More important than that, however, songs such as "The Beginning" and "Say Forever You'll Be Mine" showed just how much Dolly had outclassed and surpassed her mentor both as a writer and as a visionary. Now *she* was carrying *him* on the sessions and putting the "s" on the end of the words.

As exciting as the album was, the next one held promise of being even more so. But after Porter and Dolly finished the recording, Porter allegedly received word from Dolly's new management firm that the album was not to be released. Gossip has it that Katz-Gallin-Cleary told Porter that another duet album would be an embarrassment to Dolly, that her career was now headed in other directions. "Some of the best things they've ever done are sittin' down there in the can," says Porter's secretary, Joan McGriff.

Although Porter and Dolly won the Country Music Association's Vocal Group of the Year award in 1968, and its Vocal Duo of the Year award in both 1970 and 1971 (and received nominations the next two years, as well as a Grammy nomination for "If Teardrops Were Pennies"), their importance as a duet team is somewhat in dispute. In 1971 publicist Paul W. Soelberg wrote that their rendition of "The Last Thing on My Mind" ". . . marked the beginning of a new dimension to the industry's duet concept spawning an unprecedented number of other duet partnerships attempting to duplicate the success of Porter and Dolly." Hal Durham, manager of the Grand Ole Opry, says only that they were "darn good, fit each other's singing," and were all in all "a solid duet team." Vanderbilt University sociologist Richard A. Peterson, a country music aficionado, would probably agree with that assessment. "I don't think of them as turning the music or the notion of duets around," he says. "They were part of a time in which duets were very important and they were certainly central to that importance of the duet sound. But it seems to me that the couple that was most important in that era would be Conway Twitty and Loretta Lynn." (Twitty and Lynn have certainly been the most popular duet team of the '70s, beating Porter and Dolly out for the CMA award in 1972, '73, '74 and '75.) "Because," Peterson continues, "at the time, they were both independently strong people who came together and did songs where they often commented on each other. They were really different people talking to each other, as husband and wife or distant lovers."

But Minnie Pearl thinks Porter and Dolly deserve more credit than the others have given them. "I think they're the most successful man-woman singing duo that there has ever been," she says. "They had that combination of voices, that authenticity, and they were eye-catching. He wore the flashy wardrobe, and he's right handsome, with his blond hair, and being tall and lean, and she, of course, is beautiful and voluptuous. So they just had everything going for them. They were exciting because they were winners. The *team* was a winner. I don't know if they're winners separately or not. I'm not sure about him, but she definitely is. She's a star. A superstar. And she was ready to separate, to split and go out on her own. She would never have been satisfied to have been attached to anything or anybody in the business. It was time to move, and she did."

Fred Foster believes Dolly's association with Porter Wagoner and especially with his television show in some ways injured, or at least slowed, her career. "I didn't think she needed *The Porter Wagoner Show* to do what she wanted to do, and I still don't think she did," Foster says. "I'm not here to attack Porter Wagoner, either. While I'm sure his show did her good in many areas, I think it also confined her terribly. I think it did her some real damage. She could have made it to where she is right now much sooner without that TV show around. It was more like an anchor. If you want a universally appealing career and records that will sell to all sorts of folks in all walks of life, many of those people can't see you on the Porter Wagoner TV show. They never watch that. While by the same token, the Porter Wagoner fans and everybody, for that matter, would watch shows like Cher's special (on which Dolly appeared in April 1978) on full network in prime time."

On the other hand, as Don Howser points out, Porter was the one who gave Dolly her big break. "Had it not been for Porter, I don't think Dolly would have had that much of a career," Howser says. "Because he certainly pushed her ahead. In fact, he pushed her down everybody's throat in the beginning. She may have made it eventually, but it took the guiding and direction and exposure that Porter gave her to put her where she is."

At the show's peak, forty-five million viewers tuned in weekly as a close-up of a big, shiny, pointy-toed cowboy boot filled the screen. Then the camera would pan upward as Porter, the rhinestones on his Nudie suit sparkling in the klieg lights, strode onto the set in all his hillbilly glory, his best howdy-friends-and-neighbors grin locked into position. Porter lost no time getting into his undiluted hokum, just as they had years ago on the old country music radio programs.

Balancing Porter's hard-core, rough-edged country style was the essentially folk and traditional singing and songwriting of his girl singer. Just after acting out one of his particularly melodramatic story songs about a poor family and a calamity, or a weak-willed, but well-meaning father who just can't stay away from the bottle, Porter would hold his arms up, the wave of sequins would roll back, and "Miss Dolly," as Porter called her, would come into view. Often she would sit on a stool. Then in astonishing contrast to Porter's waxy slickness, Dolly's pure mountain soprano would pour realism into every word of her songs about life back in East Tennessee, the rich imagery of her lyrics and her understated delivery bringing a lump to the throat far sooner than any of Porter's contrivances. Even when the two paired together for a duet near the end of the show, Porter's con-man patina could not outshine Dolly's natural radiance, and anybody with 20/200 vision could see that Dolly Parton was not destined to be anybody's girl singer for long.

The show was videotaped, but for the performers, it was the same as live, since it was done in front of an audience and the director never stopped tape. If the performer made a mistake, he simply had to cover as best he could and go on. No retakes. That meant the stand-up commercials for Cardui and Black Draught cough syrup were done live, too. "Dolly was very scared on the first shows because she had to read the little line of commercial off the teleprompter," Jo Coulter, makeup artist on the show recalls. If the production technique of the show didn't allow for much emphasis of artistry, it did demand craftsmanship, with everyone knowing exactly what he would do once tape started rolling. "They could put together two half-hour shows in seventy minutes," recalls Richard Peterson, who went to the tapings of some of the early shows. "You know, they wasted ten minutes. It was an incredibly slick, professional operation." Still, the show managed to retain a relaxed country feel.

Despite the fact that Porter and Dolly supposedly never had a contract, it was understood that he was her manager, as well as her career adviser, in those early years. And while Bob Ferguson was credited as the producer of Dolly's early solo and duet albums (with Porter receiving credit for the last), Porter was the man who made the decisions. In fact, in the years they were together, Porter Wagoner ruled *everything* Dolly Parton did. His reputation is that of a tough taskmaster, and he is said to be the sort of man who has to be in control, who has to have his way. Not long ago, while filling in a reporter on her early career, Dolly said that her uncle had acted as her manager at first, "and it was a kind of bossy thing. Then I worked with Porter Wagoner, which was kind of still under an iron fist of a sort."

Porter may have been tyrannical, and he may have stifled Dolly's creativity in the studio, but he understood Dolly's voice, if not her musical vision. He realized he was dealing with a unique instrument, one that sounded like nobody else's. "My voice is not necessarily good, but it's different," Dolly told Chet Flippo. "You always know who it is. The only way I would know how to describe it is a childlike sound with a grown-up emotion, with a grown-up feeling. People think I'm singing higher than I should, but I talk high. It's the sound of my voice." Girlish, giggly, thin and soft one moment, raucous and earthy the next, Dolly's soprano could turn to a quick, high-strung vibrato and then easily glissando with extraordinary power, range and control into a hard and high nasality. Recognizing that, Porter had her record a song Bill Monroe made famous, "Mule Skinner Blues." Dolly's updated version (recorded in 1970) stirred excitement in both country *and* pop. In fact, about that time, it seemed like everything was coming together. One week, "Mule Skinner Blues" was number three in *Billboard* (number one in *Record World*), while Porter and Dolly's duet, "Daddy Was An Old Time Preacher Man," occupied *Billboard's* number eight slot. But more exciting was the fact that "Mule Skinner Blues" got air play on the FM progressive rock stations, RCA jumping up and down in its news releases that Dolly had conquered the youth market and gained an underground following. When the record received a Grammy nomination, it was icing on the cake.

Dolly's mentor knew how to resurrect a tired old workhorse like "Mule Skinner Blues" and make it sound vibrant and exciting. He knew just as well how to get the best from Dolly on a session, and he was a meticulous craftsman. When Tom Casassa and Mack Evans engineered the Grand Ole Opry broadcasts from the Ryman Auditorium, Casassa "always had to be careful in controlling the volume of Dolly's voice," he remembers. "This was the mid-sixties, and electronics weren't as sophisticated then as they are now. The Ryman was susceptible to feedback, and when we got a loud, powerful singer like Dolly, the whole thing would go. It wasn't her fault, though. She was very definitely a pro all the way." Porter had no trouble with feedback in the studio, but recording Dolly was no easy job, no matter where it was done. Toby Thompson of the *Village Voice* was there when Porter produced what would turn out to be his last Dolly Parton album, *All I Can Do,* in 1976. Here is Thompson's account of Porter as producer:

"Porter Wagoner, now a gaunt form hunched over the mixing board at RCA-Nashville's Studio A, flared at the sight of intruders, but discerning PR men and the inevitability of press shifted quickly into a semblance of his clownish TV self. Though merely a semblance. Twenty-one days of production, mixing, and nonspecific dabble with Dolly Parton's nascent LP—the big one it was hinted, the chart-buster which would cap Dolly's fall TV venture and nudge her into the arms of pop—had left him visibly exhausted. Oyster-size bags drooped below the infamous pompadour and Wagoner's spine stood bowed at the belt buckle; silver to be sure, cinching tailored denims over custom boots and a suede-piped Nudie blouse. Porter Wagoner could work sixteen hours a day any day unencumbered by the $300 or $400 worth of bespoke duds he carried on his back. That was taken for granted as Nashville aplomb. What wasn't was the special brand of pickiness an artist like Wagoner brought to the production of a fellow star.

" 'I sometimes think I'm too particular,' Wagoner conceded, 'but to me a record's like a monument. Important that it's done right. Dolly's is a hard voice to capture on record—very piercing, gives the equipment a fit. Not that our equipment's so displeased to have something that nice a-goin' through it,' Wagoner chortled, 'but it's Dolly's register. I've tried about twenty microphones in pickin' the proper one. We use an RE-15. RCA's got twenty-five RE-15s, but there's only one records Dolly good . . . I keep it in a vault, nobody else uses it.'

". . . Dolly proved not in perfect voice tonight, her throat raw from twenty-one days of touring; nonetheless, Porter waxed insistent, ever the coach, medicine man, psychologist; masking his perfectionist's distaste with affectionate concern for the artist—'That's nice Dolly, that's nearly it . . . but I do believe we can get a bit closer. . . . Her voice is *so* doggone critical,' he reiterated, indicating a solitary figure sequestered behind plate glass—a figure bobbing to taped rhythms, juggling harmonies, rehearsing for the overdub. Lost in the fishbowl shadows, a figure exquisitely alone. 'You take Dolly and a hundred other people, put 'em in this studio, get everyone to laugh the same loudness and Dolly's laugh will stand out. I'm sure you noticed that when you met her. There's not anyone in this world like Dolly Parton.' "

When Porter and Dolly got it right, the sound was something close to magic. The public had always thought so: at the time of Thompson's interview, Dolly had racked up eleven number one singles since the day Porter contacted her about joining his show. But no matter how good Porter and Dolly sounded on record, no recording could capture the excitement of their live performances.

"There was a charisma between Porter and Dolly that has never been matched," says journalist LaWayne Satterfield. "I don't think there have been any two people in country music who had the charisma they had. When he came on stage, he played to Dolly. He turned her on, and she turned him on. Then together they turned the audience on. It was a three-way feed. The audience was totally captivated and caught up in it. There was a magnetism you could feel. There'll never be another show that had the ecstatic effect that Porter and Dolly's had. There was always an excitement about them. Even backstage at the Opry, when they came in, it was like sparks jumping from a hot wire."

Though the magnetism remained all the years Porter and Dolly played the Grand Ole Opry, other things changed. Minnie Pearl remembers: "When Dolly first came to the Opry with Porter, people were impressed with the fact that she could sing. I don't think the sex image was played up so much then, or the voluptuous figure. I think people were more impressed then that she sang so well, and that she and Porter had such a great combination in the blend of their voices. She was so country. She was so *authentically* country, and she didn't dress then to call attention to her figure. I don't remember much said about her and the image she is now.

The emphasis was definitely put on her singing then. They don't talk much about authenticity now, because there's been so much crossover. But then it mattered a great deal. And she was authentic. She was also terribly sweet. We all liked her. All the women liked her. There were some sayings that began to come around after she became a sex symbol, which became so blatantly representative of her only in the last five or six years. But the Grand Ole Opry group used to say that she was such a nice girl, and she was so popular both with the women and the men, that nobody made cracks about her figure if they knew her. It was only the people who didn't know Dolly who made remarks."

Dolly, who first appeared on the Opry in 1967 by "sliding in with Porter," as then manager Ott Devine remembers, became a member January 4, 1969. Hal Durham believes Dolly made at least one Opry appearance when she was on Monument Records. She is said to have looked quite innocent and country-girlish in her early Opry days. "Yes, I thought she did," Minnie Pearl continues with a bit of wistfulness in her voice. "Of course, it's impossible for somebody to stay in show business that long and not become knowing. There's a knowing look that comes after awhile, a polish and know-how and a certain poise and change that takes place. If it doesn't, they're in bad shape. I don't know any of our people who have been a success that haven't changed considerably. With Dolly, as long as she was tied to Porter, or if you stay with any duet partner, you can never become a real star. And that's what she wanted. She left Porter not because she wanted to leave *Porter*, but because she wanted to do her own act. And then after she left, the rest of her dream was not confined to being just a Nashville star. She wants to be an international star. And that's what she's on the way to being. So I admire her. I think she's great."

Dolly's wanting to become a worldwide star in her own right—and by singing something other than straight country music—was surely her primary motive for striking out on her own, but even had Dolly's dreams not been so far-reaching, the Porter-Dolly team could not have lasted much longer the way it was. Yes, they were a top draw on the country circuit. Yes, all their records went to number one. Yes, they won numerous awards from their peers. But when Dolly joined Porter in the summer of '67, it was to be his girl singer. Porter was the star of the show, with Dolly his subordinate. He was also her boss and her manager. And he was her mentor, helping her with her songwriting and her voice, teaching her the ins and outs of recording, encouraging her, in the beginning, to develop all her areas of creativity, to use all of her talents. But as so often happens in the arts, Porter was a great teacher but a teacher with an extraordinarily talented pupil, a pupil who came, in many ways, to surpass the master. Jimmy C. Newman remembers that when Porter and Dolly played the Opry, "Porter would open with his band, and as popular as he was with the television show and his loud costumes, he'd just destroy the audience. But then when he'd introduce

Dolly, she'd tear the audience up again." There are some in Nashville who believe Porter carried Dolly the first three-and-a-half years, but that Dolly carried him the last. Their last live show together, according to Lola Scobey, was April 21, 1974, in Salinas, Kansas.

"Years and years ago, when I handled *The Porter Wagoner Show,* I booked on some fair dates," remembers Dolores Smiley, formerly of Top Billing. "And I had them booked at the Minnesota State Fair. I hadn't seen the show or been on the road in awhile, so I decided to go with them on the bus from St. Paul over to the next date. The day after the show I had to finish checking out and return the rent-a-car. Porter and the boys had gone out to play golf, and I walked into the hotel where they were. Dolly was sitting in the lobby. She seemed very happy to see somebody she knew, because everybody had checked out of their rooms and was waiting to leave. So I told her, 'I have to take this rent-a-car back, and I don't know where to go. Would you like to go with me and help me find it?' And she said, 'Sure.' So we got in the car and between the two of us, got lost several times. We finally found the place and had to get a cab back. We called it and decided to have lunch. I remember we were talking about the show the night before, and she told me she didn't want to spend her life being the girl singer on *The Porter Wagoner Show.* While we were sitting there, she told me a lot of her plans and things that she hoped would happen, and she sang me a lot of the songs she had written. One was 'Coat of Many Colors,' which came out several years later. She'd done a lot of writing then that wasn't even scheduled to be recorded. When we got through with our lunch, we went out to get our taxi, and while we were standing there waiting, some gentlemen who'd been to the show the night before walked up, and sure enough, the first thing they said was, 'Oh, you're the girl on *The Porter Wagoner Show.* Dolly just died laughing. She said, 'See what I mean?' And she told me that she had dreamed forever of becoming a big star, and we talked about her clothes and her hair and her makeup and how this meant glamour to her. It was her dream as a little girl to be able to afford all these things. And she said, 'I want everybody to like me.' She was very sincere, very, *very* sincere about the whole thing. I also remember she said, 'If I can't make it as a big star, I can always stay home and write and record.' But from that day forward, you could just pencil it down that Dolly was projected in that direction, and every bit has come about piece by piece."

Neither Porter nor Dolly will talk much about exactly why they broke up, but in many ways Dolly felt she had outgrown Porter—that she had learned as much from him as she could. With her uncanny knack of knowing exactly when to move on, Dolly knew she was ready to become the big star she told Dolores Smiley she always wanted to be.

"I don't know what information you have on this," Dolly says, shifting positions on her oriental rug and letting out a big sigh. "I'm sure it wasn't much information that came from me. But I'm sure there are stories all around. We just reached a point where it was necessary for us. It was only smart business for me to try to go ahead, because I felt I had gone as far as I could with any group. I just wanted, while I was still young, to try some of my ideas and plans that I came from the mountains to try and never had a chance to do. I was fortunate to get the chance to work with Porter. It taught me many, many things. Some lessons I learned the hard way, but even still, I learned, and I learned a lot from Porter. I did. I learned what to do and what not to do. I learned how to be, and how not to be, where you deal with the public and your career and with business affairs. I learned from Porter pretty much how to work an audience—I mean the things that please an audience." She sighs again, heavier this time. "I don't really know what I learned from Porter," she says, sounding frustrated and pent-up. "Like I said, I learned, if nothing else, the things I didn't want to do by seein' it first-hand." She pauses. "You'll kill me with this tape." She pauses again. Then she laughs a sad, short laugh. "Oh, I guess not," she continues. "Honesty never hurt. What I started to say was, if nothing else, I learned what I didn't want to be like. Half of this is for you, and the rest you know what to put in the book. I don't think the public should know all the personal things about you. I wouldn't ever tell, anyway. I'll tell some, though."

What she and Porter will both talk most about concerning their split is their conflict in the recording studio. "This day and time," Dolly says, "you can be what you want to be, especially musically, and if you don't venture out to try to be what it is you want to be, then you are a fool. You've served no purpose in life; you have failed as a person if you don't try what your heart says to do. That is, unless there are things bigger that hold you back, like wives and children and husbands and all. But if you do have a chance to do everything you can do and you don't do it, like I said, you're a fool." I ask who held her back. "It wasn't a matter of holding me back, necessarily, but working in an organization with other people, it's unfair to try to put your own ideas on somebody who is head of an organization, say like with me and Porter. When he was producing me, I got some of my ideas across and the big part of my ideas were written in the songs, you know, the arrangement ideas and all. But there was so much I wanted to do, and he heard it so differently that we just couldn't agree on so many things. It just took away the joy of me recordin' the song at all. Because then it wasn't what I created it to be. It took somebody else's personality. That's hard to explain to people who aren't writers. But I'm just sayin' that without Porter, at least I can write the songs and get them down the way I hear them."

Porter confirmed most of that in an interview with John Morthland. "We were gonna do things my way," he said. "Because that's the kind of person I am. Dolly Parton's career up until she left me was done my way. That's the only way it could be successful operating with me, because if we had done it her way it would not have worked. Had we done the songs she would like to have done, the way she would like to have done them, it would not have worked. Because I could not produce 'em that way, first of all. I would not allow 'em to be done that way on my show. I signed the checks at that time, so we did things my way, and that was the way I was born and reared to do—that if you paid a man to work for you, he worked for you; he didn't tell you what to do. If he did, that would be called an adviser. So I wasn't looking for an adviser when I hired Dolly. Whenever she talked about her career and the directions we were going, she didn't have all these ideas at that time. We were using my ideas, my guidance and my direction. That's the way it was. That's the way it would be if you were to start recording for me tomorrow and hire me as a producer. We would do it my way, because that would be what you hired me for. If you had the ideas and could do it yourself, you wouldn't need me. You would just need a place to do it. That's just the way it is.

"Back at that time, she was wanting to be more like Aretha Franklin—sing more soul stuff. She would scream and holler—'Whaaaaa'—that type of thing. [Dolly had managed to work some of that black gospel feel into her sacred album, *The Golden Streets of Glory*, particularly on "Heaven's Just a Prayer Away."] And I wouldn't allow that on my show because I knew the people wouldn't buy that, with my audience. Because had that been the case, had they been wanting to hear Aretha Franklin on my TV show, I would have tried to hire her. Because I want the best, to help my show get bigger, and to help the artist who was working to do the same. And all of these other things came after Dolly had had some success and had recorded some things that she didn't like at all. 'Mule Skinner Blues' she didn't want to record at all. It was a number one record. It did a lot of things for her career. She had written songs, [but] she would have done them in a much different manner, I'm sure. Whether it would have been better or worse, who knows? But I know that what I did was successful, so I sorta liked that part of it. When something is successful, it's gotta be a pretty workable combination. And I feel that whenever Dolly hired these other people to produce her records, it was because maybe she felt she could use more of her ideas with them. [Dolly and Gregg Perry co-produced *New Harvest . . . First Gathering*, and Gary Klein produced *Here You Come Again*, and Dolly and Klein shared producer's credit on *Heartbreaker*.] I think that was the freedom she's talking about. Because I'm the kind of person who will listen to ideas of Dolly's [if] she's working with me. If I feel that they're good, I'll use them. But there has to be someone who says yes and no. I was that person, and I would be today if you and I were making records. Because I'd always give you the opportunity to be very open with your ideas and not be embarrassed if I didn't use 'em. But there has to be one of us has a refusal to say, 'It's great, but it isn't what we need.' You cannot have two or three people giving answers, because you never really reach an end. And I felt that I did the best thing I could for her."

If Dolly felt she was "trapped" in her relationship with Porter, "I think that was the part she was talking about," Porter says. "But I feel like that trap was pretty nice to her. There were no complaints during the beginning of the show. I didn't set the trap to catch her, y'know. It was set in a very humble manner of 'Would you help me get my career started, because I'm a country girl from East Tennessee who's trying to get a career started in the country music business as a writer and a singer.' So if anyone was trapped, it might have been me. Because to me that's pretty good bait there. That'll catch a purdy big pigeon in your trap.

"Maybe later on," Porter continued, "when she saw things really begin to happen with her . . . It's awful easy, believe me, and I say this with no resentment from Dolly's career, but it is awful easy when you have something that's successful for you to convince yourself, 'I'm doing this, I'm the only one can do it, there ain't nobody involved in this but me.' It's easy to convince yourself of that. But ideas are only ideas unless they are developed, and Dolly had a lot of ideas and still does, I'm sure—a mind full of 'em—but they are only ideas unless you're able to develop 'em. What I did in her career, the production of her records, was develop ideas that came out of my own mind, with extra insertions from her mind, of different things and different other people. To me that's what it's about; that's the only way you can make it. Because you can be the greatest writer in all the world, and unless someone will be interested in what you have and work with you on it to help get it exposed to the public, all you can do is run around saying, 'I'm the greatest writer in the world.' So it takes more than ideas. I'm sure Dolly had ideas of being a big star when she was just a little girl. But I've had a lot of people tell me, 'Boy, you made Dolly what she is.' Well, that's not true. She was what she was. I helped develop her into an entertaining star. And I'm very proud of the part in her career that I played. . . . I'm involved in a lot of businesses that I'm not in control of, but as far as the music business, I don't want to be involved in production of someone unless I have a hold of the reins, so to speak. Because first of all I can't do my best at something unless I can contribute my own ideas. I feel if a person knows what they want in the music business, they don't need a producer, they need a good worker. I couldn't do a good job for someone if I had to go to them and say, 'What do you think? Yes or no?' Because I know what I'm doing in the music business. I know my limitations and I know where I excel the best."

Tom Rutledge was guitarist for both Dolly's Traveling Family Band and Gypsy Fever, and was in the studio when Porter produced his last Dolly album, *All I Can Do*. "Dolly's music is a very, very personal thing to her," Rutledge says. "It almost kills her to have to record something not the way she wants to record it. And I know that was a big part of her leaving—not to be able to express her music the way she wanted to express it. And I'm sure on stage, too, it was the same way. The way the show was presented was the way Porter said it would be presented. So her whole career was influenced by Porter, and if it wasn't the way she wanted to do it, she was miserable. She had more freedom on 'All I Can Do' than she'd ever had, or at least that's what she told me. But she had ideas of how she wanted the material recorded, 'cause she'd written it. And Porter had his ideas, because he was the producer. And I guess most of the time he would win out, mostly through intimidation, because of the type personality he is. It was very hard to work for Porter in the studio because he wasn't together as much as he should have been. At his studio, Fireside [which he and Dolly own jointly], they had a lot of trouble with the [mixing] board, with breakdowns, and he wanted everything to be just right. There would be a lot of delays, and he had a big schedule, and it had to be one way—Porter's way. At RCA, Studio A, you just never knew. We were working on 'All I Can Do,' and something wasn't coming off right. The Traveling Family Band had cut the demos. He had the demos there, and he was playing them for the studio musicians, and I was there as one of them. When it didn't come together the way Porter thought it should, he came out there and chewed some butt. But that was real lightweight, from what I understand. Really, a lot of all this is hard to believe. Because this is a business, you know. Billions of dollars flowing in and out, and you've got something like that, controlling. Four years ago, Porter was controlling Dolly's whole career, determining what was recorded and what wasn't, how it was recorded. It's incredible. That whole thing with Porter is a can of worms. The whole last three or four years were bad for Dolly. It was just a high-pressured gig for the people who worked for him, and a real depressing situation for Dolly."

Many people believe one of the reasons Dolly was depressed (aside from the fact that her records weren't turning out as she heard her songs) was that Porter had thrown her timetable for The Great Lifetime Plan off schedule. "Dolly planned the thing with Porter from the very beginning," says journalist Joan Dew. "When she left Fred Foster to go with Porter, she told Fred she had to do it for her career, because Porter could give her something that Fred couldn't, which was television exposure and the road. Fred told me he thought the only thing that didn't work out the way Dolly planned it was that Porter held her up a couple of years because he was so hard to get away from. He was . . . the one who made her into a star . . . getting her name before the public. And he did not hesitate to remind her of that. But Dolly never intended to stay with Porter. That was a stepping stone, a step on the way up. . . . there isn't anybody who could stand in her way. Not one soul. I don't think Dolly is a malicious, vindictive person by any means. I don't think she'd step one half-step out of her way to hurt somebody; she'd just step over them, instead of on them."

Porter Wagoner made that step as difficult as he could. Just why is a bit of a mystery. He surely realized Dolly was unhappy in the situation, just as he was bound to have recognized that as long as they were together people would come mostly to see Dolly instead of him. Several of Porter's former associates say he was tired of the road, and just wanted to sit at the mixing board in his studio and do his TV show for the rest of his career; others say Porter only invented that alibi after Dolly left him because he knew that without Dolly he'd no longer pack houses. But if he indeed wanted to come off the road, it's hard to believe he'd think Dolly would want to do the same, now that her star was rising higher by the day. Her underground following was growing to the extent that the duo was in demand for college tours, in which Porter is said to have had no interest. One school of thought is that Porter deliberately tried to keep Dolly from breaking into pop circles because he was sure she'd fail, sure the pop and rock audiences would reject her for not fitting in culturally or for her contrived appearance (it's all right for Alice Cooper to do that for two reasons: first, everybody knows he's just kidding, and second, he's a man). Then, too, Porter may have felt that Dolly's would never be anything but a mountain voice, and he may have worried that the pop fans would find her trills and tones too foreign. It is unlikely that Porter thought Dolly lacked the talent to excel in another field of music, although Fred Foster believes that while Porter recognized Dolly's potential in country music, he may not have recognized her potential for universal stardom. Before Porter realized Dolly meant to make a clean break, he could have thought, "Why ruin a good thing?" Their duets had made them near legendary in the South. By tampering with success (i.e. singing pop), Dolly ran the risk of alienating her hard-core country following, which could mean fewer people would attend their shows, and fewer people would buy their duet records—which would certainly mean Porter would make less money, although he hardly needed it. For print, at least, Porter is saying, "If Dolly wants to be pop, that's exactly what she should be. I certainly wouldn't want to deprive anyone of doing what they wanted." But at the same time, Porter knew he couldn't go there with Dolly—and he knew she didn't want him anyway. The whole idea was that she no longer wanted to be part of any team and sought stardom on her own. She wanted her own identity. And that was probably what hurt most of all: Porter was losing her. Not only professionally, but also personally.

Dolores Smiley says Porter's attitude toward Dolly in the years they were together was "totally protective—both of her and of her image." She tells a story about *Nashville!* magazine wanting to pose Dolly in a Santa Claus suit for the cover of their December issue, and Porter vetoing it against Dolly's wishes. The duo may have sung about alcoholism, adultery and everything else you can think of, but in real life, Porter did not want Miss Dolly on the cover of a magazine that carried listings and advertisements for clubs that served liquor, fearing it would tarnish Dolly's nonsmoking, nondrinking reputation. Porter was so protective of her, in fact, that when the two of them appeared on the *Tonight Show* (with guest host Joe Garagiola), he didn't allow anyone to ask Dolly a thing. "I just sat on the panel and slung my foot, as usual," Dolly remembers. But that very well could have been ego, despite Porter's assertion that "I'm not an ego-type person." A reporter once tried to interview Dolly as she waited in the wings to go on. Dolly answered each question as quickly and succinctly as possible, explaining Porter wouldn't like it if he saw her talking while he was performing. Two other reporters recall that in the course of their interviews, Porter came in twice in a period of an hour, checking to see what Dolly was up to, leading them to believe that Porter's protectiveness was actually in good part possessiveness. Whether Dolly thought in just those terms or not, a personal friend recalls Dolly spoke of her impending break with Porter as "getting free."

"The main reason Dolly had such a hard time disentangling herself from Porter is because he was in love with her," says one journalist. "Porter was really torn up over losing Dolly. *Really* torn up. Because he really did love her, and I don't think he'd ever been in love with anyone but himself. And about Carl Dean, well, you *know* Porter was the main man in Dolly's life all the years she was with him."

Since Dolly has told me there's no question I can ask her that she hasn't been asked before, I ask The Big One: "People say you and Porter were lovers." A mild cardiac seizure registers on Dolly's face. "We were lovers," she says, repeating my words, not certain she has heard right. "Uh, we were lovers of music, and I suppose we had one of the world's most unique relationships," she begins. "We were not lovers as you know lovers. But it really wouldn't have mattered whether we were or whether we weren't. Like I say, it was a strange kind of relationship, hard to explain to the public. It was a love of its kind. I think it was more of a . . . *ummm,* I never had that one before. Oh, I've heard people thought we were married and all that. In fact, when we split our business, I mean, when I left the show, people would come up and say, 'I really hated to hear about you and Porter gettin' a divorce.' " She laughs a taut laugh. "But anyway, I don't know how I could put our relationship into words. We got very angry at each other over workin' things. There was a . . . well, really, all I want you to write is that we were not lovers, but we loved each other. We were lovers of our music and of our work.

"But in all truth, I tell you what—I can understand how people could have made anything out of our relationship, because I think we were so involved in business, so involved with each other personally. Porter had no family,* and when we were workin'—you live together on the road. All the boys in the group are like your family. You're closer than you know. So close that you know each other's moods, you know certain things that bug you. But it was almost like we depended on each other too much. We were so involved in so many things that we had no separation from each other. To the point where we would even resent each other bein' involved in other things, mainly because we had ourselves tied so much into that. This probably sounds crazy, and I've never tried to explain this before, but it was almost like if somebody else . . . well, he was so involved with my songs that if he criticized my songs and also praised 'em, I'd get angry and hurt, knowin' both sides. But like, if say, he really was knocked out over somebody else's writin', or really almost like he was ignorin' mine, and it

* He is separated from his wife and has two girls and a boy.

wasn't jealousy like lovers, but I don't know. Kinda like a jealousy. It was like, well, how can he criticize my songs so, and then make such a big deal out of somebody else's? And then if I liked to hear somebody else sing, or if I was really close to somebody else, it was almost like jealousy. But anytime that you give that much of yourself to somebody and you're as involved as we were—we experienced the joy and sorrow of all the things. We fought in the studio, or at least there was bad times, but we also knew the joy of the same song that we might have fought over when it became a hit. But we didn't have enough separation, which is why it got to be too much for both of us. Got to be *extreme* pressure. And like I say, it was a relationship that would be very hard to explain." Most people believe Porter was in love with Dolly. "Maybe he *was* in love with me," she says. "But it was a love of its kind. It was not a love that could ever be shared, if he was."

"I have been married for a long time," Dolly told another reporter, "and I figure that if there had been anything between me and Porter my husband would have been the first to know it, because you cannot deceive people. Like I say, there was a love of a kind. We never tried to disguise that, because it was as much a respect. We got to know each other and knew our bad side and our good side, we knew our weak points, our strong ones, we knew hang-ups. Coming to know each other that much means that you—if you like that person—that you have a great respect for 'em. But I'm not ashamed to say that I cared for Porter, but it is definitely not the kind of carin' that I went to bed with him. He's the kind of person—he's so real—that I could have laid across the bed with him and slept forever and not ever touched him in the kind of way . . . People always think that male and female—that you have to be able to share sex in order to share a relationship. That's not true.

"I used to worry a great deal about that. I worried mostly because I thought so many of my friends here in town, people I worked with, never knew the difference. I'm not the kind to just go up and say, 'Well, now, you're wrong about that!' I just thought, 'Well, the time will come, if you ever knew me, if you ever loved me the way you say, or if you ever cared about me, and are as good a friend of mine as you always said you were, that you'll blame yourself for doubtin' me in certain ways.' Now, I'm not above anything under the right kind of conditions. I'm like every livin' human bein'. I am capable of a lot of things, but I will just honestly have to say that I don't worry anymore about what people think. If they want to think I was livin' with Porter, I've just come to the conclusion that they can think that. Those stories never bothered Carl. We love each other. We always have; we always did. You know yourself you couldn't live with a person and love 'em and not know if there was somethin' else, somebody else that was takin' away from that. You can't fake a feelin'. You can for awhile, but you couldn't for seven years, you know. Like I say, it was straight between my husband and me. We always knew. Porter always knew. Everybody else had it fixed the way they wanted, but I had it fixed the way it was. It never affected our marriage. There were times I wanted to lash out at people. That was in the early part of it. In fact, when I'd get all upset, my husband used to say, 'Now it don't make no difference. You're liable to hear anything. People are cruel.' "

Yes, they are, but one thing that started tongues a-waggin' in Nashville was Porter and Dolly's exchange of extravagant gifts each Christmas. The gifts got so much press, in fact, that, as one journalist put it, "People couldn't wait for the season to roll around just to see what Porter would give Dolly." Jerry Bailey was interviewing Dolly in the dressing room of a Nashville TV station in 1972 when Porter walked in to check his rhinestone finery in the mirror. "What are you gonna give me for Christmas?" Dolly asked him. "Another chance," Porter told her. "Another chance! That's what you gave me last year." "Last year I gave you a Cadillac, a diamond necklace and another chance," Porter said. Bailey wrote that Porter "had earlier estimated that he had given Dolly five rings, two Cadillacs and two necklaces during the years she had been with his show." In return, Dolly gave him 49 percent of Owepar Publishing, which she had started with her Uncle Bill in 1967. Owepar is a lucrative company with 935 songs in its catalogue, 500 of which are Dolly's; a lot of the others are Porter's. Since Broadcast Music Incorporated has awarded Dolly fourteen certificates for most air play of a song during the year, 49 percent of Owepar would be no small gift. Some thought Dolly gave it to Porter to soothe her conscience over their eventual break. That's unlikely since she gave it to him at least three years before she left. Others thought she gave it to him because he devoted a lot of time to it and had built it into the company it was. But there were others who surmised that Dolly gave Porter such a hefty chunk of the company in repayment for other favors.

"Naturally people thought Porter was my sugar daddy," Dolly says. "But why wouldn't they? I mean, if there's no mystery about an artist . . . In fact, it's real rare for me to even tell this much. 'Cause usually I'll just say, 'Well, you know, could be. Just one of them things.' But people often thought that. Even people in the business. Even people I'd known for years. Because I just wasn't the kind to go up and preach a sermon. People only believe what they want to anyway. No matter what I would say, they'd still have their own opinion. But he was not my sugar daddy, even though he was always buyin' me gifts. He just happened to get his gifts to me publicized. He often got gifts from me, but it was a personal thing with me, not a publicity thing. Like I say, it was a relationship of a kind." I point out that one reason people might have thought the worst was because it was rumored Porter explained to each of his girl singers she would have to reward him for giving her a break. "I do think that some of the girls that he had, I think he *was* involved, but that's why—they were involved before they became part of the show, and that's how they became part of it. But I don't know what he expected out of them. I don't know exactly what he expected out of *me*. I only know what he got." Was Porter as possessive as people have said? "It doesn't matter," she replies. "It was a long time ago."

One reason the gossip got so thick is because as Dolly says, she didn't feel like making a speech about it, and because Porter did everything but encourage it. "Actually, I think that love affair was more on his thinking and desire than hers," says a studio musician who worked on several of Porter and Dolly's sessions. "Naturally, she's gonna let the gossip go to the effect that it will help her, but when it comes to hurting her, or her stepping out of line, she backs up. A lot of that was his talk, his wants and wishes. He wouldn't indicate there was something going on, and as matter of fact, he always said there wasn't. But he always kinda left the door open by laughin'. He just thought, 'When you're hot, you're hot.' That was his idea. But the musicians always knew she'd break with him eventually. Because we knew she was above that. He's not in her class by any means. In every aspect—as a person and as a talent. She's a jewel. I can't say that for him. And I'll say she's an intelligent person, too." He laughs. "No remarks."

"Oh, I don't think anybody ever really believed that gossip," says Bobby Denton. "You know people start wild, vicious rumors, and the people who knew Dolly didn't believe it. Any time two people travel together on the road, you're gonna get talk. That's the way it has always been." Charlene Bray agrees. "I'm sure there'll always be rumors about that. I don't think they ever were [lovers]. I really don't think there's any truth to it. There may have been some want-to on Porter's part, because she *is* gorgeous and desirable. That could have been the problem, too. Dolly, I think, wanted it to be strictly a professional relationship. I know some tours, too, with some big male stars in country music, that Dolly would not work. They made it clear they wanted to have more of a relationship than just a business relationship, and Dolly would not work shows with them." ("If I was gonna run with anybody," Dolly told Jerry Bailey, "I wouldn't dare run with anybody in the music business because it's like a family. I mean, that would be like running with your kinfolks or something. People have had me married to Porter and Charley Pride and everybody in the business. It's not true, and I'm a better person than that.") "So as far as I know on those lines," Bray continues, "she's as straight as she can be. She feels as though there's a very strict line of demarcation that separates her professional life from her personal life. And you've got to be a strong person to maintain those barriers." Clarence Selman recalls that when Dolly spoke to a songwriting seminar at the University of Tennessee in Nashville, a student asked if she cared to comment on working the road with Porter. "I care not to," Dolly replied.

Certainly there was strong emotion between Dolly and Porter. One source says the their fighting grew to such intensity that when Dolly told Porter she was leaving his show to strike out on her own, he got a gun and threatened to kill her. A variation has it that Porter had threatened Dolly with death so often, that she got the gun herself and gave it to him, saying, according to Tom Rutledge, "If you want to shoot me, shoot me!" Several people say Porter was once apprehended with a gun near Dolly's house in Brentwood.

When confronted with the gun stories in general, Dolly gasps loudly. "Where did you hear that?" she demands. "That's not somethin' written down, is it? Well, even if that *was* the truth, it's not a thing the public should know. Porter's an artist, and so am I. But it's strange, these stories. And even if that had been the truth, I don't think I would *ever* have told anybody anything like that." I say I've been told by a lot of people that Porter isn't a very nice man. "Well," Dolly replies, "he's not. I guess he was when I first knew him." She pauses. "Well, maybe he wasn't. I don't know. It doesn't matter."

"Porter can be the most charming, sweetest person in the world," says one of his former employees, "but he is also the world's greatest egomaniac. He's a total phony. But when he's his charming self, you couldn't find anyone nicer. Now, on his other side, he's violent." A former member of Dolly's band has seen that side of Porter also. "I think that's why they don't like each other now. He may be more blatantly violent than she is, because she manages to hold it to an undercurrent rather than launch a direct attack. They're both sugarcoated on the outside and want only their good sides to show."

"Porter's band lived through that whole scene with Dolly, and the two of them went round and round. It was living hell for the band just being around Porter then, but it was lightweight compared to what Dolly went through," says Tom Rutledge. "When they broke up after a fight in Tulsa—I think that's where that particular fight happened—the band said you could hear them all over the motel. . . . I don't know too much about what went down between him and Dolly, except that she was just miserable. It was the hardest thing she ever did, breaking away from him, because he's that way, and most everybody is afraid of him. That sounds funny, but that's the reason. I saw it in her face one night. She just didn't talk about it much. See, Don Warden, who was her manager, worked for Porter at that time, also. They were both talkin' about it—how rough it was. Generalities, no specifics, but just how hard it was to do that. Because Don was next door in the connecting office, [when Dolly told Porter she was firing him as her producer], and she said she really felt better that he was there, because she didn't know what would happen.

"Porter can be very violent, from what I understand from his band," Rutledge continues. "I never heard anyone say they saw him do anything physical. But he's the kind of man, who, if you got in a fight with him, you'd have to kill him. You couldn't whip him. You know the kind of person I'm talking about? With the kamikaze complex? He can be that way. Now this is only one aspect of Porter. He can be the nicest guy in the world. And usually is. Always has been to me. I've only seen him mad one time. But that wasn't even real rage, from what I understand. He was just mildly mad. But, he's also a great storyteller and fun to be with. I know too much to know he's not always that way, though. See, being with him a few hours a day, one day a week, is not the same thing as working with him. These guys have worked with him, and I guess it's bad. He paid his band on a percentage basis, and they made good money. And most people wouldn't have left because of that reason. But most people were afraid to leave the band. You *didn't* leave the band. You just wouldn't do it. You might get fired for something. . . . when he was sleeping, you didn't wake him up. Don tells a story about sitting up late one night in the passenger seat when Jerry Owens—no relation to Dolly's family—was driving. They got stopped by a policeman. He was gonna give Jerry a ticket, and then he said, 'Is this Porter Wagoner's bus?' Jerry said yeah, and the policeman said, 'Well, I'll tell you what. If you'll get Porter up and have him give me an autograph, I won't give you this ticket.' And Jerry said, 'I think I'd rather have the ticket.' Really," Rutledge says, "all this is incredible. It's just a little glimpse into it, too. That's all I have—a little glimpse. But that's enough for me. I don't want to get any more involved with Porter Wagoner."

After Dolly fired Porter as her producer in 1976, he told John Morthland, "Had I not produced the last duet things that were number one records, had they not been that, I would possibly be in the nuthouse somewhere, trying to figure out what I had done wrong." Morthland asked him more about the nuthouse. "I guess it probably is a fear with me more than anything," Porter told him. "I've had at times—I never did think I was going crazy, but I've had a fear that it would be an awful thing to have happen. And it can happen to a person. I guess that has been in my mind all the time—it's been with me ever since I was just a kid—to not really know what I was doing, what was going on—people who get involved with drugs, not being able to know what's going on really, not knowing it as it is." Morthland asked if insanity could be an occupational hazard. "Well, I guess it would be, but I've never really thought of it heavy in that way." Porter, who wrote a song called "The Rubber Room," said he "got involved in writing these things and thinking along that line, and I had to stop, because it really got to bothering me. Because for you to write something, you really have to be involved in it, down in the deep core of it. So I wrote a couple of things, and then I quit. I felt that was bad for me."

In her book, *Singers and Sweethearts*, Joan Dew writes that Dolly finally got through to Porter that she was leaving him, one way or another, because she had a solo career ahead of her. When Porter tried to block her way again, Dolly convinced him that he wouldn't be able to stop her this time, and it would be better all around if Porter made the announcement, saying they'd worked for that day all those years, that Dolly was now a full-fledged star, ready for her own career, but Porter would still be producing her records.

"That split that she mentions—that Dolly was gonna leave the show whether we decided on it or not—is not true," Porter says. "Because we had talked about it, and I told her that I felt like it was the best thing for her career—for her to form her own show, and to work on her own things. But I would still produce her records and participate in her career and help her in any way I possibly could. But it wasn't that she was gonna walk out on the show—it wasn't the fact that she said 'I'm quitting.' It was a thing we talked over and felt like would be the best thing for her."

Dolly sighs heavily. "It was not an easy thing for me, nor for Porter," she says. "Because any time you're in business that long with people, you laugh together, you cry together, you go through hard times together, you grow together. It's hard to separate; it was hard for me, and it was hard for him. It's never easy to end a relationship, especially where business is involved, and personal feelings, and career. But we disagreed often, because we're quite a bit alike. We're both very creative, both stubborn in our beliefs, and it reached the point where it just seemed to make better sense if we didn't try to be partners in business anymore, even though I respect Porter for what he has stood for in the country music business, for what he has done in my behalf. I appreciate it. Even though there were times that were hard, there were times that were good, too. And we had problems, but any time two people are in business together and they never disagree, then one of 'em ain't doin' their job. And we disagreed often, like I said. But we made a lot of progress, too. It just reached a point to where I had gone as far as I could within a group and organization of somebody else's. I felt a need to expand, to try my wings, to have my own organization. Then that way I didn't have to feel bad when I disagreed with an opinion. I didn't have to feel I had to answer for every move I made, you know, by bein' in business for myself. And I just wanted to be responsible for my own things. It was not an easy thing for either of us, but we're still in business together. I don't know how long we will be, but we're involved in a publishing company, studio, and some other things. He has 49 percent of Owepar. I don't like to get too involved in it, because the public doesn't need to know everything. Some things I don't even like to discuss, because when you're in business together as deep and hot and heavy as we were, as duet partners, as partners on the television show and recordings and productions, tryin' to express opinions and ideas, it gets a little sticky. So it reached the point of needin' to do somethin' else. But just because we didn't agree on lots of things don't make him any less a person, nor me. It's just one of them things. Porter's a brilliant businessman and especially has been in the past. I don't see Porter much anymore." Dolly sighs again, and lets her eyes fall to the floor. The silence grows heavy. "But are you still friends?" I ask. Dolly takes a moment to answer. "I suppose so," she says wearily. "I don't see Porter much anymore."

At the time of the split, both Porter and Dolly tried to keep a calm exterior. "I was grateful to be part of Porter's show," she told a *Newsday* reporter. "When I first started nobody knew me, even though I had a few songs out. It was a great opportunity for me. It helped me build. But now I'm ready and I'm real excited." And to a reporter for *Country Song Roundup*, she said, "We always talked about the day when I would go out on my own when I got to be more successful, so after talking and waiting for some time, it just seemed to come the right time." By last March, she'd gotten some distance on the situation, and coolly and rationally told the tabloid *Star*, "I left because it wouldn't have been fair to ask Porter to change the show just for the things I wanted to do."

But Dolly's composure began to fail her at the press conference she and Porter held jointly in February of 1974 to announce they would dissolve their partnership July 15.

"Dolly is now a superstar in her every way," Porter told the reporters. "She's well prepared to go on her own. I am very happy that I have helped Dolly in preparing for this day. I think because of her being so closely woven into my show, she has been lost in the shuffle of top girl singers, especially in winning awards. [The Country Music Association had never recognized her as Female Vocalist of the Year.] Dolly is one of the finest talents I've ever seen or heard. She's a perfectionist in every way." Porter added that he would continue to be Dolly's "career adviser," and that he would plan her act and remain in business with her.

The lady herself said she had mixed emotions about leaving, but added, "I'm glad that I have reached the point where I can have my own show. Porter felt I was ready to go out on my own, which is a very unselfish decision on his part." And then with teary eyes, Miss Dolly cast an affectionate look over at her old mentor. Porter was a man she genuinely cared for, a man who had tried to fulfill her every dream but who inevitably held her back. She had outgrown him. With the tears growing larger in her blue-green eyes, Dolly paid Porter her ultimate compliment: "He took a little country girl and made something out of her."

But perhaps no one in the room realized just how much farther Dolly Parton had to go.

Not even Dolly herself.

7. "My Biggest Talent Is Being Myself"

WHEN DOLLY FIRST JOINED Porter Wagoner, she still had her own long hair, evident in some of the publicity pictures taken during her Monument days. Jo Coulter suggested to her that if she had some of it cut, her hair might be easier to manage. "She went away on a thirty-day trip," Coulter says, "and when she came back, I almost fainted. She'd cut it all off! She said she just didn't have time to take care of it on the road, and sat down on the bus, took the scissors and whacked it off. Then she wore it short for awhile before going back to the long look. But her own hair is long, you know. It's down below her shoulders, or was the last time I saw it. And it's beautiful."

Dolly without her wig is almost as rare a sight as Carl Dean. Last year, while shooting the photo session for *Country Music* Magazine's cover story, Leonard Kamsler asked Dolly if he might get a shot of her without her wig. Dolly appeared stumped for a second. "I'd have to think about it," she said. "See, that's my gimmick. Me without my wig would be like Liberace in overalls. The public has come to expect me to look a certain way, whether it's in style or not. They don't want to see me in faded jeans, braless, with no makeup and my hair combed straight back. It'd be a letdown to 'em, although I often look that way at home. That's not the character they've come to know."

Dolly, who has been known to say one thing one day and the exact opposite the next, had told another reporter only a few months before, "Lots of people see me without my wigs. But I fix my own hair about the same way, and if I tease it and puff it all up, it looks the same. I have a lot of hair. Not quite this much, but almost." She says it takes her about thirty minutes to get completely dressed in her professional Dolly costume, or to become her Dolly "character."

Another reason Dolly doesn't appear often without her wig is because her own hair is damaged from years of teasing, Dolly's band leader Gregg Perry told a St. Louis paper. But a member of a well-known back-up group remembers the time Dolly showed up for a session without it. "She was adorable," he recalls. "You'd flip over her if you saw her without that thing on. She's prettier without it." Dolly told me her own hair is blond but admitted with no hint of hesitation that "I color it a little."

The woman who has been taking care of Dolly's hair and wigs since the Cas Walker days is Colleen Owens. The number of wigs in Dolly's collection is somewhere around 200. Colleen keeps quite a few—at least seventy—of them in a room in her basement. Most are synthetic. Caring for them is a full-time job, since Dolly wears each one only twice before Colleen washes and re-sets it. Coordinating wigs and outfits is a chore, too—so much so that Colleen has had to make a chart. Even that must take constant work, because recently Stella said she'd just thrown out a bunch of Dolly's old hairpieces.

Aside from the convenience of wigs (Dolly never goes to a beauty shop), she says the idea of wearing them came almost by accident—or at least out of a criticism. "I started doin' my hair like this when I was in high school," Dolly told me. "The style—the teasin' and all—was just out then, and I enjoyed it. Then it got out of style, but I still liked it that'a way. And then when everything started changing, people got to sayin', 'You should change your hairstyle. That's out of style.' And I thought, 'Well, they noticed. So it may be a gimmick in addition to something I enjoy. I'll just keep it this way to see who all *will* notice and stir up as much interest as I can.' And the more interest I stirred up, the higher I put it, and the more extreme I got it."

Dolly has been cultivating her look for years, of course, but it wasn't until she joined Porter's show that she began to really define and refine it. "Dolly didn't really know how to dress when she came to the show," Don Howser remembers. "She still had a little bit of the rural appearance. Really, she'd never had the clothes *to* dress, since she'd come from such a large and poor family. Still, the natural beauty was there, and, of course, today, she's much more polished than she was then." Martha Hume pointed out in an article in *New Dawn* magazine that at the time Dolly joined Porter's show, the country music world was such a microcosm that it remained untouched by the dictates of Seventh Avenue. "Loretta Lynn's early pictures show a dark-haired girl with a western hat slung over her shoulders and fringes on her cowgirl shirt," Hume wrote. "Dolly Parton, now the most flamboyantly dressed of the girl singers, tended to teased blond bouffants and frilly gingham dresses. Both these outfits were accessorized with a large guitar worn over the chest. Neither had anything to do with the way other American women were dressing in the early '60s . . . Dolly's and Loretta's outfits were typical of the way female stars were supposed to look: sexually nonthreatening and apple pie plain. Moreover, fancy hairdressers and fashion consultants were taboo. Women are supposed to be able to do that sort of thing themselves."

That, of course, was not so much Dolly's "image" as it was the way she thought she was supposed to look to be accepted. It's hard to believe she could think "gimmick" in those clothes. But when she began making money, she decided to forego her sweet long flowered skirts and ruffles for custom-made apparel that matched her self-image. The logical choice of seamstress was Judy Hunt, who made the conservative western-cut clothes Porter wore when he changed out of his Nudies. Lucy Adams, a talented designer and lovely, poised woman worked at Judy of Nashville, Hunt's shop.

The first clothes the two made for Dolly were slightly sparkly but surely "innocent" in their design and cut. "She was just rural," Lucy Adams remembers. "One of the first things Judy made for her was a white, long-sleeve shift dress with rhinestones around the bottom. She wears it on the cover of her first album, *Just Because I'm a Woman.*" At twenty-two, with her hair bleached out platinum and piled high, Dolly looks a good ten years older in this album photograph. "Judy made two or three things like that—some lamés, some chiffon, with and without rhinestones—and then I started. My things weren't as wild to start with in all the styles, but we gradually built up more and more to where she'd say, 'I'd like them crusted.' Just crusted with rhinestones. Then we came up with the big wide-bottomed legs on her pants. She'd wear long dresses for conventions and special occasions, and she'd wear some short dresses, too. But she found the pantsuits more practical for the stage, for modesty's sake. From then on, just about all of her stage things were pantsuits or jumpsuits, and I just kept getting them wider and wider at the bottom."

"Modesty's sake" was not a low priority with Dolly. "She's V-E-R-Y modest, yes sir!" says Judy Hunt. "I mean she'll turn that back! Go off in another room! You're not gonna see her with no clothes on. Now, you can see her in her pantyhose, but not in just her underpants or without a bra. She won't even walk *around* in a bra. That's kind of unusual." Lucy Adams recalls she always turned her back while Dolly changed, knowing how modest she is, and when Dolly was in her garment, Lucy would turn back around and zip her up. "Dolly's one of the most modest people I've ever met in my life," Jo Coulter echoes. "When we taped the old Porter Wagoner shows at WSM, she'd go in the little tee-iny bathroom, which was like two-foot square, to change into her costume. She wouldn't change out in the big room, even though she knew there would be no men coming in, because that was the ladies' rest room, where we did our makeup. But she would never change in front of anybody."

Dolly may have been embarrassed for anyone to see her body, but she was adamant that everyone know basically what it looked like, since her seamstresses recall they could never make Dolly's costumes tight enough for her. "If she could reach down and pick it up, it was too loose," Adams says. "If she'd left it up to me, I wouldn't have done that. Sometimes I'd make things and think they fit real nice, but she'd say they were too big, for me to take them up more. It looked like it would be uncomfortable, but I'd just push her in and zip her up. That's the way she wanted it." And Dolly was just as firm in her orders that certain parts of her body be accentuated and others not. Both designers agree that Dolly wanted her waist played up and her bust played down. "Actually, she probably accentuates everything—her hips, too—but if anything, she would cover up her bust," Hunt says. "She was really into high-necked things, to cover up good." Adams recalls that if she made anything low-cut for Dolly, she'd put her hand over herself. "She'd say, 'I couldn't wear that,' " Adams quotes. " 'My daddy would whip me for that!' " But just what size the area Dolly wanted well-covered is, neither Hunt nor Adams is saying. "We had an agreement that I would never repeat her measurements," they explain. Asked if one estimate of 38-26-36 was correct, Adams replied, "I wouldn't think so." Both seamstresses also agree that despite her constantly fluctuating weight, Dolly has no problem areas that need disguising. "She's got a really nice shape. Just allow a lot for the top!" Hunt says.

All in all, Hunt and Adams remember their old client as being a "plain, sweet girl" who was very clothes-conscious, but easy to please. "She's not picky about designs," Hunt says. "She'll just say, 'Make me up something in blue, green, yellow—all different colors." (Later, Dolly would begin designing some of her own costumes. And, as she became more specific in her goals, she would ask for certain styles and designs.)

But Adams, who says she feels Dolly is a member of her family, always tried to make everything extra special for her. One Christmas, she fashioned Dolly a quilt top out of the scraps of the clothes she'd made for her through the year. Across the top, she spelled out D-O-L-L-Y in white, and put the year below it. Each Christmas, she gave Dolly a gag gift, too. One year it was an elaborate Santa Claus suit. And for Dolly's twenty-fourth birthday, her friend made her the second Coat of Many Colors, of gold and silver and velvet, lined in satin. She presented it to her on the set of Porter's show and remembers that when Dolly opened the package, big tears rose in her eyes. Then she ran off, saying she had to go back and do her makeup. Later, she sang the song on the show—and wore her new coat.

Just as important to Dolly's overall look as her form-fitting clothing was her use of makeup. On several of her early album jackets, she appears terribly over made-up, her false eyelashes too long and prominent, and her eyeshadow too garish and dark. In general, her way of thinking seemed to be "more is better." Through the years she has softened her look; she is now a breathtaking woman, possessing a beauty that has to be seen in person to be appreciated. Her flawless complexion is a gloriously radiant peaches-and-cream, set off by a beauty mark on the left side of her face, large blue-green eyes and a generous, sensuous mouth, and, of course, by her dimples, which she playfully calls "the sinkholes in my makeup." And ever since orthodontic appliances worn at night closed a gap (inherited from Avie Lee) between her two front teeth, Dolly has had the kind of smile that could sell toothpaste coast to coast.

Jo Coulter says there are no problems whatsoever in making Dolly up.

"Dolly has almost perfect features and beautiful bone structure. Her cheekbones are beautiful and high, and she has a good jawline and nose, not to mention her eyes and mouth. She can do her own makeup and does a lot of the time. She knows it because she worked to learn it, since anybody who's going to be in the spotlight needs to know something about makeup. You can't always depend on a makeup artist being there. And she has her own ideas about the way she wants to look. I was her makeup artist on the shows, both her's and Porter's, but I never tried to change her style. She doesn't necessarily always outline her lips, because her mouth is very full and sensuous. She doesn't need to do anything to make it look larger. We do put lipgloss on because it catches the lights and makes the mouth prettier. But mostly, it's just base, eye shadow and false eyelashes. One pair, not two, as one book says. They help to open the eye and make it look larger, because cameras and heavy lights tend to diminish eyes. And we apply some highlights under her eyes. She likes to change her eye shadow, to use a lot of different colors sometimes. She did a rainbow eye once that I love—all different pastel shades, painted like a rainbow over her eye. It was beautiful. It wasn't for everybody, but it was for Dolly, and we let it stay for Porter's show. She pleases herself, she loves to create, and she knows if something doesn't look right. This is all part of her nature. She loves pretty clothes, and because she is tiny, she loves high-heeled shoes and high hair. She's like a little girl. That childlike quality keeps her fresh and young and inquiring. She'll try anything. And she simply adores playing with makeup."

In her growing-up years, Dolly had few chances to indulge in such luxuries. But simply because she hadn't the money with which to buy the things didn't mean Dolly would be denied them. For lipstick she'd used merthiolate and mercurochrome, which turned out to be better than the real thing, staying on her little lips for days on end. (It earned her a whipping from her daddy but was worth it all the while: when the tears were gone, the smile remained.) For eyebrow pencil, she'd wet the tips of the long wooden kitchen matches Momma had used to light the stove and carefully apply the outline. And for powder, she'd sneak some flour when Avie Lee wasn't looking. Like the county nurse who came by the house occasionally to visit, Dolly would one day wear perfume, buy herself a gold ring, and have her hair done, the latter goal realized for the first time not long after she arrived in Nashville. She would own shiny cars and diamonds, too. And pretty clothes.

"I can understand Dolly's look completely," says Fred Foster. "She didn't have clothes growing up, and I think she decided, 'Some day I'll make it and I'll have the finest-looking clothes in the world.' The finest-looking clothes to a teenager in Sevierville, Tennessee, would be what we call gaudy-looking clothes, right? Flash. And I think she wanted that and bought it by the grossloads. It's something that you get sort of trapped into and don't know how to get out of gracefully. And she probably still does like them in a way."

Before she allowed herself to look as outrageous as her fantasies, however, Dolly curtailed her look to a vision of glamour that would match Porter's flashiness and yet was usually distinctive enough to allow Dolly's outgoing personality to reveal itself. Just as she had decided on her hairstyle because even though it was out of style, it drew attention, she picked many of her dresses and outfits for the same purpose. "My hair is out of the '60s, my clothes are the '50s, and the shoes I wear are from the '40s," Dolly often said. "Nobody's going to change me. I pile my hair high because I've always had a complex about being short. Frankly, I don't try to follow styles. I like to think I've got my own. I don't like to be like everybody else. I'd never stoop to be fashionable. That's the easiest thing in the world to do."

In years to come, after she left Porter's show, Dolly would try to impress the media with just how conscious she was of her look and her image, making sure that they understood, as Fred Foster had wanted, that she looked that way because she chose to.

Sitting cross-legged at home with her guard down, Dolly was not nearly so brave, not nearly so sure she communicated all she hoped she did. "I want to be accepted as who I am, and what I am, not as what somebody tries to make out of me," she told me. "I want to be looked at as a real person, even though my look is artificial as far as the gaudy appearance. Where you can't see is where the way I really am shows the most. That's inside. And that's what I want people to see most. I guess I want to be thought of as an honest person, as a decent person, but with enough character and enough mysetery about me to always be fascinatin', or at least interestin'. But I want people to see me as I am, and they will, I think. I just want to do whatever I can do, and do it the best I can. I'm not out to hurt anybody. I'm not out to badmouth anybody. I'm not out to destroy. I'm not out to take. I just want to give, really," she added in a hurt tone, sounding like a little girl who needed some sort of reassurance. "I just hope that what I'm givin' is accepted in the spirit in which it is given. All I have to give, really, is my music, and my love and my words. But that should be enough."

Still, sometimes people didn't understand just what Dolly was offering, the confusion arising out of the fact that Dolly's appearance said one thing, and her soul another. In a classic case of show biz irony, Dolly's physical beauty was in some ways detrimental. "Part of the magic of me is that I look totally one way when I am totally another," Dolly says. "It took a long time for some people to see I was not just a wig. I started writing a song about it: 'What difference does it make/If I'm real or if I'm fake/On the outside where it matters not at all.' " Tom Rutledge recalls that in the days when he played guitar for Dolly, "People told me they were turned off by the gaudiness and thought they didn't like her because of it. But all that stuff is totally irrelevant to where Dolly's really at. I wish people could know her as I've known her. I wish they knew what a good person she is. Dolly's really special." Rutledge and others say the preconceptions people had of Dolly based on her look—that she was the dumb blonde of the title of her early record, or that she put an inordinate emphasis on sex, or she played up her appearance to compensate for a lack of talent—hurt Dolly deeply.

"The fact that Dolly's body happens to be a little more voluptuous than other people's is a bonus, since she's also a beautiful woman underneath," says Minnie Pearl. "But in a way her body is a trap. It's been a hindrance to her establishing the kind of person she is. A lot of women would give their eyeteeth to be built like she is, but at the same time, that distracts people from her actual motives. Peculiar and paradoxical, isn't it, that being a sex symbol would be a hindrance? But Dolly's a very straightforward, plain-spoken lady."

"I don't dwell on the way I look, and it bothers me sometimes when people do," Dolly told LaWayne Satterfield in 1973. "I'm not vain at all. People think that I am, but I'm not concerned with how I look after I get dressed in the morning. That's it for the day. I may wear britches I bought five years ago with stovepipe legs when everybody else is wearin' bellbottoms. You know," she added, trying to laugh it off, "looks aren't everything. But they help in a crowd!"

They certainly impressed Richard Peterson when he saw Dolly at the taping of an early Porter Wagoner show. But like so many others, Peterson first took Dolly at face value. "In the midst of all this very slick production came Porter's then new female singer. My first reaction was, 'Well, I can see why she got picked.' Then I heard her voice. It was just so incredibly clean, clear and impelling that I was devastated. And then I learned that she had written a couple of the songs. From the beginning, then, I marked her down as someone who was unique. I don't know her, but I've always had the impression that she's cooling along at about a 140 I.Q., that she's extremely bright, and that she has a real sense about what she's doing."

Despite the excellence of some of the material Dolly wrote for Combine Music, it wasn't until her Porter Wagoner years that she developed into a superb songwriter. Her first RCA album, *Just Because I'm a Woman*, in 1968, did not do much toward lifting her out of the ranks of hundreds of other girl singers, except that it showed off her distinctive voice, and with four of the tunes she established the fact that she could write. One, "The Bridge," about what a pregnant and unwed girl resorts to on the bridge where she used to meet her young lover, sounds terribly influenced (complete with mystery ending) by "Ode to Billie Joe," which had been a huge hit the previous year. (Dolly lists Bobbie Gentry among her favorite writers. Others she admires include Tom T. Hall, Loretta Lynn and Kris Kristofferson.) But there was one song on the album, the title tune, in fact, that showed that Dolly Parton was not your average docile, stay-at-home, husband-worshiping woman. "Just Because I'm a Woman," with such lyrics as "My mistakes are no worse than yours/Just because I'm a woman," took a stand for personal and female equality that was almost unthinkable in conservative Nashville. The mere *hint* of liberation was the kiss of death to a girl singer's career, but Dolly faced it head-on, as she would many controversial subjects in her writing; her progressivism was at one time thought to be the reason the Country Music Association waited until 1975 to name her Female Vocalist of the Year.

Such songs as "Just Because I'm a Woman" soon made Dolly Parton's music almost as distinctive as her high, young-sounding voice and her look. For several years now she has been recognized as the most talented female songwriter in country music. ("If I'm the best Nashville has to offer, Nashville's in bad shape!") Now she's working on capturing that title for all of popular music. Her subject matter runs the gamut of emotions and experience. It's hard to think of another woman who has written so convincingly on so many themes. To name just a few: the search for love, unrequited love, returned affection, marital squabbles, family unity, faith, jealousy, infidelity, incest, abortion, outlaws, betrayal, suicide, joy, freedom and independence. If numbers are any indication, Dolly's favorite of all the subjects are love, country life, and, during the years in which she was with Porter, at least, unwanted pregnancy and illegitimacy. She not only wrote four songs about the latter topic, but recorded several more by other writers during this period, her penchant for such tunes eventually leading to the inevitable rumor that she knew something about the experience firsthand.

Dolly's lyrics range from the "banal and basic" to the "magical and mundane," as two writers have put it, but even the worst of them, no matter how trite or maudlin, corny or wooden, are usually saved by Dolly's honesty, sincerity and unutterable charm. (She can lay the lamest, hoariest gag on a sophisticated audience and reap gales of laughter, simply by attaching her own bemused giggle at the end.) Her real strength as a lyricist lies in her novelist's eye for setting and detail, in her poetic imagery, and in her unfaltering realism. When she combines all that with her considerable gift for feeling, the effect is often chilling, particularly in her songs about poverty in the mountains of East Tennessee. The first to appear on record was "In the Good Old Days (When Times Were Bad)": "We've got up before/And found ice on the floor/Where the wind would blow snow/ Through the cracks in the wall." She continued that theme throughout the years, the imagery brought more clearly into focus by the time she wrote "The Greatest Days of All": "A dirt dobber built its nest/On my only Sunday dress/And the roof leaked in my shoes/And when they dried they were too small/And the rats chewed a great big hole/In my only winter coat/And at night I'd hear them gnaw/The paper on my bedroom wall." But not all her imagery or memories are harsh. This from "My Tennessee Mountain Home," a milestone in her career as a writer: "Sitting on the front porch on a summer afternoon/In a straight back chair on two legs/ Leaned against the wall./Watch the kids a playing with June bugs on a string/And chase the glowing fireflies/When evening's shadows fall."

"I get most of my inspiration from my roots," Dolly says, and although it is like her to be funning and point to the top of her head when she delivers the line, her songs with the greatest depth have for the most part been those culled from her storehouse of memories of her native region. It is those songs which reach the head, heart and gut at the same time, and Dolly put out no collection of songs as moving as her concept album, *My Tennessee Mountain Home*, now regarded as a classic. "Its songs, all basically autobiographical, utilize an inborn sense of nuance and complex mixture of meters without ever losing touch with country's primal musical essences," wrote Nick Tosches. "There are often flurries of images so dense as to seem hallucinatory and lines possessed of such natural flow that rhyme seems almost incidental." Not every album is as rich as that, however. For every gem on most of her LPs there are at least four fillers, maybe more, as there are on nearly every artist's records. When the classics come along, then, they are all that more shattering.

Though labeled a "country" singer and songwriter, Dolly has always borrowed from all the musical forms and styles, working snippets of gospel and bluegrass into her tunes, and on occasion flirting with jazz and blues. Or, as Dave Hickey observed, "Taking, for instance, a country lyric, a modal Appalachian melody, and a rock bass line with a syncopated bridge, and combining them into songs like 'Early Morning Breeze' and '(The) Greatest Days of All.' " But she was most potent and powerful as a writer during her years with Porter in her folk-derived melodies and lyric forms. It was, of course, the high-pitched spirituals Dolly sang and heard at church, the old English folk songs and ballads that had been locked in the mountains and hollers since the settlers brought them over, and the foreign sounds of commercialized country coming over the battery-powered radio that had shaped Dolly's conception and vision of music as a child. "It was natural, when I wrote, to reflect back to the old songs we used to sing," she told Jack Hurst last year, "and part of my melodies kind of carried that old-timey flavor without me realizing it until after they were done. And I still do that—those folky-type melodies are the best of all."

Four of them stand out as some of the best work she has ever done. The first, "My Blue Ridge Mountain Boy," showed up as the title song of her third RCA album and was one of the first of her songs to suggest her awesome ability to evoke mood both with her lyrics and melodies, together and separately. The song is also a fine example of Dolly's creative imagination, of her talent for breathing real life into a made-up situation, making it not only totally believable, but unforgettably moving. Aside from "Down From Dover" and "I Will Always Love You," the latter song far more important for the *way* it conveys than for *what* it conveys, "My Blue Ridge Mountain Boy" is Dolly's most haunting work, heartrending in its storyline and devastating in its melody. Dolly gives the song an added emotional power by refraining from self-pity in both her lyrics and in her plaintive, but restrained delivery. And with skillful, sparse touches of instrumentation, producer Bob Ferguson underscores the mood, adds setting and points up the poignancy of the story: A lone tinkling banjo brings a mental picture of the mountain shack into view, a light-hearted fiddle introduces the cheap gaiety of New Orleans night life, and a blues guitar riff at the finish underscores the finality of the situation. The lyrics, too, are clean and succinct:

From a shack by a mountain stream
To a room in New Orleans
So far from my Blue Ridge Mountain home.
The men I meet
Ain't warm and friendly
Like the one in old Virginia,
They ain't real
Like My Blue Ridge Mountain Boy.

I was just a little past eighteen
When I came to New Orleans
I'd never been beyond my home state line.
There was a boy
Who loved me dearly
But I broke his heart severely
When I left
My Blue Ridge Mountain Boy.

Life was dull in my home town,
Lights were out when the sun went down
And I thought the city life was more my style.
But nights get lonely 'way from home
And it's easy to go wrong
The men ain't kind
Like My Blue Ridge Mountain Boy.

New Orleans held things in store
Things I never bargained for
And ev'ry night a diff'rent man knocks on my door.
But late at night
When all is still
I can hear a whippoorwill
As I cry
For My Blue Ridge Mountain Boy.

But I can't ever go back home,
Since the boy I loved is gone,
He grew tired of waiting for me to return.
They say he married last October,
But I never will get over,

Oh, the sweet love of
My Blue Ridge Mountain Boy.
Blue Ridge Mountain Boy.

Only a shade less moving, but no less powerful, is Dolly's "Down From Dover," the story of a girl who waits in vain for a boy to come back and join her for the birth of their illegitimate baby. The baby comes before the end of the song: "My body aches, the time is here, it's lonely in this place where I'm lying/Our baby has been born, but something's wrong, it's much too still, I hear no crying/I guess in some strange way she knew she'd never have a father's arms to hold her/And dying was her way of telling me he wasn't coming down from Dover." Again, the lean, spare instrumentation enhances the song's drama and effect, a harpsichord adding rhythmic fills behind an acoustic folk guitar. One small irony about "Down from Dover" is that with all its stark realism, the song appears on Dolly's *The Fairest of Them All*—the album cover depicting Dolly in her most fanciful, fairy tale pose.

The most famous of Dolly's "folk" songs is, of course, "Coat of Many Colors." Aside from the sheer pathos of the story, what makes it so endearing is its authenticity, never mind the fact that Dolly uses the word "rags" when "scraps" would probably be closer to the truth: Even if Dolly had never gone on television or given interviews saying the incident had actually happened, the listener would know. It is also to Dolly's credit that she managed to turn a painful and embarrassing experience into an entertaining piece of art, and that like all the best art, it is universal in its appeal despite its setting in America's backwoods.

Not a small portion of the song's charm lies in its rhythm, inherent in the meter of the rhyme and hammered home with a jaunty melody, appropriately simple finger-picking on the guitar, and the slightest of percussion and bass. One of Dolly's gifts as a lyricist and song stylist is making a song sound simpler than it actually is. Just as "Coat of Many Colors" has its foundation in the old English folk tunes, it retains the rhythmic aberrations of the Elizabethan ballads handed down through the centuries, although they are hardly noticeable in her delivery. " 'Coat of Many Colors' must have been extremely difficult to write," says Nashville music publisher Clarence Selman. "I'll guarantee you the sweat was sloshing in both her boots before she finished that song, because it required the best of her. She must have gotten fatigued from struggling with it. Do you know how many words she got into every line? And then she had to be able to sing them."

Back through the years I go wand'ring once again
Back to the seasons of my youth.

I recall a box of rags that someone gave us
And how my Mama put the rags to use.

There were rags of many colors
But ev'ry piece was small
And I didn't have a coat
And it was 'way down in the fall.
Mama sewed the rags together
Sewing ev'ry piece with love;
She made my Coat of Many Colors
That I was so proud of.

As she sewed she told a story
From the Bible she had read,
About a Coat of Many Colors
Joseph wore, and then she said,
"Perhaps this coat will bring you
Good luck and happiness."
And I just couldn't wait to wear it
And Mama blessed it with a kiss.

My Coat of Many Colors
That my Mama made for me
Made only from rags
But I wore it so proudly
Although we had no money
I was rich as I could be
In my Coat of Many Colors
My Mama made for me.

So with patches on my britches
and holes in both my shoes
In my Coat of Many Colors
I hurried off to school
Just to find the others laughing
And making fun of me
In my Coat of Many Colors
My Mama made for me.

And oh, I couldn't understand it
For I felt I was rich
And I told 'em of the love
My Mama sewed in ev'ry stitch
And I told them all the story
Mama told me while she sewed
And how my Coat of Many Colors
Was worth more than all their clothes.

But they didn't understand it
And I tried to make them see
That one is only poor
Only if they choose to be
Now I know we had no money
But I was rich as I could be
In my coat of Many Colors
My Mama made for me.

As impressed as most people were with "Coat of Many Colors," Dolly earned a new respect for her songwriting with "Jolene," released in 1973. The storyline itself was not all that special—the woman (Dolly) begs Jolene to end her flirtation with her husband, "the only one" she could ever love. The lyrics contained only one particularly outstanding descriptive stanza:

Your beauty is beyond compare, with flaming
Locks of auburn hair,
With ivory skin and eyes of emerald green,
Your smile is like a breath of spring,
Your voice is soft like summer rain,
And I cannot compete with you, Jolene.
He talks about you in his sleep and there is nothing
I can do to keep
From cryin' when he calls your name, Jolene,
And I can easily understand how you could easily take my man,
But you don't know what he means to me, Jolene.

Where the song became something out of the ordinary was in its melody. Beginning on a minor chord and progressing to only two more, both major, before returning home, "Jolene" harks immediately back to the purest of Elizabethan form. What made it so eerily and chillingly effective, though, was Dolly's double-tracked harmony, so close and other-worldly as to raise goose bumps. A perfect complement to that was Dolly's syncopated, hammered-on guitar lick, and the addition of bongos to accentuate the offbeat. "Jolene" shot right to number one on the country charts, and got a fair amount of pop air play, as well. Today, when asked if Jolene was for real, Dolly replies, "If she was, I probably couldn't admit it." But shortly after the record came out, Dolly told LaWayne Satterfield she'd often thought about what she'd do if someone "went after Carl."

The real inspiration, however, came from an incident that occurred while Dolly was signing autographs after a show. A child, "maybe eleven or twelve, with real fair skin, green eyes and auburn hair, in a little Girl Scout suit," handed Dolly her school picture and asked her to give it to Porter. On the back, she had written, "To Porter, Love Jolene." "I was fascinated by the name, and I thought it was a perfect name for a song, because it's unusual," Dolly says. "I write a lot of name songs." (Indeed, she has written many tunes with the names of her sisters and brothers in the titles: "Sweet Rachel Ann," "Bobby's Arms," "Randy," "Robert," to name a few.) "The lick on the intro I just started pickin' for no reason at all," she remembers. "I just started singin' 'Jolene, Jolene.' "

At the time she recorded "Jolene," Dolly was effusive about the creative touches Porter had given it, saying, "I have a big part of the arrangements in the main bulk of my songs, say like, I made up the little lick on the guitar, and it's followed all the way through." That "little lick" is so complicated that one of Dolly's most accomplished road musicians—a fine studio guitarist—had trouble mastering it at first. The night I was at Dolly's home, we played guitar together—she had just acquired an old baby Martin that she let me play—and she showed me that she picks only with her thumb and first finger. I said I didn't know how she played with such long nails. "Fairly well," she answered laughing, laying a stage line on me. "Except ever' once in awhile, I pull one out by the glue!"

"But Porter is fantastic!" Dolly went on to say. "He's a wonderful producer, and he's got brilliant ideas. He added so many other things to it . . ." Not so many years later, she would point to the fact that "Jolene," which took on a heaviness not apparent in much of her other work, had been the kind of song she had wanted, but was, in effect, not "allowed" to do for years. "That was the first time I noticed people sayin', 'That's different than what you been doin',' " she told Jack Hurst. "But I had been fightin' for that sort of thing for years. I had all these songs I was writin', and I was developin' musically, as far as a different style of pickin' and hearin' different sounds in my mind was concerned. 'Jolene' was the first good example of the fact that you can be yourself and still improve on whatever you do."

"I think Dolly's one of the best and truest folk writers and singers that we have," says Brenda Lee. But she agrees that after "Jolene," Dolly's music became increasingly harder to categorize. Of course, many of Dolly's songs through the years had really defied labels (largely because of her eclecticism), including the deliciously erotic "Touch Your Woman" of 1972. And by the fall of 1974, after the advent of "Jolene," she had managed to get Porter to allow her to put some lighter, pop sounds down on vinyl, the first shimmering example being the whimsical "Love Is Like a Butterfly," fitting no category except, as its author would have it, "Dolly Parton music." Although "Love Is Like a Butterfly" was almost a throwaway as far as lyrics were concerned (and nothing earth-shattering in melody), it pointed the direction in which Dolly was headed, and it demonstrated her increasing dexterity at handling the combination of movement and mood.

Dolly had contributed her share of mediocrity through the years, breaking meter heedlessly and turning out some truly terrible rhymes ("slip" and "sleep," when she could just have easily used "creep," and "chair" and "here," which she could have never even *begun* to pull off had she not possessed that flat East Tennessee drawl.)

Still, Dolly is very aware of the interaction of sound and meaning of language. She likes to place opposites together in phrases ("My weakness was just too strong"). And she *loves* to pun, titling one ghastly novelty song "I'll Oilwells Love You," and another "He's a Go-Getter," explaining in the body of the tune that "when his wife gets off from work, he'll go get her." But she's quite skillful at playing all the meanings of a word, as she did in her duet with Porter, "Two": "Two people too proud to say I'm sorry/Two hearts too broken to ever mend/Too many harsh words too often spoken/ Too late to find love together again." And as Dave Hickey wrote in *Country Music* magazine, ". . . within eight lines of text [she] plays off six shades of meaning from the verb 'will,' in the song 'Will He Be Waiting.'

"It is this sensitivity to the spoken language which allows Miss Parton to do what she does best," Hickey continued, "to capture the complexities of life as it is lived in the ambiguities of language as it is spoken."

Now she was getting past the verbal problems, but with "Love Is Like a Butterfly," she ran into another problem for a songwriter, one that had reared its head as early as the Monument days, when she wrote and recorded "Fuel to the Flame"—no one but Dolly Parton could really effectively carry off a good portion of her songs.

"Her major weakness as a writer is that she has so stylized her songs by the time she's written them, that it would lead another artist to believe that they're only for Dolly Parton," says Clarence Selman. "The only genuine way for her to get around that is to deliberately write a song for another artist. And I think that's a weakness that she hasn't discovered and done anything about. But, really, the word 'weakness' only applies if you think all she wants to do is write songs. And since that isn't all she wants to do, we have to assume that perhaps all of her songs are for her. As a professional writer, you have to isolate a weakness in your product and do something about it. In Dolly's case, she doesn't have to. She has an automatic record for anything she writes, because she's her own vehicle. But as a writer, I think she should hope her songs are for everybody. Maybe she does, but she just can't get them cut."

That is not to say that no heavies in the business have recorded Dolly's songs. On the contrary. Linda Ronstadt has covered the exquisite "I Will Always Love You" (one of Dolly's all-time strongest songs and one that should, in time, become a standard), Emmylou Harris has recorded "Coat of Many Colors" and had a hit with Dolly's "To Daddy" (which Dolly recorded in 1976 but never released), and Maria Muldaur has a version of "My Tennessee Mountain Home." Even avant-garde Patti Smith found "Jolene" of merit, putting Dolly right up there with Rimbaud, presumably.

(Others who have recorded her tunes include Olivia Newton-John and Merle Haggard.)

Dolly had a hip, underground following long before she knew it. Many people believe Dolly took the final steps to leave Porter when she learned from Ronstadt and Harris that it wasn't just the mobile-home set that was willing to shell out to hear Dolly live and on record, but that she'd have to change a few things if she hoped to court the other side.

"I don't think so," Dolly says. "I mean, I admire them, and I respect their music, and I think that's pretty well mutual. They were into my music before I even met either one of 'em. And I think they're super. But you see, I'm not easily influenced by anyone. They've inspired me in many ways. And they've made me feel that I should take great pride in the things I do. I know one thing. They've been great about promotin' me. They have done more for me, as far as their audience, their following, as far as talkin' me up. I'm sure they've won me a lot of fans that would not have been aware of me beforehand. I'm always jokin' with 'em that I should put 'em on salary for publicity. But as far as either of 'em ever sayin', 'You ought to do this,' or 'You should do that,' they never did. See, the things I'm doin' now," she said in early '77, "are the things I've wanted to do ever since I came to Nashville. I've wanted to be everything I could be ever since I got here. You just have to take it a step at a time."

The first time Emmylou Harris appeared on the Grand Ole Opry (for a televised special on the Opry's fiftieth anniversary) in October 1975, she faced a group of reporters sitting around a table backstage with the enthusiasm of a soldier standing before a firing squad. Nervous and insecure, she spoke in a trembling voice as she clasped her hands in front of her on the table. Finally, someone asked her about Dolly Parton. Harris lit up like a pinball machine. "We only met a short time ago, but I just think the world of her, and she's been very friendly and helpful to me, just making me feel comfortable and at home here," she said smiling. "She's that kind of person, very genuine, very sincere."

Today, she and Parton and Ronstadt are all good pals. Linda and Emmylou taped an episode of Dolly's syndicated TV show and they can be found singing on each other's albums and plugging one another in the press. They are reportedly recording an album together. Backstage at a Chicago club Harris, who does a lovely interpretation of "My Blue Ridge Mountain Boy," admitted that Dolly had been a large influence on her style.

"I heard her years ago, when I was only into country music a little bit—before I went over the deep end—and I was amazed at her voice," she said. "The first time I heard it, I said, 'Who is that?' I immediately went out and bought everything of hers I could find. As a singer, I could appreciate her voice and her style, and I did some of her material. I have just about all her records from the days she was with Porter. I like those early recordings a lot. They're very charming, very simple, with just the straightforward guitar.

She's very influenced by the mountain sound, with the banjos and the real strong melodies. I just think she's a marvelous writer," continued Harris, who used to wear a Dolly Parton T-shirt. "I mean, if nothing else, she's a marvelous writer, and an incredible singer, but then she's also amazing because of the way she can keep all these aspects of her life together and follow her career. Just to know someone like that is very inspiring. It really is. There are very few people who come close to her as a song craftsman. I mean, a song like 'To Daddy' has such a punch line that you want to say, 'Hey, that's not fair! You just set me up and knocked me over with that one.' To me, it's like an O. Henry short story. She sets you up and then whammo—she turns it all around. When I first heard it my lips were trembling and I was afraid I was gonna make a scene." (Dolly is fond of turnabout and surprise endings. Aside from "To Daddy," she used them on "Travelin' Man," "Robert," "I Get Lonesome by Myself," and "Chas," the latter song containing a surprise middle, too.)

The fact that people of such artistry as Emmylou Harris love her work must please Dolly a great deal. "It's always a thrill when people do your songs. It's a great compliment," she has said. "The great thing about music is that it's something people relate to." Many people who know Dolly well say she is far more important to her than it may appear. "People don't realize how serious a songwriter she is and how much writing means to her," Jo Coulter says. "It's her way of expressing a life and she *has* to have it. She really needs it."

"I feel like anybody can sing, but not everybody can write," Dolly explains. "My songs tell how I feel. I get more out of writing than singing. My writing is personal to me. It's my self-expression. It's me. I want to be remembered as a good songwriter and stylist and as a person who added something to this world. If I had to choose, I guess a lot of people can sing better than me. I'd choose being remembered as a songwriter, because my writing is something I take great pride in. Like I say, that's totally me." If that's true, then, the lyrics to her songs must be Dolly Parton quotes, showing her the way she really is and thinks. "A big part of 'em are, yeah," she answers. Then a mysterious smile crosses her face. "You'd be amazed at the ones that are."

The process by which Dolly writes is really quite extraordinary, her friends say, and she confirms it. "I'm not a disciplined writer at all. I'm strictly an impulsive wirter, and I write from inspiration. I get my ideas from everybody. When I feel this need to write, it comes out of my heart and soul. Because I get moods, great moods, weird moods." She laughs. "You know, really inspired moods, and I just get real involved in what I'm doin' and I can't stop. I've stayed up as long as three days before—well, at least *two* days, and *into* the third day before I could really make my mind stop enough to rest."

Apparently those creative storms are sights to behold. "Her writing is

The casual country Dolly of old, dressed in jeans and one of her many bandana shirts and scarves. "Through layers of lipstick she pushes a voice fervent with fundamentalist religion," Jack Hurst wrote, a voice in which Maria Muldaur hears "an essence and purity that chills me to the bone." *Photo: Michael G. Borum*

"She stands before the mirror, Smiles at her reflection, Striking sexy poses in the glass. She paints her lips a brilliant red, Piles her hair high on her head, Struggles to replace a false eyelash." But *voilà*! When she's finished, Dolly, who wrote those lines for "Where Beauty Lives in Memory," looks like no one else in the world. She says it takes all of thirty minutes to put herself together. Sometimes her aunt Colleen Owens (lower right) helps. *Photos: Michael G. Borum*

It's a long way from a two-room shack in East Tennessee to playing for audiences that include such luminaries as Mick Jagger, Faye Dunaway, Andy Warhol and the Queen of England. Sometimes it's worth taking a moment to look back on just how far you've come—and ponder how much further you still want to go. *Photo: Nancy Barr*

THE PUBLIC MOODS OF DOLLY PARTON: "I'm made up of so many things. I'm a bit shy, believe it or not, even though I'm an outgoing person . . . But I'm capable of anything, I guess. I'm a free spirit . . . I experience in my personality some of everything. But that's good . . . I feel like a pretty wholesome person." *Photos: First three, taken in Huntsville, Ala., May '78, by Alanna Nash; fourth, Nancy Barr*

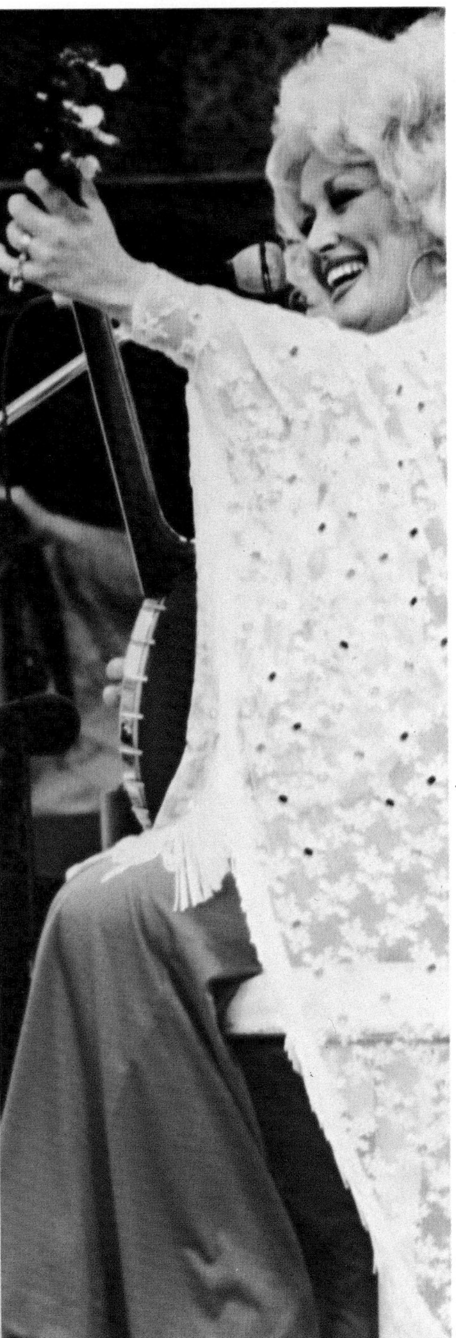

Although she has yet to become a mother, Dolly says she loves children and often dedicates songs to her young fans in the audience. In time, she may have children of her own or adopt, but for now, the lure of the spotlight and the roar of the crowd prove stronger than the mothering instinct. *Photos: Top, Nancy Barr; bottom, Alanna Nash.*

In October '75, the Grand Ole Opry called out everybody's favorite country stars for a network TV special to celebrate the Opry's fiftieth birthday. Among the stars on hand: Loretta Lynn, Roy Clark and Dolly. *Photo: Alanna Nash*

"Love Is Like a Butterfly." So was the set of Dolly's syndicated TV show, designed by Rene Lagler of Hollywood. Butterflies have fascinated Dolly since childhood ("They remind me of myself . . . They just go about their business, gentle, but determined"), and she began adopting the butterfly as her personal symbol in the early '70s. *Photo: Dennis Carney*

automatic," says a former member of her band. "I mean, she'll sit down with the guitar and the licks just come and the words fly right out of her mouth. I'm not kiddin' you. She just sits down and writes them. There's no tellin' how many she'll write once she starts—ten or twenty, maybe. And when she gets in that writing mood, forget about talkin' to her, because she's mesmerized. You ask her a question and she don't know what you're sayin', she's so into her writing." The actual writing may be automatic, but Gordon Stoker, leader of The Jordanaires, says the way Dolly comes up with ideas is purely intellectual. "Dolly's a good thinker. She thinks a lot. She's constantly trying to think of an idea for a song. While she's talking to you, she's standing there trying to think up a song. Of course, it's paid off for her, too."

I ask Dolly if it's true that's she's written as many as twenty songs in one day. She pulls herself up abruptly, as if I have bruised her dignity. "Yes, I *have!*" Then she decides I meant no harm. "I tell you, a lot of people don't believe that. They think it's a lie, even people who write. But I'll tell you something even better than that. Out of those twenty songs I wrote, fifteen of 'em have been recorded. Because when I get on a real wild streak, look out! Now it depends on the nature of the song. Up-tempo is easier for me to write, with simple words. But anyway, twenty is the most I've ever written in a setting." I ask which came out of that session. "Well, I never really tried to break it down, but there was a song—what's it called? 'Take Me Back'?—that goes 'I can still remember Momma washin' on a rub board/On the back porch while us kids played in the yard'? Yeah, that one. And let me see, let me think. Well, the song on *New Harvest* . . . , 'You Are,' came out of that batch."

"Take Me Back" and "You Are" were recorded two years apart, and yet "You Are" does not sound two years old, lending credence to Dolly's insistence that she'd always written pop songs, but she was not allowed to record them as she wanted.

"Right now I'd have to look on some of the albums for titles. I'd know 'em if I saw 'em. But I can't really judge, 'cause I haven't recorded five of 'em yet. I'm sure they'll be *recorded,*" she adds when I ask if she thinks they really will be, my tone perhaps implying that they might not all be up to quality. "I usually don't stop on a song until I'm done with it. And when I'm done with it, it's worth recordin'. . . . It just so happened that during that time, I was doin' an album, and you have a tendency— I was recordin' and Porter and me were doin' duets, so it just so happened that I recorded I guess ten of those because they were newly written and fresh on our minds. But I often write ten and twelve and fifteen, eighteen," she continues. "Sometimes I don't write but three or four." Suddenly she dissolves into giggles, catching me completely off-guard. "But I get so excited when I get inspired because I just *can't wait* to see what I come up with!" she says, reliving the experience. "Really, I *do!* I get real excited! I just think, 'I wish this was day after tomorrow, so I'd have all these on tape and know what all I can come up with.' "

Dolly, who has no technical music training, sings her songs into a tape recorder, and someone else writes the lead sheets.

"My lyrics and melodies always fall together. I just start right out with both at the same time." A common fault in country music, I say, is that oftentimes the music doesn't match the lyric. A man will sing that his wife has left him, his dog has died, his Cadillac has been repossessed, he has two weeks to live, and twenty-eight cents in his pocket—all to a wonderfully happy up-tempo and in a major key, when he's trying to arouse sympathy in the listener. Does Dolly ever have problems finding the right melody to complement her lyrics? "I have one song that I think is a terrific lyric, the title and ever'thing," she answers. "But I've got this melody—and it's good—but it's too simple for the words. It just doesn't match. And I have one song that's real up that is a real sad thing, but I guess it's just got its own sound."

"I have been to Dolly's house when she was writing and I don't think she would really know I was there," Lucy Adams says, echoing what the former band member has told me. "I wouldn't mind it because I knew what it was. When she's writing, she's living what she does. If she writes a happy song, she's happy. If she writes a sad song, that's the sad part of her."

Interesting. Dolly has often said that writing is therapy for her, "better than a psychiatrist, 'cause I'm able to put the hurtin' things into my songs and then they don't hurt me anymore. I get the world to share it." But at the same time she says she is almost never unhappy or sad, a great deal of her songs are sad in nature. "I'm not a down person," she insists. "I really have a real happy nature. I truly do. There've been times that it's been rough. *Lots* of times it was rough. But I always knew that it would smooth out. I've never got so far down I just couldn't see somethin' else. Now, I've been down, but I ain't never been out. If I didn't like the road I was walkin' on, I'd start gradin' another one. I'd try to find me a path through the woods and take a short cut. Take a detour. But that's life. If I do have a negative side, I don't know it. I just don't have a negative attitude or negative thoughts. I wake up every day just thinkin' it's gonna be a real good day. I go to sleep at night thinkin' 'Tomorrow's gonna be a good day.' I *do*. And if somethin' happens, it surprises me, usually. I love people, and I love life, and I love the joy of livin', and I love the magic of music, and I love the fact that I'm able to make music, that I'm able to create somethin' in the form of a song. Because it's like a gift I can give to people. And the only times in my life that I've ever been sad was because other people were not willing to let me be what I truly was, the person that I really am."

8. On Her Own

"I FEEL LIKE A STAR NOW," Dolly told a Los Angeles reporter in 1974, beaming proudly as the largest and most important visual sign of her independence and her growing stature in the business stood gleaming outside the concert hall. It was her own customized motor bus, done up on the outside in beige/white, with pink/purple stripe, and a butterfly on the back. "Love Is Like a Butterfly" had reached number one, and Dolly demonstrated her affection for the lovely creatures: their brightly colored wings were prominently displayed on her clothing, on the towels in her bathroom, everywhere. There would even be a butterfly wall hanging inside the bus, although, on the whole, Dolly would consider comfort and not decor the top priority for her home away from home. The layout was much the same as on any country star's coach—in the front were the driver's and two passenger seats. Directly behind that came a lounge that had a couch and a table with booth seats on either side, and a complete stereo tape system above it. Behind that was Dolly's room, with a bathroom, hot and cold water ("I can even cook in there"), and a couch that let down to become a full bed, coming all the way out to the wall, allowing her lots of room to sleep. Above it were her wig cabinets ("So here's another Dolly . . . and another one . . . and another one," she joked), and three closets along the walls held her clothes. All the stage costumes were eventually hand-washable and wrinkle-free so Dolly could rinse them out in a motel room sink and be ready to go. There were more closets on the wall across the hallway, and another at the very back, just to the side of the bathroom. In between was the sleeping section, with enough bunks for all of Dolly's very own group of musicians: The Traveling Family Band, made up of her brother Randy on bass, her cousin Dwight Puckett on drums, another cousin (by marriage) Sidney Spiva on steel guitar, and a relative only by spirit, Bill Rehrig, on lead guitar.

At twenty-eight, Dolly had seen another dream come true. "We're a close family, and I always had the idea we'd have a family show some day," she said at the time. "I was afraid at first. I didn't know how people would accept me. I'm proud I've reached the point where I could have my own show and carry it. I've had good luck so far."

They may have had good luck, but for the most part, Dolly and her Traveling Family Band got mixed reviews. "The only negative thing I would say about Dolly's show was the weakness of her band," wrote Bill Yaryan of the Los Angeles *Free Press*. "But they haven't been together all that long [three months at the time of his review], and I think the next time they make it back this way they'll be a whole lot better." John Rockwell of *The New York Times* was kind enough not to mention the group's musicianship in his review of their performance at the Felt Forum in September, just one month after Dolly headlined her first show.* A year later, he still preferred to mention the quality of Dolly's music in general, rather than of the band's specific capabilities, but he could not ignore the group's astonishingly banal, and yet somehow still winning, humor: "Both in her between-songs patter and in her musical performances, she is doing things she has done innumerable times before. The patter is often appallingly corny. But she sails into her jokes with such determined brightness that one is almost won over." "One of the rare cases when I remember anything funny happening on the stage is when Randy screwed up [a key] line," says Tom Rutledge, who joined the Traveling Family Band in 1975 as a guitarist. "I can't remember exactly what he said, but we all got so tickled we couldn't go on with the show. There was about a five-minute pause. It kinda got out of control. Dolly doesn't like it to get that way. But the feed lines in that gag had to be a certain way or the timing was thrown off. Randy would do it a little bit different about 30 percent of the time, and Dolly was always after him to do it right. This time he *really* screwed her up. He said something else, and she said something back, and it was really funny. But usually the show was all very orchestrated—the whole thing, and it is today. Really, I've tried to forget those lines. Several months ago, I was over to see Joe [McGuffee], and he'd found a cassette of the old show. I hadn't even thought of it in a year and a half, and when I heard it, it brought back disgust, it was just so bad."

As for the Traveling Family Band's musicianship, one guitarist says, "It was a joke." Rutledge says—with some hesitation—"They were a good band." About the time he joined, Bill Rehrig had taken over the band leader duties and had hired Joe McGuffee to replace Sidney Spiva on steel and Richard Dennison to play piano. None were relatives (although Dennison was to marry into the family in 1978), but bolstering the concept of the band was the addition of Dolly's sixteen-year old sister, Rachel ("a brunette Dolly," some describe her), and her brother and sister, eighteen-year-old twins Freida and Floyd, to sing harmony. Asked if the Traveling Family Band was good enough to take Dolly where she ultimately wanted to go, Rutledge stammers. "That's a difficult question," he begins. He pauses,

* With Bobby Bare and Ronnie Milsap. Dolly was billed as "The Marilyn Monroe of Country Music," Bare as "The Landlord of Rosalie's Good Eats Cafe," and Ronnie Milsap as "Mr. Country Soul."

then adds, "I doubt it. I don't doubt it—I know. She's just now getting close to where she wants to be in the business. She wants . . . a band that can play both sounds, a band she can record with, with the quality of production onstage the way she wants it. She wants the right lighting, the right material, and she wants it staged right. She's miles ahead of everybody else in the country music business, in terms of how she wants to present her show. She's aware of all the different facets of it, and she was always held back by her band, because it was just almost too country or too regimented. It was just like every other group—it was a country band. Good musicians or bad musicians, it was just a country band. She wanted a band that could do just about anything she wanted—whether it be a Billy Joel medley or 'Wildwood Flower.' She wanted it to be played and played authentically. That's Dolly. She has interest in all those fields, all that material, all different styles. And even though I was sorry to leave the band, I can see now, in retrospect, that she needed to give it up, because there's no way in the world she could be where she's at now with the old band. It just wouldn't have worked, period. I mean, leaving aside the family, it wouldn't have worked, and then she had all the tensions that come with working with a family in a business situation."

Back when she first started the Traveling Family Band, Dolly was not quite so in tune with what she wanted from a group. Mainly, she was just happy to be free from Porter. "You've gotta get rid of that band," a personal friend told her when it became apparent that a year or so on the road hadn't worked the bugs out of the family's musicianship. "Well, what's wrong with them?" Dolly asked her friend, her hands planted firmly on her hips. Little by little, she began to see and to seek the kind of group Rutledge describes. But what heavily contributed to the breakup of the Traveling Family Band was the tension that came from people who loved each other having to deal on business terms. When Matt Yancey of the Associated Press got on board the bus he saw a picture of family bliss: "Dolly Parton sits behind the booth-type breakfast table on her bus and runs her fingers through the long hair of her younger brother Randy. A little later, she and another brother tap their fingertips against each other's while a sister, a cousin and other members of the band sip on cans of cola between shows. 'It makes being on the road a whole lot easier for me than many entertainers,' she says. 'We all love each other. I can be alone when I want to but I'm never faced with being lonely.' "

Rutledge confirms: "The family has little disagreements and everything, but they are extremely close. The ties in that family are real important. The mountain folk they grew up with—your family was everything."

"We were always able to fight and scratch—growin' up," explains Stella, who was asked to join the Traveling Family Band but decided to pursue her own solo career, "but don't ever let anybody else do it to the other. Even if I've just bloodied Cassie's nose, don't you come up and say anything to her, because while her nose is bleedin', I'll knock you down! That's just how we are with each other."

"Dolly still has those feelings," Rutledge continues. "And being the kind of person she is, in an effort to keep those of us who weren't family members from feeling like we were second-class citizens, she may have treated us better in some instances. And that in turn could create hard feelings with the family. But we had an awful lot of fun, too. We'd listen to a lot of music, and we'd have picnics . . . pull off and party for a few hours. Then we'd jump back on the bus and sleep, especially on the cross-country journeys, where you've got a lot of time. Made it a lot more tolerable. Life on the road with Dolly was the best. When we were in England the first time, a lot of us hadn't been to Europe before. We got up one morning and called down to the desk. There was a message from Dolly that she'd rented a tour bus and guide to take us around London, just to show us around. And she got the bill. Now what artist would do that? She was always doing things like that. She's said the way to have the finest musicians and the way to have moral support is to take care of them. She's got that total support."

Back at home, though, things were not running as smoothly. Part of the code that binds people from Dolly's part of the country, or at least from Dolly's circumstances, dictates that whichever of the clan "makes it out" and is able to establish himself in better conditions then helps the others. That was the whole reason Dolly's brothers and sisters had come to Nashville to live with her and the reason Judy Ogle had come, too. So when Dolly got in a position to do so, she hired as many of her relatives as she could—but not out of nepotism, she makes clear. "Any job that I have open, if there are any relatives I have who are qualified to fill that job, they have first shot at it," she told me. "My sister Cassie runs my fan club; my uncles travel on the road with sales—pictures and books—and I had an uncle that drove the bus for me for a time [when she had the Traveling Family Band]. I have relatives all in my organization but only if they're qualified. Oh, there have been times I had relatives who were not qualified. That works itself out, too."

In the beginning of the Traveling Family Band days, Dolly's uncle Louis, who had run Owepar for awhile and who now sells T-shirts and souvenir books on the road, served as her manager, opening the Dolly Parton Enterprises office out in a Brentwood shopping plaza in early '75 to further emphasize Dolly's break from Porter. From all accounts, Louis was a less than satisfactory manager. Or, as one member of the band put it, "He didn't know what the hell he was doin'." Dolores Smiley says she had a lot of dealings with Louis after Dolly's split from Porter and that in the year or so he managed Dolly she became "very fond" of him, getting along well with him when they were booking Dolly. "And," she adds, "he was very helpful to me, because the split between Porter and Dolly was a nerve-wracking experience, to say the least. We worked very closely." Louis may be a fine person, the band says, but when it came to motel reservations and schedules, Louis was delinquent in his responsibilities, "sittin' around the office, not knowin' what to do." Realizing that Louis was simply incompetent to run Dolly's show, Bill Rehrig is said to have taken on the responsibilities of a road manager, in addition to playing on the show and leading the band. When he found he couldn't get information from Louis, Rehrig bypassed him and dealt directly with Dolores Smiley. On top of that, after personal problems prevented Dolly's other uncle from driving the bus safely and subsequent drivers failed to work out, Rehrig began driving the group from date to date. Dolly used him for one more function. "Dolly didn't know how to deal with the family without putting them off," says Tom Rutledge. "Instead of going to them, she would go to Bill and say, 'Bill, tell them to do this or that.' Bill would tell 'em, and they'd ignore him some of the time, partly because they didn't respect him. He was in a real bad position." The other reason they ignored him, another band member says, is because Dolly's brothers and sisters told *her* what to do, instead of the other way around. "They felt like it was just their sister, not Dolly Parton. They gave her a rough time. There was no business there. Dolly would say, 'I want to do this and that,' and if they wanted to do it, OK, but if they disagreed with her, they let her know."

The upshot of it all was that on September 29, 1975, Porter and Dolly held a joint news conference at which they announced that they had completely restructured their business organization. "Due to the diversity of their organization and the mushrooming of Dolly's career," as one trade paper put it, Don Warden was named Dolly's professional manager. Porter called Warden "the most qualified of anyone I know in the music business." Louis Owens was to "become more involved in new areas of production and publishing." News stories went on to say that Porter would continue to produce Dolly's records and to negotiate her business as well as keep up his concert schedule. But he was to take on management of Fireside Recording Studio, the studio directly behind Porter's office still owned jointly by Porter and Dolly. Porter also announced the shifting and addition of several people at Owepar, which is still under their joint ownership. At the time of the news conference, Dolly's single, "We Used To," off her *Dolly* album, was just beginning to head up the charts, at number 63 with a bullet. Her duet with Porter, "Say Forever You'll Be Mine," was number one. Porter said at the news conference that they would continue to record duets.

Behind the scenes, Dolly had realized that she was in trouble. Not only on the road but also at home, with Louis. Her enterprises office was in some financial difficulty. She was getting an average of $3,500 a night, with some $5,000 dates, and paying each musician $125 a day. With road expenses being what they were, and with her left hand not knowing what the right was up to, things just weren't shaping up the way they should. She needed help. Don Warden had been a man she'd liked and respected since she started on Porter's TV show. A fine steel player, a singer and a publisher, Warden also possessed a level head and an unfaltering sense of responsibility and know-how. Even though Warden had been with Porter for more than twenty years, acting as his road manager for a good part of them, Dolly went to Porter and asked if she could have Warden to straighten out her affairs. Gossip in the industry had it that Dolly had Porter do the actual "firing" so as not to incur blame and ruffle family feathers, and that her subsequent deal with Louis allowing him to market the official Dolly souvenirs and memorabilia was only "throwing him a bone" to soothe hurt feelings. "It killed her—I mean it hurt her so much" to have to replace any member of her organization, let alone family, says one of her Traveling Family Band musicians, adding that in the past, she had always called the departing member herself, offering him a bonus. Others say the action was in part a scheme "to deceive Porter into thinking he was in control of her affairs when in fact, he was next," as one Music Row executive observes. Apparently Dolly can be a pretty icy business woman, too."

Whether or not she's icy, Dolly is proud to say she's a good business woman. "Yeah, I am," she says, and then repeats it for emphasis. "I'm pretty well qualified in that area." I ask how she came to be so. "By bein' all the things I am, and seein' all the things I see, and doin' all the things I do. That depends on what business, but I think I know this business pretty well. I don't have to be a business person, and I don't necessarily like to be, but I really could be. In fact, I am. That's just somethin' I know."

Dolly also knew by this time how to win awards. In two years, she racked up seventeen major awards and citations for her accomplishments in country music, and 1975 alone saw her being named Top Female Vocalist by *Record World* and *Cashbox*, and Female Vocalist of the Year by *Billboard*. She also won four BMI "Country Citations of Achievement" for "I Will Always Love You," "Kentucky Gambler," "Love Is Like a Butterfly," and "Please Don't Stop Loving Me" (which she recorded with Porter). But 1975 brought an even bigger recognition—being named the Country Music Association's Female Vocalist of the Year, an award she had no doubt wanted for years and an achievement that certified to Dolly Parton that she had been right to break away, to carve out her individual niche. Did Dolly, in all those years she was overlooked, ever feel as if she should have won the CMA award then? "No, I felt like I wanted to," she says. "But I figured that when the time come for me to get it, if it was my time, then I'd get it. It was like a dream come true, but if I never receive it again, at least I got it once in my life, and that's enough if that's the way it needs to be. But I wouldn't have worked any less hard if I'd have never got it. I would have put the same pride in my music. In fact, I might have even taken more pride, because I would have thought, 'Well, they may never recognize it, but I do have something to offer. It may not be as good and as beautiful, but it is different and original.' Whether I would ever have got an award, I've been rewarded time after time. My reward is being able to know that I can look at my royalty sheets and know that it's being accepted. The award is a nice thing to have. It's something you can show your kids and your grandkids and say, 'Look what your momma and your grandmomma did. One time in my life, people thought I was really important.' That's really what the trophy is for, but your work stands on its own."

Dolly's former dealings with the CMA had not been without a little controversy. In 1974, when she was scheduled to make an appearance on the awards show, "They mentioned that I should wear less hair," Dolly told Jerry Bailey. "They said, 'Has anybody approached you with the fact that you should wear less hair?' I said, 'No, and if they do, I'll say I'll not wear less hair because if I can't be comfortable, I'm not going to be on the show. I'm not selling nothing but my talent, and I'm wearing what I please.' " That same year, a much bigger controversy erupted in the CMA—over Olivia Newton-John's nomination for Female Vocalist of the Year. Jerry Bailey asked Dolly about it before a winner was named. "I maybe shouldn't mention this, but I don't reckon it'll hurt nothing to be honest," she began. "I won't say who it was. They said, 'Have you heard any controversy about the people who've been nominated for the awards?' They said, 'All kinds of people are mad because Olivia Newton-John and Mac Davis are nominated. They said, 'Have you heard anything?' I said, 'No, I don't even know who's nominated. I know that I am because they told me at the office. And I know that Olivia Newton-John is because I heard it on the Ralph Emery Show.' I said, 'It doesn't make any difference to me because all the country people are trying to go pop and all the pop people are trying to go country. So whoever wins, I figure it's equal."

Two weeks after Newton-John won (beating out, in addition to Dolly, Tammy Wynette and Loretta Lynn), a group of about fifty established country entertainers gathered in Tammy Wynette and George Jones' living room to discuss "the future of country music." Much confusion and misunderstanding has come about as to exactly what those entertainers meant to do in forming the Association of Country Entertainers (ACE), but, at that first meeting, they were most upset about four of the CMA awards going to musicians they did not consider "country": Charlie Rich, Ronnie Milsap, Danny Davis and the Nashville Brass, and Newton-John, who was not only an Australian but who admitted she did not think of herself as a country singer! The entertainers who sat in the Wynette-Jones living room for the first meeting (and who came to be known as ACE's "charter members") decided there had to be a new definition of country music, one "that would exclude the cultural carpet-baggers coming from the field of popular music," Richard Peterson wrote. Among the charter members were none other than Porter Wagoner and Dolly Parton. When Dolly won the CMA award the following year, a lot of people thought she got it as much as an anodyne for the 1974 decision (and to appease ACE) as she did for her talent, which may explain Dolly's accepting remark, "I hope I deserve the award." But the irony was that Dolly's recent success had come from her pop-tinged singles, which she had written herself, five of which, including "I Will Always Love You" and "Love Is Like a Butterfly," had reached number one. Several journalists wondered in print how Dolly could be both for the purity of country music and record pop songs and how she could consider herself an ACE founder.

"A founder?" Dolly asks me, getting visibly uptight. "OK, I'll tell you about ACE, as far as my involvement. When they first started ACE, Tammy and George were the people who called us together. We didn't even know what it was about. I didn't. I knew it was to do with country music, but evidently they had thought this all up. And I'm sure a lot of people agreed. I'm for anything that's to better country music, so Porter and I went to the meeting. So many people were there. Then the conversation was about the awards and all, and people got so distorted about ACE. The press got so distorted, as if it were some monstrous thing. And all it was in my mind to begin with— I don't know what it is now. I've only been to three meetings since it started. I never served on anything. I'm not braggin'. I just didn't have the time. But it got so distorted in the press and on the radio stations and things, as if it was somethin' that was against anybody outside. But I don't think that's true. From what I got out of it, at the first they were just talkin' that a group of people should insist that CMA had different categories for crossover country, instead of givin' the award to somebody who didn't want to be considered country. 'Cause there are people who *do* want to be considered country and nothin' else. And from my understandin', that's what it started out to be. But then it got to be where it was just a fightin', arguin' situation. To be honest with you, if ACE is for protectin' and preservin' country music, then I am for it. And I think there is a lot of good that will come from ACE, and has come from ACE, as far as benefit shows and helpin' people that were at one time big artists that can't even get a record played now. But really, it's somethin' I'm not qualified to talk about. I'm not really sure [what it's for]. It was confusin' to me from the start. I didn't know what it was everybody was tryin' to get at. I never made one comment. I was just there as a group of people tryin' to find out what it was, what the main complaints were. I don't know, honest to goodness, what all is involved in ACE, but all I can say is this. I'm proud to be a member of ACE if it's to preserve country music. Now people can say about me what they want to, about what my music is, but if it's something that means that much, if it's somethin' that can help country music in any way, I want to be part of it. But I don't even know what they're doin' now. I've been so busy. I tried real hard to make those meetings, because I wanted to know what it was exactly they were tryin' to do."

When I ask Paul Soelberg, formerly with the organization, if ACE sees Dolly as saying one thing and doing another with her music, he replies,

"That's it exactly. It's very confusing. She has a lot of people disillusioned, on the one hand, and on the other hand defiant, and on still another hand, thoroughly confused."

The same could be said for ACE itself. While it protested the awarding of CMA prizes to several artists, it still maintains it does not condone censorship. "What Dolly is doing today with her music doesn't run contrary to what ACE is about at all, as far as I know. ACE is primarily interested in seeing to it that all varieties of country music get very heavy, very fair exposure," Soelberg says. "In addition to the other functions, such as providing health care for its member artists, it's interested in doing whatever it can to help them pursue their careers more effectively and professionally. But ACE is not trying to dictate any particular style of country music. [It] is vehemently opposed to rigidity in any kind of country format—any kind of play list on radio stations, for example, or the endless recirculation of the same records. If that recirculation happens to consist of records that some people would think of as not exactly country, then the problem becomes even more severe."

One thing ACE fights is "the hazards of the new high-pressure industry," as Richard Peterson wrote. " 'These days I sometimes have to bear in mind just how country I can be,' " Peterson quotes Roy Stingley of WJJD-Chicago as saying in 1972. " 'I have a new Porter Wagoner record maybe, and I can't play it 'cause it's *too* country.' " Peterson went on to write that "Many people continue to hold a disparaging view of ACE. For example, a knowledgeable music industry executive told me in January 1978, "They named it wrong. It should have been called the Under Fifty Thousand Record Sales Club."

From Porter: "Country music never got to where it is today because of the Charlie Riches and the Olivia Newton-Johns. It got there because of the *country* singers . . . I don't think it would be good for country music, or for pop music, to mix it all together."

I tell Dolly it occurs to me ACE might be critical of her new direction. "Well, if they are, I don't know about it, and I really can't help what they think," she answers testily. "At least I'm out doin' somethin'. I ain't sittin' around bitchin' about it."

One of the most important ways a country artist can show his fans how much he appreciates them is by appearing at Fan Fair, an annual migration of about 12,000 fans from all fifty states and at least ten foreign countries who flock to Nashville for a week of conventioning and fun. For a $30 registration fee, the fans are treated to concerts and allowed access to the fan club and record company booths set up in Nashville's Municipal Auditorium, where the stars autograph and pose for pictures with the people who have made them what they are. Thirty dollars does not seem too much to them, certainly not when it might mean getting a kiss from Freddy Fender or a hug from Jeannie C. Riley, and it is not too extravagant a price for a fantasy come true or for a memory to last a lifetime. Such as a glimpse of Dolly Parton.

Porter had always told Dolly how important it was that they mingle with the people who bought their records, that they get out and let them shake their hands and allow them to get their own personalized pictures and autographs. The stars owed the fans that, Porter thought. So in 1975, Dolly had gone all out for Fan Fair, building an elaborate fan club booth with a "Bargain Store" facade to celebrate her current album of the same name. The booth would win awards from both the Country Music Association and the International Fan Club Organization. But it was Dolly the fans had come to see. "Every year, you knew Dolly had to be there if the crowd started rushing," says Joan McGriff, Porter's secretary. But in 1975, the year of "The Bargain Store," Dolly came down with food poisoning and missed her Fan Fair appearance. "When they announced to the crowd that Dolly wouldn't be there, I don't think it would have had any more adverse effect if they'd said Dolly had just been killed," remembers LaWayne Satterfield. "It was like a black shroud had been draped over the excitement, over the whole Fan Fair congregation. It even affected the promotion people from RCA." For most at Fan Fair, then, the closest they'd get to Miss Dolly that year would be either at one of her concerts or on a turntable.

Dolly's performance on vinyl was uneven, at best, in 1975. The title cut of *The Bargain Store* is no less than extraordinary, its eerie melodic structure harking back to the old Elizabethan ballads, but the instrumentation is just upbeat enough to give it a certain excitement. The overall effect was helped out, no doubt, by the lyrics, more leading than suggestive, but questionable enough to get the record banned from several radio stations: "My life is like unto a bargain store/And I may have just what you're lookin' for/If you don't mind the fact that all the merchandise is used/But with a little mendin' it could be as good as new./The Bargain Store is open, come inside/You can easily afford the price/Love is all you need to purchase all the merchandise/And I can guarantee you'll be completely satisfied." Another strong song on the album is Dolly's "Kentucky Gambler," the story of a man who left his wife and kids in the bluegrass. Merle Haggard's "You'll Always Be Special to Me" is about the only other pearl on *The Bargain Store;* the others are more like paste. The lyrics are quite strong all the way through, but the melodies are weak.

Also issued in 1975 was *Dolly,* an album of romantic love songs, with the exception of "The Seeker," Dolly's pop-gospel talk with God: "I am a Seeker, a poor sinful creature/There is no weaker than I am/I am a Seeker and you are a teacher/You are a reacher, so reach down/Reach out and lead me and guide me and keep me/In the shelter of your care each day." Music publisher Clarence Selman analyzes this song and Dolly's writing in general: "One of Dolly's strengths is the way she can deal with a subject," he says. A songwriter has . . . just a little over two minutes to communicate . . . With 'The Seeker,' Dolly leaves no doubt in your mind as to who the seeker is and that's her. She has a way of personalizing those songs so that whatever message there is in one is made even more believable because she says it with conviction. And this is a gift. ['The Seeker'] follows every basic pattern of legitimate and good use of the words available. The meter is absolutely perfect. Then it also has an exciting tempo and melody. It's just an extremely well-written song." After "The Seeker," though, the upbeat tempo dissolves into nine of the saddest-sounding love songs on record. Even the few positive songs are encased in gloomy melodies. Most of them sound fresh off Dolly's assembly line, the product of one of her two-day writing storms, and several are almost indistinguishable from one another. One of her most uneven albums ever, *Dolly* contains both the weepy "The Love I Used to Call Mine," which would have fit in well on one of Porter and Dolly's maudlin duet albums (and featured some truly awful singing), and the bittersweet "We Used To," a lovely, poignant remembrance, a genuinely moving performance and a well-crafted song, underscored not by fiddles, but by violins! In the arrangements and instrumentation, Dolly was getting her way at last, it seemed. That was even more evident on her next album, *All I Can Do*, which came out in 1976. Or at least it was obvious in the country-pop arrangements and production, credited jointly to Porter and Dolly. But *All I Can Do* turned out to be disturbingly disappointing, with Dolly opting for form over substance. There is nothing close to "The Bargain Store" or "The Seeker" here, only shallowness in the lyrics of six of the eight Parton originals. (Of all times to include a lyrics sheet!) As for the melodies, some of them are quite catchy, but all are nearly as mindless as the lyrics. Dolly rode this one out on automatic pilot. On the title cut, she tries to make up for the song's nonexistence (two chords all the way through!) with gimmicky production techniques, having the gospel-like tune sound as if it were recorded in a barrel. That description makes Dolly laugh. "It's just the voicin'," she explains. "It's my brother and first cousin and the guy who sings in my group. I came up with this smothered kind of sound on the voices, just to muffle 'em. It wasn't through a machine, or anything. I was just tryin' to create a sound, something a little different to catch your attention. But I like that muffled kind of sound. I thought that was part of the success of it, really. I'd done everything else." Including half-talking/crying and half-singing her way through Emmylou Harris' fine "Boulder to Birmingham," which, other than its sentimental delivery, showed Dolly was on the right tract to finding her new style. And the album was not without other bright spots—the harmony in "Falling Out of Love with Me," and the skilled use of metaphor in "Shattered Image." "Shattered Image" ends up in true Dolly form: with the woman and the singer turning from defensive to defiant ("Stay out of my closet if your own's full of trash"), and going on her way. Still, *All I Can Do* was mistitled.

Just as Dolly had made concessions to Porter to win her freedom, she sacrificed a great part of her sensitivity and talent as a writer in an effort to hook a pop audience. But in 1976, the Country Music Association judged Dolly's latest efforts to be of such quality that she was again named their Female Vocalist of the Year.

Porter seemed to be doing his best to comply with Dolly's wishes now, since he saw he had indeed lost her from his organization. In 1975, he quit the road to devote all his energies to recording and to his television show. That same year, he played writer Dave Hickey ten of thirty unreleased tracks he'd recorded on Dolly. "The songs were all first-rate quality," Hickey wrote "and the production was as daring and original as production can get while still sounding country. If you released those ten songs in an album," Hickey told Porter, "you could make Dolly a pop star overnight."

Dolly's usually happy spirits were boosted sky-high at the end of '75, when it was announced that she would soon begin production on her own syndicated television show, *Dolly!* Bill Graham, of Show Biz, the TV production company responsible for the then sixteen-year run of *The Porter Wagoner Show,* handed out interviews saying the show was going to be a first-rate production, the budget for each program ranging from $85,000 to $100,000—quite high for a non-network series. Making its debut in September 1976, the show would in time feature such guests as John Hartford, Linda Ronstadt and Emmylou Harris, Anne Murray, Kenny Rogers, Jim Stafford, Karen Black, the Hues Corporation, Pure Prairie League, Ronnie Milsap, Bobby Goldsboro, K. C. and the Sunshine Band, the Staples, La Costa, Tennessee Ernie Ford, Tom T. Hall, The Fifth Dimension, Mel Tillis, Captain Kangaroo, Marilyn McCoo and Billy Davis, Jr., Anson Williams and Rod McKuen. The idea was to entertain Dolly's old following while developing a new one. Show Biz hoped guests such as Karen Black and K. C. and the Sunshine Band would help sell the show in New York, Los Angeles, and other big markets. "Just as Dolly is a country singer with appeal in both big cities and small towns, so is our program," Graham said. The set designer would be Hollywood's Rene Lagler, whose credits included *Dinah!* and *Tony Orlando and Dawn.* The show, shot at Opryland, would open each week on a shimmering butterfly perched on the "Y" of "Dolly," the camera then picking up Miss Dolly wafting down onto the set in a red velvet swing—all to the instrumental strains of "Love Is Like a Butterfly." Jo Coulter would be responsible for makeup, and Lucy Adams would handle wardrobe.

The primary look was Dolly stuffed sausage-casing tight into a bright-colored, one-piece jumpsuit, although the footage shot on remote and the sketches she did with such guests as Captain Kangaroo called for special dresses and costumes. "She had to hold her breath to get into the jumpsuits," remembers Adams. "Of course, I made a lot of the jumpsuits out of swimwear material, and it's stretchy. They really weren't as tight as they looked. They just fit her snug. But even the material that wouldn't give had to be tight. She wanted 'em to fit—nothing loose or baggy. You can imagine the zippers she popped. I even had to have a little portable machine out at Opryland. We always had to watch to make sure her clothes didn't make her look big, because everybody looks heavier on TV. Dolly would always ask, and her friend Judy was a good critic, and she'd tell her. Then I could usually come up with something that would be better."

Dolly left the actual designs up to Lucy. "She didn't give me too many guidelines. There were times when she would have to have something in particular, and she'd let me know, but I just usually worked like I wanted to for her. It was very exciting. Sometimes it was tiring, too—I just had to hurry so fast. They'd call me like Thursday and say, 'She's gonna start Monday. We need four or five things.' And they would tell me what it would be and I had to get out and get the material, cut 'em out and make 'em. Sometimes I had to go out there and fit 'em on her and maybe have thirty minutes left. I remember sometimes I couldn't even stay because I had to come home and make her up something for the next day. It rushed me, but it was fun. Sometimes I made mistakes, but they turned out to be interesting. Once I was cutting her a dress and was cutting the sleeve and cut off the material under it. So I just cut the other sleeve off and sewed it in. But anything different, she liked. She didn't have many ideas of her own. One time I got her to go shopping with me, but she said, 'I don't see anything in the material. It's just cloth to me.' She likes red, and pink, but I would say she likes to wear white above anything else. Sometimes I'd put a design of rhinestones on 'em. I got me a rhinestone machine. Those rhinestones got as expensive as diamonds. There was times I'd order two hundred or three hundred dollars' worth a week. But Dolly's as down to earth as any country person I know. I think she would have wanted to wear these things even if they didn't get her attention. Because she liked 'em, and rain on the rest of 'em if they didn't like it."

A lot of the television critics throughout the country flipped out over Dolly. "Can she be genuine, this five-foot, heavily corseted creature who dresses like a dance hall hostess and wears enough hair on her head for three? Can anyone be *that* corny?" asked Howard Rosenberg of the Louisville *Times*. "The only thing that used to be worthwhile about 'The Porter Wagoner Show,' besides taking bets on what color Wagoner's hair would be each week, was Miss Dolly . . . Tonight, for example, she girlishly sings 'Me and Little Andy' to a dog and a group of children. How could anything so maudlin be so good? . . . Never has corn been so digestible."

Although the show eventually made it into 130 markets, where it was seen by more than nine million people each week, most of Dolly's friends thought the series did Dolly a disservice. Certainly she looked foolish dancing with the Hues Corporation in a white Afro wig and singing "My Funny Valentine" to a basset hound. And she had absolutely nothing in common with some of the guests, nor could she sing some of the material well enough to do so on TV. Despite Show Biz's understandable desire to reach all audiences and to allow Dolly to display her numerous talents, it was often difficult to figure out why Dolly was made to do so many ridiculous things in front of nine million people. "I only saw one of those shows," says singer Marty Robbins. "That's the one with that Captain Kangaroo on it. I saw this guy feedin' this little monkey popcorn while she was singing 'Abba Dabba Honeymoon.' That made me so damn mad—Dolly playing second fiddle to a monkey—that I turned it off. That's not Dolly Parton."

"I didn't like the TV show at all," says Tom Rutledge, who played guitar in the house band. "The best show of the season was the one she did with Emmylou and Linda. Because it was real. They had tracks cut for 'Jambalaya' and the different songs Linda was supposed to do, but she told 'em to stick it, that she wasn't gonna use tracks. She said, 'We're gonna sing like we sing when we get together. And the band's gonna play the music live right here.' And Reggie [Dunlap, the producer] went, 'Uh, uh, uh.' And that was it. She told 'em what they were gonna do. But the reason the show came off better than any of the others is because they had something in common, and they had a mutual respect and interest in each other's music.

"Everybody workin' on the show became miserable," Rutledge continues. "It wasn't organized well, and it was time-consuming. They had a lot of technical difficulties. They wanted a more contemporary show, and that's why they chose some of the guests . . . It just wasn't very classy, and Dolly could do a classy show. I'm sure in the big league, in the center of it all in L.A., there are some producers who could put something together that would be of some quality. They could use her assets to best advantage."

"Here, again," says Jo Coulter, "they wouldn't let Dolly be herself. Innately she's a very funny person . . . all you need to do is turn a camera on Dolly and let her go. But some of the lines that were written for her were just not what Dolly would say. But she had a contract, and she had to abide by it. It started working better, but she sure put in a lot of long, hard hours on that show. Dolly needs to learn to be a little bit tougher. [There were times] when she should have said, 'No, that's it.' There were times when at 10 o'clock she needed to go home, and we would be there 'til 12. People should have had more concern for her. If you're going to work your star to death, you're not going to have a star."

Dolly thought the same thing. For months she'd been troubled by throat ailments, and doing a television show did not help any. She also knew better than anyone how *Dolly!* perpetrated the image of her as a wig and a smile. She asked to be let out of her contract. Show Biz consented but reportedly has plans to resyndicate the show in late '78.

"I think I would take more of the blame for the show not being what I wanted more than anybody," Dolly says. "It was prematurely done, and it was too time-consuming, leaving me very little time to be creative, to write.

And I was in the middle of health problems and business changes. Doin' a weekly television show is real hard. Plus, I think their idea of what would be a good television show for me was different from my idea of what would be good for me. But since they own the company and since they are the ones supposedly in the know, I didn't feel it right for me to keep bringing up what I thought. But it wasn't capturing me the way I really am. It seemed senseless to continue something like that. I just had a different idea of what I should do. It was misunderstood."

As for the guests, "I liked all of the people who were on. We became friends. But I would have had a totally different lineup of guests myself. I was so involved in so many things that I didn't have time to book guests, and a lot of the people I wanted on, they didn't seem to think would be of the right caliber for what *they* had in mind for me doing.* If we couldn't see eye to eye on who we should have on, I wasn't about to stand and argue about it. But I think the show hurt me more with what I was trying to do, as far as people understanding me crossing over in a way to where I'd have broader appeal or at least promoting it that way. What I did on television was sing songs that were totally out of my category, like 'My Funny Valentine' and 'Singin' in the Rain,' when I could have been singin' 'Lying Eyes.' I couldn't sing them songs anyway. That's just not me. That's just like a hypocrite, and I am not a hypocrite! So, yeah, it was really bad for me, that TV show. It was worse for me than it was good, because the people who didn't really know me who liked the show thought that's how I was . . . I mean, I still come through as myself, even with all the other stuff, but not really like I should. Not my real, natural way. And the people who did know me thought I was crazy. They knew that wasn't me. Including me. I didn't know that woman on TV!

"There were about three really good shows—my family show, where I had all my family on, the Milsap show, and the Emmylou-Linda show. I was especially proud of them." I ask the significance of the ending of the Emmylou-Linda show, in which the two guests were seated in the audience, and Emmylou threw popcorn to Dolly. "Aw, it was just a joke," Dolly answers. "It was somethin' we really didn't want to do. It was a production thing, and that's why we made a joke of it ourselves. We didn't want to do it that way, but like I say, you kinda have to meet halfway, because Linda and Emmylou had already refused to do it on cue cards, because we're just too good friends to try to read, and they're just not that kind. But when they were sittin' in the audience, it was funny, because Emmylou wouldn't say what she was supposed to say, and that's when she threw that popcorn at me. It was real cute. And when I said, 'The Apple Sisters—Seedy and Cory,' that wasn't part of the script, either. But lots of things in the TV show had

* One of the people Dolly personally invited on was Bob Dylan, said to be a Dolly fan. "He said he would do it later." Dolly, wide-eyed, assured Chris Chase. "Later. He don't like to do TV too much I don't think."

no significance. And that's one of the things I didn't need. I wasn't on Broadway. I just wanted to sing, to have good guests, and have a down-home-type glamour. But that's what I *didn't* get, so that's why I'm not there no more."

Nineteen-seventy-six proved to be a long, hard and harrowing year for Dolly. At the beginning of the year, she was booked into Harrah's, in Reno, and found to her chagrin that she had developed "Vegas throat"—a real and legitimate ailment common to entertainers who play the Lake Tahoe-Reno-Las Vegas circuit. "She'd been having some throat problems before this," remembers Dolores Smiley, "and they advised her not to do this date, but she wanted to do it badly enough that she took the chance and went. It was the first time she'd worked any place like that. All the years we booked Dolly, I don't guess we ever had to take her off but two or three dates, because even if she was ill, she went ahead and made the dates. And the only time we did cancel her was when she was legitimately, totally in bad shape and under extreme doctor's orders. While she was in Reno, they had to take her to some specialists for her throat, because she was having real tremendous problems. When she came back, she had a couple weeks off and then we had to reschedule a couple of dates because her throat problems didn't improve as it was. Then she went back on the road."

When she did, she encountered another problem of greater seriousness, a problem that, unfortunately, is not a stranger to many country singers, especially the women. Dolly was scheduled to play the Wheeling (W. Va.) Jamboree when WWVA, the sponsoring station, received a phone call saying Dolly would be killed if she appeared. WWVA phoned Don Warden in Nashville, and when Warden showed up at the job, Dolly knew instantly that something was wrong, since even though Warden was Dolly's manager, he never traveled with the band. "We had our stuff backstage, unpacked and ready to go," Tom Rutledge remembers. "I was next door eating, and word came down that we weren't going to play. We packed all our stuff up and put it in the bus and took off. Dolly was real upset. She couldn't go on stage thinking that someone would actually try that and maybe shoot one of us or something. It just really freaked her out." When the band played Louisville the following day, the threat came again. This time, the band went on, although Dolly had police ring the stage, and told the crowd why they were there. "It was kinda scary," Rutledge says. "Most of those things are just pranks, but you don't really know." Within days, police arrested a thirty-year old Wheeling man and charged him with the threatening calls. Not long after, Dolly was asked to star in an episode of *Starsky and Hutch,* playing a famous female singer who received similar threats. "Dolly wanted to do the role, which would have been her first TV role of any kind," says Charlene Bray. "But since she'd already had this sensationalism around her, she did not do the role. Lynn Anderson ended up doing it." Even though the incident was over and done with by the time

Dolly received the TV offer, she probably did not want to give anyone else the idea. It was not uncommon for Mr. and Mrs. Parton to answer the phone to an anonymous caller informing them that Dolly or Randy had just been killed, and, more than once, Dolly's household help had been followed home.

According to Don Roth, Dolly carries a small gun with her on the road. "It's a little princess pistol or whatever," he says, "mostly just to have in the hotel room. You know, she spends an awful lot of time by herself in hotel rooms. She's often said that she's not sure she'd even know how to use it, but she's got it. Before Gregg [Perry] came along as the ultimate protector and constant side-by-side bodyguard, confidante and companion, she and Judy spent every night of their lives in a strange hotel. And she runs around those hotels. She eats in the restaurants, she doesn't try to hide, and she goes in the bar and has a glass of white wine, or at least she always did with me. And everybody knows she's there. If some sleazy old perverted weirdo drunk decides to follow her up to her room and knock the door down, she's got the gun. I think that's why she has it—that it's more of a womanly thing than a star thing. It's just a little ol' snub-nose .22 or something. It's a toy gun as guns go, but I suppose it could kill you if it hit you in the right spot." Dolly recently told Dave Hershey of the New York *Daily News* that she carries the gun at all times and recalled that on her first trip to New York eleven years ago, she and a girl friend were followed walking out of a dirty movie by a man who mistook her for a prostitute. At first, Dolly told Hershey, she took the man's comments as flirtation, and turned around and smiled in country naiveté. When his flirtation turned to harrassment, Dolly calmly informed him that she carried a gun and would have to pull it out if he didn't leave her alone.

Dolly wasn't one for trouble of *any* kind. Especially not in her organization. "I just *can't* have trouble," she told a reporter for *Country Song Roundup* not long after she put together the Traveling Family Band. "My work is very important to me, and it is to them, too. I don't have them working for me just because they're my family, but because they are qualified as well. I feel like these boys in my band are as good as you can find. In fact, I went to listen to them play before I asked them to work for me. If the time ever came that personal family problems would affect my work and my business then I would just have to get another band."

The time had come. By now, Dolly had caught on that the Traveling Family Band was not traveling in the direction she thought it would; she realized that country music was booming all over the nation, and she, in relation, was not. She may have been grossing $600,000 a year, but night after night (120 dates a year by two estimates, 250 by another) she found herself screaming over bad public address systems in high school gymnasiums, not only wounding her pride, but injuring her vocal cords. If she was going to run herself into the ground, she was at least going to put her energy into reaching as many people as she could. And that took some planning. Looking back on just how Dolly achieved her goal, Charlene Bray says, "She pulled off quite a thing here. It was quite a tactical maneuver for her to keep as many people loyal to her as she did through the change."

On May 28, a story appeared in the *Tennessean* saying Dolly had canceled all her appearances from late June until October (with the exception of Fan Fair), as ordered by her physician. "It's mostly a case of overwork," Don Warden told the paper. "It's nothing serious, but as I understand it, if she continued her schedule like it was planned, it could become serious." The news came during Dolores Smiley's last week at Top Billing. "When Don called, naturally I took several aspirin and pulled all my records," she recalls with a wry smile. The dates were worth $350,000 by one estimate (probably high). "When she had gone back on the road, she was told, 'It's not so bad to sing, but don't talk,' " Smiley says. "Well, Dolly is a talker. She'll talk to the wall, you know. She is most friendly and would meet anybody or do anybody's interview. But instead of doing what they told her, going out and keeping her mouth shut after doing her shows, she did just the opposite, because she didn't want her public to think she was not what they thought she was. So she really had bad throat problems." Charlene Bray corroborates: "She was indeed under a lot of strain and having a lot of voice problems, because she's got that high, high voice anyway." (For relaxation, Dolly went on a second honeymoon with Carl to Yellowstone National Park, and then took all her nieces and nephews to Disney World.)

But not all that strain was on Dolly's vocal cords. She knew she was stuck with a mediocre band, she was working herself to death, and she wasn't realizing as much money from it as she should. And people with half her talent were making more headway in country music than she was. It was time for a change. A *big* change. The kind of change Fred Foster had talked about years ago and still every time she spoke with him on the phone. She could see every dream she'd ever had come true. And then some. But she would have to change everything. Totally. She needed some time off to think about it and implement the changes.

In June, she called the Traveling Family Band together for a meeting. She told them she was sick and had to disband the group, and would probably regroup in six months, however long it took for her to get her business and health straight, one of the members recalls. "Really, what it was," he says, "she wasn't gettin' nowhere. She'd been workin' for two years now since she left Porter and didn't get nowhere. Absolutely nowhere." Dolly says the family took it well. "I'm real, real close to my family, and we're all very close, just like you saw for yourself," Dolly tells me, referring to my introduction to Rachel and a scene I had just witnessed in which Stella brought her big sister a ring in the shape of a duck for her birthday. (Dolly squealed and cackled in childlike delight. Her housekeeper ran in and fussed around Dolly as if she were a mother hen. "I heard you cacklin' and came to gather the eggs," the housekeeper said, lifting the hem of Dolly's overblouse as if it were tail feathers.)

"We were all anxious to try not travelin' on the road together," she explains with a small sigh. "We would have preferred to be family, and they were all talented writers and singers and some desired to have a group on their own, to record on their own, which was makin' it hard for all of us. It wasn't fair for me to just keep them tied up in a group when I didn't have time to do any more than just my work, or to expect somebody to just play for me when they had talent of their own. We certainly parted on good terms. In fact, we just decided that it was best. Because they all saw what I was doin' to myself, tryin' to work every place and do everything that everybody wanted me to do. And it was hard for them to see me work like that. It was hard for me to make *them* work like that. So there was so much personal love that we were all glad. We were glad we got to do it, and we were glad when we decided it would be best if we didn't."

Meanwhile, the cancellation of dates started a flood of rumors "Dolly has cancer." "Dolly's silicone has gone haywire and she's rotting away inside." "Dolly's had a nervous breakdown." "Our biggest problem is the rumor that she's just got a little while left on this mortal plain and wants to spend it in private," Don Warden told reporters. "I've never been in the hospital for exhaustion, and I don't ever intend to be, because it's just about time for me to say 'whoa.' You can only do so much, and then you're a fool if you do more," Dolly told the *Tennessean*.

But Dolly actually had a whole lot more to do. There were a few trips to make out of state, a few people to talk with. Some of them were at RCA in New York. "I love to be with RCA," Dolly said in 1975 in an interview with Sally Duncan. "I have worked with different labels and I have been a very lucky person. I've worked with good people. I know there are so many bad people. Especially in a big business like the music business, but I've been lucky enough that all the people I've worked with have been good to me and I've been good to them. They are behind me all the way and that's great. Everybody I know there is for me 100 percent, and I am for RCA. So I am very happy there, too. If you're happy, it doesn't kill your creativity." When Dolly got off the plane from New York, she had their full support to embark on a crossover career, one that would cost a rumored $3 million in promotion and publicity (one estimate has it at only half a million), one that would change her image and make her palatable to the hip young audiences but not endanger her standing with the country constituency. Sort of Country Girl Goes Uptown. And there was one other request. Porter Wagoner was not to have another thing to do with her records. She wanted to produce them herself. RCA would have to make good his contract. She told him that June, fearing the worst and dreading the day, grateful Don Warden was in the next room. Porter was said to be in too much shock to think about retaliation. He didn't talk to reporters about it for a long time, and still doesn't much today. One of the interviews went to John Morthland.

"It's hard, in fact it's very difficult for me to tell the story exactly how it happened without injuring Dolly's career," Wagoner begins, explaining why he's stayed silent so long. "I don't ever wanna do that, or have people think I'm saying something because I am bitter or because I am jealous, or anything about her move. It's difficult for me to tell the thing exactly the way it was without injuring that part of her story. First of all, you know I would want the bigger and better things for a person I had worked seven years of my life for, given the bigger part of my energy toward her career rather than my own. You know I would want the biggest and best things for her. It was the way the move was done, the manner in which it was done that was so wrong. Because at each meeting that we would have with RCA, or with the record execs who were talking about directing Dolly's career more toward the pop market, I never failed to mention at any time that if the production of her records was short in any way, I would be happy to work with or step aside and let anyone else get involved who they thought was better qualified. And even with this happening, the entire move was done behind my back and with her and RCA. And that's a very discolorful way to do a person, regardless of who they are ... So that's the reason I haven't told the story the way it is, because it's not a colorful thing. But it is exactly the way it happened. It's something I wouldn't do to anyone. I would rather say nothing more about it ... I was just surprised, to say the least."

Porter did manage to continue talking about it. "I worked the road a little more than a year after that. But the schedule was so heavy, in having to put time in on her records and our duet records, that I decided to quit the road. Had I not been producing Dolly Parton's records and the duet records, I would not have quit the road, 'cause my schedule would have been loose enough that I coulda done the things they wanted to do. That's the reason I felt that it was such an underhanded thing to do. After I had made this concession, had given her a man who had worked for me twenty-three years as her manager—because she wanted him and because I felt like it would be best for her to have a man like that handling her business—and after doing all this in good faith, because she wanted me to spend a lot more time as an adviser in her career and producing her records— Well, after I had quit the road to do this, to make this possible, and then things happening like they did. You can see the appreciation shown, you can see the loyalty shown, you can see exactly what I'm talking about. That's why I say it's really a discolorful picture if it's brought out exactly the way it happened.... She went to New York without me knowing it to discuss about her getting 'free,' so to speak, getting her ... whatever it was that she wanted. Naturally, RCA would talk with her, because I felt they were sort of happy to see the thing happen. Because at that time, I represented three of their top acts, which was Dolly, Dolly and Porter, and Porter Wagoner. I could go in and get things done that Dolly Parton couldn't do, or Porter Wagoner couldn't do. But with the combination of those three acts that I represented, they did pretty much the route that we decided to go. So by them making this other arrangement, it sorta split the soldiers up.

"I don't know why she did it," he continues. "And that's the thing. I can't understand why a person with any kind of background and any kind of soul would be afraid to tell a person that. Because I feel that's something I should know, why it happened. And until now, I don't know. It's a heavy thing for you to have that much of your life wrapped up in a certain area and spend as much time and as much energy in the production of records, then all of a sudden see it crumble and not know why. The thing that kept me from being in the nuthouse is the fact that number one is not bad, and they were all number ones up to that time. Had it not been for that, I would have been in serious trouble. With myself. Because it did an awful lot to my confidence in people, [to have someone] tell you one thing and be thinking something else. Because I was born and raised in a family where your word is your bond, because if I tell you something is a certain way, you can bet your life it'll be that way. It's hard for a person who has that kind of upbringing to guard against anything else. So I was off guard completely from the thing. There was no way I could have been on guard, because I was not born and reared that way and never had done business with anyone that way. Because what I have done for Dolly Parton's career, I don't want a lifetime of thank yous for; I don't want a lifetime of money. I need none of that. But for chrissakes, why couldn't you be a friend to someone that has given you six or seven years of their life's energy to try to build a career on, to launch on? That's why I find it very difficult to feel in my heart, 'Boy isn't she a wonderful girl?' "

Porter was no less candid in an interview with Mike Kosser of *Country Style*. "I put a lot of energy into making her records great, and my own records suffered. In 1975, I spent 568 hours in RCA studios, and 95 percent of the time was on Dolly's records or the duets . . . Believe me, I wish her well [but] if she's number one for ten years she won't be happy . . . All of this changeover came to me secondhand," Porter insisted. Kosser wrote that Porter told him he was informed of the change of producers not by Dolly, but by RCA. Charlene Bray says the same thing.

But two of Dolly's friends say that isn't so. "No, that was the hardest part," says Tom Rutledge. "She had to go and face Porter and tell him, 'I don't want you producing my records anymore. I want to do it myself. I want to totally divide our careers.' *That* was hard. Of course, she'd given concessions to him. She'd have given Porter anything if she could have divided it all sooner. She would have given him Owepar and the studio if it would have made things easier." Dolly did not give Porter her share of the studio and the publishing company, but she never visits either, some say out of fear of running into Porter. "She doesn't come to Owepar because she really doesn't have any reason to," says Owepar's general manager, Carla Scarborough. "We talk to her on the phone some, not too much. We don't really need to, unless there's something that we need, like a tape, or information on what she's done with a song, or whether she wants us to pitch it or to hold it. She's awfully busy."

Dolly and Porter haven't spoken in two years, it's said. But she read Porter's comments in *Country Style.* "It just broke my heart what he said about me, that he didn't know why I left him, which is not the truth," Dolly told another reporter for the magazine. "Me and Porter fought all the time. We've fought for years. I tried to tell him what I was trying to do. I tried to tell him my dreams and plans, but it was too touchy a thing. I had to go because we couldn't share it together because he wouldn't accept it. The article made me look like I had done a bad, vicious thing. It was as if he was trying to make me look bad and him good. He's no better than me. I think we're pretty equal. I don't want this to sound vicious if you can print it right. That was an embarrassing article to me. Very touchy because he had . . . When he said he had worked in the studio for all those hours, it was what he *chose* to do. He got paid as my producer. I'd like to think I was not so bad, the way I sounded, like he had to spend all his life trying to make me sound good enough to sell. I appreciate the things he's done for me. I have my own kind of respect and admiration for him. But he knows better than to make it sound like I just left, that he didn't know why. My dreams were so big that they were turning into nightmares because I didn't have anyone to help me carry them out."

Nashville is divided in its reaction to Dolly's dumping Porter as her producer. "That was really like the final blow for Porter, I think," says Joan Dew. "Because the way she got partly away from him was by more or less promising him that he would still be producing her and they would still be doing records together. Well, the minute she got away from him, she quit doing records with him, and the next step was he was no longer producing her, either." Dolores Smiley has a different view. "All that went on for a long time before the final break, and there were a lot of ill feelings during the period of time, and then they would be smoothed over. I can honestly say for Dolly that she went the extra mile for a long time to try to make it as congenial as possible, and I know she could have broken out on her own a lot sooner, but she felt she owed Porter and she respected him and really made more of an effort than was called for. She did appreciate all Porter had done for her, and when Porter finally decided that he was ready to quit anyway, it all began to get real bad in the breakup thing."

Now that Dolly had gotten two of the main stumbling blocks out of the way, it was time to find someone who dreamed as big as she did, someone with the know-how and the contacts to make her a first-rate star. She needed big-time management. And she found it. On July 31, a story ran in the Nashville *Banner* announcing that Dolly had signed a personal management contract with the Los Angeles firm of Katz-Gallin-Cleary, an agency with such clients as Cher, the Osmonds, Paul Lynde, Mac Davis, Tony Orlando and Dawn, and, ironically, Olivia Newton-John, the biggest burr under ACE's saddle. "What we are going to do," the paper quoted Sandy Gallin as saying, "is to supervise Dolly's career. And that includes all phases—TV and personal appearances, recording, etcetera. We think she is the best writer in the business and that she is going to be a huge superstar. Contrary to rumors, we do not plan to change Dolly's image."

Not one person in Nashville believed that. But some thought she had done a smart thing. Others were undecided and still others were appalled. To them, Dolly had a lot of explaining to do. Seeking management outside of Music City was heresy. "I shopped around," Dolly says. "I needed really professional people. I talked to a number of management agencies, a number of individual people who had reputations for being great managers. Then I talked to Sandy Gallin of Katz-Gallin-Cleary. You know who all they handle. But it wasn't who they had that impressed me; it was why they had 'em, which I can certainly understand after talkin' to 'em just a little while. I just asked 'em,' OK, tell me what you can do for me.' I didn't say, 'Here's what I want you to do.' I wanted to know what they could do, and they told me. And it was just right there on the line—what I felt like all my life should be. And I thought, 'My Lord, this is just too good to be real!'

"It was Mac Davis, really, who was responsible for me goin' to them when I did, because I happened to see Mac the day I totally stopped everything and decided I was gonna totally change everything. I was goin' to L.A. to look for management, or I was goin' everywhere I needed to go. But he told me how great they were, how happy he was with 'em, and he thought I should talk to them. There were several people like that. I found out later that Mike Post—a wonderful man—had been tellin' Sandy Gallin they should try to manage me, that he just believed that I could really do all these outrageous things, which I hope someday I can live up to, but whether I do or not, it's just great to have people believe that much in you." I ask if Mac Davis is a good example of the sort of crossover career Dolly wants. "Well, I think Mac's great. I think he's a great writer and singer, but it's still totally different, what I'm doin'. I'm not tryin' to fool myself into thinkin' I can be somethin' I can't be. I'm just sayin' mine goes in a different way than that. I don't compare what I'm tryin' to do with Mac, or anybody." I ask what specifically Katz-Gallin-Cleary can do for Dolly that no one in Nashville could. "Well, there are no management people here," she answers. "Well, that's not true, I guess, but I don't know of any management companies where— You see, they [Katz-Gallin-Cleary] can do pretty much what they want to do. They have been in business for years. They have all the connections with all the things you think you need to do. Like with network television. And they have connections with movie people, producers." But perhaps Dolly's comment to *Country Style* sums it up best: "They make me look important because they make me *feel* important," she said of her management firm. "I have a need to be important. Now I'm happier than I have ever been."

"Oh, they know what they're doin'," says David Skepner, the man who made Loretta Lynn into a household word, and who comes from Beverly Hills with a background of rock and pop with Music Corporation of America. "They're no pushovers. Sandy has a great track record. Mac swears by him." I ask what tack he thinks they'll use in guiding her career. "Very simple," he answers. "There's no tack. They're gonna make her a star. I think she made a very good move."

"What Dolly says is right—there probably wasn't anyone in Nashville who could help her do what she wanted to do," says Marty Robbins. "People in Nashville don't have the contacts the people on the West Coast or in New York have. And the contacts she needed are the contacts she didn't have. It's been proven. She's gettin' all the television exposure she needs, and that's what it takes. A lot of television. And evidently, they couldn't do it in Nashville. Now she's working with people who are probably gonna make RCA put out her records. And that's what you have to have. You have to be working for somebody who's gonna work for YOU. And the group of people she's with aren't in it for 10 percent. I don't know what percentage they're getting, but it's definitely a lot more than 10 percent. Of everything she makes."

One of the first things the new management helped Dolly do was put together a new band, Gypsy Fever. "I made the name up myself," Dolly says. "I just always was fascinated with gypsies—people who travel around with no roots, love to travel, love music. Most of 'em do, you know, the fables you hear about gypsies. Plus, I just thought it would be a nice idea if I wanted to get into costume things, it would be like a gimmick, to dress the band and myself as gypsies. . . .have things that suggest that, like the jagged skirts and the bandanas. I always wore the jewelry. I always sorta looked that way, anyway. But the name just had a lot of possibilities for a lot of things. It just came to me as a good thing; it just sounded like a good-ringin' thing, a good name for travelin' rogues. Gypsy Fever sounds like a good group name.

"I have this idea in mind to have a self-contained group, because a lot of the people in it are so talented. I want to record them as a group, put out singles, have different things featured. We're gonna be producin' a lot of things together, where they'll be a star on their own, and eventually, in a few months or so, they can go out and have enough of a name to where they can put on a show and do thirty minutes or so before I come out. That's what I'd really like to see happen. I'd like to see us all be involved in the production, in the publishing, and where everybody really has a chance to do something more than just make money as a sideman. Because I have no sidemen in my group. They're all terrific musicians to me, and they're all terrific friends. We just do a different thing, but in my mind, they're equally important to me."

Dolly culled the band members from different places. "From Atlanta, Milwaukee, and New York, from Indiana, Louisiana—from everyplace, really. A couple of them worked in a studio in Chicago for years doin' jingles. There are eight in the group, and the number will remain the same for awhile. I'm lookin' for a bass and drums now. Later I'm gonna add fiddle and banjo. Ten people is what I'd really like to have, and myself, so I can have some of everything. So I can do the country and do it really well, and do the bluegrass and do it really well, and to have people who can double on other things and do that really well—flattops, acoustics when I want to do the folk things, and then also where they can play rock things and play in the studio when we record our own albums. They're really terrific people, very, very talented."

Rock? And no more using Nashville's studio musicians on her sessions? Unspeakable, to a good number of people in town. They'd heard that she had gathered some of the oldest, most established names in country to sing on one of her tunes, "Applejack"—Roy Acuff, Kitty Wells, Chet Atkins, Minnie Pearl, Ernest Tubb, Grandpa Jones, Ramona Jones, Carl and Pearl Butler, Wilma Lee and Stoney Cooper, the Willis Brothers, Bashful Brother Oswald, Joe and Rose Lee Maphis, Kirk McGee, Hubert Gregory and the Fruit Jar Drinkers, and Johnny Wright, plus Don Warden and Mr. and Mrs. Lee Parton. But some Nashvillians were beginning to wonder if part of the reason for that wasn't to offset the hostility that was beginning to grow over Dolly's choice of outside management and her fondness for rock. It was looking as if Dolly didn't think Nashville was good enough for her, they thought. And some of them had the audacity to wonder aloud if Dolly had really been sick when she canceled all those dates, or if she had faked it to get out of playing traditional country venues.

According to Charlene Bray, Katz-Gallin-Cleary may have tried to get Dolly out of some of those dates by various means, the most important being the rider on her contract. "I remember when the rider first came down to Top Billing, it was just tremendous," she says. "I would say anywhere from twelve to fifteen stipulations about things that she either could or could not do, or things that had to be provided before she would do the date. And this was such a departure from the Dolly that we knew and loved to work with ... It was a rider that most of the country music promoters just could not live with. We felt it was a direct result of Katz-Gallin-Cleary. Strictly a management decision."

"That's not true," Dolly says with anger in her voice, when I mention faked illness. "And that's really not fair. I take great pride in my work. In fact, that's why I screwed up my voice to begin with. Because I worked under every condition to try to *not* cancel, because I had been through that before. A big part of it was workin' under poor conditions, just over-doin' it, and then a lot of emotional strain, tryin' to change things around. I really think that was as much it as anything. I had nodes on my vocal cords. But I have a great responsibility to the public, and I just will not cancel unless I have to. Never have I canceled a show just because I didn't want to go or didn't feel good. When I canceled because of my throat, it was when the doctor said, 'If you sing, and if you strain against the nodes, it'll do permanent damage.' But it just didn't make sense for me to continue under the conditions I was workin' under. My throat couldn't improve like that. So I just finally went to the doctor and said, 'I don't believe I can go any farther.' And he said, 'You can't if you're ever gonna go again, if you continue this.' You know, it's a frightening thing. That's how I make my living. So I canceled all summer. Had to. During that time I was off, I was makin' preparations to change my organization, because I had to let my musicians go, anyway. I couldn't keep 'em on the payroll. I didn't know when I was goin' back to work. It all depended on my throat and what I decided to do about my new plans and all. So I was off all summer and got organized, got a new group, new management, the works."

It was also said there was another reason that Dolly got rid of the Traveling Family Band. "I've heard a lot of people say that what happened to Dolly is that she got rid of all those country pickers and just sat around on the bus listening to these rock cats until she acquired a feeling for it, and then went after a rock career," says one music the executive. "I've been told that's why she fired her band and all of the country people that were around her. She felt they were beneath her. It makes sense she fired the family because she didn't want them around. They're the people who had special privileges with her, whereas the new faces wouldn't have known her when. And the places she wanted to go, she didn't want anybody who knew her when. Because they could reveal her climb. The new image she's creating for herself wouldn't hold up with somebody saying, 'That's phony. That's untrue.' "

"That's one thing I'm touchy about—that my family was fired," Dolly told *Country Style*. "That hurt me and that's embarrassing to my family. It was difficult to tell them that they were not doing the kind of job I needed. I knew I had to do it and it tore my heart out." She explained more fully in an interview with *Record Mirror:* The move toward rock ". . . was something I'd wanted to do for years, but I wasn't in a position to. I wanted to do country but also heavier things. I don't necessarily want to be a rock and roll star, but I want to be able to go into any market, to express myself totally. The toughest part of all, when you've decided what you want to do, is to tell people. Even though you love them dearly, having to tell them for no reason that it just doesn't fit in with what you have in mind is difficult. It was very hard emotionally. But I've always suffered pain for my music—and my music stops me suffering pain. My family was very understanding. I don't want you to write there was any problem with them . . . You don't want to see your family have to go through all the pain of being on the road because it's something you want to do. You don't like to see your own blood being battered around." Or, as she told Cynthia Heimel of the *Soho Weekly,* "It was a heartache and a headache and the most emotional strain I ever been under in my life to say to the people I'd been with for years and years, 'I can't use you anymore. I'm gonna make changes, do this and that.'. . . It just broke my heart; every time I'd do it, I just cried like a baby. They understood, as much as anybody *could.* I'm sure they didn't know for sure if I knew what I was doin', but I did. I got through it. It's the best move I ever made."

One person who couldn't quite understand was Bill Rehrig, whom Don Warden had often called Dolly's greatest find. When Dolly signed on with Katz-Gallin-Cleary, she told Rehrig she would hire him as her road manager. Dolly told him to find work for the summer and they'd get back together in the fall. In September, Dolly called Rehrig to a meeting of her Los Angeles management, where he was offered a good salary and complimented on his work in the past. When Rehrig accepted, Dolly informed him he was in charge of Nashville operations. After two months and two weeks, Rehrig was fired. No explanation was given. Dolly didn't phone or write Rehrig to express her regrets, although he had often volunteered to make the hatchet call in the past when Dolly let someone go but Dolly always refused, making the call herself. Dan Cleary made the call this time, explaining that Dolly didn't have the heart to call because she felt he was one of her family. Instead of the usual bonus any departing band member got, Rehrig received a regular two weeks' pay. "Dolly has to have the right-looking guy with the right personality now," says one former band member. "I don't know if that was it or not, but one thing led to another and Bill was just let go. He never knew why."

The fall brought further cancellations and dismissals. "Keeping a band on a payroll, you've gotta work," Dolly explains. "And I had to finish out the year of things I hadn't canceled. I still had the throat problems, but I was gonna try. I started back the first of October. I lasted for a week and a half, and then my throat just absolutely gave out. This was before the new management was in effect—it didn't start until the first of the year—and I still didn't have better sound to where I could hear myself in the monitors and not have to ruin my throat under a poor sound system."

What gave rise to some doubt about Dolly's throat was the fact that she was seen out at Opryland in production precisely at the time she was supposed to be so ill. "I was told by an unofficial representative that she was sick," says Dolores Smiley. "I can't say anything truthfully beyond that. But I do know that after I left Top Billing I went to work for Opryland Productions on a show called *Music Hall America,* and I was at Opryland a great deal. One particular day it was very, very cold. We were working inside, and when the crews came in from outdoors, they said they'd been filming all day on Dolly's television show. The guys were just freezing. And I said, 'Well, surely Dolly wasn't out there.' And they said, 'Oh, yeah, she was out there all day.' So, it's common knowledge—everybody knows that she went ahead and did her television show at the time she was supposed to be unable to work because of throat problems. Now she *did* legitimately have throat problems. But she was also doing the TV thing." After Dolly announced she would no longer do the show, some people speculated there was a reason behind it other than exhaustion and dissatisfaction with the scripts. "I don't think she voluntarily gave it up except that she knew there was so much more money to be made out of rock concerts, and she had already been polishing apples with people like Emmylou Harris and Linda Ronstadt," says a record company executive, "and I would imagine they had advised her and encouraged her to stop doing a syndicated TV show when she could do network guest shots and that kind of thing. There was a tremendous amount of business involved in it, I'm sure."

"I was trying to put up with [everything] emotionally, and tryin' to do an album, and I was still doin' the television show," Dolly explains. "It was just more than I could take." In November, the wire services carried a story that Dolly's doctor had ordered her not to sing for the rest of the year and that she would have to severely limit her talking for a few weeks. Dolly canceled twenty-five concerts. In March of 1978, Abe Hamza, president of Packaged Country Music, Inc., one of the leading promoters of country music, sued Dolly for $375,000 for breach of contract. Hamza claimed that Dolly gave two-days' notice before canceling her fall '76 tour, on which he had booked thirteen (or sixteen) concerts, and that she "never made an attempt to make up the dates." The suit was submitted to arbitration.

Dolly's bookings were to make the news for another reason late in '76. In December, it was announced she was leaving Top Billing, Inc., a company Porter had originally formed with Bill Graham, but which was now owned by Tandy Rice. Dolly had broken with the company once before, shortly after she left Porter, but returned to Top Billing after a short stint with Bob Eubanks in California. Her new booking agent was Monterey Peninsula, of Carmel, California. A small firm, Monterey Peninsula came to Dolly's attention through her new friend, Emmylou, who was one of its mostly-rock clients. "Well, in a roundabout way, yeah," Dolly says. "Really it was through Bob Hunka. He works for Happysack Productions, which is their company. I don't know if Emmylou was involved in that or not. Bob really helped me with good advice on things I should do and shouldn't do in certain areas, things like what I needed as far as sound and certain songs he thought would be good for me to include in my show, in addition to my own. He believes in me, and that means a lot." (Dolly was to remain at Monterey Peninsula for about a year before leaving to go with International

Creative Management—ICM—a huge entertainment booking agency. One reason for the break is said to be because Monterey Peninsula has no fair outlet, and fair dates can mean as much as $50,000 to an artist.) When Dolly first went with the Carmel firm, she said she was "possibly" going to tour with the Eagles and would do a tour with Emmylou and Linda Ronstadt "for sure," adding she had planned to do a March 1977 tour with Harris, but canceled when some of the dates conflicted with her bookings with Mac Davis. "We've talked often about doing a concert—the three of us—doin' a tour to see what kind of reaction there would be," she said. Asked if Monterey Peninsula planned to change Dolly's image to that of a country-rock or pop-country performer, owner Dan Weiner replied, "Definitely not. What we are going to do is book Dolly in places where audiences know her—from recordings and TV appearances—but haven't seen her in person. For instance, her first concert tour is at college campuses in Texas."

Charlene Bray, still with Top Billing at the time Dolly left, remembers how the parting came about. "Any booking agent hates to loose a major artist. It hurts; it really does. Not only in income from the artist's percentage of bookings, but prestige-wise. It hurts your relationship with other artists that you're negotiating with to come to the agency. They always wonder why an artist leaves. But Tandy is a genuinely nice fella, and he wished Dolly well when she left. We tried to tell him we saw the handwriting on the wall and knew she was going to make a terrific change. I had been talking with a PR outfit on the West Coast and they said, 'Hey, what gives? I saw Dolly in our building on Sunset Boulevard and Katz-Gallin-Cleary is in our building, and she was getting on the elevator going up. And she wouldn't be talking with them if they were not talking about a management role in her career.' And we tried to tell Tandy this, and he sort of shrugged it off, as if, 'No word has come down the pike to me from Dolly or Don Warden, so I've got nothing to say until they tell me she is indeed leaving.' And they had put the quietus on me not to book any more interviews or do anything else for her, so I knew by that she was leaving. And Tandy kept talking with Don Warden about these offers that were coming in on important dates, and he would say, 'I really can't make any decisions on this for X number of reasons.' And Tandy said to Don, 'Well, is Dolly gonna call me? Don't do anything and let me be the last to know.' And Don said, 'You'll be informed. I don't know. We'll call you. As soon as I know something, I'll tell you.' And finally, one afternoon, Dolly called Tandy and talked to him herself, and I think even then, she was at the airport somewhere, and the deal was already made. But the bargain had to be sealed before she told Tandy and before the Nashville music community knew about it. Once you make up your mind, you can't have people second-guess you. So that's why I say she just made her decision and held fast to it, and then she called Tandy and talked with him, and I think she was crying when she told him. Tandy loves her and completely supports her in what she did." (Dolly chose to leave Top Billing's public relations division, also, going with Solters and Roskin, of Los Angeles and New York.) "Naturally," Rice told the Nashville *Banner*, "we didn't want Dolly to leave us. She has been with the agency since it was formed in April 1968. We had no signed contract with her—only a verbal agreement. Yet," Rice continued, "these things happen in our business. I sincerely wish Dolly the best. She's a super performer."

Not everyone in Nashville was so charitable in their reaction to Dolly's choice of L.A. management and booking agent and "foreign" pickers. It seemed to some that she was not only going Hollywood and going pop, but she was turning her back on the people who had made her what she was. "I haven't turned my back on Nashville," Dolly told me. "I wouldn't move to L.A. You couldn't *give* me that place. But it just so happens that that's where the best management I could find happened to be located. If Katz-Gallin-Cleary had been in Nashville, I am sure I would still have wound up with them. I just had big plans and I just had big dreams . . . Every country girl wants to go to the city, and every city girl wants to go to the country. But a person who is free to go where they please can go to the country and the city and can come and go as they please. And that's exactly what I'm doin'. I love my home in Nashville. I love the people here. I would never leave here—never. And I still do business here. [Owepar is her only Nashville office.] I do interviews here. But, well, like I say, I can't preach it. I have tried too hard. I'm just gonna have to let my work stand on its own. . . . I just thought, 'Well, I'm thirty years old now. I have held these dreams and plans in my mind for thirty years. I have seen a good many of my dreams come true and I have, because of some people, seen a lot of my dreams turn into nightmares.' But I knew that was nobody's fault but my own for allowing that to happen. So, I thought, 'If you really want to do these things that you believe you can do, you are gonna have to make preparations for it. You're gonna be ridiculed, or condemned, or whatever. But if that's what you really want, then nobody's gonna live for you. You gotta walk that lonesome valley by yourself.' "

Back in 1970, Dolly recorded a song she and Louis Owens wrote called "When Possession Gets Too Strong": "If you try to control me/Then you won't ever know me . . ./So if you want to love me/You just understand all of me."

A lot had changed since she conceived that song. She had meant it then, and she still meant it now. But she had broken all the chains that bound her, and for the first time in her life, she was free to be all she could be. It was a glorious feeling.

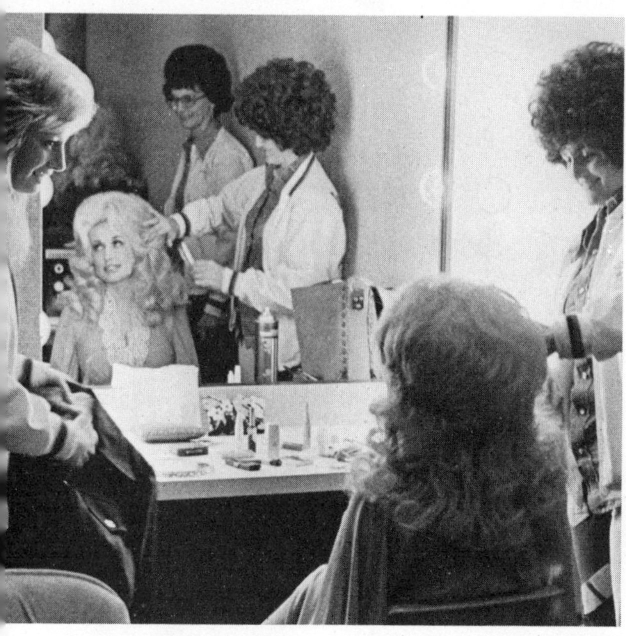

Above left, backstage at Dolly's TV show: secretary Judy Ogle, Dolly, hairdresser Colleen Owens. Wardrobe mistress Lucy Adams appears next to Colleen in the mirror. (MICHAEL G. BORUM) Left, "When they had Dolly playing second fiddle to a monkey, that made me so damn mad I turned it off. That's not Dolly." —Marty Robbins. (SHOW-BIZ) Below, poet Rod McKuen makes a guest appearance on *Dolly!* (MICHAEL G. BORUM)

Dolly dons a white afro and boogies with the Hues Corporation. (SHOW-BIZ)

The Queens of Country Music: Lynn Anderson, Dolly, Loretta Lynn, Dottie West and Tammy Wynette. (ALAN WHITMAN)

Left, Dolly's last appearance at Nashville's Fan Fair, June 1976. (DAN LOFTIN/THE TENNESSEAN) Right, and below, Dolly in Soundshop, Nashville recording studio, putting down tracks for *New Harvest . . . First Gathering*. (MICHAEL G. BORUM)

Above, there's no mistaking whose form *that* is! But Dolly warns that she's liable to have a whole new look. "I may throw away the wigs tomorrow, next month, next year, maybe never. I might do something drastic, when I'm ready to shock the people again." (ALAN MESSER) Left, The Bicentennial cover photo of *Country Music* Magazine. (LEONARD KAMSLER) Below, Dolly in 1974—determined to become a universal star. (MICHAEL G. BORUM)

9. "Light of a Clear Blue Morning"

It's been a long, long time
Since I've known the taste of freedom
Those clinging vines had me down
Well, I don't need 'em;
I've been like a captured eagle.
You know an eagle's born to fly,
Now that I have won my freedom, like an eagle,
I am eager for the sky.

"Light of a Clear Blue Morning"
Copyright 1976 Velvet Apple Music

It's a good five hours before the concert is to begin in the Waco Convention Center, and the stage crew and a few cowboy disc jockeys are waiting for Miss Dolly to show up for her sound check. Dolly has played two dates in California earlier this month, but starting today, the twenty-first of January, she's off on her first tour of the year, a cyclone ride through Texas with its favorite native son, Willie Nelson. The promoter, Tom Gresham, has billed his concert "The Outlaw and the Lady," the idea, he says, to present a mix of the traditional and the progressive. But if Dolly has gone with Katz-Gallin-Cleary and Monterey Peninsula to lift her bookings from corn to class, this is certainly somewhere in between.

The disc jockeys in their felt cowboy hats and a reporter for the Waco *Citizen* think it'll be an interesting crowd tonight. "You'll be able to tell who they've come to see as soon as they walk through the door," forecasts the reporter, Steve Ray, who has come early hoping to get not only a Dolly interview, but an autograph, as well. "If the guys have long hair and wear dungarees and flannel shirts—that progressive country look—then they've come to see Willie. If they're rednecks with flattops who bring women who wear short skirts or tight pants, then they've come to see Dolly." I ask one of the disc jockeys what he thinks of Dolly's crossover career. "She needs to go commercial," he begins. "A lot of people will miss out on her talent otherwise. Dolly's goin' a little more where she needs to go—to the top forty, where people get high. I guarantee you'll see everything from super rednecks to super freaks here tonight. You'll have your old establishment folks, too."

As the afternoon drags on and turns into supper time ("dinner" is served at noon down here), it becomes increasingly apparent that there will be no sound check. Steve goes out and gets us Kentucky Fried Chicken and Cokes. I spy Don Warden sitting up front with Tom Gresham and ask him what's going on. A diminutive man who puffs a large pipe and says as few words as he can and still communicate, Warden tells me Dolly's been up all night. "Plane trouble." Don Roth, guitarist on the tour, is later to remember the semi with the sound system arrived too late. "See, Willie doesn't need a sound check," says Roth. "They play night club type music and volume and you just sort of open up the mikes and it's OK. But we needed a sound check for the acoustic guitars, acoustic piano and background vocals. The fact was, when it was time to go on, they hadn't finished setting up the monitor system. We were supposed to have a sound check at four, and at four when the bus pulled up, the semi was backing up to start unloading the equipment. Right away, I said, 'I don't think we're going to get a sound check.' I had this strange feeling, you know?"

Dolly's custom is to stay on her bus until just the moment before she is to go on stage. Tonight two local acts perform first, but when it comes time for Dolly to go on, she is still outside on the bus. By now, Steve Ray's assessment of the crowd has proven correct. But the rednecks with the flattops and the ladies with the beehive hairdos are definitely in the minority. Mostly it's guys in Willie picnic T-shirts (a few have bought the ghastly Willie-Dolly T-shirts on sale in the corner) and hand-tooled leather belts with their names on the back (lots of Dwaynes). In every other seat, high school boys dip snuff and spit ambeer into open-topped Coke cans, accentuating the action with a kick of their cowboy boots. Up front, a fat man in a red James Dean windbreaker with two "Dolly Parton—Backstage" passes sells programs and buttons ("Hello, Dolly!") by the stage. Linda Ronstadt's "Hasten Down the Wind" blares from the speakers. And the Lone Star product is flowing freely as the Brazos River.

Finally the backstage door opens with a rush of January air, and Dolly steps inside, resplendent in a pink-and-black sequined gypsy outfit. And, oh, my gosh, yes, it's true what they say about how beautiful she is, and that her coloring can only really be appreciated in person. Steve Ray walks in behind her, numb and red-faced from having waited for her outside her bus. But he has gotten what he wanted, both the autograph and the interview. He asked about the changes in her music. Was she indeed making a radical departure? "We're not changing my style," she tells him. "We're just doing things a little different. We're experimenting with new music. The truth is, I am country. I am Dolly Parton from the mountains. I can't be anything but Dolly Parton, and that's country." Ray flips through his press kit hurriedly. The quote had sounded vaguely familiar. He turns to a reprint of John Rockwell's *New York Times* story; Dolly has given him the same quote she gave Rockwell. This will never do. Ray knows his editor will think he copied it right out of the press release. "I'm anxious to see how this crowd accepts me," Dolly adds, and Ray scribbles it down. But he needs more. "I'll talk to you after the show," she promises. She walks past a row of black instrument boxes marked "Dolly Parton: Fragile."

Sim Myers, one of the head honchos at RCA in New York, has said over the telephone that he imagines Dolly will be nervous about the tour. "It's a new show," he tells me. "And really, after the first of the year, it's the beginning of a whole new career."

The lights dim, and Gypsy Fever whips into the opening strains of a rousing rock rendition of Jackie Wilson's "Higher and Higher." Dolly walks out on stage and the audience—thoroughly sodden by this time, since the concert is about an hour behind schedule and there's been nothing to do but drink beer—hoots and stamps and whistles, cowpunch style. They have not quite expected what they're about to get, however. The Miss Dolly who used to swing through Texas on Porter Wagoner tours is up on stage belting out songs with a hand-mike, reaching down to shake hands with the kids down front as if they were customers sitting around tables at the MGM Grand. By the second tune, Willie's crowd has blissed out, and they laugh and talk among themselves as Dolly stands up front singing a Ronstadt version of "Silver Threads and Golden Needles." Not only has Dolly lost a good portion of her audience, she has also lost the better part of the sound system, which squeals loudly as it cuts through Dolly's soaring soprano. Dolly finishes to enthusiastic cheers and applause from her faction. "Thank you!" Dolly says. "It's good to be back in Waco. You know, the thing I remember most about Texas is everybody is always so friendly, and I'm glad to see you ain't changed!"

"Willie!" drunken voices shout in unison. Dolly pretends she doesn't hear that. "I'm havin' a little trouble hearin' you up here. Can you hear us?"

The fans yell no; the drunks yell yes.

Never mind. Dolly is brave enough to try "My Tennessee Mountain Home" on an acoustic guitar. "Well, I hope you can hear, 'cause I've got a red-hot lick I want to try here and take you back to the Smoky Mountains in East Tennessee!" The sound system goes from bad to disastrous. Halfway through, all I can hear from the third row is the throbbing bass line under Dolly's high notes. She's washed out altogether in the lower registers. She attempts to make it through the stanza about holding hands on the porch swing when feedback cuts like a laser beam. "Turn that thang loose!" Dolly yells good-naturedly, and giggles, not about to let anyone know she's rattled. The bass thumps on, and she brings the song to a close—"In My Tennessee Moun-"

"Wi-i-il-l-ie!."

". . . tain home."

"Wi-i-il-lie . . ."

It's beginning to show in her speaking voice now and in her eyes when she turns around and gives the band direction. A combination of anger and fear. The crowd is far from hers. In some ways, it's "Where's Norma Jean?"

all over again. But she goes ahead, making a joke about getting up on a stool in her tight britches ("This may be a show in itself"), and picking up the banjo for "Applejack." The crowd gets off on this one. It gives them a legitimate excuse to hoot and holler as if they're driving the cows in. But she loses them again on "Coat of Many Colors," her personal anthem that she dedicates to "all the mommas in the audience." The guy sitting next to me thinks Dolly is calling him a nasty name, country style. His girl friend tells him to hush and listen to the song. "I'll tell ya what," Dolly says at the song's end, "since y'all seem to be feelin' really good—"

"Yeaaaaaaaaaaaahhhhhhh . . ."

"Why don't we do a real happy love song, and everybody can clap and sing along, called 'All I Can Do.' "

They don't want to clap and sing. They want to talk. Talk about anything but Dolly Parton. Mostly they talk about Willie. And when he'll be there. But in doing so, they miss her breathtakingly beautiful version of "My Girl (My Love,)" a lovely, languid arrangement to which she gives her all. It is so lovely, in fact, that it takes the edge off the shock of Dolly Parton singing soul. The biggest surprise turns out to be how very well she does it, her voice tremulous with emotion. From there, Dolly moves into some traditional tunes to try to soothe the savages—"Honky-Tonk Angels" (they like this one, since it reminds them of the corner tavern) and "Mule Skinner Blues." Then she gives them "Jolene," done up not on acoustic guitar but on an arp and to a tempo so fast that Dolly can barely spit out the words. The haunting, chilling effect from the recorded version has vanished. But she redeems herself with her closing tune, "The Seeker," into which she pumps real fire-and-brimstone conviction, the white background singers sounding as gospel/black as you could find in any Pentecostal church in Alabama.

As Dolly leaves the stage, only a small portion of the 4,000 in the crowd sounds sorry to see her go. Warden says Dolly was pleased with the performance, but upset about the sound. She has reason to feel both ways. Despite laboring under the worst possible conditions, Dolly has proved that she is ready to be heard by every audience—country, rock, pop, what have you. And to anyone who saw the dancing figure in the pink-and-black gypsy outfit there tonight, the little girl who sold Cardui tablets between numbers on the Porter Wagoner show is but a dim memory.

"I don't really know how the tour came about," Dolly tells me. "I just know that I thought it would be a good idea to do some things with some people like that, 'cause I have quite a following in what they call 'underground,' and I especially like Willie. I found it to be an experience. Now, Willie's people treated me great. We had some problems with a few things—not with each other—but, like the night you were in Waco we had some sound problems and all that. And the crowd was different. Different for me even than they were for Willie, but they accepted us both very well.

I mean, Texas people just love music. But I'm glad I did it. The first night was the worst night we had. They'd just built a new sound system, and we had some problems. But the first night was the only night like that. I'm just sorry that had to be the one you saw."

"It got better because we started demanding sound crew," Don Roth recalls. "The sound got to where it was mediocre—all the way up to mediocre. But that first night, it was absurd. But the rest of the tour went about the same, as far as the crowd. We did only twenty or thirty minutes in front of Willie. We took our money and ran. I don't know why we were there. Oh, yes I do. RCA wanted a throwaway tour for Dolly to polish up the new band. They didn't know the new band was all professionals and didn't need polishing. RCA thought, 'Give 'em a chance to get out and work with a big sound system' that we'd never had. Eight cities in two weeks. That was a dumb thing to put her and Willie together." Roth feels that Willie's fans gave Dolly no fair chance, and the inadequate sound system left her no way to win their attention. "All they wanted to do was drink whiskey and scream. I mean, she'd be trying to sing 'Me and Little Andy,' and they'd be rolling whiskey bottles across the room." As back-up singer Mary Fielder put it, "The Texas tour wasn't one of the highlights when I was with her."

The mistake of booking Dolly on that tour aside, anyone who saw it who had also seen the Traveling Family Band could not help but be amazed at the difference in quality of the stage shows. "Well, as I understand it," says Don Roth, "the first show was real country bumpkin. They would just sort of walk out on stage and everybody started tuning up, and then Dolly'd come out, and then they'd stop and tune between songs. But then they got Gregg [Perry, Dolly's band leader and piano player], and with his experience on the road, he said, 'If you want to tune your guitar, you tune it offstage. You walk out, the show starts, and that's it.'

Everyone who was ever with Gypsy Fever comments on how invaluable Perry is to Dolly, both in holding the performance together and giving it direction and in communicating Dolly's musical ideas. "She used to try to give us direction, but it was real hard for her, because she hasn't had a lot of technical training," says Tom Rutledge, who was a member of Gypsy Fever from July '77 to January '78. "She couldn't communicate what she wanted. When she got Gregg, it became a lot easier. She would talk to him, and he could communicate to the band in musical terms what she wanted. Or try to. We'd just do it over and over until we came up with what she wanted." On the first tour, Dolly left all the communicating up to Gregg, because the two of them had just coproduced Dolly's forthcoming album, *New Harvest . . . First Gathering*. Gregg wanted everything like the album, says Mary Fielder. "I would say Dolly is pretty dependent on Gregg musically," she offers. "They work pretty closely. She's on the creative end, and he's on the technical. He can say, 'This chord is wrong,' or 'That particular rhythm is wrong.' She also depends on him for a very close friendship—both musical and otherwise. But in a performance situation, where she's the star, she appears to be very strong and very superior to him."

The man who actually produces Dolly's road and stage show is Mike Post, out of L.A. "Oh, he's *very* L.A.," says Don Roth. "He's got a shirt open down to the navel—the whole bit. But he's a neat guy. He's super dynamic, and he's a talented orchestrator. I think he's got three [TV series]. Very busy person. But Katz-Gallin brought him in, said they needed him. He comes to rehearsals and says [here Roth goes into a flamboyant impersonation], 'I think it has to build here,' or, "We need more of a flourish here,' and 'Let's make this into a medley.' Gregg does a slow burn when he's around; he just keeps his mouth shut. See, Gregg is a very fine piano player and arranger, and he's perfectly capable of doing what Mike Post does. He's even capable of *managing* Dolly. I mean, except for the absolute business, money end of things, he's worked his way into a position where he really does a great deal more than Don Warden. I think that's an ambition of his, to make himself *very* valuable to Dolly, because now he'll have a good job for a number of years, whereas bands basically come and go. He's created a certain stability for himself to the point that even if she didn't need a band anymore, I think he would go along with her as her conductor, the way Barbra Streisand takes a conductor with her everywhere she goes. Gregg doesn't get a lot of sessions in Nashville, because he's very quiet. He was really starving when Dolly first took him. He'd moved down from Chicago and had been here about two years and had really just run out of money." (Perry, twenty-nine, now owns a home in the exclusive Bellemeade section of Nashville.) "Dolly's very dependent on him musically, but when Mike Post's around, he keeps his mouth shut. He's very businesslike, very somber, very much the opposite of Dolly's vivacious bubbly personality."

Gregg Perry is not the only one put off by Mike Post. A lot of people in Nashville are unhappy about him, too. Not really about Post, personally, since they've probably never met him. It's the *idea* of Mike Post that they abhor—the very idea that he takes native, pure folk music (or country, if you will), and makes it sound as contrived as Dolly looks, the contrivance and the slickness more apparent with each of Dolly's tours. And, of course, Nashville objects to the fact that both *Here You Come Again* and *Heartbreaker* were recorded in L.A. with West Coast studio musicians (although *Heartbreaker* does feature several members of Gypsy Fever), when Nashville pickers were good enough for Dolly for ten years of her career. Some of them understand, however. "You need to change your setting, you need to change your studio, you need to change your musicians, your engineer, and everything, really, to do a complete about-face," says Gordon Stoker, leader of the Jordanaires, who worked on a lot of Dolly's early sessions. "This is one reason we've never done many albums. Because it's so hard for us to go into the studio here in Nashville and record an album with the people we work with day in and day out. Remarks are made, jokes are made, they put you down, and they don't give their best. The best album we ever did was done in Hollywood. It was a completely different setting with a different set of musicians. And that was the reason. Dolly's management just thinks about getting a complete about-face, as far as musicians and studio are concerned. It's best for her. Now, a lot of session people here call her words and say to hell with her—things like that. But let me say here again, that isn't Dolly as much as it is her management and RCA."

That's exactly right. *New Harvest . . . First Gathering,* Dolly's first long-playing declaration of artistic independence, was recorded in Nashville (although mixed in L.A.), and featured, in addition to Gypsy Fever, a great many Nashville studio pickers and singers, including Dave Kirby, Buddy Spicher, Bobby Dyson, Janie Fricke, Lea Jane Berinati, and Ray Walker. The album liner even included the commercial prod that had appeared on all Dolly's previous albums: "Visit the Country Music Hall of Fame, Nashville, Tennessee" (a message that was to "mysteriously" disappear by *Here You Come Again*). Although *New Harvest* became Dolly's first album in six years to make the pop charts—as well as her biggest to that date, reaching number seventy-one in July after a February release—the only single released from it, "Light of a Clear Blue Morning," failed to become a crossover hit. (The record peaked at number eleven on the country chart in June, but made it only to eighty-seven on pop.) "When Dolly came to me she wanted very badly to write and produce her own material," Sandy Gallin told Paul Grein of *Billboard.* "She had always been under the auspices of Porter Wagoner, and I felt it was only fair she be given a chance to produce her own album. But we made an agreement that if it wasn't a sales success or if it didn't produce a hit single, that I could pick an outside producer to do the next album."

New Harvest . . . First Gathering is a very good album. The playing on it is solid and first-rate, as is Dolly's vocal performance, especially on "My Girl (My Love)," which, along with "Applejack," the most played track on country stations, should have been released as a single, given the song's proven hit track record. As for the songs, Dolly wrote eight of the ten, the other two being the rejuvenated soul classics, Smokey Robinson's "My Girl" and Jackie Wilson's "Higher and Higher," two of Dolly's favorite songs from her teenage years. Both were songs she had wanted to cut before but was prevented from doing. ("Everyone thought I was *crazy* when I said I wanted to record them," she says, and indeed, on the album's release, several critics wrote that Dolly's voice was just "too country" to handle "rock.") Of the Parton originals, her statement of purpose, "Light of a Clear Blue Morning," "Applejack" and "Holdin' On to You" stand out as the best, the magic of the last probably lying in the infectious arrangement. But once again, form triumphs over content on *New Harvest.*There are no songs of the depth of "Coat of Many Colors," or "My Blue Ridge Mountain Boy" or "Down from Dover," or even "My Tennessee Mountain Home." And it's hard for a Parton-supporting critic to have to write that two of the most memorable and exciting songs on the album are reworked R & B, especially when Dolly is one of the most gifted songwriters in any style of music.

But perhaps that is not really so terrible. Dolly's purpose here was two-fold. The first was that she wanted to hook a new audience, and she surely did, even though her one single was not a hit. Maybe her thinking was, "After I get 'em interested, I'll lay some of my *real* stuff on 'em," and in subsequent albums, she will return to being sensitive and introspective in her own special brand of folk poetry. Dolly's second purpose in *New Harvest . . . First Gathering* was to show what she could do. "I wanted to try to give everyone a good shot at something," she explains, and that's obviously true enough. *New Harvest* is a smattering of country, rock, rhythm and blues, Latin/disco, folk, ballad, and almost anything else you can think of, all done up with pop/rock coloration but still retaining country roots. And that is no small feat.

But the danger in saying, in essence, "I can do everything—I can write, sing, play, produce, arrange—the works" is that Dolly got so carried away with her freedom as a producer that she resembles a child let loose in the kitchen for the first time, throwing in everything she thinks will make her concoction taste better in the end. The result is that *New Harvest* comes perilously close to being over-produced. At least three of the tunes, "Light of a Clear Blue Morning," "There," and "You Are," nearly reach production-number status. It's a wonder even Dolly's big voice can carry over some of this, the way she's piled instrument over instrument and voice on top of voice the same way she wears her makeup and jewelry. To use Dolly's word, *New Harvest* comes close to being gaudy in spots.

Most of the new songs were copyrighted by Velvet Apple Music, a BMI company Dolly started in September '76, after she broke with Porter. Dolly is fond of velvet. "Yeah, I am," she tells me. "But if you wanna know where I got that name—I was in Los Angeles back in the summer of '76 when I was makin' these changes, and me and Bob Hunka—we're best of friends, and he works with Emmylou—were gonna go on a picnic. But first we had to go to the store to get some things to take, 'cause we were gonna go to an outdoor concert to see The Band and the Flying Burrito Brothers. We were just gonna fix us a picnic lunch. So, anyway, to make a short story longer, we went to this grocery store. We's walkin' down in Beverly Hills, and that's the rich part of town, and I saw this grocery store and I said, 'Oh, here's one.' And Bob said, 'You don't want to go there. They're outrageously priced.' And I said, 'I can see why.' In the window they had their apples layin' on velvet pieces of cloth. And I thought, 'Velvet Apples.' So it just kinda stuck. It sounded like a title of something—Velvet Apples. Anyway, that's where I got that." In the spring of '78, Dolly started another publishing company, Songyard Music, an ASCAP company set up to handle the songs of other writers Dolly has under contract.

Gaudiness aside, *New Harvest* is a marvelous "first effort," one of which she can be proud, even if she didn't get a hit single. Who cares if a couple of the songs don't actually *go* anywhere, or if two of them sound too much alike in melody and feeling? More important to Dolly's hard-core country fans, *New Harvest . . . First Gathering* is really not all *that* radical a departure, at least not to anyone who heard "Love Is Like a Butterfly," "I Will Always Love You," and her version of Emmylou Harris's "Boulder to Birmingham." In many ways, it is still the old Dolly Parton—only better.

The album is very precious to her. "Even if it doesn't sell a nickel's worth, it will always be my special album, because it was the first time in my whole life I got to do something totally on my own," Dolly tells me as we sit in her living room listening. Her visitor can tell. A moment ago, Dolly was sitting on the floor by the fire, looking lost and wide-eyed and vulnerable as she sang along to "There," seeming as much a little girl as the children who sing off-key in the recorded background. "This is my favorite one to listen to," she says, and I feel slightly like a voyeur. "I ended with an inspirational song because I think all good things come from God, and I didn't want to do an album of all joy without a song about the One that makes it all possible. I had a lot more songs that I couldn't fit on. My songs are like kids to me, and to take one out is like takin' off an arm or a leg. 'Light of a Clear Blue Morning' is very personal to me 'cause I wrote it when I decided I had to make necessary changes. I'd gone as far as I could under the conditions I was workin' under. I didn't feel the people I was involved with were dreamin' as big as I was. In certain areas, I was workin' under pressure. It broke my heart to have to relieve several people, but I had to do it. This is by far the best thing I've ever done. It was the first chance I had to have total musical freedom and self-expression—the first time I've ever produced anything. I got all my ideas down and also had some great ideas from the creative people in my group, like Gregg. But it's the first thing I've done of this nature, and it's not the only kind of thing I'm ever gonna be doin'. I just wanted to do these things because I've done the others. And in the next albums to come I'll be doin' the kind of things I did in this album, in addition to the things I've always done—simpler things, and not so big on production. I'll go back to simplicity and production. But I am really proud of the album. It's one of the greatest, most fulfillin' things of my life. There was just so much *joy* in it. It's an album of pure old love, as far as I'm concerned."

Most of the critics thought *New Harvest . . . First Gathering* was deserving of praise. A few called it an artistic triumph. In Nashville, the reaction was, as usual, mixed. Those already bent in that direction considered the album further proof that Dolly had abandoned both Music City *and* her country music fans, and those a little more liberal in their thinking realized Dolly was feeling her growing pains and doing the only thing she could about them—and rather well, at that. Both Dolly and RCA were obviously nervous about how people would react to the album, even taking out ads in which Dolly proclaimed, "Any time you make a change, you gotta pay the price. A lot of country people feel I'm leaving the country, that I'm not proud of Nashville, which is the biggest lie there is. I don't want to leave the country, but to take the whole country with me wherever I go. There are really no limits now." The ad was signed with Dolly's signature, almost as if it were a document or a declaration.

One of the criticisms leveled at her was that such music as hers contributed to the breakdown of country music, that like Glen Campbell and Mac Davis, she was blurring the distinctions between country and pop, destroying perhaps the one last pure musical form, turning it into homogenized pap. For years, country musicians had suffered the humiliation of being called "white trash" and "hillbillies," thought of as being one of the lowest socio-economic groups in the country, just a step above "niggers." Now that country music had finally gained respectability, it was hard for some of the old-timers to accept the fact that the woman the CMA had twice elected Female Vocalist of the Year was joining "the other side" and would probably be writing no more songs that celebrated rural America. It was not only traditional sounds that were in danger here—it was country heritage.

"I thought that was true for a time," says Jimmy C. Newman, who's been a regular on the Grand Ole Opry since 1956. "But now I think the new forms of music have a way of bringing back the old forms stronger than ever, because it eventually revolves. The grassroots music—the hard country—was taken for granted because it was heard so much. Now it's dwindled some, and you don't hear it as much and you think maybe this other music is taking over. But the fact is, when it's real, as country music is, you can't keep it away. Eventually people starve for it again. There's a day coming when people will demand a whole lot more basic, real country music than you're hearing today. I saw this happen with Cajun music. People are seeing it as it really is, now more than ever. The only thing I update is the beat. There's no way it will be lost, because people really dig it."

Most of the back-biting that went on was not really about Dolly's change of "music," though. Glen Campbell, Mac Davis, John Denver, Olivia Newton-John and others had been doing country/pop for years, and aside from the ACE controversy, nobody really complained about them—certainly not the way they did about Dolly Parton. No one minded that Linda Ronstadt and Emmylou Harris recorded country/rock and lived out West. But perhaps these people just had country *hits*, and the fuss is that Dolly and Willie and Waylon wanted to extend the music from *within*. What it really came down to with Dolly Parton was that she was the first establishment female country superstar to branch out from "solely" traditional music. And that let all sorts of worms out of the can. One was that Nashville had a set pattern of behavior—both musical and personal—that Dolly was expected to follow. First, simply being a country superstar meant she was to perform one kind of music and one only. "I know the words to 'Stardust,' " says Jimmy C. Newman. "If I got a network television shot and did 'Stardust,' or a country song *and* 'Stardust,' too, there would probably be very little thought of it until I became a big superstar. However, if Dolly did 'Two Doors Down' or 'Coat of Many Colors' and then came back and did 'Stardust,' people would be very distressed about the situation. That's funny and very strange to me." Indeed. And yet Willie Nelson—the very essence of Nashville rebellion—can do an entire album of such standards and nobody minds. "Nobody raised cane about Johnny Cash, either," says Jo Coulter. "I mean, that was his right. But let a *woman* do it—the first woman—and somebody with Dolly's talent, and they want to keep her right there. Well, that's wrong. Especially if you have the drive and determination Dolly has had since childhood."

Chauvinism aside—and there is no worse chauvinism than *Southern* chauvinism—some people in Nashville just don't want to be left behind. They don't want Dolly out on the West Coast where she would (A) Forget them, (B) No longer bring them business, and (C) Outgrow them. Judy of Nashville, for example, no longer gets orders from Dolly for clothes since Dolly has the majority of her current fashions made in California. I asked her if Katz-Gallin had ever contacted her about making outfits for Dolly. "No, uh-uh," she says. "They don't like us Nashville people. They really don't. That's sad, but I guess they think we're dumb because we're from the South. I'm really proud for Dolly, for anybody who can blossom out, and she's definitely done that. But it's a shame she couldn't do that with Nashville people—people who really do care, instead of people who want the money they can make off her. A lot of people don't want to accept it. They think, 'She's just disappointed us.' Especially people who were close to her. Then, a lot of other people *have* accepted it. I was very skeptical that she'd make it at first. I thought, 'Gosh, she's too country.' But she's comin' right along." Lucy Adams, Dolly's close personal friend as well as seamstress, likewise has little work to do for Dolly these days, even though she is her chief dressmaker. "Well, I was," Adams says. "I don't say now, because she's gone on to bigger and better things, and she's outgrown me, I think." But because she loves Dolly, Adams says she doesn't feel slighted. "She has to let go a little bit to reach her goals," she says with quiet resignation. "She can't keep holding on to everybody if she's going to reach them. It's just like a child growing up and leaving home." Dolores Smiley understands that, too. "I think you'll find that resentment over anybody they think isn't gonna stay in our own little convent here, but frankly I think Nashville is beyond that at this point," Smiley says. "Nashville has grown, whether we like it or not. Our old country music situation was awfully good and secure to us. But now we are in a highly competitive world of show business."

Buddy Killen says it's a combination of all those things that brings people to criticize Dolly. "People fear change," he says. "And when you become accepted in an area of the music business, people fear you'll leave them behind. But anybody who just sits there and says, 'I'm gonna try to conserve country music,' has a wrong attitude, for the simple reason that country music today has been bombarded by every kind of sound in the world—all the influences of outside music, rhythm and blues, pop, jazz, you name it. And because of that, it continues to stay popular and contemporary. You can't stay thirty years ago. That constant state of evolution is always there. If you can't accept it, you'll be out of the business. It hasn't hurt country music. It's made it greater. Some people are very jealous of others' success. I'm glad to see it. It makes country music more accepted all over the world. Dolly hasn't turned her back on Nashville. She did what she thought she had to do as a business woman. She reached out of this, out of Nashville for management that she felt was capable of getting her all the things that she needed. And they have. She's become a popular thing for people to kick around like a little football. I don't like it. I think it's very small-minded, foolish kind of talk. Anybody who does it shows me their minds are just a little smaller than they ought to be."

Bob Beckham agrees. "When you say 'they,' " he corrects, "or when you say 'Nashville' when you talk about this—that's bullshit. There isn't a 'Nashville.' There are only people. The people I know and do business with have always been proud of Dolly. I don't go for this petty resentment bullshit. I don't think that has any place in the music business."

Like it or not, it exists. "I think a lot of people *have* thought Dolly sort of left the country field, but they're people who are not quite ready to accept the fact that if you intend to be an international star, you have a wider concept than Nashville," says Minnie Pearl. "When I say 'international star,' I mean Johnny Cash, and several others. But I think that's commendable for people to want to add dimension to their act by going into a little wider concept, and still keep Nashville more or less home base, as she has done, or has said she wants to do. But I don't blame her. I know that she has had some criticism, but it's impossible for a woman as attractive and as talented as Dolly to not have a lot of jealousy connected with a lot of the comments. And envy. It's impossible not to be envied if you're beautiful and talented and attractive and cute and funny like she is. And I think that a lot of times—not every time—people have accused her of leaving country because they probably wished they could do the same thing, but they don't have what she's got." Barbara Mandrell, who has several of those qualities working for her, naturally agrees with Dolly's change of direction. "I couldn't be happier about what Dolly's doing," she says. "Because she's taking country music in some places it hasn't been. This is what I've had occasion to do many times in my career. I think it's just fantastic, because there are a lot of fans today who used to be closet country music fans. Now that it's the in thing to like—and Dolly's certainly helped—they're coming out of their closets. I think it's great."

Marty Robbins thinks if there are any hurt feelings among management in Nashville, "naturally it was because they wanted that fifteen or twenty-five percent that Dolly's giving that firm out in L.A. *That's* the hurt feelings. If they'd really wanted, they'd have gotten out and done what she wanted. And I admire her for doing what she wants to do and not waitin' around for somebody else."

"The people who seem to feel the resentment say a lot about it," says journalist Bill Littleton. "I don't feel any resentment, and I feel like I'm as much a part of the music community here as anybody else. It's just another direction. But there's an awful strange quality that I can say that I feel is a little bit unique to the country idiom, because I've had enough exposure to other areas of musical expression. The only thing as close to this is jazz. What I'm talking about is a little bit of clannishness. These people have the idea that the very presence of the label 'country,' or 'jazz,' as the case may be, bestows some kind of virtue on whatever is being done. The people in the country situation who really get fanatical about that resent anything that might call their loyalties into question. Now I don't give any credibility to the resentment that says, 'She's trying to be a big shot.' But a legitimate reaction is the resentment that Katz-Gallin-Cleary is trying to change Dolly Parton. If that's true, I don't feel a resentment. I just think that's sad. And I think that kind of resentment is related to mystery. Nobody seems to really *know* what's going on between Dolly and Katz-Gallin."

"I'm not leaving the country," Dolly says, twisting the six or seven rings stacked up on her fingers. "All I want is a chance to do everything I want to do in life, which is the same thing every human being wants. Most people don't get to do a whole lot because they ain't brave enough to try. Well, I'm a pretty brave little number, and I'll try. It's as simple as that." I ask if she considers everything on *New Harvest . . . First Gathering* country. "Oh, no, no, no! But I consider everything on that album me. Country is what you make it. I'm a country person. I love to be country. I'm glad I was brought up just like I was. I love the old traditional country. I sing it often and in my show. That's why I used a lot of the people who had meant a lot to me and really influenced me on 'Applejack.' I could have used background people. See, I really feel like I'm fighting a battle when I didn't start a war. I'm just doing what I want to do, because my music is me, however it sounds. If I wanted to do R and B, it's still me, because it was something I felt I wanted and needed to do. But then I'll turn around and do something so country that it'll be appreciated by the hardest country-lovin' people in the world.

"You see, country and gospel music are my favorite music, but I like other music as well, and in order to not get left behind, I will keep up with the times the best I can. Plus I have a lot of creative ideas—things you wouldn't classify as just country music, what you'd think of as old country music, with fiddle and flattop—even though I would do that very thing in an album. But I can do things like 'Light of a Clear Blue Morning,' which is just so totally me—my thoughts, my feelings. Like I say, I'm having to fight for something I already *have!* So what I'm gonna do is just do the best I can at writing songs and recording them. I'll do my best at everything I do, and if the people like it, then that'll make me real happy. If they don't, that'll make me real sad. Everybody wants me to do something different. So in order not to get confused myself, I just do what I want to do for me. There's nothing I can say now. It's at a critical time in my career. People are just waiting to see what it is I'm doing. They've got it all confused. They've talked it up more than I have. I'm just trying to make progress. I want to be everything I possibly can. Ain't that what life is about? I'm a big enough person that I can accept success without it affecting me personally, or I'm a big enough person that I can accept failure, if that's what I should see. But either way, I'm also a big enough person that I can be happy either way. Just because I fail at one thing don't mean I'm a failure.

"I cannot be bitter. I cannot be resentful, and I can only defend myself because I know myself. I will still do what I felt I had to do, and that's everything I could do. Because I am a gifted person. I am not necessarily great, but I have a gift and I think it would be wrong for me to not try to exercise what talent I might have and to do with it whatever I can, to reach as many people as I can. There are other people in the world besides the ones I grew up with. But I will always be here, and I will always be able to help country music in many, many ways." I ask how. "Well, by becoming as big as I can in the music business and the entertainment field, and then by doing things like I did on the Johnny Carson show, when I know that at times there have been people on there that have really downgraded country music, or people who said they were not country. Like Buddy Rich comes on there sometimes, and he says country music is music with no class and all that, which makes me furious! You talk about country music in a bad way and that's like sayin' my momma is a whore! Them's just fightin' words! So I think I'll help it by sayin' things like, 'I love country,' and that I'm proud to be part of it, and I'm proud of Nashville, and that I think country music is a music with a lot of class. It's ordinary stories told by ordinary people in an extraordinary way. I want to be able to walk out on the stage of the Grand Ole Opry and have people say, 'Well, you know, I saw her on so-and-so, and boy, she's still on the Grand Ole Opry.' Well, I *am* proud to be on the Grand Ole Opry. I love it. I would like to take it with me everywhere I go. And I do. I would never walk out on the Grand Ole Opry or on Nashville. I hope they'll always let me be a member, because that is something I wanted to do all my life. If I walked out on the traditional country and the people I love most, like the Grand Ole Opry, that would be like turning your back on your momma and daddy, when they have been the ones that's raised you and took care of you. Well, I could talk forever, but the best thing to do is just let the people see."

Dolly wants no labels put on her music. But if it has to have one, she says she will always call her music country. "Because I *am* country, don'tcha see? Now, a lot of people would be furious with that. I'd call it country because it's me. But I really prefer to call it Dolly Parton's music. Why should it have a label? But I would stand up for country, and if somebody said I was in rock 'n' roll and we were in a discussion and they said, 'Well, you can't say that last album you cut was country,' I'd say, 'You may be right as far as what *you're* talkin' about country, but because I'm country, it's country in my mind.' Oh," Dolly sighs, exasperated. "I don't know what I'll say. I'll just have to say whatever is right. If it's good music, people are goin' to buy it. If they don't like it, they ain't gonna buy it even if it *is* country. It's just as simple as that, really. It's like politics, and it shouldn't be. See, if you're gonna try to stay in the music business, you've gotta put something out you know can be played at the radio stations. Because there are so many people that are so stubborn they will not change in any way. They keep putting out records and nobody plays them. Well, you could take that same song, and if you were smart, you could do something to it where it would not change it from what it is, but do something to it to where it would at least get considered. I hope we never lose traditional country, like the sound of the Carter Family. The new movement in music has been taken from the old country. A lot of people are doin' Carter Family songs, Louvin Brothers songs."

I tell Dolly some of the criticism directed at her comes from fear that she and others who sing a homogenized country contribute to the dilution of traditional music. "Well, maybe they are saying that," she concedes, "but what am I supposed to do? I have a song to sing and I have a heart that is full of love and compassion. And I have dreams and desires to do things. And I will *not* sit and grow stale. I *will not* do it! The years will tell what I'm doin'. I can't explain it, because what I'm doin' will stand on its own. This is probably real confusin' to people right now, but I think real soon it will all be real obvious what it is I'm tryin' to do. Time will tell if I'm wrong or if I was right. I *believe* in what I am doing. I believe in God, and I believe in myself and in the people. I want to be a universal artist. And I will someday. But if I don't, it's because I wasn't good enough to be. I like to think that I'm a stylist. And I know that I am, because I don't dwell in other people's music. I'm too busy makin' somethin' up—too busy creatin' my own, singin' it the way I sing it and feel it. I'm not tryin' to keep up with the Joneses and sing or write the way somebody else would, just because it's the goin' thing.

"But now, about this jealousy, I don't know any people who are jealous. A lot of people live in a soap opera world. My world is very real. I have no time for horseshit. I don't have time to worry about what everybody else does. I'm too busy doin' what I know I have to do. But people have misunderstood. When I said 'change'—that word just flew through the country like a plague. By 'change,' I meant I was changin' things that were not right for me, like my management, my organization, my band, my bookin' agent. Not that these people weren't great, or not qualified for what they do. They were. But our qualifications for each other were not really jellin' that much. My dreams were just so much bigger than theirs. I'm not changing. What would I change into? A pumpkin at midnight? I am so totally me that it would scare you to death. I know myself very well, and I don't trick myself. I don't fool myself. I know exactly what I can do, and that's just about anything I choose to do, mainly because I'll work hard enough at it and I'll believe it. And if I can't actually do it, I'll bluff my way through it. It's like a saying I saw on a shirt: 'If you can't dazzle 'em with brilliance, then baffle 'em with bullshit!' Music is a gift I give people. But it's also a gift I can give myself. And that's why it baffles me. I don't hardly understand why anybody would want to criticize whatever kind of music you make. It's somethin' you're givin' of yourself. What difference does it make? I mean, you wouldn't complain about somethin' somebody made you for Christmas. If they took their two hands and the time and the mind to be creative with makin' you somethin', why should you say, 'Why'd you have to make it like that?' Because then you've killed the whole joy of the gift for yourself and the person that gave it to you. It's the same with music. Why should I have to explain it? I haven't gotten any hostility back from people, though. I think mostly it's concern. People are afraid I don't know what I am doing. But I do. I think they're thinking I'm headed toward that land of the lost. When in all truth, I have been found all the time."

A great deal of that concern—and the hurt—that Dolly's old friends feel in Nashville is over the way they say Dolly has changed in her attitudes. It's not just Porter she's cut out of her life, but almost everyone who was ever close to her there, even Lucy Adams. Nashville may still be Dolly's base of operations, but an RCA representative says, "She's never here," and when she's not touring, she spends most of her time in California, where she now records. Rumors fly that she's bought a house there, but her family denies it. That would be the final straw for a lot of people back home, the ultimate symbol that Dolly had "gone Hollywood." When she is back in town, Dolly is inaccessible to her old friends, they complain. According to them, for a long period of time, she refused to answer messages on her Code-a-phone. Finally, she simply changed the number. And now that she no longer maintains a Nashville office, it is impossible to find her short of going out to her house, where a gate blocks the drive. Once Dolly could be seen out in Nashville's shopping centers, doing her marketing just like anyone else. But no more. In short, they say, she is acting like a Star. Not like a Grand Ole Opry star—and there are reports that she had a guard on the door there on one of her last appearances—but like a Hollywood Star, a Star created at a board meeting of a management firm.

"I don't feel like I know Dolly anymore," says a woman who saw her and worked with her every day for seven years. "She's excluded everybody I know in Nashville. Nobody hears from her anymore. You can't get in touch with her. There definitely has been a change. Whether it's that she's busy, or what, I don't know. But she used to go shopping, and stop and talk with men, women, children—whatever. Now it's like she's disappeared from the earth. All this just happened when she went to the West Coast."

"Yeah, it's a shame the way Dolly's gotten away," says Nashville photographer Michael G. Borum. "She used to be real accessible, but she's not any longer. To get to her at all, you have to go through three agents. You just can't talk to her at all. I used to practically call her—just call her aunt [Colleen Owens] who does her hair and say I needed to see her, and I'd get a reply. When she'd be shooting her TV show out at Opryland, RCA would call and say, 'We want to do some shots of Dolly. You want to come on out?' That kind of thing is long gone."

Brenda Lee has an idea of what it might be. "Maybe old friends are a threat to Dolly," she says, "inasmuch as she's trying to live a life that's in accordance with what she's doing. She's leading a jet-set life now. Let's face it. That's how you live when you're in those circles. And there's nothing wrong with that. There are a lot of great people in that circle. But I think maybe she's afraid to relate to the sort of semi-stardom and fans that she had before. She doesn't want to lose what she's gained. She's worked hard for it. Maybe she's afraid for herself—how she feels inside. That's only one way to look at it. I've been in those circles myself and I know sometimes you're told that you can't socialize with certain people. There are all different things that go on. I know she's definitely trying to do a lot. And that must take a tremendous amount of time. It's a hard grind. Especially to stay up in the pop field. But I hope everything good happens for her, because I think she's a good person. Let's just hope she keeps her perspective and remembers all those things she's said—that she's not ashamed of her heritage, that she's not ashamed of having been poor. Because the values of the heart and soul should not change."

The insinuation that Dolly has rejected her old friends brings fire to her eyes. "I don't even have time to see my kinfolks!" she says, her voice shaky with anger.

Stella confirms Dolly's remark. "I used to share a bedroom with Dolly, and now I never see her," says her sister, as her own bus travels down the highway in the moonlight. "I saw her in February, when you were at the house, and I saw her in May, when we taped *The Mike Douglas Show,* and then again at Christmas, and that wasn't even alone. I was watchin' TV the other night and she was on, and I thought, 'That's my *sister,*' you know? And now we don't even . . ." Her voice trails off, and I look out at the moonglow and try to concentrate on the revolutions of the wheels beneath us. When I look back, Stella is gently dabbing at her eyes. Last year both she and Dolly were staying at the Sheraton-Universal in Los Angeles, and neither of them knew it until an operator mistakenly put a call for Dolly through to Stella's room. "I said, 'Well, is she here?' Stella remembers. "And they said yeah, and they rung her room for me, and she said here Stella goes into a dead-on impersonation of Dolly, 'Stella, where you at? What are you doin' callin' me?' And I said, 'I'm downstairs, probably the next floor down. Look out your window and you can probably see a little nekkid body goin' across the window.' So she came down, and we visited. It was kind of a pleasant thing. But I didn't know she was there, and she didn't know I was. If she had of, she'd have gone with me the night before to the Palomino Club where I was workin'. She'd been busy tapin.' Mac Davis and Tom Jones and her were doin' the TV special."

Dolly's anger passes. "About not returning phone calls—I don't know of but one person who would have said that. I guess," she begins again, collected now, "that because I don't have management here now and my booking agent is not here, people think they can't get in touch with me. Well, I'm out on the road. I'm busy writing songs. I'm busy making records. I'm busy trying to further country music, the name of country music, and myself. I am busy trying to leave something good behind. I don't have no time to gossip or sit around criticizin' and condemnin' people. I have not turned my back on anybody. If there's a person that I have not returned an important phone call to, it was because the message didn't reach me, or because I just couldn't do it. Because there are a few people that I don't return their calls because I don't want to talk to 'em. And they are people who have hurt me in the past. And I think, 'Well, why put myself on the line again? Why put myself on such a spot? All they want to do is tell me how I have turned my back, which is a lie.' And about goin' out shoppin'—now I go shoppin' at midnight at one of them all-night groceries. I can't do no Christmas shoppin' at all anymore. People won't let me. So that's the reason. And that's the *only* reason."

That, in part, was due to Katz-Gallin, who by this time were doing all they could to make Dolly a star and to get her name and face in front of as many people as possible.

Most important to Dolly's name and face recognition, undoubtedly, were the two appearances she made on *The Tonight Show* in January and February. The first time she appeared—on her thirty-first birthday, January 19—Johnny Carson introduced her by saying, "We have with us a young lady, Dolly Parton, who's very big in the country and western field," as if he were telling the audience about a newly discovered antediluvian artifact. Carson, who had not met Dolly backstage before the show, was clearly taken aback by her appearance and vivaciousness from the moment she stepped out on stage in her peach-pink pantsuit and gypsy scarf to sing a rocking version of "Higher and Higher." Afterward, she walked to the desk to cheers and hoots, and, the mandatory show-biz kiss exchanged, Carson invited her to "sit down and take a load off your feet." Dolly giggled and blushed and covered her face with her hands, her feet giving a little kick in the air. "How come you've never been with us before?" Johnny asked, realizing he had a real find here. "Well, mostly 'cause you didn't ask me!" Dolly shot back. Carson was smitten, and for the next fifteen minutes proceded to play straight man for his guest, who told him all about her family—using all her standard po'-folks jokes—and about her husband, who never missed a night of Johnny Carson, but would tonight, since she would be on. All America was intrigued and charmed, but no one more than Carson himself, who sat dewy-eyed as Dolly sang "Me and Little Andy."

"I wasn't a bit scared," Dolly told me two weeks later. "It just seemed like a real natural thing to do. Now, I did *Hollywood Squares,* too, and I don't think I done good at all. But I feel perfectly natural and comfortable with all the people on *The Tonight Show.* To me, a human bein' is a human bein', and me and Johnny Carson are made up of the same things. He just happens to made up of more of 'em, I guess. But anyway, we just fit good together, and I had a good time, and they asked me back right away. Now they asked *me* back. Katz-Gallin and Cleary got me on the show, but Johnny asked me back. Which is a nice compliment."

On Dolly's second appearance in February, Johnny pulled story lines from her first appearance and led her into anecdotes along the same lines. But the appearance was no less winning than the first, with Dolly singing "Light of a Clear Blue Morning" and "Travelin' Man," one pop and one country song—a little something for everyone—just as she had her first time on. As before, she was irresistibly charming, causing millions of male hearts to pump coast to coast, and winning female fans, too, for her pluck and zeal and beauty. NBC reported viewer mail was stupendous.

Carson announced that Dolly would be appearing at the Anaheim (Calif.) Convention Center with Mac Davis on February 27 as part of their three-week tour of the West and Midwest. One review said, "The evening's show was a masterpiece of crowd control as both Parton and Davis took the audience on a musical trip . . . The tempo wound down to a point where the audience was in complete silence as Dolly Parton, accompanied only by an autoharp, entranced everyone with a few strains of 'Poor Wayfaring Stranger.' " As the opening act, "Dolly was kinda scared before those huge crowds that came to those shows on the Davis tour," Don Roth says. "I think she felt she wasn't quite in her realm." But Mary Fielder remembers it as "a great tour. I think the audiences were very responsive. The band was more together than it had been on the Texas tour because we had longer to work together. And it was just really enjoyable for all of us because the people in Mac's group and our group got to be good friends. I really enjoyed that tour a lot." Don Roth didn't. "Mac's band is just real Hollywood and even though we were making a lot more money than they were, they treated us like a bunch of country bumpkins. They'd invite us to their parties once in awhile, but they were just very much into their own little thing . . . We were all more professional, to be perfectly honest." No matter how the bands got along, the tour was good experience and good exposure for Dolly, who found the contemporary country audiences appreciative of her talents. Also good exposure was her appearance on Mac's TV special, aired April 26, on which she sang "Coat of Many Colors" by herself, and "Applejack" and "Naughty Girl" with Mac, the latter song one of her best-ever television spots. Dolly and Mac proved a good team, their youthful, fresh-faced sexuality complementing and sparking each other into thoroughly believable performances, Dolly being particularly fetching as the sixteen-year-old high school cheerleader who, after a night in a pickup truck parked in the woods, persuades Mac to give up football for other recreation. Lucy Adams made Dolly a "dress of different colors" for her first spot, and a shirt and matching scarf for the second, and ran them out to the airport so she'd have them in time.

As valuable as the Davis tour was for Dolly, it was only preparation for her April bookings, which included headline club dates at the Roxy, in Los Angeles, and at San Francisco's Boarding House—the most prestigious concert appearances she had been offered since her change of direction. But Dolly's reputation had preceded her actual performances, and in the audience for the three-day Roxy engagement were such jet-set names as Barbara Streisand, Linda Ronstadt, Bette Midler, Faye Dunaway, Jack Nicholson, Cher and Glenn Frey of the Eagles. L.A. *Times* critic Robert Hilburn asked, "Can Parton, the tiny, five-foot buxom blond, maintain her excellent country music instincts despite the cute, but sometimes excessive Mae West-meets-Minnie Pearl manner on stage? If she can, Parton could emerge as the most important hard-core ambassador for country music since Johnny Cash. Like him, she touches on the joy, poignancy and sociology of country music in her beautifully crafted songs." But, Hilburn continued, "Her strength is still her songs. When she sings of childhood memories ('My Tennessee Mountain Home,' 'Coat of Many Colors') in that clear, lovely high soprano voice, Parton is as commanding a figure as country music has to offer. She can also write contemporary love songs with effectiveness. It may be Parton's peppy enthusiasm and the good-natured jokes about her wigs that attract the wider audience, but it'll be her music that holds it. That's where Parton's talent lies, and it's an immense one. With so much to offer, it's no wonder she is seeking wider horizons. If she can maintain her standards, the move should be beneficial for everyone involved."

The audiences and critics at the Boarding House shows in San Francisco several days later were no less enthusiastic. "It was gush at first sight," wrote James Kelton of the San Francisco *Examiner*, who added Dolly "was greeted by a standing ovation as she whirled onstage wearing pink chiffon and tossing roses to the down-front customers." As for her musical contribution, "she obviously sees herself as a performer in flux and she means to make the best of it," Kelton said. "Her new songs such as '... Blue Morning' and 'Your Memory Keeps Getting in My Way [sic],' combine the best of her instincts with pop superficiality. The result is a kind of bittersweet euphoria that is more honest than the dedicated plagiarism of some country-oriented pop singers but at times is less interesting. There's no challenging Parton's talents as an entertainer, however. She exudes a warm awareness that virtually shines from the stage ... The worth of country artists can sometimes be determined by how rigorously they maintain their individuality. In Parton's case, the question never arises ... And her Boarding House appearances—two a night—were sold out weeks in advance. If that is any indication (and it should be) of her potential drawing power among the unstuffy masses, Parton could be the first hardcore female country singer to bridge the gap between country and rock from the wrong side of the gap."

On the last night of the Boarding House engagement, Dolly was to come face to face with a new, avid following that she'd never had with Porter Wagoner. "The whole audience was gay," says Mary Fielder. "They had bought the whole floor. They're a great audience. The strange thing was that one of the guys was dressed up like Dolly—in drag—and he had on this big blond wig. It was from a distance, kind of eerie, because here I am behind Dolly to her stage left. I could see the back of her head and then to look out into the audience and see Dolly out there too, well, it was just really bizarre performing in front of this face that looked like her. The whole audience—you could tell, the vibes—were just waiting for her to say something. So, for the first two or three songs, we just went along with the show as usual. Dolly was making a joke about her fingernails—something about pulling one out by the glue. It was a standard joke and everybody laughed. Then she looked at the guy and said she supposed he knew what she was talking about. It was really funny." After that, Dolly got quite adept at handling gays and transvestites. Spotting a couple in country-queen drag at another concert, she interrupted herself to ask, "Girls or boys?" Told boys, Dolly gave her wig a toss and flashed a big smile. "Well," she said, " 'tis the season to be jolly," and continued her song.

Dolly brought roughly the same show to the heartland at the end of April and first of May. After a club booking at Denver's Ebbetts Field, she played two days in Chicago (probably taping *The Phil Donahue Show* at this time) and then went to Charlotte, North Carolina. In contrast with the exuberant response she'd gotten on the West Coast, Dolly walked out on stage in Charlotte to a lulled crowd that demanded to be entertained. Dolly won. "She came on with so much energy and radiance that it was like 'MMMMMMMMMMM,' " remembers Mary Fielder. "She's got a lot of power, and she put forth everything she had. It was amazing." Fielder remembers Dolly met with another kind of potential set-back in Atlanta, the next stop on the tour. "There was this crazy lady in the street with a sign—something about 'I wrote Dolly Parton's songs,' or 'She stole her songs from me.' She was really deranged—claiming that Dolly was a fake. That really upset her. She acted like it was no big deal, but I could tell it really disturbed her. Seeing anybody less fortunate always disturbed her. So did being misquoted."

From Atlanta, Dolly brought her show to Louisville for the Kentucky Derby Festival. It was as beautiful and well-crafted a show as ever to hit town, the weeks of rehearsal and performance in the West Coast clubs having polished it till it sparkled brighter than any of the rhinestones in Dolly's finger bracelet. From the first chords of "Higher and Higher," the band was crisp and tight, as professional and competent a group as could be found anywhere, Rod Smarr wringing stinging notes from his guitar and holding them fast in the air. If the level of excitment had not already been set, Dolly raised it to a fever pitch as soon as she stepped on stage in a costume typical of her new look—a filmy red chiffon sequin-encrusted cape designed in California to be worn over pants, her gypsy look now discarded. From there on out, Dolly was no less than brilliant, undeniably at the top of her form. Her voice, strong and soaring, despite having to cancel several more dates because of throat troubles, breathed new power and emotion into even her oldest numbers—"Coat of Many Colors," "Jolene" (done almost at normal speed here, not quite at the cabaret tempo she performed it in Waco), "I Will Always Love You" and "My Tennessee Mountain Home." Even the tunes from "New Harvest" that had not really worked on record came startlingly alive. And "Light of a Clear Blue Morning" sounded like the true celebration it is, rather than simply a testimonial. If she sang everything that night with the freshness of a first performance, it was probably because for one man sitting somewhere in the audience, they *were* first performances. Carl Dean had finally decided to break down and attend one of Dolly's shows. And she gave him a performance worth the drive up from Nashville, as she kicked like a Rockette to accentuate the disco beat of "Getting in My Way," and shook her tambourine wildly over her head in unabashed joy.

It was rock, and it was country. But most of all, it was all the things Dolly Parton had said it would be, taking from nothing, but adding so much. Had the show been taped for a live album, it would undoubtedly rank among the most exciting and infectious recordings on the market. It was, to use the word Chet Flippo would give to her concerts, "purifying," with not just a few people leaving the show that night as if they'd just attended a revival. "If you enjoyed our show tonight, you tell all your friends and you come see us somewhere else," Dolly said when she was called out on stage after the last song. "If you didn't like the show, you keep your big mouth shut!"

But there had been almost nothing to complain about—one sour note from the piano and one flat note from Dolly, perhaps, but neither worth mentioning. Still, there had been one other thing—a fleeting, probably inconsequential thing, I told myself. But pat jokes and lines aside (all high-class this time), Mike Post had convinced Dolly to put her "down home" songs into a medley. And even though Dolly's strumming the dulcimer on the lead-in—"There's No Place Like Home"—added a nice, authentic mountain touch, the essence of Dolly Parton, the true soul of Dolly Parton, was being marketed here in a most unflattering way—in a plastic-wrapped, lightweight, disposable container. In time, it would get worse. "When they put 'My Tennessee Mountain Home' in as part of the mountain medley," Don Roth would say a year later, "that should give you a little idea of how much real belief Katz-Gallin-Cleary has in Dolly Parton's music."

That night in Louisville, Dolly had impressed the backstage people in different ways. To Joe Dice, of Philip Morris, the cigarette company that sponsored the free concert (with Kenny Rogers as the opening act), Dolly was professionalism personified. "When she finished a very quick little rehearsal, we asked Dolly if she and her band would like to have lunch as our guests," Dice recalls. "She said she really wouldn't, that the band liked to stay together. I said, 'Well, fine, you can stay together. We'll just pick up your tab over at the hotel, and you can eat together in the dining room if you like.' And she said, 'Oh, no, no. I came to work for you. I didn't come to freeload. I'm here to put on a show. You don't have to entertain me.' That," Dice says, "is kind of unique in this business today." I asked if her contract carried an exorbitant rider. "No, she didn't ask for a thing," he says. "She wanted to know what the lighting effects were going to be, and we told her. She dressed accordingly, and it came off beautifully because of that. But that's the extra effort she apparently takes to make a good presentation." But backstage, the brother of one of country music's most respected stars stood waiting for Dolly to get off her bus and mingle with the musicians the way she always had for years. Kenny Rogers came and introduced himself and chatted. But Dolly, the man says, got off to do her rehearsal, did the things Philip Morris asked of her, and went off on her own.

After several more concert dates in the South, Dolly went to Philadelphia, where she would co-host a week on the *Mike Douglas Show*, letting housewives throughout the country know they could relax—Carl had finally made it to one of her concerts. Mike was entranced by Dolly's stories of mountain poverty—so much so that he had her demonstrate the making of rock soup, Avie Lee style. But then Mike Douglas was a pushover. The real test of her powers of charm and persuasion was to come in just a few days, not far up the road: Dolly was to play New York's Bottom Line for three nights, beginning May 12. This was indeed the Big Apple.

And Dolly charmed it to the core. In the audience opening night were Mick Jagger, Candice Bergen, Phoebe Snow, John Belushi, Lily Tomlin, Eric Idle, Patti Smith and Janis Ian. For starters. John Rockwell of *The New York Times* was there, too. "I was a little nervous—on the brink of being scared," she admitted to him in her dressing room after the show. "But when I walked out on stage, I was at ease. The crowd was just great." But then, so is Dolly. Rockwell termed her engagement "a triumph."

On the second night—the night every music journalist in town packs in for a special RCA press party show—Dolly literally runs on stage laughing, picking up the handmike and launching headfirst into "Higher and Higher." She's chosen the apricot-peach cape for tonight, with "Dolly" spelled out in sequins and big, fat strawberries trailing down the side. And she is exhilarating. She shouts and cries and stamps and wails in even greater animation than she did in Louisville, and the band is right behind her. And she's feeling good. The jokes begin to flow. "You know, these britches weren't always this tight—only since I got in 'em!

"This is a song I wrote about an old red-headed girl who tried to take my man," Dolly says. "She didn't get him, but she nearly did. I fought that red-headed woman like a wildcat. She jerked my wig off and nearly beat me to death with it. I had another wig, but I didn't want another man. Her name was Jolene!"

From there, she does the mountain medley.

"I'd like to do a song for you now if I can get my guitar off without jerkin' my hair off. You know it comes off, don'cha? Whew!" she puffs, the guitar disposed of, "I didn't pull it off, but I set it back three years!"

The big- city journalists don't quite know what to think. A lot of them have come because they've thought this would be a giggle. A slicked-up hick with a wig and big bosom has come to New York to pick a guitar and talk about down home. She will make cute copy. But she is also wonderful. In every way. First she sings a rocker, then a bona-fide country tune, and now she is imitating her own record being played at 78 rpm's. "You flip your record player down on thirty-three and I'll sound like Porter Wagoner," she quips with a flash of the dimples. And the city boys melt. They don't realize she has beaten them to the punch, resorting to self-parody because she is so frightened they won't take her seriously. So what? New York says. The press is in love.

"I wanna dedicate this next tune to all the good mommas in the audience," she says, leading into "Coat of Many Colors." "You bad ones can hear it, too."

Two hundred and fifty people have received orange buttons from RCA signifying admittance to a gala press party at Windows on the World, the top of the World Trade Center. Five hundred and fifty show up. Among them: Andy Warhol, Olivia Newton-John, Mick Jagger, Robert Duvall, Sylvia Miles, John Belushi and Terry Southern. Jagger looks in awe. Warhol looks paler than usual. Duvall looks under the weather. And Dolly is literally on top of the world, 107 stories high. When she first came to Nashville not so many years ago, she hadn't the social grace nor the courage to go to a cocktail party or even a restaurant. Now all of New York's Beautiful People are standing in line to meet her. And to have their pictures taken with her.

I stand with them. The line reaches halfway across the room. It takes half an hour to get to Dolly. When you get there, she hugs you, asks you what you're doing there, smiles for the camera (*everyone*, just in case they're *someone*, is photographed with Dolly) and tells you she didn't like your past piece on her. She then gives you an ever so subtle but understood nudge, and the next person files into place. The party lasts until 4:30 A.M. It costs $35,000, by one estimate. When the clippings begin rolling into RCA's publicity department, it has been worth every penny. Sometime after four, Sandy Gallin escorts Dolly back to the Statler-Hilton. Every synthetic hair is still perfectly in place, and despite 550 hugs and kisses, Dolly's makeup has not smudged or budged. Dolly is, after all, a Star.

"I can fit in anywhere," she had told John Rockwell some years earlier. And she has proven herself right.

The press goes back to its typewriter and writes from the groin. Dolly runs the interviews. "I hate to talk about my throat. I hate to dwell on it. But I want to clear up the rumors. I hear people talking that I have throat cancer, or that I'm having surgery." Not true, she makes clear. Just stress and strain. "There is not a lick of danger of me doing that," she says when asked if she's moving to Beverly Hills. "I would *never* move there. I love to go there. It's excitin' for me, just like New York is. Why, I could sit there on the corner of Hollywood Boulevard and watch those freaks forever . . . Nobody is going to change me or ruin me. I am as stubborn as a mule. I have my own idea about who I am, and what I am, and I am very happy and content with that . . . That I am brave enough, that I have the gall to go out there as gaudy as I am, it makes it fascinating . . . I always figured all I needed was promotin'."

But that worries one astute critic, Ken Emerson of *New Times:* "What makes Parton fascinating (apart from her sheer talent as a singer and songwriter) is the contrast between the gimmickry of her self-display and the sincerity of her music. What made her triumph at the Bottom Line somewhat disturbing is that contrivance held the upper hand. She seemed more intent on capturing attention than on rewarding it." Still, not even Emerson can deny that even though she often sounded "coy or brassy rather than heartfelt" at the Bottom Line, she was also "thrilling." He doubts, like everyone else there that night, that "her genie will soon be bottled again."

It has been a very heady experience for Dolly. "I can tell you one thing," says Don Roth. "If she seemed snooty, it's because she was scared. Because she's scared of big city people and New York, to begin with. But if there's one thing Dolly ain't, it's snooty. She's open and funny—until she gets in a situation that she can't handle, and then she goes into the shell a little bit. Because she doesn't know how to be New York. She doesn't know how to be Barbra Streisand. See, Dolly's not jet-set. She's often said when she goes to a party at Ronstadt's house, she just wants to get out of there as soon as possible. Everybody was saying to her for a long time, 'Isn't that great? You'll go to Linda's party and meet a Rolling Stone and all these people will be there . . .' But she said, 'I'd really rather not. I like Linda and all, but boy, I'm sure not into her crowd.' One thing I learned a long time ago is that Dolly Parton is still very much a little girl. She's very uneasy in surroundings she doesn't know. I think that's the only reason she likes her bus. It's a security blanket to her." ("I can sleep better on the bus than at home," Dolly says.) "She leaves the concert, she goes back to her little room on the bus," Roth continues. "And I know she's very insecure at these press parties she does only because RCA or Katz-Gallin says do 'em. She'd rather go back to the bus and get into a sweatshirt and a pair of jeans. Really, she would be much more at ease meeting the Queen of England. The Queen would accept her as Dolly, but she feels insecure around big-time people, and she considers New York big-time people."

Two days after the press party, Dolly left for an RCA promotional tour of the British Isles, where, in Glasgow, she finally found someone with whom she could be at ease. The Queen of England. And Prince Philip, the Duke of Edinburgh. Dolly's performance at King's Theater was a royal variety gala staged as part of the Queen's Scottish Jubilee tour. David Soul and Shari Lewis were also on the bill. Meeting "a real live Queen," as Dolly put it, fulfilled another of her dreams. "A lot of people thought I was silly, or seemed to, when I said I got so excited. But I really did, because that's something we grow up with in the United States," she explained to a reporter from *Melody Maker*. "Thinking of fairy stories, kings and queens are kinda like fairy tale characters to us as far as the glamour goes. I was fascinated by her face and by her eyes, how clear they were. I always wanted to build my home like a castle, with a real drawbridge and everythin'. Maybe the Queen could come and live with me. Forever and ever."

"That show was fantastic," Mary Fielder says. "To hear about the Queen all your life and then there she is. The Queen told Dolly she enjoyed the show. There was some remark made—I guess it was actually Prince Philip who said it, but Dolly went to shake his hand and she had on a diamond glove—I guess that's what you call it—and she withdrew her hand and said something about her diamonds being fake and knowing that he was used to real ones. And he laughed."

When the band returned to the States May 30, Fielder received a phone call from Gregg Perry telling her in essence that her services were no longer needed. "Dolly travels a whole lot—160 days out of the six months I was with her—and at the time I took the job I was sort of under the impression, at least from talking with the band members, that it would mainly be weekends and sometimes a week out of the month. I was really into studio work at the time. That was my income. I wanted to take the job with the understanding that it was on weekends. When we actually started working, we really worked and we had very few days at home and I missed doing studio work. She just really essentially works too much. I wanted to spend more time at home. So, by the last month, at the end of the European tour, I was really pretty discontent with the schedule. Dolly was discontent with me because I was discontent. It was a mutual thing. So we had a parting of the ways. When Gregg called he said Dolly had sensed that I was not happy, and she didn't want me working for her if I wasn't happy. That was fine, because I had made the decision to get out. I guess technically I was let go, but essentially, it was a matter of who called who first."

By this time, Don Roth was gone, too. Aside from the fact that Roth, also a well-paid studio musician, joined Gypsy Fever on a temporary basis, "I quit because I really disliked that bus. She always gives you the option of saying, 'You can quit, because I'm going to fire you,' but I was the only guy who ever quit her. We did things like leaving Springfield, Missouri, and driving nonstop for forty-three hours to Anaheim, California, without brushing our teeth, without a shower, without changing clothes. The wheels never stopped turning except to get gas. And you don't eat until the bus stops at the Union Seventy-six truck stop and you run in and say, "Extra order of grease, please.' That's fine for a lot of people, and if you haven't got anything going for you, it's good money—about a thousand a week—and you put up with that. But what Dolly considers big-time and what I consider big-time are two different things. She thinks the bus is the cat's meow. She rides it on purpose. To a country and western person, owning a $150,000 bus with two bathrooms and hot and cold running water and a full-time salaried driver is a big feather. But I didn't get off on the bus. And I didn't get off on Mac Davis's group staying in a first-class hotel with single or double rooms to themselves, when we had roommates at the Holiday Inn, and us traveling forty-three hours on a bus, only to find they'd swam in the pool and laid in the sun and jumped in a plane.They always had the best, and they were making maybe $500 a week and expenses. That kind of stuff is not Katz-Gallin. That's Dolly Parton Enterprises. On top of that, a good many things promised by Dolly did not happen. I think she promised them in all good faith, but they just didn't happen. Gypsy Fever was supposed to be a band of professionals, a family unit, a business unit, a corporation. We were going to do all the sessions and TV shows and all the road work. We were going to do demos for her publishing company. She didn't want to treat her backup group like a backup group. And she didn't. She rode the bus with us, and she hung out with us. We were together all the time. She liked us and we liked her. She's a nice lady. But she listened to her big L.A. management firm, and slowly, but surely, we weren't doing any TV shows. We didn't do the Mac Davis Special, and we didn't appear on camera on *The Tonight Show.* And I knew none of us would be playing on *Here You Come Again.* She would have loved to have had Gypsy Fever be all the things that Gypsy Fever was going to be, but it didn't work that way, so I got out. A number of other people got fired and, of course, all the people that got fired say, 'Oh, that___Dolly! She promised this and that—,' and some people are very bitter."

As a result, Dolly has a reputation of not being able to keep a band. Roth says Gypsy Fever has never consisted of the same people for more than six weeks. "She wants studio quality people, but the way she likes to tour, you never see your house for six to eight weeks at a time. And you just don't hold onto people, no matter what you pay 'em. They can make that much back in town in the studio, if they're good," Roth says. "She can't get people to go out for a grand. They won't go. First of all, everybody's afraid they're gonna get fired; there's no stability. Because if she doesn't like you, and chances are she won't, she will fire you. If she doesn't like your attitude, if she doesn't get 'good vibes,' as esoteric as that is, from you on or off the stage, she doesn't care if you're the best player in the world. She's not going to keep you in the group. She carries it to extremes sometimes. She will simply say, 'Gregg, I don't *feel* his playing.' I've heard that many times. I guess she felt mine, though, because she has called me many times since and asked me to go back on the road."

Dolly is not oblivious to the talk. "I've probably gone through more musicians than anybody, but it's not personal, it never is," she told the *Star.* "I have a reputation in Nashville—you can't keep a job with Dolly Parton—but that's not so, really. I have to have the perfect sound for me, and I've nearly achieved that. I can't work with squirrels or dope addicts or drunkards. I expect goodness from my people, and I expect them to be qualified for what I need, and I want to be proud of the band I've built."

"Then, too, she wanted to find people who could really work together, personality-wise," says Mary Fielder. "So I guess they just really haven't found the people they're looking for." ("We've had to get rid of band members in the past because Dolly only likes to have nice people around her," Gregg Perry told the St. Louis *Globe-Democrat.)* Roth estimates Dolly's gone through four or five guitar players, four or five drummers, four or five bass players, two or three lead guitar players—"fifteen or twenty players." Tom Rutledge came back into the band after Roth left. "I'd say they've been through five or six guitar players—maybe more like seven or eight—five bass players, and I don't know how many drummers. I was let go after six months, along with another guitar player and the drummer. Something to do with a management decision, or something in L.A. She's been trying to find 'that' sound. It's kind of hard for me to say exactly what it is, because I don't think Dolly knows. She'll know it when she hears it, though. That's why it's so hard. She said she was as happy with the band as she had ever been, but Katz-Gallin wasn't happy with it, and she went along with their decision because they're running the whole show now. They say that Dolly's different, that she can be sold and she's a good product—if she's packaged right. They saw it and they're doing it. When I was let go, it was done very professionally, very cordially, good feelings on both sides. Gregg told me. Apparently, Dolly was pretty upset about it, because she had let me go with the other band before and felt real bad about it. It was real hard for Dolly to do. But one of the reasons that Gregg is in the band, besides him being a really fine musician, is for him to take on some of those responsibilities."

"Toward the beginning," says Don Roth, "she would call the person in the room and fire them face to face. I walked in and quit face to face and we cried. When I walked through the door on the bus after the last concert on the tour, she said, 'Well, come on in and shut the door. If you're gonna quit me, quit me like a man.' She knew I was unhappy."

"Dolly once told me how sensitive she was, though," says Fielder. "She didn't ever want to hurt anybody. She was concerned with personal feelings and all that, and firing someone or hiring someone or correcting somebody—anything that could bring about feelings—she just didn't want to have to deal with. She didn't want hassles. I think it was easier for her to tell Gregg that she didn't like the way so-and-so was playing."

Roth says Gregg is in a bad position. "See, his idea of keeping that job has been to do anything that Dolly says to do. He's just so afraid not to do everything Dolly wants. It really is too damned difficult for her to fire people when she loves them, and it may not be totally right for her to have somebody else do it, but Gregg was all too willing—always. But he just does his job. A great deal of talk is going around town—'That son-of-a-bitch fired me.' All the poor bastard did was make a phone call because he was told to. I like Gregg. He's a good friend of mine. But to Dolly, he got to be a convenience. To the point of where she'll say, 'I think I'll call Don,' and he'll say, 'I'll call him for you.' His title is band leader, but he has taken it upon himself to always carry her suitcase for her and to do just about everything. We'd get into a new city after an incredibly long bus ride, and it'd be four o'clock in the afternoon and we'd have a couple of hours 'til concert time. The phone would ring, Gregg would answer and say, 'Yes, I'll be right there.' I'd say, 'Where are you going?' He'd say, 'Well, Dolly's got some radio interviews, and I gotta go dial the phone for her and get the DJ on the line and say, 'Miss Parton will talk to you now,' and hand her the phone. I'm sure Dolly's taking care of Gregg. He's getting paid good money, I would guess $50,000 or $60,000 a year."

Judy Ogle used to take care of a lot of things Gregg now does. But early in 1977, she and Dolly parted company. "Boy, that was a shock," says a former member of the Traveling Family Band. "I figured she got fired, but I heard she left, she quit. She couldn't stand it because it's altogether different now." Dolores Smiley was surprised to hear that Judy was gone, too. "Because they were very close, and Judy appeared to be more family than employee. She was a lovely girl, and she took care of an awful lot of things for Dolly. But they were just inseparable, as far as I could tell. I understand that Judy just got tired of being on the road and wanted to stay home."

Some people in Nashville thought there was more to it than that, one line of reasoning being Katz-Gallin probably decided she was superfluous, figuring a band member such as Gregg could handle her responsibilities. "Since they were so close, I imagine Dolly probably said, 'Judy, I hate it that it has come to this, but I have turned every aspect of my career over to Katz-Gallin-Cleary, and I will have to abide by what decisions they think are in my best interest.' And Judy, being the friend she is, would have to abide by that decision," says a Music Row executive. But several members of Gypsy Fever say that while Dolly listens to Katz-Gallin, she has veto power over their decisions. Several people think Judy was let go because Dolly's management people felt they were too close. "Could be it had gotten to the stage that it would jeopardize Dolly's career," continues the executive, "and Dolly could no longer tolerate that. But of all the changes that took place in Dolly's career within the last few years, that was the one that was most shocking to me—that Judy was no longer with her."

"Dolly and Judy just had a falling-out," says Tom Rutledge. "I don't know that much about it. But just a few days ago [April '78], they spoke to each other for the first time in a year. It's no big deal. They haven't been uncivil to each other, but they just had a parting of the ways. Judy felt she could no longer work the road, I guess. She was living back in Sevierville for awhile, but she and Dolly are fine friends right now. They just don't work together anymore. They don't have any ill feelings toward each other. She used to stay over at the house with Richard [Dennison] and me, because she and Rachel [now Dennison's wife] are very close, and Rachel would come over and stay. Anyway, Dolly called over there just this last week, and talked to her. They had a long talk, and I guess got everything straightened out. I think she invited her over to listen to a tape of the new album, but she wanted to talk to her, too. They're too close. They've been through too much together. See, they went through that whole Porter thing together. And anybody who went through that with Dolly has got to be close, because that was a bad time."

"Nobody talked about it much," says a former member of Gypsy Fever, "but when Judy quit, there were quite a few words said between them. It was high emotion. Of course, nobody ever just floats away. It's always high emotion."

"I went on the road when Judy left," says Don Roth. "Judy was really fired. Gently, and for her own good. Judy's a very quiet, very intelligent, soft-spoken girl, who just basically does her job and keeps everything inside. She worries a lot about Dolly when Dolly's having a bad time of it on the road, as happens to stars when things get too busy or too hectic. And Judy would take it all personally. And too seriously. She used to get so upset when the band would be complaining about things, just as everybody does. They'd be bitching, and Judy would always say, 'Well, it's not Dolly's fault.' She'd take this all too personally, like we were really cutting on Dolly personally. We were just cutting on the way things were. I think she was really run-down, and Dolly just finally said, 'Judy, you're my friend, and the best thing is for you to quit the road.' It was the best thing Dolly could do for Judy, in Dolly's estimation. I haven't seen Judy since. She sent her home. And they made up some excuse about Judy's parents being sick and she went home and never came back. Now, about that rumor—I would say no way. I am pretty sure that I would have sensed it. Cats have fleas, and stars breed rumors." Stars and gossip, he says, are "just attracted to each other."

In May '78, Judy was in Birmingham for Dolly's concert. And in June, Carla Scarborough of Owepar said Judy had been in the office the day before. She confirmed what several people had said— Judy has new plans for her life. "Judy's joined the Army. She wanted to do that for four years. She acted as Dolly's personal secretary and traveled with her a long time, and Dolly's been her world, but I think Dolly felt that it wasn't quite fair to Judy, that she was just absorbing her and she wasn't making a life of her own. So she's gonna try this for four years and see how she likes it. She's meeting Dolly on the road this week to travel with her some more just before she leaves—Dolly's in Hawaii and Judy's gone to meet her. She'll be down at Fort McClellan for basic training and then she'll be based in Washington. I don't understand it exactly, but that's what she wanted to do. I'm just crazy about that girl. She is so sweet. She was saying yesterday that no one's been taking care of Dolly's office, that she's gonna have to get in there and straighten it all out."

Several people have said they thought Judy was further irritated by Gregg's increasing responsibilities within Dolly's group, and that Dolly no longer spent as much time with her old friend as in the past. Whatever, Gregg has now worked himself into a position as "the last shield, the final authority—the new Judy," according to one of his personal friends. "He's with her everywhere, all the time." As a predictable result, of course, talk is widespread in Nashville that Dolly and Gregg are more than just good friends and colleagues—as has been the rumor about almost every male Dolly has been associated with in a business situation. Several reporters who have traveled with the band on the bus were surprised to see Dolly and Gregg holding hands in full view of everyone aboard.

Barbara Walters asked Dolly if any hanky-panky went on in the bus. "Hanky-panky!" Dolly said. "Well, that depends on what you mean by hanky-panky. We do a lot of celebratin' on the bus. Let's put it that way. If there's really something to celebrate, if we want to stop and buy some wine or some champagne, if there's somethin' really nice. So it's all fun, but, it's very rare that anybody in the bus . . . I don't have anybody in my group involved with each other as lovers. I have worked in groups where there were people, the musicians or singers, whatever, were involved. It makes it very hard for everybody because if they have a lovers' quarrel or that sort of thing, then it affects everything."

But, as Matt Yancey pointed out in his Associated Press story of some years back, Dolly is affectionate with all the members of her band, and treats them as family. "See, Dolly's a great snuggler," says Don Roth. "But she's totally loyal to Carl Dean. Maybe not totally loyal in the sense that a Southern Baptist would say you should be loyal, but totally loyal in her own mind. But I would say Dolly's an extremely moral person. *Extremely* honest, to the point of it almost being an obsession. About Dolly and Gregg, they did spend lots of time together. Gregg was my roommate and I didn't see a lot of him on the road. But Gregg's a pretty platonic guy. He's as vanilla a person as you could ever want to meet in your life. But you have to understand a lot of rumors that were started about Dolly were fertilized and conceived in Nashville. If you went out to L.A., you wouldn't hear any rumors about Gregg and Dolly, as much time as they spend together there. See, Nashville in general still feels cheated, betrayed and divorced from Dolly. Bobby Dyson, a bass player, studio musician, says, 'Boy, Dolly used to be able to sing.' I said, 'Oh, really? What happened?' He said, 'Well, you know, she doesn't use us anymore.' Now that was great logic. When he was playing on her records, she was great. When she records in L.A., she can't sing. If anything, she sings better.

"But Carl is the perfect husband for Dolly because he doesn't demand anything of her, and he'll always be there to come home to. They seem to have a very stable relationship. I don't know if she would ever leave Carl because somebody better came along. It certainly would be within the realm of possibility. She's such a private person to strangers, but if she started something with some incredibly sophisticated Hollywood-type person, Carl Dean couldn't hold a candle to that boy. Carl Dean is only capable of being Carl Dean. But apparently, that's what Dolly wants. And she is very *Bible*-believing and Christian-professing. I'm relatively sacrilegious and would make Easter jokes about Jesus turning water into wine by palming a grape fizzy, and she would just *cringe* and say, 'Oh, please, Don, don't.' It wasn't that she thought lightning was going to strike the house, but she really didn't like it.

"And Dolly really loves Carl, besides all that. He's a neat man. Carl's one of those rare individuals who could be married to Dolly Parton because he's got his head on straight. He's a good old country boy, extremely funny man. Kind of guy you can say, 'God, Carl, you're a country bumpkin.' And he'll just smile and say, 'Yeah, probably right,' and put the gold American Express card in his pocket and go fishing. Now, he may be incredibly Beverly Hillbillyish naive, but I have a feeling he's more like Buddy Ebsen was in the show—he really knew what was going on. [When a woman from the New York bureau of Solters and Roskin, Dolly's PR firm, called the house recently and left a call back number for Dolly, Carl reportedly took down the 212 area code and asked, "What side of the mountain is that on?"] In Hollywood, Carl would run up and down Sunset Boulevard having a ball, being as tourist as he could be in a pair of blue jeans and a tacky shirt. That's Carl. But he and Dolly pretty much know where they stand with each other. When we'd be playing some place, like in Missouri, he'd drive up and Dolly would jump off the bus when she saw the car there. She'd say, 'Now I don't want any of you botherin' me. I've got some serious___to do,' and she'd head straight for the room with Carl. She doesn't mince words, and she doesn't have a particularly clean mouth. But to show you the true Dolly Parton, what makes her so damn neat is that as she was walking down the stairs of the bus, she turned around and looked at everybody and said, 'I sure talk a good story. Hope I can live up to it,' and walked off toward the motel room. I thought that was cute as hell."

Carl spent a lot of time with Dolly in the summer of '77, traveling with her on her six-week tour of Eastern dinner theaters with Mac Davis. A journalist who attended several of those shows privately calls them "the East Coast version of Waco. The people were there in their leisure suits to see Mac Davis and just barely tolerated Dolly with polite applause. They had her on one of those revolving stages, and she got so disoriented, she'd reach for her banjo and it wouldn't be where she thought she'd put it." Dolly herself was to remark, "It was a typical Mac Davis audience."

"After that tour," says Don Roth, "she told Mac she wouldn't work with him anymore. I don't know why, but I would assume it was because she was still warming up for him and felt she was ready to headline." Dolly was still on the tour in June when she missed putting in an appearance at Fan Fair. The fans thought she'd shown up after all when an announcement came over the loud speaker that Dolly Parton was autographing at the RCA booth. When the herd of fans stampeded over there, they found Vic Willis dressed up with balloons in his shirt. With the controversy over Dolly leaving country still thick in the air, it was a bad year for Dolly to miss a Fan Fair appearance. "She *had* deserted her country music fans," says a Music Row executive. "She has to realize that she's starting all over again with the pop fans, and they're nowhere as loyal as the country music people. That was the dumbest thing possible not to come to Fan Fair." But the no-show at Fan Fair was not to disappoint the country fans as much as Chet Flippo's *Rolling Stone* story on Dolly, which appeared that August. "Ooh, you got cherries for dessert," Dolly said to Flippo, who had taken her on a picnic. "Um, good. I ain't had a cherry in a long time." Dolly then looked at Flippo mischievously. "I don't think I ever had a cherry. If I did, it got shoved so far back I was usin' it for a taillight!" Says Loudilla Johnson, co-president of the International Fan Club Organization, "I couldn't believe she said all that stuff. It's not doing her any good with some of her fans." Some may have expected the article would anger Dolly, but, to the contrary, Flippo's wife, Martha Hume, says "Dolly loved it." Shortly after the piece was published, Dolly appeared on a television news show in Nashville complimenting Flippo by name and saying how pleased she was with both the photos and text. The country fans were also unhappy with the outrageous rooster costume Dolly wore on the CMA Awards show in October. "She came out there in that garb lookin' like a peacock," says one. "She thought she was a million bucks, and she didn't get nothin'." (Dolly was nominated for Entertainer of the Year and Female Vocalist of the Year but lost in both categories.) "She used to be my favorite," says the fan. "Now I like Anne Murray and Tammy Wynette. Dolly's just changed. On her shows, she always dressed so pretty." Judy Hunt, Dolly's old designer, felt about the same. "That was horrible. Sick-lookin'. Like somethin' you'd wear to a costume party to be funny. I want the whole world to know I didn't do that! I don't know why she'd wear somethin' that hideous, unless it was to get attention." Of course, not everyone felt that way. Jo Coulter thought it was "gorgeous–and she looked fabulous in it." But the majority agreed with Judy Hunt and the fan. "I really thought it was one of the most tasteless outfits I've ever seen her wear," says Charlene Bray, "and when she came out, the audience gave a collective gasp. But then she had that big song, and I began to see a little bit of sympathy and comradery expressed for her in this town."

The big song was, of course, "Here You Come Again," the record that landed Dolly right smack in the middle of mainstream pop, and the title track from her then new album. As per their agreement, after the disappointing sales of *New Harvest* . . . , Sandy Gallin brought in an outside producer, a producer he felt sure would guarantee a hit single, earn Dolly new (pop) fans and yet not alienate her old (country) following. The man for the job was Gary Klein, then thirty-five, a proven hitmaker who had produced Barbra Streisand's *Superman* album, a top three effort that satisfied not only Barbra's MOR fans, but the young fans she picked up from *A Star Is Born.* Klein had also handled his share of country/pop, producing Glen Campbell's catchy *Southern Nights.* Executive producer on Dolly's album was Charles Koppelman, who had been a staff writer for Don Kirshner and Al Nevins's Aldon Music in the mid-'60s, along with Barry Mann and Cynthia Weil, the writers of "Here You Come Again." The song had kicked around some, Mann having recorded it himself for Arista Records and pitched it to his friend Brenda Lee, who knew it was a hit and held it for eight months and then passed it up, since she wasn't recording at the time. "I knew it was the single before it was even mixed," says Klein, "but it was a little bit scary for Dolly to make a pop record. She was afraid her fans would say, 'Oh, Dolly's selling out.' She did ask to have pedal steel guitar added to the record, so I added a few licks. But I pointed out to her that records like Engelbert Humperdinck's 'After the Lovin' ' make the country charts now. People don't realize how broad country is." Gallin agrees. "She was questioning whether it would be a country hit. She told me, 'I'm not going to trust you again if the country people don't like this.' She's very sensitive to not offending her country fans. That's important to her."

Dolly's fears were partially laid to rest when the album went number one country. "I knew the song was a hit, but I wasn't sure if it was the kind of hit I wanted," she told reporter Bob Allen. "I wouldn't want to get labeled with this slick production because my own songs are a lot more gutsy and a lot more soulful. The album is slicker than I've ever heard myself, or would probably ever want to hear myself again. But it was somethin' I purposely did. We were purposely trying to get a single and an album that would cross over. And we did. In three weeks, the single sold more than anything else I've ever had out. And in two weeks, the album outsold any other album I've ever done."

Dolly has only four originals on the LP; Klein decided to emphasize outside material in further quest for the pop listeners, although the title track is the most contemporary of the outside tunes, with several of the others, John Sebastian's "Lovin' You," Kenny Rogers' "Sweet Music Man," and Bobby Goldsboro's "Cowgirl and the Dandy," not far off the country path. "Evidently," Dolly told Allen, "my own songs, as they were, didn't quite hack it, so we purposely included songs that were recognized by the pop world. But once I crack that market, my own songs *will* be accepted. And when I get to where I want to go—which is a long way from here—I'll still be going back and doing the old traditional songs and preserving them that way." One of her tunes on the album, "Me and Little Andy," which she'd been doing in concert for some time, is another of her "child-dies-and-goes-to-heaven" songs, except this time her dog up and dies, too, so "Sandy" won't be lonely! (Why is it always a *girl* and never a boy who dies in her fundamentalist-inspired songs?) A favorite of her own songs, "Me and Little Andy" is as maudlin and mawkish as anything she's ever done, and yet it's arranged and orchestrated with an ever-so-light touch to fit into the style of the album and still retain its folk base. "God's Coloring Book," another of her songs, is one she wrote several years ago, the melody highly reminiscent of "Coat of Many Colors." Ironically, the two follow-up hits to the title track, "It's All Wrong, But It's All Right," and "Two Doors Down," Dolly dashed off at the last moment to fit the feel of the album. (Six years earlier, she had recorded a song by J. and B. Eggers called "It Ain't Fair That It Ain't Right.") The fact that she had no trouble whipping off the two in such short order and having them blend so well was no accident. "Even things on *New Harvest* I wrote four or five years ago," Dolly told me. "I've always written songs like that. It's all a matter of arrangement. But that is where people think you are not country if you use a different instrument on things. But you know, I am me. I am a person who is creative. I am thankful for everything good that has happened to me. I will never neglect or turn my back on any person who has ever helped me. I will give my country fans what they want and what they need from me, but I have other fans that I must give what they want and what they need. And I must give myself what I want and what I need, because I have to live with me, and I have to know that I have done my best. That's what I'm doing. The last two years I haven't gotten to write as much as I used to and as much as I'd like to, but I'm sure as soon as I let up some of my road schedule, I'll be able to be back to my writing. I want to do better as a writer, I want to have more songs recorded by other people, and I want to make better records myself, have bigger sellin' records." (Dolly told Bob Allen basically the same thing, but added, self-confidently, "I plan to leave myself more creative time. It's not fair to me or the world for me not to.")

The reaction in Nashville? "Dolly's sound has gone slicker'n a greased pig and she's not at all embarrassed about it," wrote a reviewer for *Music City News.* That's because Dolly has nothing to be embarrassed about. *Here You Come Again* has the highest overall quality of any album she'd released to date. Yes, "these are Hollywood cuts, with Hollywood producer, Hollywood musicians, and Hollywood studio," as the Nashville paper snips, but the production is not nearly as heavy-handed as that on *New Harvest* . . . and once Dolly makes it past the forced-sounding phrasing of the title cut, she sounds perfectly at home throughout—especially on "Lovin' You," done up with come-hither sexuality, and the wonderful "Baby, Come Out Tonight," far more sensual in Dolly's cool but passionate delivery than any heavy-breathing disco record on the market.

But it was obviously disco the RCA art department had in mind when they designed the plasticized cover, showing Dolly caught in the middle of four disco moves—which has absolutely nothing to do with the music inside, other than an ever-so-slight disco feel to the title song. It is in fact the cover (smacking of market research) that has angered people in Nashville more than the music. "I don't think they're resentful of her switching over as much as they are of the pictures on that album," says one studio musician. "And people resented her standin' in front of that muscle man [Arnold Schwarzenegger] in *Rolling Stone*. They're wondering if the sweet disposition and the clean mouth that she's maintained all up to this point will stay the same. They're worried that she's not a clean-minded person anymore."

"There were some people who care enough about me as a person," Dolly told *Country Style*. "They were afraid I might be making a mistake, and they didn't want me to. ["Careful, Dolly," read the headline of one *Country Style* editorial.] Then there were those that said, 'Well, I can't believe it. She's going to get her rear end in a sling some day.' Those are people who are eaten up with jealousy. People who do not have the nerve or the grit to do what I did. Now they're embarrassed. They thought I was messin' up. Now they sort of wish they hadn't said it to me. They had hoped I'd fail, but I was determined I would not."

All in all, it was a busy fall for Dolly, with lots of press coverage, some earned, some manufactured. In October, on the day he threatened to quit his network television series rather than apologize for a skit he did satirizing the family of Farrah Fawcett-Majors, Redd Foxx appeared on the tube making fun of Dolly's bosom. According to Marsa Hightower of the L.A. office of Solters and Roskin, the skit alleged that if Dolly imprinted her breasts in the cement in front of Grauman's Chinese Theater the indentations would be so large that midget actor Billy Barty could get lost in them. Dolly, off on a concert tour, stopped her bus long enough to send Foxx a telegram: "Regarding the remarks made about me on your show last night on the ABC-TV network, which inaccurately made reference to mammoth-size 'imprints' of certain portions of my anatomy in the forecourt of Grauman's Chinese Theater in Hollywood, I must take exception. Imprints of these or any other parts of my anatomy are not currently in the forecourt . . . Further, the dimensions attributed to me are more than slightly incorrect. I would be the first to admit that I am well-endowed, but I seriously doubt that even your show's little person, Billy Barty, could be lost in such alleged imprints . . . I hesitate to add to your current woes, but I feel that in this case you owe me two equally ample apologies." The skit may indeed have embarrassed Dolly, and the sentiment of the telegram could easily be hers. But the wording—and the prompting to send such a wire at all (and copies to the press?)—had to come from none other than Dolly's new bosses.

She was getting genuine attention and recognition from the press about this time, too. In November, Solters and Roskin sent out a release announcing that on December 6, Dolly would be one of Barbara Walters' three interview subjects on her ABC network special. That one appearance—in which the most ferociously ambitious and often taxing interviewer on TV found herself not only matched but also awed by the little country girl from the mountains—earned Dolly more respect in the eyes of many viewers than all her records put together. She had an answer for everything.

"Dolly, did you look like this when you were a kid?" Barbara asked.

"Not quite."

"I mean you didn't have the . . . the blond wig . . . ?"

"No . . ."

"But when you went to school. When you were eleven, twelve, thirteen. Was it . . . this about you?"

"Well, you mean . . . the . . . full figure?" She laughs.

"Yeah, that's what I'm after."

"Yeah, I thought that's what you meant. Well, actually, I've always been pretty well blessed. As a child I grew up fast. Other members of my family have done the same."

"My assistant asked me something," Barbara says, sounding embarrassed. "And I'm going to blame it on her 'cause I wouldn't have had the nerve otherwise. Is it all you?"

Dolly chuckles. "Well, I can't show you here right on television."

"I'll take your word for it. When you talk to me—and we've talked a little bit today—do you feel that we're very different?" Barbara asks, sidling up.

"Not so much," Dolly replies, not nearly as chummy. "I feel we came from different palces . . . different backgrounds. . . .

"Yeah, we sure did." (Barbara chuckles.)

"But I really can relate to you in many ways. Probably more than you might relate to me," Dolly concedes.

"No, I felt the same thing," Barbara says, pals now. "I mean, I think that if people took the two of us together . . . we are very different women and yet, I relate to you very easily."

It takes Dolly no time to figure out why. "Well, I think that's that drive."

"Maybe . . . Dolly, you've said of yourself that you live in your own imagination. That sometimes you remind yourself of a fairy tale. I want to try a fairy tale on you . . . Once upon a time there was a little girl from the Smoky Mountains. Her name was Dolly Parton . . ."

"She lived in a small town in the mountains," Dolly picks up, knowing the story well, ". . . which she loved, because it was a comfort, because she knew there was love and security there, in her family. But she was a child, very curious. And she wanted all the things that she had always been impressed with. Like the fairy tales of Mother Goose stories and Cinderella and the lost slipper. Well, I guess she kinda wanted to find the other slipper in sort of a way so she worked hard and she dreamed a lot. And one day, it came true. She was a fairy princess and she lived happily ever after . . ."

10. Dolly Doll

The people at the Goldberger Doll Company in Brooklyn just couldn't picture it. "Does she really look like that?" they asked Ann Warden, who described her friend and business partner with elaborate gestures, hoping to interest the manufacturer in marketing a Dolly Parton doll. "They didn't know her," Mrs. Warden, the wife of Dolly's road manager, Don, told United Press International. "They were thinking about Barbie dolls with conservative clothes and Dolly's face on them. They just didn't understand." So Mrs. Warden showed them Dolly's picture. That helped. But it wasn't until she slapped modeling clay on Barbie's chest that the Goldberger people got the point. The twelve-inch poseable Dolly ("getting ready for showtime," "playing guitar and piano," etc.) came dressed in a one-piece red jumpsuit with silver trim and arrived in stores everywhere in June of '77, yours for only $9.95 Other costumes were promised soon, including a Coat of Many Colors. "Why it looks like Dolly *everywhere*!" Carol Channing exclaimed on *The Mike Douglas Show*, turning the doll over in a close inspection. In truth, it did not look much like her at all, but a lot of people thought it did. Chain stores put in big orders, and Ann Warden got letters from mothers throughout the country. One enclosed a snapshot of her delighted son clutching his new playmate. "Little children love me most," Dolly says. "I guess that's because they're too young to know better. They like me because I have a childlike voice, a silly laugh, and my name is Dolly. Something they can relate to—a doll. And I think they sense I love them, too." Mrs. Warden says children see Dolly as Cinderella. "She's almost too much. Someone that beautiful is hard to be true." Don Roth remembers 'Mrs. Warden' caught up with the band in Phoenix and brought the preproduction model for Dolly to approve. "Dolly looked at it and said, 'Yeah, that's swell. We'll take some pictures.' She was never really knocked out with that doll, but Ann is like family, you know." From toys, Mrs. Warden moved on to coloring books. The Great Selling of Dolly Parton was on.

There was a lot of money to be made from Dolly's likeness, for sure, but the real selling of Dolly Parton was in the image. And that was done not in the toy departments of chain stores coast to coast but between the covers of America's most prestigious magazines and newspapers and on TV.

"I'm not sure Dolly could have done that Barbara Walters interview two or three years ago," says Hal Durham. "She might not have been that outspoken. She would probably have been that honest, but I'm not sure she would have said as much as she did. It's probably a matter of confidence. When she made the move to cross over, she knew that people were going to criticize her for it, and for that, you have to have a certain confidence in yourself."

Part of getting on with being Dolly these days includes a high knowledge of the press, or at least of which magazines should carry Dolly features and which should not. But then she had good teaching. Early in '77 when Roy Blount, Jr., a contributing editor to *Esquire* magazine, wanted to do a cover story on Dolly, Tammy and Loretta, Dolly's L.A. people threw a fit at the idea of their client being lumped with country queens. Word has it L.A. said if *Esquire* wanted to do a "Dolly only" story and cover, Blount could have his interview. *Esquire* did not. Blount did his story without talking to Dolly and wrote that he believed Dolly herself wanted to be profiled, having answered an ad in the newspaper for a reducing belt, telling the owner she needed to shed a few unwanted pounds for an upcoming *Esquire* interview. It was just L.A., then, that balked. That disturbed Blount, as well it should have: "I tell you what I hope to hell," Blount wrote. "That those L.A. people aren't going to ruin her. Have her referring to her hair as 'the hair' and her work as 'this business' on the Carson show." The *Esquire* incident was not the only one of its type, however. When Joan Dew planned to write *Singers and Sweethearts,* about the five most successful women in country music, L.A. sent word through Charlene Bray that if Dew left Dolly in the book, they would sue her publisher. "They're hard-nosed, full of themselves, tough to do business with—egomaniacs," Dew says. "They think they're as big a star as their clients."

From an experience journalist Martha Hume had, Solters and Roskin can be just as hard-nosed as Katz-Gallin. In January '78 Hume was assigned a story on Dolly for *Us* magazine. Between the time the story was assigned and published, the magazine changed editors twice. One editor guaranteed the cover, and the next editor pulled it. And then they came back and . . . well, Hume tells it better.

"Apparently, they decided to let Dolly talk to me on the basis that she was getting a cover," Hume says. "I never spoke to Sandy Gallin. I talked to Don Warden, Sim Myers at RCA, and Katie Valk at Solters and Roskin. It was Sandy and Lee Solters who were plugging for the cover. I had just called and put in the routine request through RCA and Solters and Roskin, because I'd called Sandy Gallin's office and they wouldn't even let me speak to him. They were really rude and said, 'Call Solters and Roskin,' So I called them. At that time they were having a feud with *Us* magazine over Barry Manilow. Lee Solters was furious at *Us.* Meantime, *Us* had fired their person who'd been dealing in music, so I was it. So, finally I called Herb

Hellman at RCA and said, 'Herb, maybe I should talk to Lee Solters and explain to him the person who screwed up the Barry Manilow thing is gone, and we'll do our best to deal honestly with you.' So I put in my call to Lee Solters and explained to his secretary what I wanted to do. And Lee Solters called me up. He said, 'Martha, you want an interview with Dolly? I'll tell you what I'm gonna do. I'm gonna call 'em up over at *Us* magazine and I'm gonna demand that they put up a $100,000 bond. And when I see Dolly's picture on the cover, I'll give 'em back that $100,000 with interest.' He said, 'Do you think that's fair?' And I said, 'Mr. Solters, I think that's probably one of the most audacious things I've ever heard of.' Meanwhile, I panicked. But Solters called up Ron Martin, the then-editor, and not a word was said. Everything was hunky-dory. Ron Martin said, 'Dolly's probably gonna be a cover story, don't worry.' Meanwhile, I don't get my interview, I don't get my interview, I don't get my interview. And I'm still calling, and they say 'Lee's still making up his mind.' Finally, I only got it when I told them I didn't want it. Just to preserve my friendship with Dolly, I told Don Warden to tell her not to worry about it, that I wasn't all that upset, and we were going to skip it. I said, 'Please give her the message that I'm staying out of the fight between Solters and Roskin and *Us* magazine, and I think she should stay out, too. And when they come to an agreement, we can get together.' Then I told Solters and RCA that I didn't want to talk to her. I said, 'I'll just make it up. I don't want her to call me, nothin'. Zero. Forget it.' They called me at midnight from California and said, 'Dolly's gonna call you tomorrow at noon.' And she did. I told her what was going on, and she said, 'Oh, Martha, I'm so sorry. It's not personal. I just have to do what my manager says.' I said, 'Dolly, my feelings were really hurt, because I knew no more than you what was going on, and I thought you were mad at me or something.' And she said, 'No, no, no.' She sounded sincere, but then, of course, she always does. And, as always, I'm so charmed by Dolly. But I think she was sincere. Sandy Gallin's bad PR for her. Solters apparently is not that much of a bad guy. He has the reputation for threatening to do things like $100,000 bonds. But he's just one of those old-fashioned PR guys with flamboyant gestures. That's his thing. But they hung me up from January to May. And then it was not a cover."

Dolly is not yet at the point where she talks about "the hair" (although she does say "this business," but not quite the way Blount means). But one fears that is not far around the corner. She is already insisting on photo approval on several projects. In a press conference in Huntsville, Alabama, in May, '78, a male reporter asked Dolly how she managed to keep from being exploited like Farrah Fawcett and Cheryl Tiegs. "Well," Dolly shot back stern-faced, "they're models, and I'm an entertainer." "That's true," the reporter conceded, "but have you tried to control the exploitation?" "Well, we always try to control the type of publicity that we have," Dolly said matter-of-factly, as if she had been running one of the big movie studios in the Golden Age of Hollywood. "And we have a great PR firm, Solters and Roskin, that do all the publicity. And we try to limit it to what makes sense for me. I don't want to be places where I really wouldn't have a reason for bein', you know, without a good story or in-depth story." And then she knocked his hat off. "The wildest thing I guess I've ever done in the line of publicity is in October, if I approve the picture, I'm gonna be on the cover of *Playboy* magazine. But it's only because there's a real lengthy article in there that I'm quite proud of. So they wanted me to do the cover, and I said no for a long time. I wouldn't even do the article for a long time. So if I like the pictures, I'm gonna be on the cover. If I don't, I'll still have the article in the magazine." Dolly said the pictures had been shot, but she hadn't seen them yet. "I have to see how fat I look, I guess," she added, and laughed.

Hoo, Porter! And you wouldn't let her be on the cover of sedate little *Nashville!* magazine because it carried ads for eateries with liquor licenses! Last year, when Chet Flippo alluded to Dolly's remarkable chest, Dolly told him, "I have never been the one to play up that sort of thing about myself. It's always been the public and the press. I have really tried to not promote nothing but my talent." And just a few years ago, Dolly had told LaWayne Satterfield she wasn't trying to sell her body. Perhaps *she* isn't now, but *somebody* sure is. The *Playboy* interview may be just that—an interview, and a cover, and some nice respectable pictures without emphasis on Dolly's monumental physique. But there is no denying the fact that the Dolly poster, which went on sale in May '78, was designed to play on the libidos of college boys everywhere. The Dolly who was so modest that she wouldn't let her seamstress see her undressed or allow anyone outside her family to see her in shorts, appears reclining in a haystack, dressed in a Daisy Mae outfit—short shorts and an off-the-shoulder polka-dot blouse. A paper moon hangs in the painted background, just underneath the "Love, Dolly Parton" signature. "Now, *that* surprised me, coming from the Dolly I know," says Don Roth.

Dolly's reaction to the poster? "I haven't even seen it," she told me in Huntsville. "It's so new, and I've been on the road ever since it's been out. I have no idea how it's doin'. Now, I saw the one in *Time* magazine [another pose taken at the same session, in which she gives the camera a colder, but less castrating look than in the official poster version], and I didn't think it was too cute. I looked like I was sittin' on somethin' in the hay, like somethin' was stickin' me. Whoa!" she laughed. I asked how the idea for the poster came about. "I was doin' publicity shots, and my manager and some of the people thought it would make a cute poster, so we released it. I enjoyed doin' it, I guess."

There's something distressing about Dolly posing for such a blatantly exploitive photo and allowing her management to release the poster without her approval, something that suggests she has turned absolutely everything over to them. Roy Blount, Jr., appears to have worried not in vain. It's also slightly confusing that Katz-Gallin would nix a book and a magazine article that includes Dolly in country company and yet sanction a poster that sets her right down in Dogpatch. ("When I think of hillbillies, am I thinking of your kind of people?" Barbara Walters asked Dolly. "I think you probably are," she replied. "The people that grew up where I was were the ones that you would consider the Li'l Abner people, Daisy Mae, and that sort of thing. They took that kind of thing from people like us, but we were very proud people. People with a great deal of country class.") But then perhaps it is not so very confusing after all. Dolly went on to tell Barbara that "As a business person I like to think that there's more money to be made than the money I've been makin'. I've been workin' too hard, too long, for too little. The most money that I've made as a country artist would probably be maybe five, six hundred thousand dollars a year, not countin' expenses or records and this sort of thing. But when you say that you can make millions compared to thousands, and if you are going to be *in this business* [take note, Roy Blount!], if you are talented, if you do love it, then why not touch as many people? My dream was always to make as many people happy as I could in this life."

From the first reports, Dolly's poster is going to make a lot of people happy. "It's the fastest-selling poster we've ever had," Jerry Tupler, vice-president of Star City, Inc., the marketing company, told Laura Eipper of *The Tennessean.* "We don't have any exact sales figures yet, but I'd say we've easily sold several hundred thousand so far, just less than a month. The response has been just fantastic—it's a dynamite poster. It's something different in posters, not like what you usually see. The country image appeals to people. Some people have also said it reminds them of that old picture of Jane Russell in a haystack. I guess they do have the same physical attributes." The attributes are available at $2.50 per poster and the fact that they're selling like hotcakes pleases Dolly as a business woman but amuses her in other ways. "I know people are talking about me as a new sex symbol," she told Tom Zito of the *Washington Post.* "I think I'm more like a cartoon character, this big hair flipping all over, big hips, big bosom. It's a gimmick. I don't want the responsibility of being a sex symbol. I'm too lazy to stay on a strict diet. Really, I don't feel about it one way or another. It's always just amused me, the way men responded to me. They made pictures of me in a little bunny outfit for the cover of *Playboy,* and I just thought it was a real cute idea."

Dolly has been saying she dresses as a gimmick for years. But it's only lately she's been so up-front about money. ("If I was doin' this for the money . . . ," she told me in early '77.)

Three months later, Dolly was to tell other reporters: "I wasn't making all that much money—you really don't in country music unless you're a real superstar—and I knew I could make more," she told a British reporter for *Melody Maker.* "I mean, no matter how country you are, you hope for a crossover hit. why not? There's more money and recognition involved. Why are most of these people working if not for that?" And to the *Star* Dolly said, "You know, I have money left over, something to see for my work for the first time in my life now."

Just how much is open for debate. The *Star* estimates her crossover could make her richer by $10 million. Over how many years, the magazine fails to say. Still, that figure seems excessive. Several other estimates put Dolly's gross at about $1 million a year. But that was before the success of her poster and before *Here You Come Again* went platinum, signifying one million units have been sold. *Country Music* magazine reports that terms for the average recording contract would earn Dolly about $500,000 in royalties on the album, with her writer's royalty for the four Parton originals on the LP bringing her another $100,000. (A Nashville music publisher guesses that Dolly makes about $65,000 a year out of Owepar, from writer's royalties and publishing rights. Another says Dolly probably realizes $1 million a year—before taxes—from Owepar alone.) No figures are available as to how much Dolly makes from her cut of the Dolly doll, the coloring book, the T-shirt transfers on which she has the copyright, and the souvenir posters and books sold at her concerts. (One journalist suggests a Dolly wig should be the next marketed item.) *Country Music* magazine also reports that the agreement Dolly has with Twentieth Century-Fox is rumored to be "a multimillion dollar, three or four movie deal," and that she could gross $50,000 or more from the haystack poster. The magazine goes on to quote an insider as saying that stage shows, fairs and TV specials could pull in "well over a million dollars this year," or "maybe two million" for Dolly. Dolly was booked to do the rodeo at one large state fair in August '78. An insider there estimated in June she would receive $30,000–$40,000 guaranteed and a percentage for her five 30–40-minute shows over three days. "The guarantee might be under $30,000," the insider said, "but the percentage will be high. Either way," he said, "she'll walk out of there with a lot of money." A promoter who handled two of her concerts in May told me he paid her $10,000 for one, and $7,500 for another, despite rumors that she was commanding $50,000 for several dates. "To get $50,000," the promoter said, "she would have to play an outdoor date." He and other booking agents doubted Dolly was getting $50,000 for many shows, adding, "That's what the Bee Gees get!" (Dolly has publicly said that is one of her goals.) One booking agent told me he paid Dolly $6,000 flat for one concert in November '77, adding, "She turned down two dates for us for $12,500, simply because we wanted her to do two shows. It was not because of the money." The promoter says that two years ago, Dolly played Huntsville, Alabama, for $4,000. (She was getting $5,000 per concert in 1976.) He also said that when Katz-Gallin set up her spring 1978 tour, the dates were arranged with first-class promoters at $10,000 a night. "But business turned out not to be what they anticipated or hoped for, and they had to come off that figure in some cities." Still, that adds up, considering that Dolly does in excess of 200 concerts a year. But, as *Country Music* says, "Before you decide that Dolly is a country Rockefeller, remember the expenses. First agents, managers, publicists and so on take a big slice off the top, at least 25 percent." (Katz-Gallin probably gets 15 percent, says Don Roth.) "Then touring expenses, salaries for the band, costumes, arrangements all add up to big numbers. Take what's left, send half of that to the IRS, and you know why Johnny Paycheck worries about '. . . Uncle Sam's hand in my pants . . .' "

Several years ago, LaWayne Satterfield asked her about the line in "Kentucky Gambler": "When you love the greenback dollar, sorrow's always bound to follow." "A lot of people twist the *Bible* around and say money is the root of all evil," Dolly told Satterfield. "That's not what it says in the *Bible.* It's the *love* of money that's the root of all evil. So in my mind I thought, 'When you *love* the greenback dollar . . . not when you want it.' Money, I enjoy. A person would be a liar to say they didn't want the money. I don't want the money first. I want the joy and thrill out of this business. I want the feeling of accomplishment and I want to give what I feel that I need to give. But money is a bonus to me. I'm proud to have the money, and I would be telling a lie if I said I didn't. But my music is– Money is secondary to the things I want." But last year, Dolly reversed her order of preferences to *Time* magazine: "Sure I'm in it for the money, but also because I love music." And to Tom Zito, she said, "You can be a number one country star, and you're still not selling lots of records. People used to think I was making millions of dollars; I was making thousands. But now, my dream in life is to be successful at the movies."

She told me that in February of '77. "I want to be a recognized songwriter. I want songs recorded by people in country music and outside of country music. I want to leave things behind for the public and for my family. I want to see my records go into any territory they can go. I want to do TV, some specials, and I want to write some movies." Scores or scripts? "Both." Later the same year, she indicated to Bob Allen that she hoped she was building a legacy: "One hundred years from now, I would like to be thought of as one of the greater writers or somebody people would pick up on and analyze what I was sayin'. I care to know I might leave something for future generations to enjoy, and that's important to me now."

I asked her if she wanted to act in the movies she'd write. "Yeah, well I never wanted to be a movie star. That never appealed to me at all. I've always wanted to do a comedy, though." Just a few days before the press conference in Huntsville, the *New York Post* reported that Dolly was about to sign an unusual contract with Twentieth Century-Fox "wherein the high-riding studio will develop properties for her. In light of Dolly's highly individualistic style, this could prove quite a challenge." In Huntsville, Dolly announced that she had signed a three-movie deal. "I don't really know what I'll do yet," she said. "But I think one of the things will be my life story. [Dolly told Martha Hume that she didn't think she'd be able to kiss another man—not even for the movies. And for the heavy love scenes, the movie people would just have to turn the lights down low so nobody could tell she had Carl in bed with her and not an actor.] It's kinda hard to write your life story when you ain't lived it yet," Dolly continued in Huntsville, "but anyway, I think we're gonna sell that to Twentieth Century this week. We already signed the deal with them. And then probably the other two things will be a continuation of the story, or it could be a comedy thing. There's a few people talkin' to us, writers we like. I think I'd like to do somethin' comedy. Maybe one of 'em will be a musical. To be honest, I don't know."

A reporter asked if Dolly likes to act. "I don't act," she said. "I don't know how to act. I'd like to be in the movies if I don't have to act." She laughed. "That's what I told them. They wanted to sign me up to this deal. And they came to me. I didn't even want to be in the movies. I'd never even thought that much about it. But they thought they saw somethin' in me that I would do well in movies, and I told 'em, 'If you're willin' to put out that kind of money and take that kind of chance on somebody who's never had an acting lesson or a screen test or anything, I'll be glad to gamble with you.' Which makes a lot of sense. The main thing in movies is the fact that you don't act, where you can be what you are, be yourself and say the lines the way you would naturally say 'em and all. So if we can get somethin' like that, I think I'll do well. If not," she added with nervous laughter and a furrowed brow, "I guess I'll be awful."

Some people who know Dolly say she has natural acting ability. Lucy Adams suggests Dolly may have been a little haughty and snooty in New York because she believed that's the way a star is supposed to act. "And she knows to get there she has to do some pushing," Adams says. "She could act like that, but I don't think when it comes right down to it, she is like that. Because she can act. I said something to her once about being a big shot one of these days and going off to Hollywood, and she said, 'I'm not an actress.' She isn't an actress, but she can act. She's put on some skits here for me that were hilarious. I got her the overalls, and she said, 'I need a sack of Country Gentleman tobacco.' She wanted cigarette papers, and she squatted down like some man, poured the tobacco in and tried to roll a cigarette in one hand. Then she talked real country, about digging taters and all that. It was an act, and she was good at it. Yet, you can see her act just as dignified as anybody."

The personality she plays best, though, is Dolly Parton, creative artist, sensitive person, gimmick with a heart of gold. Like Joan Crawford, Dolly conceived her character years ago and eventually became it. "Well, that's fine," she told me. "A character never grows old. A character lives forever, just like Mae West, like Zsa Zsa Gabor, Liberace. I guess I *am* a character. In more ways than just by look. I guess I'm a character only because I'm just totally what I am. I'm not afraid to be that and say what I want to, and just do what I want to." Don Roth has played for several big show-biz stars such as Tony Bennett and Frank Sinatra. "They come backstage, and they're just regular people. They'll offer you a beer. But Dolly is always Dolly. I've never seen her without her wig, without her makeup. After we got close, I asked her why. She said, 'It's my opinion the reason I'm so successful is that the masses expect to see Dolly Parton sparkle and shine, and I don't want them to ever not see that.' And even though I was a member of the band, I was closer to being the masses than I was to being a friend. I don't know if there is a character other than the spangles and sequins. If there is, it's buried really deep. I don't know that it's an act at all, because the character has overtaken her."

"I was sent down to do the 'Dolly Parton—Is She For Real?' story—what's behind the cornpone charm," says Dave Hershey of the New York *Daily News*. "And it's a very well-cultivated act, I think. I tried to catch her at odd moments when she wasn't hooked into her stage persona, but she always seems to be on. She's just a very, very charming person, and you can't catch her with her guard down. I've done a lot of big-time celebrities in the last year and a half, but she is as tough to catch off-guard as anybody. She's very guarded about her childhood. Everytime I would say, 'It sounds like you had a miserable childhood,' she would say, 'Oh, no, no, it was really quite happy, joyful.* I'm not like Loretta Lynn. I've had a very happy life.' She's afraid to appear human, and that's sad. It's just a matter of time before people see through it. I went out there totally objective, and I could tell it was an act the whole time."

Dolly's better at that at some times than at others, and she's more convincing on some particular subjects. "She can convince me of anything in an interview," says journalist Joan Dew. "You've heard all these stories about her marriage being an arrangement, and you've heard that she is so ambitious that nothing stands in her way. And then you spend an hour with her, and she shines those big blue eyes on you, and that soft, little-girl voice, and she's *sweet*. There's a sweetness, an innocence about her, that can't be all phony. Unless she's the world's greatest actress. And you leave an hour or two later, or maybe two days later, and you're convinced. You believe she's got the best marriage in the world. She calls it that, and it probably is, for her. But it nevertheless is not a marriage in the conventional sense. You're convinced that her relationship with Judy is no more than she says it is, that they're girl friends from grade school. You're convinced that as far as her career goes, yes, she's very ambitious, but everything that's happened has more or less been predestined anyway, that she hasn't really had that much control over it. It was just meant to be, from three or four reincarnations ago, I guess. She *can* convince me of anything when I'm in her presence. Have you ever read a cynical, bitter interview with Dolly Parton? An

* Although Dolly constantly talks about how much love there was in the Parton family, she told freelance writer Carol Botwin, "I never got enough personal attention when I was a child. Not enough caressing. How can you pick up twelve children!"

interview where the reporter doubted in print her sincerity? Never. And you probably never will. Did you read the *Rolling Stone* interview? Now, you know how cynical they are. The guy was eating out of her hand!"

Lucy Adams doesn't want to believe Dolly really said all those things in the *Rolling Stone* interview. She doesn't know the side of Dolly that told Flippo, "When I was a teenager I wrote a lot of *real* hot and heavy love stories, I was just so horny myself." "I have read articles like that one that to me are just not Dolly," Adams says. "I think it's their own writing lots of times. I can't see Dolly changing that much, 'cause I don't think Dolly would change basically from what she has always been. I told her when we were doing the show, 'Dolly, don't ever change.' She said, 'I can't. I have to just be me.' I hope she never does, and I don't think she has to. I don't think she could better herself by changing in any way."

Joan Dew doesn't think *Rolling Stone* put words in Dolly's mouth. "If she said those things in front of a *Rolling Stone* reporter, she said it because she wanted to see it in print, for whatever reason she wanted that to be in the story. Because whatever else she is, Dolly Parton is not a stupid woman. She's not naive, she's not dumb or gullible. You're not going to con Dolly, or outsmart her. And you're not going to get her to say anything she doesn't want to say. I think it's instinctive. It's just something she's got."

Rolling Stone's accompanying photos of Dolly with Arnold Schwarzenegger caused as much hoopla in Nashville as the article. Some were aghast. Others, like local TV personality Huell Howser, were exhilarated. "Tell me the real story behind that picture session," Howser asked Dolly on camera shortly after the piece came out. "Well, actually, there was no real story," Dolly said. "[Mac Davis and I did] a six week tour, and so Chet [Flippo] came out on the road, and we spent two or three days just doin' the thing. So he told me that I was to go to New York on the day that they had set aside to do the pictures. I just thought I was just gonna take regular pictures. But when I got there, this girl, it's a real popular photographer, Annie Leibovitz, she's really, really sharp, and she comes up with some real good ideas. But when I walked in, here was this naked man. Almost naked—had on these little skin-tight, uh, shorts, and all this . . . body, and it was just . . . I just almost fell over. [Laughter] And I said [she gets a mischievous glint in her eye], 'What are me and him gonna do together?' [She squeals on the last syllable, and then begins giggling so hard she almost can't tell the story. Howser can hardly contain himelf.] And the idea she had was the male and female body. And it turned out really neat. It's got a lot of . . . attention, yeah, and they made some posters up of 'em. And he was such a nice guy to know. We had a fun day takin' the pictures, but, like I say, it was new to me." Howser razzed her a little. "I saw your face in those pictures. You were smilin' awful big." "Well," Dolly said, laughing half from embarrassment and half out of the high of the moment, "He was, too!" Arnold agrees. Dolly was "the nicest weight I have lifted in a long time," he told *Time* magazine. "I did a one-arm curl with her. She was about 110 pounds, good resistance. My biceps felt very good after that. So did I."

Dolly has kept her promise to Lucy Adams. She hasn't changed. She's simply been revealed—and on purpose. "I do have this image that I have to protect among some older country fans," Dolly told Matt Yancey in 1975. "But that doesn't mean I don't like a good time." But now Dolly has another image to work on, one that will let her young, newly acquired hip fans know that she's just kidding when she wears all her sequined trappings. "Young people cannot only enjoy my music, but they can appreciate what I have been doing with my appearance," she told a reporter last year. "They think it's funny that I would be so bold to do it." And by being bold enough to tell Chet Flippo about her "cherry," she was letting all his hip readers know that Miss Dolly is no longer (or never really was) country-naive and innocent. While I was interviewing Dolly in her home, Dolly asked me not to quote her saying "boobs." The word seemed hard for her to say, even to another woman. In May, Phillip Rawls of the Montgomery (Ala.) *Advertiser* asked Dolly if she tired of hearing jokes about her "endowment." "You mean boobs?" Dolly asked back. Just as she told Rawls, "I had to work extra hard to show I was more than gaudy," she now apparently feels she has to work extra hard to prove she can fit in with Linda Ronstadt and Emmylou Harris's crowd. Dolly will now tell an audience, "A lot of you brought your binoculars tonight. I guess you just want to see if they're as big as people say they are." Sometimes she'll add, "My wigs, of course." Sometimes she won't. Then again, Dolly could be sneaking a few of these in for another purpose, for a reason that was denied her public under Porter's iron hand. "You can use sex as a threat, or you can use it like Dolly uses it," Linda Ronstadt says, "as a celebration of your attractiveness, with nobody left out."

Manipulation of the press has turned out to be one of Dolly's greater talents. "She courts reporters," says Dave Hershey. "She went through a whole rap to me about how nobody's ever been mean to her in the press." Odd, since I have heard her tell reporters how much she disliked their stories, how they embarrassed her in print, and how, as a result, she and the reporter could never be friends, since she didn't trust him anymore. And doubly odd, since Dolly is hypersensitive to any criticism of her work. Just as she was hurt that Porter told her both the good and bad points to her songs, Dolly cannot understand how a journalist who basically praises her work and considers her a major talent could write that "Me and Little Andy" is an unbearably sentimental piece of claptrap. "She couldn't even understand if you wanted to sit next to someone else on the bus," says Don Roth. And while Dolly insists "I'm not temperamental at all," one semi-critical line in an otherwise glowing story or review is enough to upset her all day. "A horrendous writer in Green Bay tried to write a negative piece, but it didn't come off," says Dave Hershey. "The woman quoted Dolly as sayin 'Ah' for 'I,' and Dolly got a little rankled at that. She said, 'She tried to make me sound like a country bumpkin.' But there was a line in the story that really angered her. The woman wrote, 'Dolly Parton is so sweet you'd almost hope she had a cocaine stash somewhere.' My wife showed the piece to her, and she was livid for the rest of the day. This was nothing except a woman trying to be clever at Dolly's expense, but Dolly said, 'This is the nastiest thing anybody's written about me in quite a while.' The day after, she seemed really down and wouldn't do any interviews—just the fact that it was not a rave. What's amazing to me is that she knows every magazine in the country and what they mean to her. Our circulation is three million, and I got a two-two hour interview. My wife is a senior editor at *Family Circle,* and its circulation is nine million. She got a four-hour interview. Dolly knows *Family Circle* is the heartland, she's got her hard-core fans out there."

Hershey and his wife ran into the problem Steve Ray and many other journalists have in interviewing Dolly—once she comes up with a line that sounds good or looks good in print, she continues to use it over and over. Every celebrity does that to a certain extent—but usually only those without Dolly's intelligence and quick wit. "Dolly knew we were married, or maybe she forgot, but she knew we were traveling together, and she repeated the same anecdotes to us as if they were fresh," Hershey says. "She's really got the lines down. That's what disturbs me more than anything. I went out there, thought I got really good stuff, and then came back and read the clips and got a little depressed, because most of the anecdotes were in the clips. She gave me one great quote—she said, 'I can't run or jog, 'cause I'd black both my eyes,' and my friend at *Rolling Stone* who does Random Notes was all excited about it. He said, 'Jesus, what a great quote. Can I have it?' I said, 'No, it's one of the few things I have that I haven't read in the clips.' And then I found out she'd given it to you a year and a half ago. I was sick. She's got like twenty lines that she just keeps trotting out every so often, and it's very calculated. Occasionally, she'll slip and give you something different, but very rarely. Like Rodney Dangerfield she has one hundred rehearsed bits. She even has a rehearsed giggle. Everything is recycled. But she didn't give me the same anecdotes that she gave *The New York Times.* She knows the market."

The giggle is indeed rehearsed. "She likes the little girl image," says Judy Hunt. "You know how she talks like a little girl? Well, now she's got that little squeaky laugh. She didn't use to have that. Well, she did, but it's different now. It's more noticeable. It's put on. She acts like a little girl a lot. But if she and I were just talking, she wouldn't be like that. She'd be real serious. She'd be fun, but she'd be real sincere about things." Whereas Dolly used to be quite serious in the majority of her interviews, she now tends toward a certain flippancy in her answers. Not out of rudeness, but out of a need to convince the interviewer that she is aware of what she's doing. "This is my Beverly Hills wig," she told journalist Dick Kleiner. "It's only eight inches high. I think wigs are such fun . . . I started wearing them because they're so handy . . . Then it got to be a publicity gimmick—a least

I'm not going to be overlooked in a crowd." In the same article, she said, "The stories that I own Tennessee are not true. Most of my money is in land in Tennessee, but I don't own the whole state. I will say that I do own a large chunk of it, however."

All of that—the giggle, the wigs, the self-mockery ("Show business is a phony world anyway so why not dress the part?") and the self-aggrandizement—has been concocted for basically one reason. "I think the most important thing in Dolly's life is that people like her," says a friend. "Because it's real obvious that she does not think they do. She once told me, 'If I showed myself just like I was, nobody would like me. No one would think that I was a star.'" (And, in fact, when reporter Bob Allen first interviewed Dolly on her bus, he waited up for her to change clothes. When she appeared, "I turned once and turned back and then I looked again and realized that was Dolly sitting across from me. She had on a shapeless dressing gown and slippers, and she just looked real ordinary and casual.") "This woman has been put down quite a lot, but I think most of the putdown came when she was a kid," continues her friend. "I think she gets along better with men than she does with women because she likes to be courted. She likes somebody being overwhelmed by her. Maybe she has this dream of being able to dangle fifty men on a string. Since Dolly's whole life is fantasy anyway, maybe she sees herself as having all these men who really, really love her and think she's beautiful, and she can be a capricious bitch. No matter how she treats them, they'll like her anyhow. With Dolly, she wants you to love her, but maybe she doesn't want to have to give it back. She really enjoys the adulation. It helps her. She has a poor self-image. Dolly doesn't think she's pretty. If she did, she wouldn't wear wigs and rhinestones. People making over her is enjoyable to her."

And the press has certainly made over Dolly, focusing much of their attention on the incongruity of her look, her intelligence and her talent. "Dolly Parton," wrote Josh Mills, "is a blend of unlikely proportions. 'Five feet tall' she says of herself, 'but 6-feet-4 in my wig and my heels.' Half of her is pure country, jes plain folks, her life a joy and her marriage perfect, li'l farm girl made good. The other half, from those stacked heels right to the top of her ridiculously piled blond wig, is pure show biz. It's a most peculiar package ..." Jack Hurst has spent a lot of time talking with Dolly, and thinking about her, too. "Inevitably," he wrote in *High Fidelity* magazine, "the recent national notice accorded Dolly Parton has focused more on the improbability of her image than on her art. A voluptuous woman with a childish giggle, she finger-picks the guitar, the banjo, and the mountain dulcimer with inch-long, painted nails. She composes delicate lyrics of Tennessee mountain innocence and performs them in finery a stripper would happily peel. And through layers of lipstick, she pushes a voice fervent with fundamentalist religion. Today she would like to be a little more listened to and a little less ogled. But the reams of copy about her fashion and physiognomy can hardly be blamed on anyone but herself; she donned the gaudy garb and high-piled hair specifically to make us stare. 'If you have talent, people are gonna overlook it,' she cynically observes, 'unless you've got somethin' to get attention.' Parton has a lot of both." And in the *Chicago Tribune Magazine* Hurst commented, "With her physical attributes, it is hardly surprising that she has attracted a lot of press coverage. What is surprising is that she has emerged as a highly intriguing personality, a very quotable combination of mountain innocence, frank ambition, unpredictable grammar, bubbly sincerity, and attractive modesty . . . her movements began to be reported by such diverse journals as *The New York Times*, the *Village Voice*, *People* magazine, and *Rolling Stone*. And they all proclaimed that they had made an identical, astonishing discovery: Behind all the paint, hair and frills, Dolly Parton is one of the most charming and real performers on the American scene." And most journalists waxed not only poetic about Dolly Parton but also favorable. "Even off stage, she looks like the quintessential truckstop fantasy, with gobs of yellow curls, an easy smile and a body that has more curves than a good knuckleball," wrote one reporter. *Time* magazine's Jean Vallely took in a couple of Dolly shows and pronounced, "A Dolly Parton concert is a treat, like a hot fudge sundae after a month of dieting." And *TV Guide*'s Neil Hickey, obviously smitten, wrote that "only scoundrels, scamps and scapegraces would take aim at the splendent, clinquant image of Dolly Parton—such fun is she to look at and to ponder."

That is exactly the reaction Dolly wants everyone to have, and if they don't, she's liable to get testy about it. "I think she's terrifically talented at manipulating people," says Joan Dew. "If she couldn't get what she wanted with her big blue eyes and her smile, she was accustomed to being able to intimidate people. I'm not easily intimidated. So consequently she never showed me her claws, as it were, where I think she might have liked to a couple times, especially when I implied that Carl was possibly henpecked. Then I said, 'Well, if you look at it from an outsider's point of view, the way it looks, the man never gets involved in anything. You do exactly as you please. You do what you do when you want to do it. And he never says anything about it one way or the other.' And then she backed down. She was very cold to me a couple of times about questions I asked or insinuations I made. She can shut you out in a second, but then she can turn around and flash that smile on you two minutes later."

Dolly can be disarming in other ways, too. After I had been at her house for about eight hours, she suddenly stopped in the middle of our interview and said, "You ain't been to the bathroom all day, have ya?" I blushed and told her no. "Well, come here," she said, "let me show you where it is." I followed her down the hall, but declined use of the facility. Later, after we ate dinner and were about to continue the interview, she suddenly asked, "Have you peed yet?" Again, the answer was no. "Well, here," she said, "you use this one and I'll go upstairs. I've just got to go!"

However, Charlene Bray can remember a time when Dolly was not always so accommodating to visiting journalists. "I've never seen her get mad at a writer, or be ugly with anyone," Bray says, "but she can be surprising. All of a sudden, something can hit her that's all wrong. It can recall something that maybe she's wanted to get you about for some time and hasn't had the opportunity, and all of sudden, she can nail you to the wall. She'll do that if she thinks she's misjudged you, too; if she didn't play you just right, that frustrates and aggravates her, and she'll nail you. One of the first inklings I had that Dolly could be temperamental and hard to work with if she wanted to be was when she was doing the filming for her TV show. I brought a journalist down from Pennsylvania, from *Grit*. She had known for weeks that he was coming. They were going to give her color coverage. And the backbone of their circulation is the small towns across the country, where so much of her grassroots support comes from. This boy was so enamoured of her, anyway, before he got an opportunity to meet her, and I had the photographer ready to do pictures anytime we could get them. And she was uptight. I knew she was when we got there that afternoon to do the pictures. He was not gonna interview her then. He was just, like many others, hangin' around, watchin' what was takin' place, and he was gonna write about it and take the pictures anytime we could get them. Well, we got a cute idea to do a picture inside the makeup room of twenty wigs setting in there on a pedestal. She would have no part of it. Slammed the door. 'Not now,' she said, and almost did not do the interview, and kept the poor guy on pins and needles from the time he got there in the first part of the week until Friday. And Friday was his very last day. He'd already made his reservation. And we ended up doing the interview in the office of Don Warden. We walked in and she said, 'Alright now, I'll give you twenty minutes. I've got to do something.' He was not a cub reporter, but he was not accustomed to that kind of treatment. And I could look in his eyes and know that he was already disappointed, was gonna be workin' under a handicap. But the piece came off beautifully. That was my first inclination that she could be other than her sweet, saccharine self. She never did give a reason for it. It could have been something that had taken place earlier that day and she was taking this frustration out on the next person at hand, or it could have been she didn't look as good as she wanted to that day. Could have been that the music was not going well. This was a big production for Show Biz, too. It was the first time that they had called in a set designer from the West Coast. They were uptight and nervous about the whole thing, and I think Dolly sensed by that time that it was not the proper vehicle for her. So she was uptight about the whole thing. She's a complex person. She's got a lot of determination, she's gutsy, she goes after what she wants, and if it affects her career, she can afford now not to be nicey-nice all the time. She can afford to express her opinion. And that's what she's got a management company for—to cover her on all bases. And if something needs smoothing over, then they can do it and so can their PR outfit. They've got the clout to do it with. I never saw Dolly be intentionally mean to somebody. She gave the boy the interview, so he went away happy with that, but he did it under not the best circumstances."

For some journalists, that smile and the look and personality behind it is overpowering. One of the most astute country music journalists in the country, a fine writer to boot, admits that she's lost her objectivity when it comes to Dolly Parton. "I've come to the conclusion that what I want to believe about Dolly Parton is what she'd like me to believe," she says. for me. I want there to be a Cinderella. And I'm going to let her be it. There's a lot that's magical about her. I'm not saying I don't understand how calculated it all is. I'm just saying I've *chosen* to believe it. I've chosen her as my symbol of a pretty lady that I'd like to be like and never will. There is a certain loveliness to her personality, and I'd like to have that."

Such quotes and reports must thrill Sandy Gallin, who is doing his best to create an aura of mystery and intrigue about Dolly Parton, and to make her as inaccessible as the top rock—or movie—stars. The truth of it is that Katz-Gallin, to a large extent, is only packaging and promoting an image that Dolly set up for herself long ago. Such as a comparison with Elvis. In 1975, at the press conference to announce Porter's giving Don Warden to Dolly to be her manager, Dolly looked into the television cameras and said, "Don's gonna be my Colonel Parker."

When Peter Manso of *Playgirl* magazine asked Dolly what musicians she'd most like to work with, Dolly answered Roy Buchanan and Bob Dylan. "And also it makes me real sad that I'll never have the opportunity to sing with Elvis. This is something I'd always wanted since he had that vibrato in his voice and we both were brought up with the same background, you know, the same mother thing and all. And when I wrote the story of the 'Coat of Many Colors,' even before I recorded it, for some strange reason, I thought it should have been sung by Elvis Presley. I always felt like I was kin to Elvis, like he was a brother, and there was something between us that if we'd ever gotten together something would've come of it."

Dolly and Katz-Gallin are not the only ones making comparisons. "I think she'll be the female Elvis," a young fan was overheard to say after Dolly's concert in Huntsville in May '78. But Don Roth thinks Dolly considers herself bigger than Elvis right now. "I think she wants to be bigger than anybody—she wants to be the *biggest,*" he says. "She puts no limits on her accomplishments." Nor does Katz-Gallin or Solters and Roskin. And to make sure everyone understands what a hot prospect Dolly is, they ration her press conferences, her interviews, the amount of promotion she does in connection with concerts, and her autographing. The rider for the dates she did in the spring of '78 carried stipulations that she would have a barricade in front of the stage, that no mail or gifts were not to be left in the dressing room but held in the box office and given to her at one time, and that she would sign autographs only if her schedule allowed. Apparently, her schedule never allowed it because she was always whisked away immediately following the concert, in a limousine carrying two security guards. One promoter says the rider was "more than for most country artists." Don Roth says he's glad Dolly's no longer "coming back on stage and kissing little children and letting everybody in the audience get an autograph," because "part of the reason Dolly used to lose her voice every now and again and have to quit tours was strictly nervous tension. Dolly is a sweetheart, and she will stay up twenty-four hours a day signing autographs for just anybody standing outside the door, and somebody, either Gregg or Don Warden, has to say, 'That's it, she's wasted.' She does this six nights in a row, and then gets up at six and goes to radio interviews, gets on the bus, drives for six hours, does the concerts, gives interviews before and then stands on stage and does the show. Or at least she used to."

But while Dolly will give so much of herself physically that she wears herself down, she realizes the value of holding back psychologically. She knows that Greta Garbo's aloofness and mystery got her as far—or further than—her acting ability, and she's pleased that a lot of people say they think nobody really knows her. "That's probably true," she says with a sly smile when the subject is put to her. "You can know a good bit of me, but that's why I say I'm made up of so many things. I'm a bit shy, believe it or not, even though I'm an outgoing person. I'm very modest and I have a shy side. But I'm capable of just about anything, I guess. I'm a free spirit. Not that I do everything, but I'm honest enough to say that I'm capable of it, under the right conditions and all that. But I have many secret thoughts and many secret places in my mind. I'm real deep. I don't mean that as a compliment to myself, necessarily. I just mean there are so many caverns in my mind that nobody ever explores except me and whoever I want to go there. I have secrets. But a person needs to have secrets—if nothing else, certain emotions that you feel that you have to keep secret, or that you want to keep secret. I'm even fascinatin' to myself, because there are so many things and ideas that I have—creative ideas and things—that I excite myself when I get real creative and come up with these harebrained ideas. They come so fast that I get excited about it and I can't get to it soon enough. And then I turn around and do something so dumb and so stupid that I'll tickle myself, and I just won't believe it. I'll get mad at myself for certain things, and then sometimes when I done somethin' really good, I'll take great pride in that, to myself, and I'll just think, 'Oh, boy, that turned out real good. You done a good job on that'n.' But I never know. I'm very—what would I call it? Impulsive? I never know from one minute to the next what I might do. I'm mischievous, I'm very playful. But like I say, I guess, I experience in my personality some of everything. But I guess that's good, though. I feel like a pretty wholesome person. I don't want any of that to sound vain. I mean, it's so easy to get to talkin' too much by tryin' when somebody asks you what you're like and what you are, but I guess I *am* mysterious, because there are so many things that I don't tell. But I don't want to. I mean, I'm sure everybody has lots of things that they do that they don't want people to know they do, or things they feel that they wouldn't want to say for fear somebody'd think they're perverted or crazy or somethin'. But you still feel 'em just the same."

William Carlos Williams knew something about what this country does to its favorite sons when he wrote "The pure products of America go crazy." No one is suggesting that Dolly has lost her mind, by any means, but several of her friends fear that she may be losing her identity and her sense of self in her capitulation to Katz-Gallin and the quest of stardom. In the spring of '78, this woman who was so self-conscious about her large bust that she preferred turtleneck sweaters to almost any other shirt or top, appeared on the Cher special in two low-cut gowns that revealed plenty of cleavage. Perhaps only Dolly's Nashville dressmakers realized what a compromise that was for Dolly. Aside from the fact that Katz-Gallin was having Dolly dress fashionably, which Dolly had never wanted to do, the purpose of the low-cut gowns was, of course, "to get her away from that innocent look and into something more sexy," as Judy Hunt puts it. It wasn't just a sexy wardrobe Katz-Gallin hung on Dolly last spring, though. A month before the Cher special, she appeared at the Radio and Records convention in Dallas, where disc jockeys were given laminated "eats" passes that featured an autographed picture of Dolly from *Here You Come Again,* with "I Spent the Night With Dolly in Dallas" printed across it. "Talk about sloppy," says Richard Peterson, tongue in cheek. "Can you believe nobody thought that was tacky?"

"If she were a man, Katz-Gallin would already have Dolly in a shirt open to the navel with false chest hair and a big medallion," Don Roth says. "They'll do everything in their power to drag her down the Donny and Marie route to Vegas. I don't think she's realized how much she's changed. She has to have control over everything around her, but she doesn't realize that Katz-Gallin really is controlling her. I know why she went with them. She couldn't go on being the girl on the Porter Wagoner show all her life, and she didn't know what to do. She wanted to be a superstar. And even though I'm sure she disagrees with them a lot, it's like going to a doctor. He's supposedly a professional, and you'd be stupid not to take the pills he prescribes for you. After the first week of rehearsals, we were a little irritated. We said, 'Who are these bozos telling us what to do?' She said, 'Just remember this. They work for me. I hired them. I pay them to do what they do and I'd be a fool not to at least listen and try and explore what they say I should do. But when I don't feel it's right, believe me, I won't do it.'

"But some of the band thought way back there that she was compromising herself musically, in doing such things as putting together that Vegas-type show with the mountain medley. Look at Emmylou Harris's and Linda Ronstadt's shows. It's a natural musical show. It's music. They don't sing and dance. They don't tell funny stories in between. They say, 'Here's our next song,' bammo. That's how Dolly used to be. And now they've got her doing stories and medleys and everything with time changes. They've turned it into a Vegas show. They've turned it into a Mac Davis show. Katz-Gallin has done wonders for people like Cher, Mac Davis, Olivia Newton-John, Paul Lynde, Donny and Marie. You know why? Because they need them. They would have gotten up on stage and fumbled and stammered and had nothing to say between tunes. Their music ain't very good, but their stage presence is exquisite because they've been taught to do that. One of the reasons I went with Dolly is because she was a natural knockout stage performer. In my opinion, they have . . . taken all the balls out of her performance. She now takes steps. She's always at the right place on stage from the choreographer's point of view. I wonder if Katz-Gallin couldn't have taken Dolly as she was and simply promoted her into superstardom without asking her to change very much. If you could only have seen her like she was in a place we played in Tennessee. We hadn't done that long a concert and people were really clapping. We ran out of material, and the bass player and drummer were new and just didn't know any more than what they'd rehearsed. So she came out and did about another forty-five minutes with just a guitar slung around her neck. It would have knocked you dead. Would have knocked *anybody* dead. It was a killer. She was hoarse, but she gave them a great show. Told some great, natural stories about her songs and how she wrote them, and it was just beautiful. But that first Mac Davis tour, Dolly had to fight to keep 'Me and Little Andy' in. You and I may be very jaded and sophisticated and think that song transcends the boundaries of good taste, but that's Dolly's song. And the average person out there will cry when she sings it. Dolly could turn out to be a created entity that ends up failing because the thing that made her good in the first place—her naturalness and originality—is being taken away from her. She was such an original, and they're trying to make her the same as every other performer out there. I don't think Dolly is sure of what she's really like anymore, or what she's supposed to be like. Katz-Gallin has told her so long, as I'm sure any manager would, 'I know what you'd like to be, but here's what you should be.' She's scared. And she's insecure and Sevierville enough to still listen to them because she just doesn't know what else to do. Dolly backs up very quickly from situations where she isn't in control. But somehow, Katz-Gallin's managed to intimidate her, and I don't know how. She's not easily intimidated."

"These are the aspects of the change that I think are the legitimate complaints," says journalist Bill Littleton. "I think that homes in on where it stands. The individuality of the human being is that person's greatest divine gift. We are all here for some purpose that has to do with our individuality. And it really disturbs me to see people undermine their individuality and fall prey to the conformity of convenience. I saw Dolly at the Opry last summer and it was just like the world had been turned upside down, like the coming of Christ, or something. It was incredible! So it disturbs me when somebody as naturally unique as a Dolly Parton comes along with some staggering contributions to make and sings material that is hacked out in some L.A. songmill."

Other people who know Dolly or who are familiar with her career are concerned with what effect all this is having on Dolly's psyche. "I imagine a lot of these stories you're hearing about her change of behavior come from her insecurity with all this new direction she's getting," says Clarence Selman. "These people are totally phony in my judgment. All those West Coast people do is believe in the image. They never seem to attach very much significance to the person. You're fine as long as you're hot, and then they start building another one. They have no regard at all for the person. All they want is the picture of that person." One of Dolly's journalist friends concurs. "There's just so much that Dolly doesn't understand," she says. "She's naive. Take that poster. She doesn't know anything about women being degraded, although if anyone's been degraded, she has. She just figures, 'Well, if they like it, we'll give it to them. If that makes me some money and sells me some records, why let 'er go. Here it is, folks. You can look at my body, but I, ha, ha, get to eat and support my family.' She doesn't see it as degradation. She's never heard the word." Adds Fred Foster, "In the final analysis, Dolly's going to have to grab control of this situation and get approval on everything that goes out on her, like that poster, which is beneath her. Or she's going to have to have somebody she trusts implicitly to have the taste in her absence, to approve only those things which are becoming. There should have been a Dolly Parton poster, but it should have had a lot more thought put into it, and a lot more taste."

"I have a little made-up Dolly in my head, just as Dolly has a little made-up Dolly in her head," says one of her friends. "I don't think she knows where the real Dolly ends and the fake Dolly begins. I think she's real confused, that is, if there ever was a real Dolly. Maybe the last time she actually appeared in public as the real Dolly was in the cloak room when the kids ripped off her blouse. I like her an awful lot. I really like that woman. I wish I could just sit down and give her the facts of life. But I can't, really. Because she jokes with me, and she won't allow me near enough to say something. She keeps me at more than an arm's distance. There's no opening for me to say anything like that. Besides, is it any of my business? I don't think anything I say or you say or anybody says is going to make any difference. She's set on a course, and boy, that's it. I could sit and talk to her all day, but that woman has never taken anybody's advice. If she wants any advice, she can ask me, but as long as she never asks me, I'm never going to give her any. What I'd like to say to her is, 'Get rid of Sandy Gallin. Get rid of him, get rid of him! You need somebody who understands you, who knows what to do with you and understands your particular talent and your intelligence. And you need to tell Johnny Carson if he ever tells another boob joke on his show, you'll personally come over and bash him in the face.' But it's gotten to the point to where she's telling Dolly Parton jokes herself. She thinks they're a big yuck!"

Jo Coulter says contrary to what Dolly may say, the jokes about her look "hurt her very much. The remarks have often been cruel, and she's very vulnerable and sensitive. People must think she has a shield of armor around her." In 1975, Dolly was asked how the bosom jokes affected her. "You know, you'd have to know me pretty well in order to know, but it embarrasses me and it hurts my feelings. But, then, again, I'm smart enough to know that anytime anything is over-exaggerated like that—well, like my hair—and I'm such a small person that my figure is over-exaggerated. I will admit that I have aplenty, but I'm not as ungodly and outrageous as people have made me out to be. People just dwell on it all the time now, so it naturally—I want to be appreciated for what physical appearance that I may have as far as if it's anything extraordinary. But I wanna be loved as me and appreciated as me first. There are so many women that just take physical things like that and build a whole career around it. That's all they have to offer, because they have no goodness and realness from the inside. It's almost like me being trapped in some other form. The real me is so different from the way I may look on the outside." But by 1977, when I asked the same question, Dolly had developed a philosophy about the subject. "It used to kind of embarrass me," she told me, "because I didn't know quite how to take it. But anymore I just kinda play along with it myself, and come up with some funny things. There's no way to hide it, you know. That's something you're gonna have to accept. I could be ugly about it and say, 'Don't do that,' but what is it they say about impersonatin' somebody bein' the greatest form of flattery? But anyhow, that's just something I'll have to live with."

Sitting in her hotel room after her May '78 Birmingham, concert Dolly was not finding it all so amusing. Only 3,200 people had come to the show, in this, one of "her towns," if past concert attendance is any record. (According to Carl Reagan, the brother of Dolly's aunt by marriage, Colleen Owens, "She had twice the crowd in Birmingham after she changed over.") A worried Dolly sat in a long dressing gown and pondered what all was happening to her. "Everybody's treating me like a product, wantin' to write books about me, wantin' to write my life story," she said anxiously. "You, Lola Scobey, even my sister. It's my life. It should be my book, my story. But I ain't lived yet. I'm just beginnin' to live. I'm miles yet from where I want to go." She sat with her legs folded under her and stared at the floor, her eyebrows knitted in thought. Her fingers unconsciously worked the hem of her gown, resting in her lap. Perhaps she was tired from the show, or maybe it was the new wig, shorter and more suburban housewife than those of the past, but she seemed older and tired not just in body, but in spirit. "Of course, everybody's treating you like a product," I said. "Don't you realize you've brought this on yourself?" Dolly looked at me blankly and then returned her gaze to the floor.

"She *is* a product, let's face it," says Mary Fielder. "She's a marketable product. Everybody is getting on the bandwagon. That's what a star is. I think it's probably a whole lot different from what she thought it would be. I don't know that she thought it would go where it has. She may lose sight of herself. Because she wants to become a superstar more than anything. She just wants it so badly. If Katz-Gallin tells her something will really help—well, I don't know how far she will go," Fielder continues. "She has strong morals, and there are certain things she's closely attached to, such as respecting her mother. But she really wants to succeed. Dolly in the movies—she may not be the best actress on the screen, but she has the belief, and that's all you really need. I don't know if she could ever do a role that wasn't Dolly. Her personality is so strong that she will always appear to be Dolly. But given the right role, she could be good at it."

"Listen, anybody with a bosom like that is *bound* to go to the movies," says Clarence Selman. "And there's going to be a Dolly Parton legend and it could be propagated by the movies. I think it's inevitable that she be in the movies. And I think she could probably do a pretty good acting job, because singing for a living gives you a tremendous background for that."

"Dolly's bright and she's talented and if some director would have the intelligence to let her be Dolly Parton on the screen, she could be great," says Don Roth. "But they won't. Burt Reynolds does well. He plays Burt Reynolds, and he's good at it. When he's angry, he's an angry Burt Reynolds. When he's sad, he's a sad Burt Reynolds. When he's in love, he's an in love Burt Reynolds. If they would do that with Dolly, she'd be a killer. But they won't and she'll come off real dumb. A few years ago, she would have had potential. If they just got her on the set and let her go and then edited it, catching Dolly at her best, it would be terrific. Because the natural Dolly Parton is unbelievable. She's just unbelievable."

Still, even though Dolly may be confused about having made the right move in her career, she has always had that unfaltering sense of knowing when to stop and when to go, or when it is time to change. The only thing that may block that sense now is that having climbed the rainbow and found the pot of gold half empty; she may not realize that Katz-Gallin does not own the only rainbow in town. But although it may take some time, Dolly's better judgment is almost sure to win out. No matter how big Katz-Gallin's ideas are for Dolly, they aren't nearly as big as her own.

"I think you're right," says Don Roth. "Because if you took Dolly Parton and parachuted her into the middle of Alaska, she'd show up on the Opry two weeks later and you wouldn't know how she got there. She has a tremendous sense of survival. She'll survive through this whole thing and she'll continue making a lot of money and wearing the fancy clothes and wigs and hair and being Dolly Parton. As soon as she figures out Katz-Gallin's not doing anything for her, she'll drop them in a New York second."

Roth and other of Dolly's personal friends aren't the only ones concerned. "I still fear a bit for Dolly," wrote Pete Axthelm in *Newsweek*. "As a country loyalist, I know that there are silver-tongued devils lurking behind every hill in Beverly, ready to smooth the wonderful roughy edges off her high notes or drown out the peaceful front-porch voice with arrangements featuring Mantovani or the Mormon Tabernacle Choir. But in the end, I believe that Dolly will prevail with what she calls 'country wisdom, cutting through the bull and getting to the point . . .' Dolly Parton has put most of her crises behind her. 'When it's all said and done,' " Axthelm quotes Dolly as saying, " 'you've got to listen to your own self.' "

Jo Coulter believes Dolly will do just that. "You can't take a human being and turn him into a product and have it successful at all," she says. "That person has to come through, and if that person feels like just a chunk, he's not going to do anything. It doesn't work at all. And Dolly is a very human young woman and she needs people. I'm sure she could never accept the fact of being just a product per se and a commercial artist. She'll do something about it. If she's changed, she'll turn around. If you've known her as long as I have, there's no way you can doubt that she's going to come out fine and on top of everything. Now, she may go through a trying period for a time, but she'll come out fine. There's no way a person can change that much in a short time. And if she is that way now, she'll handle it and be bigger for it. See, Dolly is very good at learning lessons and then not making the same mistake twice, which is a good way of living. You don't have to look at things as a failure if you have learned something from it. And if Dolly has done something or people are doing something to her, she'll turn about. It won't take her long." Coulter takes a sip of coffee and stares at me out of the corner of her eye. She swallows, and a slow smile comes across her face. "You'll see," she says, setting down her cup. "I have all the faith in the world in that child."

Dolly's Spring '77 tour culminated in an SRO triumph at New York's Bottom Line. Olivia Newton-John and Andy Warhol pay tribute at RCA's Windows on the World party for Dolly. (STEPHANIE CHERNIKOWSKI) Rehearsing for the Bottom Line engagement. Steel guitarist Joe McGuffee is in back of Dolly. (ASSOCIATED PRESS)

Right, The most spectacular male and female bodies in the world? Who else but Arnold Schwarzenegger and Dolly Parton! (COPYRIGHT 1978 BY ANNIE LEIBOVITZ/CONTACT) Below, Gregg Perry—bandleader, keyboard man, friend. (HARRY HAMBURG)

Dolly's Summer '78 tour with Eddie Rabbitt comes to Holmdel, N.J. At the end of Dolly's set, he joined her singing in "Let It Be Me." When he put his arm around her waist, she cracked, "You're getting me stirred up." Laughter. And blushes? (HARRY HAMBURG, ALANNA NASH)

Dolly found love for each child who greeted her at Holmdel in August '78. (HARRY HAMBURG) Below, Born to fly. (STEPHANIE CHERNIKOWSKI)

11. *There You Go Again?*

CHRISTMAS OF 1977 brought Dolly no Cadillacs or diamonds from Porter Wagoner. But the holiday week brought something Dolly infinitely preferred—something she hoped was a sign of gifts to come in the next year and for the rest of her career, really. The Recording Industry Association of America certified *Here You Come Again* a gold album, signifying 500,000 copies had been sold. RCA issued a press release that said the company expected the title single to have sold a million copies by the first of the year (making it a gold single), and with album sales at between 50,000 and 100,000 a week, it was sure *Here You Come Again* would go platinum, meaning a million units sold. Waylon Jennings had been the only other artist on the label to earn a platinum album in the past year. "Thus, RCA's year-long campaign to break country singer Dolly over into the pop market without causing her to lose any of her country identification has paid off handsomely," the release boasted. "Both album and single have hit the top of the country charts." In other words, it looked as if Dolly had successfully crossed through the country/pop divide.

While Dolly had been at the center of the crossover controversy for well over the past year, she was certainly not the only Nashville singer desirous of a career in both country and pop. Quite a few country singers had enjoyed crossover hits through the years, among them Marty Robbins, Lynn Anderson and Charley Pride, but now the idea was to be a big star on both fronts. Crystal Gayle, a lovely young woman with a piano bar voice who just happens to be Loretta Lynn's baby sister, was a prime example of the twin careers to be had. Her heritage was enough to make her a natural country singer, and both MCA, her first label, and United Artists pushed her essentially country until they caught on that her exquisite uptown looks and sultry singing style could propel her across the divide. And yet because she had never really established herself as a product of backwoods rural America, as Dolly had, the country music fans felt no threat when Crystal showed up singing "Don't It Make My Brown Eyes Blue," about as non-country a tune as you could find. Crystal had, after all, grown up in Wabash, Ind., singing along to Lesley Gore records (not Kitty Wells) in her backyard, so no one, especially not Crystal, was flabbergasted when, in addition to the aforementioned song, she put a Cole Porter number on *We Must Believe in Magic*, her first platinum album, one of the few platinum albums awarded to a female "country" artist (she received hers before Dolly). It looks as if Kenny Rogers and Dottie West are finding a pop following as well, based on his former pop success, the tremendous appeal of his "Lucille," and their fine duet, "Everytime Two Fools Collide." Now that "country isn't redneck anymore," as one magazine headline had it, probably as many who can will follow. The Nashville country music industry grosses more than $300 million a year, and by no longer restricting records to one market, singers and record companies could likely up that figure by millions. "Some people are afraid for me. They think I'm going to embarrass myself, or already have," Dolly told *Melody Maker* in the spring of '77. "Others are resentful, I think, because they've always wanted to do the same but haven't had the nerve."

Porter Wagoner has been called the Last of the Hillbillies. How does he reflect on the changes in country music through the years? In an interview with John Morthland, Wagoner said, "I think Nashville and the industry are just sorta searching for a direction. Country music is great, and country music is big, but a lot of times a person just gets discontent or something if there isn't something real big or exciting happening at the moment, and they start searching for different areas and different directions to go. Sort of like a guy lost out in the country that don't know which road to take. And I think that's probably the way a lot of the people in the industry have gotten. But people love country music, believe me, they do. The sales, reviews, compliments, everything of my latest album [are] good proof of that to me."

Morthland asked what the songs say. "Honesty, I guess," Porter answered. "Country songs are of a more honest nature than the other songs. They have more honest characters in 'em, more honest stories. Because a big part of the country songs are actually probably true stories . . . with maybe a little extra imagination added to it. I think there's a part of that still left behind in the writers of today. They seem like today they're searching for more of the now-happening things, things that will appeal to more people at this particular time. I think what makes a song popular is people can connect with what it actually says. Either that, or the melody has a certain reminiscing that makes them think of something. It seems to me that writers now, instead of writing an honest, straight-out song of something that happened, will try to write something that will 'fit' with today's happenings. Songs from the day of the big golden standards were written truly from the heart, [by] a writer who poured his heart out in words. I don't think that happens as much anymore."

Are there many people like that in the real world? Morthland wanted to know. "I think there's as many as ever—more, I would imagine, because the population has gotten bigger, though the country really hasn't changed all that much. The new highways down through the town . . . I don't feel made the town all that different. The songs are about the same things happening today, but maybe in a different setting. I feel like the trend is going towards more of the Larry Gatlin thing, because the disc jockeys are going more towards a modern country thing. Maybe that's great. I think anything that's successful and healthy for the industry is fine. But not for me, because I have no desire to be a follower. The modern country songs—I have no desire to make my records sound that way.

"I love all kinds of music. Any kind of music that I can understand at all. The part of the business that has changed the most to me is that it has become more political. You have to be a politically inclined person to really launch a career at this time. I think the days where a man's talent really speaks for itself . . . for instance, Stonewall Jackson came to Nashville with a guitar and a flour sack, drove up here in an old car, but he was a good country singer with some good country songs, and he sang 'em and got on record, started a career. I believe those days are gone. And I think it's sad in a way that a man doesn't have a chance to just display his talents, and if it's great, there'll be a place for him. If he don't have political connections he don't have a chance. I think that's really bad for the business. So many people, like artists, they have their own publishing companies, they have their own managers, they have their own little world, their own little . . . powerhouse, and in order to get something done with them, you've got to have a connection inside this powerhouse. And I think a person's talents should be given an opportunity . . . If I've got a song that I think you should sing, I think you oughta listen to it whether you own any of the publishing or not. But if I wanna get into your little empire, I'm gonna have to give you some of the publishing just for you to do that song. That's bad."

Morthland asked if Porter had any temptations to record pop. "No, not really," Porter said. "Because if I was tempted, I would do it. To me, it don't take no more talent to cut that kind of record than it does to cut any other kind."

"I think Dolly's tremendous crossover success should be inspiration to anybody's who's got the talent and wants to branch out and not stay in one particular form of music," says Charlene Bray. "She did take a terrific chance. There were people who said she'd be washed up in country, that promoters would turn against her in country, and I don't think it's gonna happen. If the few [fans] that she's lost cannot be compensated by the tremendous following she's got now in the pop audience, well . . . anybody who's got an overall view of the music industry knows that she's bettered herself and increased her audience, and that's what she said she wanted from the very beginning."

But now that Dolly has earned a pop audience, she has to keep it. Unlike the country fans, pop fans demand their heroes keep proving themselves. To say then that Dolly is a pop star on the basis of one hit album is to jump the proverbial gun. And that, of course, raises the question of what is to become of Dolly Parton. Have a great number of the people who bought *Here You Come Again* done so because Dolly's the current thing, popping up regularly in Johnny Carson's monologue and showing up in the pages of slick national magazines that have nothing to do with country music—or music at all? Do they consider her a serious artist with staying power? Or, in time, will her current success seem as short-lived and trendy as Tiny Tim's moment in the spotlight, with Dolly remembered as little more than one of many country musicians dragged into national prominence by a public curious about a Southern President's roots?

The likelihood of the latter seems slim. Although Dolly has indeed traveled far on her "gimmick," she has a substantial talent to keep the fans satisfied once they've fallen for her external trappings. But it takes far more than talent to survive in the pop ratings, a place where the old Hollywood adage certainly applies—you're only as good as your last record. Pop fans are as fickle as the country fans are loyal, and while several of Dolly's friends think she'll find that a rude awakening, Dolly showed the interviewer from *Playgirl* that she already knows it. Country fans are ". . . definitely more loyal," she told Peter Manso, "and that's 'cause they're good, stable people to begin with. They've got their work and their families, and after that, if they're devoted to you, they're devoted forever. The public doesn't really get to know their rock heroes. Rock artists themselves just usually go on stage and then immediately leave because there is such screaming and hollering. It's a different kind of audience. Rock fans will tear you to shreds, they get so excited. They'll have a different poster hanging in their bedroom every six months, and while country fans may not love their artists any better, they love them a lot longer."

Not even Dolly's staunchest supporters in Nashville guarantee that the pop success of *Here You Come Again* means Dolly has a secure future on the rock charts. "I don't know how much success she's going to have, and neither does she," says Marty Robbins. "It'll be a long time before you can say she's really crossed over. And it's not the artist that crosses over, it's the song. It's pretty hard now for her to follow that first song. Actually, it was a bad thing for her to have that big song first. If she could have had a couple more songs that got some pop play and then come out with that, it would have been a lot better. But first cat out of the bag with a big song—and a great song, too—it's hard to follow a big hit. You can't just follow it with 'The Star Spangled Banner.' It's got to be something that's different. If you're not ready for a big song like that, it's bad. Just the same as a new artist having a great big hit and nothing to follow it with . . . She'll have a hard time for awhile yet." Fred Foster agrees. "Dolly has gone platinum on her album, and she's going to have to cut really good material to go platinum on the next one. There aren't many people who can build up a devout following that will snap up whatever [the performer records]. That's sort of not done anymore. Elvis, maybe, was one of the last of those." Bob Beckham says Dolly's crossover success means four things: Talent, good song, good producer, and "a ton of money. But when it's all said and done," Beckham maintains, "the people determine, and you can spend all the money you want to, but if they don't buy the record, that's it. All you can do is make sure that it's heard in the proper circumstances, on the proper stations, by the proper people and all that. And then if the people buy it, you were right. If they don't, bad mistake. They bought it. So it has opened up a new field for Dolly, which she is perfectly qualified in filling. But it's a hell of a calculated risk. And we'll see what happens from here."

Some people in Nashville fear that because Dolly achieved crossover success so soon—and on such a large scale—that she may have already peaked. But just as many feel Dolly has just started her career, saying, as Clarence Selman does, that "she hasn't reached her peak yet, but ultimately she must, and when it's all over, she'll be an old lady and have a scrapbook. And she has the possibility of doing it with a great sum of money. People who call her a novelty are wrong. She's someone who is here to do it big and stay."

"I think Dolly's will be a long-lasting success because she has tremendous talent as a songwriter," says Bobby Denton. "The reason some careers bomb is because the people are unable to come up with that song to keep it going. You have to keep getting good songs. Dolly can sit down by herself and write a hit. She can decide which way she wants to go—ballad or up-tempo—write it, go into the studio and produce it herself. So I think it will last because the exposure she is getting now is not like the exposure she had on the country shows, like *The Porter Wagoner Show, Pop Goes the Country,* and *That Nashville Music.* Now the kids are into Dolly Parton's music, and she's a new artist to them. A lot of them have never heard of her before. But why should she care? She wouldn't have to work the rest of her life if she didn't want to. She's got over five hundred songs published."

Dolly can indeed write hits. But at the moment, the first singles that RCA has released off her two overtly pop albums, *Here You Come Again* and *Heartbreaker,* have been songs written by established pop songsmiths. One reason is that Dolly simply has not had the time to devote to her writing that she had in the past. Late in '77 she told reporters she would arrange her '78 schedule so that she'd have two weeks on the road and two weeks at home. "I can write anywhere, but I really like to have a few days off the road to sit and think and write," she told Wes Hasden of the Chattanooga (Tenn.) *Times.* In Huntsville in May, she said "Soon as I let up some of my road schedule, I'll be able to get back to my writing." Charlene Bray believes Dolly hasn't peaked by a long shot, but that "if she doesn't find time to write, it will hurt her development as an artist because she loves to write and is a tremendous songwriter. I don't think within the last few years she's written tremendous songs like 'My Tennessee Mountain Home,' which is a classic. In fact, even say in '75, when I was setting up interviews for her, the writers who are really steeped in country music and know the history didn't want to talk to her about flighty songs, like 'Love Is Like a Butterfly.' They wanted to talk to her about 'Jolene,' and 'My Tennessee Mountain Home' and 'Coat of Many Colors.' Those are gutsy songs that really tell a story. It takes time and depth to write songs like that. You can't write 'em on the go. And I don't know how much solitude she has for writing. She's on a heck of a schedule. But if she doesn't have time to write, I think she will be judged in the long run by saying her best and creative years as a songwriter were in the '60s and very early '70s."

Rumor has it that one reason Dolly has relied primarily on such sure-fire commercial material is that she feels obligated to RCA for supporting her through all the months she didn't work due to throat problems, and for lending her a sizable sum of money ($100,000 has been mentioned), no strings attached, at some point in 1977. Another reason for such blatantly commercial tunes, some think, is to assure that as many people as possible know the name Dolly Parton, so that Dolly can branch out into other forms of entertainment and creativity (movies and books, TV, etc.) and have a ready audience. Dolly has said as much herself. "I want to continue touring and recording for five or six more years," she told Wes Hasden. "By then, I hope I'm established enough to record often, do occasional guest appearances on TV and reduce my traveling on the road."

"Oh, I think she'll just get bigger," says one music and film journalist. "Bigger than she is now even. I don't think it'll be through her music, though. For two or three more years she'll grow and become a *cause célèbre* and more and more people will realize she's a lot more than hair and boobies—that she's funny and cute and interesting, and something'll come along, like a *Laugh-In* or some vehicle that will do for her what that show did for Goldie Hawn."

One thing that certainly could alter the course of Dolly's career is her recurrent throat problems. While the condition was diagnosed as nodes on the vocal cords at the time Dolly canceled a large block of dates in '76, early the next year she told me, "I went to a specialist just a few weeks ago, and he said I did not have nodes, that I had swollen membranes and tissues in my throat, which was evidently caused from just improper breathin' and improper use of my throat, singin' too much from my throat instead of usin' the diaphragm." Dolly said at the time of our interview her throat was giving her no trouble at all, but Mary Fielder remembers that when Dolly went back on the road, "There were times she was taking medicine for her throat, and one time we had to take off because her throat was just no good. The nodes are worse at some times than they are at others, and she just has to rest and get proper sleep." It is rumored that Katz-Gallin has seen to it Dolly receive instruction not only in how to sing from the diaphragm but also in speech and elocution. (She has lately been heard pronouncing certain words in an accent far different from the East Tennessee drawl. I was thunderstruck to hear her pronounce "line" with a hard *i.*) A speech therapist is often called in for singers suffering from nodes, in an effort to get them to speak higher or lower than normal to rest the swollen area of the cords. After Dolly canceled a few of her Roxy Theater performances in the spring of '77, John Rockwell interviewed the physician who treated her, Dr. Edward A. Kantor, of Beverly Hills, whom Rockwell described as "the best-known throat doctor in Los Angeles specializing in singers' problems." According to Rockwell, Kantor described a node as "a small tumefaction—like a rounded corn—on the vocal cord, a swelling or a growth. It is noncancerous, benign. But it's still something you have to check; hoarseness for more than six weeks is cancer until proven otherwise. There is no pain with a node. The major symptom is hoarseness, and eventually a loss of vocal control. It's the thing singers fear most," Kantor said. Rockwell went on to report that after rest, cortisone is the second cure, with surgery being the "third and most radical cure . . . the trouble [being] the singer risks altering his or her familiar vocal color or even losing the voice altogether."

Several people have remarked that they just can't see Dolly Parton in the movies. "Shoot, yeah!" says one writer. "First of all, Hollywood will *love* her! They'll eat her up. They don't know that she's smarter than any of them. It'll take 'em five years. Because they're so smug out there. I mean, 'Here's this dumb little girl from Sevierville, Tennessee, that wears those silly clothes and does her hair like that. Isn't she cute and precious and different and wonderful?' And all the time, she's outsmarting every one of 'em. As an actress, good Lord, the way she can con you and me in an interview, her resources as an actress haven't even been tapped yet. I think Dolly Parton will be around as a star, a personality, when Loretta and Tammy and all the other country music stars we know of now are forgotten. Whereas most of the other girls in country music are limited to singing and writing, I think Dolly could run a show business empire. I think she could direct movies—any of that. It makes you almost believe in reincarnation. But Dolly in the movies? Heck, yeah."

It is just for those very reasons, though, that some of Dolly's friends worry that she may be taken as a novelty, as a Professional Personality, and that the public will soon tire of her. Journalist Bob Allen could see that happening. "It could be that her music will never catch up with her," says Allen. "Right now, it seems like a vehicle for her personality—like her music is almost coincidental. I can see her becoming a female Kris Kristofferson. He came so far so fast that his music never caught up with him. He's doing acting roles beyond his capabilities now, and nobody takes his music seriously anymore. He makes crummy movies and crummy records. But he over-extended himself. He never really got good at any of them. He became a star on the sheer force of his physical presence. He's become a Personality, and he's got it all, but actually, he has less than he had five years ago. And it's sad, because you know he's a brilliant man. I wonder where Dolly's identity is going to fit into all this. Because here was somebody with her own integrity, who sang about her heritage and refused to have a producer stuff songs down her throat. That was the real Dolly Parton. Now she's doing this disco stuff. Is this the real Dolly Parton now? There's no focus to it anymore."

On the other hand, Richard Peterson points to Dolly's new music and direction as proof that she is a genuine song stylist, capable of just about anything. "When I first heard *Here You Come Again*," Peterson says, "my first reaction was, 'Damn, she's done it!' She really has made something of this. Because there are lots of people who have tried for crossovers and gotten stuck between the cracks. But there she is singing something which is appealing. And the title song wasn't just another 'Jolene' or another one of her former hits. It showed that she could do something different, and that she could move. And with some of the other songs on the album, she showed she could rise above mediocre material. When she can make songs that are just decent sound really good, she has a chance to be something more. Of course, the major way to insure that is to start working movies. Because a lot of people—Elvis, Frank Sinatra—whose careers cooled off were sustained by their movie performances, and then they came back. So one thing you would expect in the move to L.A. would be putting Dolly in the movies. That seems to work better for country music entertainers than a television show, for some reason. She's probably going through a period where she's being given a lot of advice that may or may not work. All performers that end up being called great have done dumb things along the road and been involved in strange or unusual or inappropriate things that were formatted for them at one time or another. But her new stuff is very strong music. I think she has a chance to be something more than a novelty hit." Asked if he thinks Dolly runs the risk of falling into the Professional Personality trap, Peterson said he was recently in California lecturing on the country music industry to various universities. "For some of them, to talk about country music is to talk about polka, right? But they all knew who Dolly Parton was, and I found if I could just mix her name or *Here You Come Again* into the title of the talk, that made it legitimate. So she's at least become a personality, and she's in that group you'd expect to see on Johnny Carson or some of those celebrity game shows, but I also found she was a way of introducing the idea of country music."

Fred Foster is one who worries some about Dolly being taken as a novelty. "But any time you get a hit, the record and radio business looks at you as a novelty and rightly so, because your chance of making number one is what—one in eight million? But I'm sure they don't take her as seriously as she needs to be taken. Because there isn't anybody on the pop charts any better than Dolly Parton, I don't think. There are some as good, maybe, but not many of them. Ronstadt's great, but she can't write those songs. Emmylou [Harris] can do some of the things Dolly can, but not all. Carly

Simon can't write either, over a long period of time. The one thing that could hold Dolly back, though, is trying to do too much, too soon. She really ought to take off a little while and stand back and evaluate where she is. She needs a month off to herself with no influence, to really look at it. Dolly has a lot of personality and a lot of depth, and she could, in time, if she didn't want to sing anymore, become Dinah Shore, if she wanted, with a sense of humor even better than Dinah's. I don't know where she's going. She could go anywhere she wants to go as far as I'm concerned. If she wants it, she can go get it."

Charlene Bray thinks the public does indeed see Dolly as a novelty, but that it's nothing to worry about. "She *is* a novelty," Bray says. "She's the only one of this particular class or gender that acknowledges that all these trappings are just that—they're her gimmicks. A woman who had something to do with Dolly's *Vogue* magazine spread was on the *Today* show, and she said she just loved Dolly, that she was the genuine article. She was talking about Dolly's jewelry, where she said she had a lot of it, and she wore it all the time, that it was junk jewelry, and she didn't worry about the bus being robbed, because unless she was on it, they wouldn't get anything because she wore *all* of it all the time. All of this—the wigs and her look—is just part of Dolly's makeup. She's the only one who's flamboyant right now. David Allan Coe was, but he's dropped off of that right now. I don't think the public will tire of Dolly if she keeps comin' up with good material. And not as long as she's as open and genuine about it as she is. When she was on the Carson show, Johnny was talking about wigs, saying she must have a fortune tied up in them, and she cracked, 'Not these cheapos!' Johnny loved it. So as long as she maintains this genuine uniqueness about herself, the public will not tire of her. But if they saw a crack in that demeanor, they might refer to her as a phony."

And that is exactly what one of Dolly's journalist friends is worried most about—that Katz-Gallin will force Dolly to compromise herself to such an extent that her fans perceive a difference in the things she says and the things she does, and Dolly will lose her credibility, long one of the things that has made her so special. "I don't like what they're doing to her at all," her friend says. "I can't tell you who I talked to, but a very heavy-duty Hollywood press agent—about the heaviest of the California press agents—said he thought Dolly was being seriously mismanaged, and her career is gonna be ruined. She doesn't know what to do. She's never dealt with these people before. They've made too much of a joke of Dolly . . . I'm afraid no real work that she does will ever be considered seriously and that nobody will consider her a serious artist. They consider her a joke. Maybe a pretty joke or a sex joke, but a joke. So she's got to rescue herself, and she'll be the only one who'll do it, because everybody else is gonna exploit her. She's got to stop and retire from the world and really start putting out some creative stuff. The real talent she has—which is immense—is lying fallow. And if she doesn't revive that, Dolly's gonna go down in the books as Mae West, or something. And Mae West had some talent, remember? And yet nobody today ever says Mae West is a talented woman. And I think that's what's gonna happen to Dolly, but she doesn't understand that, because she doesn't have any experience or anything in her life to prepare her for undertaking this. She's making a big mistake, and she doesn't know why *in hell* it's a mistake. She isn't educated enough. She finished high school to prove she could do something, not because she was interested in it. Not only that, I don't think Dolly has any self-respect. So she's gonna bomb out. The woman is a victim. A victim of every kind of exploiter you can think of—of record companies, of managers, of anybody. But she says Katz-Gallin are her managers and she's gonna do what they say."

"Dolly's going nowhere fast," continues the friend. "But she can take it over. That woman is immensely intelligent. If she'd come in and take it over, she could save herself. If she had started with *New Harvest* . . . and kept going, she might not be on the Johnny Carson show every night, and she might not have people mentioning her everywhere, but she would be a hell of a lot more respected. The shame is she just doesn't have the background to understand that. What's respected? Does respected bring you money? Does respected make you famous? Does respected cure all of the things that happened to you when you were a child? Of course not. She is just not equipped to understand that she's a product. She's not equipped to understand a lot of things. If she had her boobs enhanced—and I don't know that she did—it was because she got so goddamn mad she thought, 'They want boobs? I'll give 'em boobs. All the boobs they want.' It's a hurtful thing. You get kidded. Boys bump into you in the hall by accident. There are jokes around school about you. And it's not pleasant at all. And yet she's taken that and finally gotten mature enough to say, 'OK, here they are—boobs. Make all the jokes you want to.' That's why she tells Dolly Parton jokes herself, and talks about 'knockers.' It's because she's just so defensive. But if she doesn't stop all this, she's gonna go down the drain. I think there's a chance she *can* stop it, but she's gonna have to take over and change her management. And I'm afraid she doesn't understand enough about the pop music business to see *how* she can take it over."

Most of Dolly's friends are more confident that she will prevail. "Because, you see, Dolly has the one thing that is more important than any innate talent, and that is the belief that she can do anything," says Mary Fielder. "And because of that, she can. I guess I would have to say that power is the key to Dolly Parton. She's a very hard worker, very bright and sensitive, but she's also tremendously powerful, in that she's so strong-willed and strong-minded. She is probably *the* strongest-minded person I have come in contact with."

Dolly described herself in similarly positive fashion when I asked her if she had any thoughts about why she's been successful. "Yeah," she shot back. "Because I'm ambitious, because I'm determined, because I'm positive, because I'm a worker, because I'm willin', because I'm brave enough to try the things that some people say won't work. See," she said, "I don't think it's because I'm that talented. I think it's my attitude. It's because of my attitude that people think I have far more talent than I do. I'm not hard ambitious. I never get anywhere at anyone else's expense. The worst mistake you could make is to think of me as one hard business woman. See, I don't have a negative side. Or if I do, I've never given into it enough to know it. They say everybody has a negative side, but I've just never exercised that. I just don't have any negative thoughts. I believed I'd have a good marriage, and I do. I believed that I could keep my marriage separate from my business, and I have. I believed that I could be an ordinary person, even bein' a celebrity, and I am. And I believed that I could be a star as big as I wanted to be, and I will be. I don't like the word 'star' myself, but I just mean 'to accomplish' so many things. I just take great pride in what I do. Everytime I accomplish somethin', I just feel that much stronger about accomplishin' somethin' else. Which puts that negative side farther and farther away. I'm a real strong person. But yet, you know, I'm the most sensitive person you'd ever want to know. I'm very emotional. Very sensitive and very caring about people. But I'm talkin' about things I can tolerate—I'm very strong with my own emotions. I love strong, I work strong, and I endure. I can endure more things without it affecting me than I guess nearly anybody. It comes from that faith I told you about—the mustard seed and all. See, I like myself. I do. I like the kind of person I am, because I like compassionate people. I like caring people. I like energetic people. I like people with determination. I like people with a strong will, with a strong drive. I like all people, but I'm just sayin'—people'll probably take that wrong—that I'm content with myself. I'm happy with myself, and if I wasn't, I'd be changin' the things that I'm unhappy with. As long as I treat people fair, long as I treat myself fair, long as I do my best and keep my nose out of other people's business, then I'm pretty well satisfied with that. I'm real content."

Dolly expounded on the subject of positive thinking to Chet Flippo of *Rolling Stone:* "I'm always sure of the goals I set for myself," she told him, "but I like for them to be flexible because I may get midways and get a big brainstorm. Then I can change. I just set new goals. There will *never* be a top for me—other than the one I am famous for," she cracked, while Flippo tried unsuccessfully to keep his gaze directed at Dolly's face. "I mean there is no top and no bottom to my career because once I accomplish the things I decide I'm going to, then I want to get into other things. I am a list maker. I like to write my goals and plans down and keep them in a secret place where people can't see them. You'd be *amazed* that even *years* ago the things I'd written down on my list, that I just mark 'em off as they come true and I think, boy, if that ain't proof that positive thinkin' is a marvelous thing." Flippo asked if it really works. Dolly came forward in her chair. "Yes! It *does!* If I get sick, I think myself well. That's why I never did worry when my throat was botherin' me. But you see, I had practiced that all my life; *that's* what got me out of the mountains. Even as a little child, I daydreamed so strongly that I saw these things happen, and sure enough, they would, so it was just a matter of growing up to meet that."

To many of Dolly's friends, positive thinking has not only brought her an extraordinary career, but it has made her an absolutely joyous person, a person who is delightful to be with, a person of overwhelmingly fine traits, a person with no dark side. "Dolly never really sees the dark side of things," says Jo Coulter. "Not ever. She always sees the sunlight. She bubbles all the time, and very seldom have I ever seen Dolly depressed. I have seen her tired and sick and go out and work under those circumstances and do a whale of a job, but I don't think I've ever seen her angry. I could imagine she could be, but she's a very considerate person, particularly around the people she works with. I'm always up when I'm around Dolly. I'm on a natural high, always. And she's not only considerate, she's thoughtful, and she doesn't work around you as if you are a machine. To her, you are a person, and she's not so self-involved that she forgets that there are other people with feelings. She looks deep inside those around her. She isn't all that self-centered, which is a beautiful trait. And I don't think—except for the growth that she's had in all these years—that she's changed that much, basically. She's still a charming, beautiful, childlike person, and I hope she keeps that childlike quality all her life."

Coulter, like many other of Dolly's friends, can recite story after story to illustrate Dolly's positive qualities. "I'll just tell you one, though, to show you how thoughtful she can be," she says. "I'm sure Porter doesn't know about it to this day. Not too long after she came with Porter's show, I had some really bad personal problems. Now I'm not a nervous person, but all of a sudden I became very nervous, which is bad if you're trying to do an eye-line on somebody. Dolly knew there was something wrong, and I told her about it. She said, 'Well, I'll do my makeup for awhile, until you get yourself settled down.' And every time Porter would walk into the makeup room, he'd say, 'Jo, you through with Dolly?' she'd say, 'Oh, yes, we're all finished.' And she did that for two months, until I got myself under control. Porter, I'm sure, would not have said anything at all, had he known, because he's a very special person in my life, as is Dolly, but she did it because she knew I was in trouble and she was the only girl I had to make up. The guys I could handle because I didn't have to put an eyeline on them. She helped me, and I'll never forget her for it. And I know if I needed help today, I wouldn't be turned down, no matter what it was. Dolly is a friend, not just a client. And you can't ask for more than that."

Don Howser says Dolly is so open and loving that she looks at *everybody* as a friend. Lucy Adams says that's true. "She has a way of reaching out to people in a way that you can't forget her. Oh, I could say anything I wanted to her, and my family is bad about joking, but we could tell her if she weren't so fat, she'd fit her clothes better, and she'd know I meant no harm by it. Now, she's hurt if people mistreat her, but still she loves them." And no matter the situation, even under the most trying conditions, Dolly was always "genuinely nice and warm and outgoing and gracious," says Charlene Bray, "even at a show in Huntsville, Alabama, where she was there 'til one o'clock in the morning, signing autographs. I've never seen her get tired or snap at somebody when I knew she had to be exhausted." All in all, then, Dolly's friends think of her as a person interested in making others happy. "Dolly taught me a lot of professional things," says Mary Fielder, "but she also did one neat, personal thing that I'm grateful for. She knew I was really interested in doing professional comedy, and out of the blue one time when we were in New York, she said Lily Tomlin was backstage, and I got to meet her. The next day she told me she and I and Jim Morey from Katz-Gallin were going to see Lily's one-woman Broadway show. It was the neatest thing out of the whole tour. She knew that would mean a great deal to me, and I'll never forget it."

Out of all the people I interviewed, only Cas Walker could remember ever having seen Dolly angry, and his memory was of a child's anger. Back in '75, a journalist asked Dolly what it would take to make her angry. "I can't really think of any particular thing," she told him. "See, I'm not expecting it, and I don't think about it. If I sat around and thought, 'Boy, if they ever do that to me, I'm gonna really be mad . . .' But I don't expect it. Now, I have a temper, but it takes forever to get there. And when I get mad . . . I don't have a bad temper. But all God's children got a temper. You're a fool if nothin' ever bothers you." Several things do indeed bother Dolly, though. "She once told me that she didn't care who said she was a bad singer, but she never wanted to be known as a bad writer. "Writing is very important to her," says Mary Fielder. "If anybody slandered her writing, that would be very sensitive to her. And I think her marriage is real precious. She always made it a point to say that they are very happy, and I honestly believe that they are. I don't think it's any kind of front. She seems to be pretty protective of him and the way he feels. She's sensitive to his feelings."

Another area in which Dolly is sensitive is her press coverage. And that is one thing that will definitely provoke anger, perhaps resulting in hostility if she happens to see the journalist again. The incidences of confrontation are rare, however, mostly because Dolly is extraordinarily well-controlled in her emotions when she wants to be. Several journalists who have spent days with her in preparation for a story have come back thwarted, saying they never saw Dolly lose control of herself, or show any emotion other than what she wanted to be seen. "I never saw Dolly turn her back on anybody," Dolores Smiley says, "and I've never seen her do anything unkind. If she's changed for any reason, I don't want to know about it. Because I love her." And if she's changed, or if she has a blue day, Dolly doesn't want anybody to know about it, either. In the course of our interview, I asked Dolly several questions which clearly shook her equilibrium. And yet while she answered them with long, heavy pauses in between her words, she insisted I had not depressed her when I apologized for getting into areas which were obviously painful for her to discuss. Over and over, she said she was not "down," because "I'm just not a down person. Now I get serious," she said. "But if I didn't get serious, I wouldn't be real at all. I mean, you can't laugh all the time. I have dimples, but you don't always see them, and if you did, you'd know my smile was phony." Still, I said, there did seem to be a sorrow about her in some ways, in ways I couldn't quite articulate. "Really?" she said. "Sorrow. Well, if there is, then it must be the sorrow I feel for things that are not right with others, 'cause I'm—I suppose—I never said that, but I guess maybe right now what you see as sorrow is concern with the new things I'm doin'. I'm made up of many things—of depth, of joy, of *extreme* emotion, of love, of a child. I'm very excitable, and very sensitive. I hurt so deep because I love so deep. How do you say how you are? I have many moods, but yet I'm always the same. I mean, I do not take my moods out on other people." Lucy Adams has spent a great deal of time with Dolly through the years, and she remembers times when Dolly would call and ask if she had finished an outfit or two, saying, "I just thought it would make me feel better," as Adams recalls. "I would say, 'Come on over—I got you some things,' and she would come and say, 'Oh, I feel better already.' But I never saw her too depressed," Adams says. "She never lets it show. I'm sure she has her days, though. But she has told me, 'I'm always a happy person, and I don't want to ever be any other way.' "

There's another reason few journalists who have incurred Dolly's wrath have actually felt it, and why Dolly rarely lets anyone see her when she's not her usual effervescent self. Not only does she not ever want to be unhappy, but she doesn't seem to want to admit to herself that she might *be* unhappy. Most of all, she appears to want to avoid conflict at all costs. After one journalist absolutely insisted that the two of them talk out what Dolly considered a negative and embarrassing story (and the journalist considered only fair reporting), Dolly, who had been confronted about the issue almost against her wishes, having turned down two requests from the journalist to talk, ended up saying, "I can see I've been more wrong about it than you have. I won't run from you anymore." Then she volunteered a hug.

"Anything that could bring about [bad] feelings, Dolly just doesn't want to have to deal with," says Mary Fielder. "Like in firing or hiring someone or correcting somebody. I think that's why it was just easier for her to tell Gregg that she didn't like the way so and so was playing and would he call them and tell them they weren't needed anymore. I feel Dolly is a good person, but I don't personally understand why she handles situations the way she does. Maybe because she was so naive when she started out with Porter, those years changed her a lot, and she just doesn't want to get too involved emotionally. She told me once, 'I am the star. I am the star. I am the *only* star in this group.' Meaning, we take a back seat, and it is a business situation. She'll love you as a person, but it is a business, and if she sees that you are not working out or someone else isn't, it's still a business situation. But it bothered her, just the same.

"Another thing about her I didn't quite understand," Fielder continues, "is that she wouldn't recognize her own sadness. She was always saying how up and positive she was. I really feel that she wanted to keep that [sad] side of her hidden. There was a side she wanted to present to the world, of being real happy, kind and cheerful and positive and glowing. But there has to be a side which she doesn't want anybody to see. Maybe sad or sometimes cruel. She denies a lot of things to herself, and she has a real vulnerable side. I think if she thinks you see that, you're gone. She doesn't want to have anything else to do with you. A lot of this is just what I felt from her, and I've tried to be real objective about it, because I don't want to hold personal grudges. But that's the way I saw it."

Don Roth saw the same thing. And both he and Fielder saw a change come over Dolly during the months they were with her. Little by little, the woman who insisted on riding and eating and doing everything with her musicians began putting more distance between herself and her band. She began to act aloof, and to emphasize more and more that she was indeed the only star of the group. And as various members of the band were fired, they were replaced by musicians who were "no-threat people," musicians who had a good deal of technical talent, but very few creative ideas. For the most part, they were musicians who took orders and asked no questions, who had no objection to being looked upon as extensions of Dolly Parton.

"Dolly sincerely loves me, and I sincerely love her," says Roth. "And she sincerely loved a song I wrote that she demoed and wanted to go on the new album. But when it got shot down at a production meeting at RCA, she simply had Gregg call me and tell me that it wasn't going to be on the record. She's never called me since I left the road; it's always been through Gregg. I can understand it, though. I'm not hurt by it. Stars don't call people. In the year or so I've known her, there's been a change. When I first knew her, she was definitely one of the band. Now she is no longer one of the band. I still love her—a bunch—but we're just on different plateaus. She respects my playing, and she would always put in a good word for me. There's a certain loyalty there. But there's also a certain star aloofness now, too. The loyalty would end, I think, if she thought it stood in the way of business. That's something that scares Gregg Perry. Gregg has said to me that, invaluable as he is, he's very, very insecure about his job and very frightened. Even as close as they are. Because he knows that if it ever got to a point where his being around was only so that he'd be making a living and she didn't need him, she'd let him go. It's kind of sad, in a way. Back when, Dolly was the kind that if she really liked you, she'd call you up and say, 'Boy, I liked the way you sang that song.' She's real natural that way. That's why I still find it difficult to believe all this. Because the Dolly I knew, even a year ago, when she got back to town, would have called me up and said, 'OK, are you ready to eat some spaghetti? I promised to fix you a spaghetti dinner, remember? Is your house clean enough for me to come over? I'm gonna be there in about an hour.' But even though she meant it when she told me she'd come over and fix dinner, I doubt seriously that she'll ever walk in that door. She really hasn't got the time, and if she did, I really think she's to a point in her career to where it just grates against her to go out and visit regular people in regular neighborhoods.

"The change came about the time they went to Europe." Roth continues. "Two people in the band got fired and she let Gregg do the firing. Dolly had sort of grown distant from the band by then. I think Katz-Gallin had influenced her whether she wanted to be or not, with the fact that Mac Davis doesn't always go out with his band after a concert, implying that she was still running her life in a little-girlish, naive sort of way. She finally got a great deal more into being a business woman. It was the business woman in her that simply realized that the president of the company calls personnel and says, 'So and so is not making it. Get somebody else.' She had too many other things to think about. Dolly needs people around her who are either in awe of her or who know how to act in awe of her."

Such actions might leave one with the impression that Dolly is hardening up. "Yes," says Roth. "But I think she's toughening up in a positive way. For years, she's been ultimately nice. Porter took advantage of her all that time, and so did the fans. If you feel like signing a few autographs, fine, but she would go out and stay two hours after the show signing because she wanted everybody to get their money's worth. That's what she's getting away from, and that's why I say she's getting away from it in a positive way." Fred Foster says if she is indeed toughening up, it's a natural progression. "You show me somebody that can go all those places and do all those things and not get hard," he says. "You have to, to survive. You can't go out there and be the little flower. You'll be crushed." Still, it is this sort of thing, in addition to the way some people perceive the way Dolly broke from Buddy Killen, Foster, Porter Wagoner and the Traveling Family Band, among others, that has led (rightly or wrongly) to one person in the music industry dropping such lines as "So and so is as cold and calculating as Dolly Parton." People such as Bob and Charlene Bray and Minnie Pearl take exception to such a statement, saying that Dolly has always known just what she wanted and gone after it, with Pearl adding that management can often give such an impression when the client is not really at fault. But Don Roth and Mary

Fielder, who have worked much more closely and recently with Dolly than either the Brays or Minnie Pearl, say there's some truth in those words. "She's a lot more cold and calculating about her career than she'd like to come off," Roth admits. "I mean, believe me, no matter how much she loved—and I mean sincerely *loved*—that Family Band, when it was time for them to go, they went." Fielder pauses before she addresses the question. "Sometimes she *is* cold and calculating," she finally says. "I don't want to give the impression that she is a cruel person with an evil side, because I don't feel that way. There are times when, I would imagine, she *has* to be cold and calculating. It's a hard business, and it's hard to contend with. Dolly is basically a good person. But people expect an awful lot from her, and they put an incredible amount of pressure on her. She then puts the demands on other people, because she wants to be a star."

Several people believe that when the pressure gets to be too much for Dolly, she retreats into her own fantasy world, where everything is rosy and beautiful, and she is unencumbered by reality. Dolly is aware of the belief, one which is rather commonly held in Nashville, and she counteracts it by frequently saying, "My world is very real" in her interviews. But Dolly has perpetuated the idea somewhat herself ("I used to love stories, fairy tales. I used to just live in them"), in her song lyrics, in her explanation of her look, and in her constant reference to storybook figures such as Cinderella and Snow White. "When you see Dolly Parton, you see the gaudy girl, the country Cinderella, so to speak," she told *Melody Maker*. "And in a lot of people's minds it's totally ridiculous. And in *my* mind it's ridiculous, but it's fun." A member of the Traveling Family Band recalls that when the group played Disney World, they performed on the stage at Cinderella's castle. "She felt like she *was* Cinderella," he says. "She was really happy that night. She said it was the greatest thing that had happened to her up to that point—that the feeling she got from being in Disney World and playing on that stage with that castle behind her was the greatest thrill of her life. That was the way she always thought of herself, she said, with the blond hair and rhinestones. She was absolutely ecstatic." While it's interesting to remember that it was to Disney World that Dolly went when she was having to decide on the major changes in her career in the summer of '76, Mary Fielder sees Dolly's fascination with fairy tales not as an escape from the present, but from the past, as Dolly herself has often said. "She made a lot of references to fantasies, to fairy godmothers and all of those things, but so many times she's said she never had the riches when she was a little girl, and I guess she's trying to make up for it. There was one time there when she was coming out on stage with a wand with a star on the end and glitter inside and the glitter fell all over the stage when she waved it around. She was getting really crazy with this wand, but it was kind of neat. The crowd loved it. They thought it was a bizarre thing to do. But she loves to be extravagant, and she's intrigued by that whole thing. I guess when you grow up as one of twelve children, you don't have time for fantasies, because you're out working, and that takes your childhood away. She's probably just trying to catch up."

There does seem to be more to it than that, however, since fantasy shows up so often in her work. "Believe me, it's easier for her to live in a fantasy world than it is to face reality," says one of her friends. "If things get too hard for her, then she'll just skip into her fantasy world, where everything's fine and she's the fairy princess. In her mind, she can make it any way that she wants it to be. You know her song that goes, 'In my mind I've made love to you often/But only in my mind can this be so'? If you go through her songs and examine them, you'll find out a lot of things about Dolly Parton. There's a song on *New Harvest* . . . called 'Where Beauty Lives in Memory.' That's Dolly Parton up one side and down another. See, life doesn't always work out the way Dolly wants it to. But she would like to believe that she can control everything, and if she can't control the people around her, she has no use for them. But in her fantasy world, she can control everything, and make it any way she wants to. You go listen to that song."

The song, for the record, describes a once-beautiful woman who loses her mind when her beloved prince leaves her, and after forty years of waiting, she finally succumbs and falls dead on the floor. Apparently she spent all that time doing one thing: "She stands before the mirror/Smiles at her reflection/Striking sexy poses in the glass./She paints her lips a brilliant red/Piles her hair high on her head/Struggles to replace a false eyelash./She powders up her face/Paints her cheeks to match her lips/She wears a dress cut low in front/Fitting tight around her hips./And there inside her room she stands and gazes at herself/Where Beauty Lives in Memory/She lives in fairy tales./Mirror, mirror on the wall/Who's the fairest of them all?/She sings as she goes waltzin' 'cross the floor./She keeps a candle burning/And she waits for his returning/When Beauty Lives in Memory/It lives forevermore." * Dolly talked about it with Chet Flippo. "I knew a woman who was beautiful. She was married to this man, and she was crazy about him. But he would do bad things to her, and he got to tellin' people she was crazy. She almost grieved herself to death, and now she is like a child. She still talks about him; she has kind of gone back in time. She still thinks she is as young and pretty as she ever was. It just touched me so deep, and I could just imagine that happening to *me*."

"One time she told me her mother had a dream about her, in which she saw Dolly up on a hill wearing a long white dress trimmed in gold, and she had wings," Lucy Adams says. "She said, 'I want you to make that dress, and to put wings on it, too.' So," Adams adds, reaching for the sketch in her book, "I made the dress. I couldn't put wings on it, but I made sleeves like

* Copyright 1977 Velvet Apple Music.

wings, and I put the gold trim on it. Then I went to the florist to pay my bill, and I saw this white dove. I bought it, and when Dolly came over, I had it on her dress form with the dove on her shoulder. And she just squealed. She said, 'It just makes chill bumps come all over me. I'll take it home and wear it for Christmas.' When she saw things like that, she'd get so excited, she'd jump up and down. It was always such fun to make her something like that, 'cause she'd act like a little kid."

Dolly not only has a child's fantasies, but some of a child's fears and insecurities. She told Barbara Walters, "I can afford to piddle around and do-diddle around with makeups and clothes and stuff because I am secure with myself." Yet when I asked her if she thought she was insecure, she paused a moment and then answered, "Ummmmmmmmm." "Don't you still feel a need to leave a light on at night?" I asked. "Yeah, but that's not bein' insecure," Dolly told me. "I have a fear of darkness. That could have come from bein' brought up in the mountains where we didn't have electricity. Country darkness is the darkest darkness, and wild animal noises at an early impressionable age can— Well, then, too, I'm a fanatic about seein' everything around me that moves. I have to see every sound. I'm so curious and so aware of everything. But one reason I don't like the dark is I must see. I *have* to see. I just can't stand it if I can't see. I like lots of windows and sunshine, and I like the windows open. If somethin' moves, I want to see what it was. I hear it; I can't help but notice it. That's just a natural reflex for me. I don't know if it's the fear of not seein', not bein' able to see, or what. It's not what I'm afraid I'll see that bothers me, but what I *don't* see that bothers me. I can't help bein' that way. That's part of my personality."

But as Lucy Adams has mentioned, Dolly can be several people, and drawing a bead on the sum total of her personality is no easy job, partially because as Dolly says, "There's so many sides to me." Tom Rutledge knows about that. "I'm just fascinated by how deep she is," he says. "She's got so many facets to her personality. The longer you know her, the more you learn about her, and the more you learn, the more you're fascinated." Jo Coulter believes there are two sides to her personality. "Well, the childlike quality is the one I used to adore," Coulter says, "but then Dolly's a very serious songwriter and an intent listener. So it's not just all makeup and hair and glorious costumes."

Perhaps there is more. "I think there are three characters who skip in and out of her personality unconsciously," says a former member of Dolly's band. "There's the sensitive little girl, the hard-core business woman, and the intellectual observer, the character that stands back and looks at Dolly Parton somewhat objectively. It could be that number two has taken over."

Could just be. In 1975, Dolly told John Rockwell, "I'm a woman when I have to be, but I'd prefer to be a child. I have more fun that way." In the last couple of years, since Dolly embarked on her new course, she's been working so hard (all but twelve weeks on the road in '77), she's hardly had much time for fun. The result is that quite a few people in Nashville believe Dolly's personality has greatly changed, LaWayne Satterfield going so far as to say, "The Dolly Parton we knew and loved died two years ago. She's sold her soul. I understand what she's doing and saying. Anytime you make changes, even minimal changes, you're going to have seventy-five percent of the people giving you flack, and twenty-five percent on the cheering line. But when the changes were made as abruptly as they were in Dollly's career, the timing of her going out to the West Coast after the cancellation of all those dates when she was sick, you had ninety-five percent flack and five percent on the sidelines believing she could do whatever she wanted to do. And five percent can't fight ninety-five percent. I don't necessarily condone the way she's done it, but I'll stand up and fight for her right to do it, and I'll fight for her."

All in all, several of the people in Nashville who have seen Dolly in the past two years have noticed a change in attitude on her part, which could be attributed to a growing confidence or assertiveness. Some have stronger words for it. Joan Dew, Tammy Wynette's biographer, tells one such story. "I can't remember which show it was, but it was some sort of TV thing that Dolly and Tammy did together," Dew says. "Tammy was backstage and had been posing for pictures. She had on an outfit with some little scarf with rhinestones tied on her head. Dolly saw her, and came down to the dressing room and said, 'Are you gonna wear that for the show tonight?' And Tammy said, 'No, why?' And Dolly said, 'I was afraid you were, because I'm wearing my gypsy look tonight, and I didn't want anybody else to dress like that.' Which is not the kind of thing Dolly would have done prior to when she went with that Hollywood management firm. She's more assertive now, but she's also jealously guarding her image, or whatever image she currently has. She was determined she was going to be unique or very different from anybody else on the show, in costume as well as performance. But the women in country music aren't that way. They aren't the kind of women who sit backstage at the Opry worrying about what another's going to wear. If the TV director says, 'OK, there are six of you, and we can have one white, one pink, one blue, one yellow—,' I've never know the big women in country to fight about something like that. They'd all get together and say, 'What do you want to wear?' 'Well, I don't know. I've got a white dress if you want to wear black.' Or they would just let the director tell them. There was never any pettiness, unlike you'd find in Hollywood. And that was the first time anybody'd seen Dolly act that way. They're just not used to that, because they *don't* act that way."

Don Roth has thought about it a good deal. "I don't know if she's ever been any different than she is now, because to make it, I think you have to be as clutching and as determined as she is now. I think it was an 'at all costs' thing to make it even to Porter. Now she's just starting to let drop the image of the sweet little girl from the mountains, so people think she's going through a personality change, but I personally think she's probably pretty much the same as she always has been. She's just finally starting to get secure enough that she doesn't have to play that little girl all the time. She still plays it a lot. Sometimes I think she really thinks she still *is* that little girl from Sevierville. I only spent three months of her life with her, and then not every waking minute. But she certainly comes across differently to people now. I get the impression that now, possibly, when she refuses to give an interview, that's being more real on her part. I think it was *unreal* on her part to never refuse an interview and to always stand around for two hours after the concert letting everyone with a Polaroid One-Shot take a picture of her with the kids. It's probably more a revealment than a change."

Back in '75, LaWayne Satterfield asked Dolly if she felt success had changed her. "It hasn't changed the person I am," Dolly answered. "Because the more success I have, the more humble I become." Jo Coulter, Dolly's ever-faithful friend, believes if there is indeed a change, "I'm sure it's only temporary, because the Dolly that I know will be, I think, the Dolly I'll always know. Sweet and giving and loving and considerate and thoughtful. It's still there. She could never outgrow it. Why would she want to? I don't think Dolly will ever change, except to become the biggest thing that's ever hit the country or the world. Absolutely. Because she has the talent, number one. She has the know-how, too, and then, of course, she's brilliant. She may have come from the hills, but she didn't stand behind the door when the brains were passed out. And don't forget—Dolly knows where she wants to go. She'll be an international star, I'm positive."

Dolly has one other thing that Coulter failed to mention, something that may be more important than all her other attributes put together. It all goes back to positive thinking. Hunter S. Thompson put another name to it in his *Fear and Loathing: On the Campaign Trail '72*: "Later, when the big rain started, I got heavily into the gin and read the Sunday papers," Thompson wrote. "On page 39 of *California Living* magazine I found a hand-lettered ad from the McDonald's Hamburger Corporation, one of Nixon's big contributors in the '72 presidential campaign: PRESS ON, it said. NOTHING IN THE WORLD CAN TAKE THE PLACE OF PERSISTENCE. TALENT WILL NOT: NOTHING IS MORE COMMON THAN UNSUCCESSFUL MEN WITH TALENT. GENIUS WILL NOT: UNREWARDED GENIUS IS ALMOST A PROVERB. EDUCATION ALONE WILL NOT: THE WORLD IS FULL OF EDUCATED DERELICTS. PERSISTENCE AND DETERMINATION ALONE ARE OMNIPOTENT. I read it several times before I grasped the full meaning . . . Then I put a Dolly Parton album on the tape machine and watched the trees outside my balcony getting lashed around in the wind."

No doubt Thompson heard a great deal of determination and persistence in in those songs oozing from the speaker of his tape player. And it is perhaps there, as one of her friends has suggested, that one learns the most about Dolly Parton. "In my songs, I can do and say almost whatever I want," Dolly told Peter Manso. "I can live out my fantasies, and 'cause of this, I'll be flying until I fall dead. I just won't give up. I won't be a-dyin' on the ground. No way. I just won't let that happen."

12. *Iron Butterfly*

FROM THE OUTSET, 1978 looked to be a very exciting year. Not only for Dolly but also for her fans, and for the fans of Emmylou Harris and Linda Ronstadt, too. Late in January, music journalists throughout the country received a press release from Elektra/Asylum Records, announcing that Dolly, Emmylou and Linda had begun recording an album together for spring release. Emmylou's husband, Brian Ahern, would produce. To a lot of people, that was far more exciting news than promise of a Beatles reunion had ever been.

Details of the project were kept as big a secret as the combination on the vault at Fort Knox. "We got the official clamp from all concerned," said one RCA spokesman. One version had it that Linda and Emmylou spent New Year's at Dolly's home in Nashville figuring out exactly what they'd do; another account said that they indeed met at Dolly's but on January 16. "Dolly and Emmylou sat down with their guitars and figured out the parts, and then each of them sang into a cassette recorder to hear each of the others' vocals," said someone who was probably in a position to know. But nobody wanted to talk about material (except to say a good number of the tunes were Dolly's) or much else, other than to add that the members of Emmylou's Hot Band were the primary musicians, along with Nashville session men David Briggs (piano) and Larrie London (drums), and that Linda's usual players would do the overdubs. Continuing the idea of equal input, no one singer would handle the lead vocals, the three trading off even on the harmonies. Quotes from anybody were hard to come by. "It was like a week-long slumber party," Dolly was reported to have said, but that was about all. Chet Flippo made twenty-seven phone calls to everyone involved. "You know more than I do," Ronstadt's press agent Paul Wasserman said. "The three girls made a pact not to talk."

While Ronstadt-Parton-Harris were experimenting with their own particular brand of crossover, the trade magazine *Record World* carried an item in its first issue of the year that said the country music industry had not only enjoyed its best year yet in 1977, but that a large number of country artists, including Crystal Gayle, Kenny Rogers, Waylon Jennings, Dave and Sugar, Dolly Parton, Ronnie Milsap, The Kendalls and Don Williams found continuing success on the pop charts, as well.

Everywhere you turned, it seemed, somone was talking about Dolly Parton. Three days before Dolly's thirty-second birthday on January 19, *New Harvest . . . First Gathering* was selected as the favorite country album, beating out two Waylon Jennings LPs, in the American Music Awards, based on the nationwide polling of 30,000 record buyers. Dolly had also been nominated as favorite country female vocalist, but lost to Loretta Lynn. But if she felt any slight over that, she had a bigger honor in store; she was the hostess of one of three half-hour segments of a network special, *Fifty Years of Country Music,* set at the Opry House. True to both her old and new fans, and to herself, Dolly gave the audience her new pop single, a sample of what she calls "Dolly Parton" music, and a country music showstopper—a duet of "Mule Skinner Blues" with the father of bluegrass, Bill Monroe. It was both an aural and visual treat, Dolly certain her bubbly effervescence would crack Monroe's flinty stoicism, Monroe certain that it would not, Dolly finding the song a good excuse to whoop and holler, Monroe determined to stay close to the music's roots. The fifty years of country music came together in that one performance.

The beginning of the year was also a good time for Dolly the songwriter. Emmylou Harris's version of "To Daddy," a song Dolly wrote after the near breakup of her parents several years ago, had been picked as one of the most active country singles, and newcomer Zella Lehr was doing well on the same list with a version of Dolly's "Two Doors Down." Eventually, it would make it into the top 10, sparking a lot of rumors as to Dolly's reaction. In its April 1 issue, *Billboard* reported that Dolly ". . . resisting the advice of her label, agents and managers, held off releasing 'Two Doors Down' . . . when she heard that Zella Lehr had released a version of the song, giving the newcomer a chance." But Music Row scuttlebutt had it that the reason Dolly held off release of the song as a single was because she was dissatisfied with her album version. Whatever, Dolly went back into the studio and recorded a loose, laid-back rendition of "Two Doors Down" and released it as a pop single, to follow up "Here You Come again," seeing to it that the new version replaced the old on subsequent album pressings. Gossipers wouldn't have it any other way but that before Dolly got her new version out, she phoned Zella and "warned" her not to try for a crossover on the pop charts, something she'd allegedly heard was in the offing.

"Oh, no, no," Lehr, who also records for RCA, said backstage at Fan Fair in June. "I've never even spoken to her. But if I ever meet her, I want to thank her. I was lucky to have gotten the song for the country charts. I've heard a lot of people say she's a very nice lady—as nice offstage as she is on, everybody says—and if it hadn't been for her I wouldn't have a hit right now. I wouldn't have any say over releasing the record pop anyway. That would be the label. She might have called [RCA vice-president] Jerry Bradley, but I don't know. I didn't even have anything to do with recording it. My producer, Pat Carter, called me and said, 'I've found a song on Dolly

Parton's album that's a smash hit for you, and we talked to Jerry Bradley and he says you can do it and Dolly says you can, too. She's not going to put it out.' So I recorded it and it *was* a smash hit. Dolly decided she wanted to put it out pop, so she had the pop hit and I had the country. She would have been a fool not to have released it, because it was her tune to start with, and all the pop stations were already playing her version before I came out with mine. I thought hers was a great pop vocal, and, of course, the song is excellent writing. A disc jockey in San Jose interviewed me recently, and he said he'd just interviewed Dolly and that he played her my version and she said it was fantastic. I'd love to do some more of her songs. If I ever get a chance to talk to her, I'm going to ask her to write one for me."

For the time being, though, Dolly had about all the work she could handle. Aside from the Emmylou and Linda project, she was busy working on her own album, tentatively titled *Sure Thing*, after one of her original songs. March found her appearing at two conventions, for Radio and Records in Dallas in the first part of the month, and for the National Association of Recording Merchandisers in New Orleans at the end.

Early the following month, Dolly appeared on the network Cher special, along with Rod Stewart and the Tubes. For her initial segment, in which she sang "Two Doors Down," Dolly, dressed in her first public low-cut gown, moped around her apartment, poured herself a drink, and generally felt sorry for herself before she exited in search of the man with whom she would have "our own party, two doors down." In her next segment, she appeared talking with Cher in an absurd sketch with dialogue composed entirely of song titles. The only thing more surprising than the realization anything this dumb could be taking up space on the national airwaves was just how well Dolly pulled it off, proving to anyone in doubt that Dolly really could act and deliver prepared lines. Nothing could save the last sketch, however, a heaven/hell scenario with Cher and the Tubes, in which Dolly appeared in a white dress as the archangel up on high. It was almost Avie Lee's dream come true.

Most of Dolly's friends thought she was used badly in the special. "I didn't like it," says Tom Rutledge. "Everyone I talked to didn't like it. There again, it was the wrong format, though I thought she handled herself fine, as well as can be expected. I just didn't like the way the show was done. The song title sketch didn't seem to go anywhere. But you give Dolly anything and she'll pull it off. I don't like what they did with her, but she carried her part of the show." Fred Foster had mixed feelings about it. "I was happy to see she didn't have on a very large wig, if she had one on at all, and she had on some toned-down dress. I thought it was super, although I'd never seen her wear anything low-cut before. But Cher was the one who was really underdressed. I'm not prudish, but when they were rockin' around singing 'I'm Saved,' I couldn't tell if Cher had anything on at all. That struck me as sort of far out. And Dolly joined in rather uncomfortably, it seemed to me. Maybe not, but I would have been looking for the light." Still, a few days later, Red O'Donnell wrote in the Nashville *Banner* that "... after favorable reviews for her appearance on the recent Cher special, [Dolly] seems to be rapidly en route to super stardom.... She's wearing wigs that are shorter. Understand the cropped hair pieces were designed in Hollywood." O'Donnell went on to report that CBS-TV professed no knowledge of truth behind the rumor that Dolly and Carol Burnett would tape a music-variety special at the Opry House in January of '79. The rumor was confirmed as truth not long after. Despite her eagerness to appear on network TV, Dolly insists she does not want another series of her own. "I would never take a regular TV show," she told *Country Song Roundup*. "I would never take anything on a weekly basis, because my own TV show, even though it was just syndicated, proved to me what a time-consuming thing television is. You always have to devote all your time to that. I've been offered chances to do network shows. I'll be doing specials and guest shots, but unless I want to get out of the business in a hurry, I don't think I'd ever do a network show. In a few years from now, if I decide I want to quit traveling and quit the business, or stay home and write and do my stories and things, then I might decide to take a series and let it run two or three years. Usually once you've had a network show, as you've noticed, once it goes off, you're through, all washed up. People get too familiar with you."

April brought other events in Dolly's life and an especially big thrill to Nick Damico, a Nashville advertising executive. At WDCN-TV's Action Auction, Damico won against stiff bidding to have Dolly make an appearance at his private party. The price? A cool $3,000. The next day, Damico's name was all over the papers, strangers were stopping by his house to shake his hand and ask if they might drop by some special night, and people in faraway states were writing him letters. What the papers didn't say was Damico did it as a PR stunt for a client. When the Dollar General Corporation, Damico's client, found their official country music spokesman, Jim Ed Brown, was booked in Orlando, Florida, for the very day they wanted him to appear at the company's Christmas party, the corporation president turned to Damico and said, "Why don't we just buy Dolly?" the account executive recalls. "Now this is not to take away from my love for Dolly Parton," he hastens to add. "Because I've been following her and liked her ever since she came out of the hills of East Tennessee and got her break with Porter Wagoner." Luckily, Damico says, Dolly wasn't booked for the day of the party. "But Don Warden told me if she gets an offer—like to play Las Vegas for two weeks in December—I'm shot. That's the chance you have to take."

The day after the Action Auction, the Academy of Country Music in Los Angeles named Dolly Entertainer of the Year, over nominees Roy Clark, Loretta Lynn, Mel Tillis and Kenny Rogers. (Rogers ended up winning just about everything else that night.) Dolly lost the competition, however, for Top Female Vocalist and Album of the Year, the other categories in which she was nominated. Because she was on vacation from April 13 to May 4, Dolly was not in Los Angeles to get her award. So Stella, who was nominated as Most Promising Female Vocalist and sang "Four Little Letters" on the show, accepted it for her. "Poor little thing," Stella said on camera. "I'm glad she finally got something." Two days later, Rachel, Dolly's baby sister who had lived with Dolly and Carl for the past five years, married Richard Dennison, Gypsy Fever's backup singer, in a large church wedding in Brentwood. Relatives, including Reverend Jake Owens, came in from Sevierville. Contrary to published reports, Rachel's brother Floyd, and not Dolly, sang at the wedding.

Dolly was to be doing a lot of singing in the month ahead, though. On May 5, in Charleston, West Virginia, she began a four-week tour of the South and Southeast. Opening for her was Andrew Gold, a former member of Linda Ronstadt's band who had found solo success with "Lonely Boy" and "Thank You For Being A Friend." If there was any doubt in the promoters' minds how the advertising for the show was to be handled, a letter from Abbey Konowitch of International Creative Management made it all quite clear: "With respect to your Dolly Parton engagement with Andrew Gold," the form letter opened, "it is important that you be reminded that Dolly's management is expecting this show to be promoted basically as a top 40 presentation; not country. We do not want to find, once the tour is on the road, that a country station has its call letters on a show or is a presenting station. We do not object to radio time buys on country stations as long as the top 40 stations are purchased as well."

Steve Gudis of Entam Productions handled a couple of the early dates. "She looks real good, and her voice is super," he said shortly after the shows. "She's gotten a couple of new band members since I last worked with her. Both her guitar players are relatively new. But it was just excellent. She did real well. The business was reasonable. She's getting between $5,000 and $10,000 a show, and we had 3,000 or 4,000 people, which is not bad for Dolly. Having Andrew Gold on the show was a little strange, but that's the new mix of music, you know. She played about seventy minutes, which I thought was a little short, but it was very well received. Everybody liked it a lot. I did, for sure." Was it true that Dolly was doing the Elvis-style getaways? "Yeah," Gudis said. "Dolly comes right off the stage now and goes right out the back door, right into the limousine, and splits. We did a press conference in the afternoon at sound check. That way she got all her major press commitments taken care of so they wouldn't get mad at her 'cause she hit the back door on 'em. I do the Elvis exit with a lot of people—Mac Davis, for one. I didn't ask her about it. I didn't say, 'Why aren't you going on the bus and signing autographs like you used to, Dolly?' That's just what was told to me to arrange." And they really did have guards on the door? "That's just regular security that I'd do for any major rock show," Gudis answered. "She has a police officer who goes with her back to the hotel 'til she gets in her room. But I'm security conscious, 'cause there are a lot of nuts in this world. I think it's a very good idea. It's very different from the old days, though. She's got Sundance doin' her lights and Stanel for sound, to give the show a little polish, you know. I've known Dolly since she was a little girl. I grew up forty miles from her. In fact, I used to book the prom at her high school."

It was a perfect time for Dolly to tour. The flip side of "Two Doors Down" was "It's All Wrong But It's All Right." While the first song was dancing its way up the pop charts, the second was capturing the top positions on the country charts, making the single one of those rare double-sided hits in two different markets. RCA had expected this to be the clincher for *Here You Come Again* to go platinum, and early in May, Dolly posed for publicity pictures with Jerry Bradley, a dozen roses, and her platinum disc. The record company stirred up a hornet's nest by announcing that Dolly was the first female country artist to receive a platinum album for a solo recording effort. In actuality, Crystal Gayle had beaten Dolly to the punch; the RIAA had awarded her a platinum album on February 15, 1978, for *We Must Believe in Magic*. Dolly did not receive hers until April 28. But neither was the first to sell more than a million copies of one LP. *Tammy Wynette's Greatest Hits* had sold more than a million years ago, as had Lynn Anderson's *I Never Promised You a Rose Garden*. But the RIAA didn't get around to establishing the platinum award until 1976 and made no restitution for million-selling albums before that date; Tammy had to settle for a gold disc, the top award given at the time.

Meanwhile, everyone was asking where the Dolly-Emmylou-Linda album was. Rumor was the LP was indefinitely postponed. Some people said the album would never be made because of a conflict of egos; others said the three couldn't coordinate their schedules to do the overdubs until December. Still others said the three were dissatisfied with the basic tracks and would begin anew. To complicate matters, Solters and Roskin issued a press statement that said the album was finished. Cornered backstage in Chicago, Emmylou wasn't much help in clearing it all up.

"I can't discuss that," she responded when the subject was put to her. Could she talk about how the idea came about? "It was just one of those things, where we spent a lot of time together. Well, not a lot, but a lot considering we were never in the same spot. But we do all appreciate each other's music, and it just seemed like the natural thing to do. That's all I can say." Would there be a time when we'd know more about it? "I really don't have any idea. I'd rather there not even be questions about it, because that's more publicity about something that isn't even in existence. I'm just not supposed to talk about it. I'm sorry," she added genuinely.

Perhaps Emmylou's road manager, Phil Kaufman, could say more. Why were they all so secretive about the project? "Because they all agreed," he said. "All three ladies agreed that until the project is complete, nobody will hype it. In other words, it's three ladies doing a project that they enjoy. They love singing together, and they're all such good friends and they've sung together before, so they decided to do their little album. It's not so much a commercial venture. It's three broads that are really tight—I mean, friends, really tight friends, who just got together. It's not merchandising. It's a project they love doing, and they want to do it right, so they're gonna do it in their own time. It's not something that's gonna be knocked out." So it isn't finished? "No, it's not finished. It's not even near finished, but a lot of the tracks are done. They work on it in their spare time." Why were Solters and Roskin sending out press releases saying the album was finished, then? "They're full of shit," Kaufman said and broke into a grin. "How's that?"

The album was one of the first things reporters asked Dolly about at the press conference in Huntsville, the last gig on the tour. "It's postponed for now," Dolly said. "We had hoped to get it finished in the spring. There was a lot of press about it, which we really didn't want. We tried to keep it pretty secret, because it was a big project. We just wanted to do it real casual like, but they did a press release on it, and the strain, the pressure of the project from the public and the people in the business got to be so much, we couldn't even get our work done, for publicity questions and people showin' up at sessions who weren't supposed to know we were *at* the sessions." (When Ronstadt's friend California Governor Jerry Brown and Willie Nelson showed up one evening, they found armed guards on duty, *Rolling Stone* reported.) "So we had to postpone it," Dolly continued, "because we ran out of time. Now we've rescheduled some more [time] in the late autumn to get back at it. I don't know if we'll get it done then, but we'll finish the project sometime in the future." A reporter asked if the three were disappointed in the existing tracks. "Well, we just didn't get enough done," Dolly said. "And we didn't have enough variety in the things. So it just takes awhile. We will eventually finish the project, one way or another, I'm sure. I sure hope so. I think it would be a shame for that to fall through. It won't fall through because of the three of us. If it falls through, it'll just be cause of the time, or something."

It appeared to one reporter that Dolly was doing more rock music these days. "Not really," she said. "The last album, *Here You Come Again*, which was my first platinum album, and the new album I've just done, *Heartbreaker*, are more directed at that than anything I've had so far, but I still have some country things in the new album that are countrier than the ones that were in the album before. But I am personally tryin' to do that, because I'm tryin' to establish myself in both fields of music so I'll have total musical freedom to be able to do whatever I do and do well and be able to sell it. I'm real excited about the new album. It's got more of a variety than the *Here You Come Again* album. I coproduced it with Gary Klein. 'Heartbreaker' is the name of the first single that'll be released off it, and about six of the songs on the album are songs I've written. I think it's real different from *Here You Come Again.* It's somewhere in between what I always did and the *Here You Come Again* album. I love country music, but I like all kinds of music. I like anything that I can do, and I feel I can write pop music or rock music as well as I can country. But I like the country things, 'cause I have more room to tell stories and things. And I grew up with that, so naturally I'd be partial to that." Dolly added the album was recorded in Los Angeles, sparking someone to ask if she spent much time in Nashville anymore. "No, I don't," she said. "Not as much as I'd like to. But right now, everything's going full blast, so I have to get it while it's hot, and make hay while the sun shines." She laughed. "I should have enough hay by now, but I guess I don't. The Daisy Mae is the most hay I've had in the haystack. But, anyway, sometime within the next year, I hope I'll be able to let down and maybe work half the year and be off half the year to do whatever I want to."

One of the things she wanted to do, she said, was work on her prose writing, and she confirmed that she was writing her life story for the movies. "For awhile I thought I wouldn't write my story," she said, "but several people are beginnin' to, so I thought I would write it up to the point it is." I asked if she were also working on a novel. "Oh, I've always written," she answered. "When I ever get time to publish some things, I will." Late last year, she had announced contracting with Bantam Books. "I write a lot of stories," she had said then. "And I write a lot of poetry and children's stories. Maybe I'll be the new Mother Goose. Bantam is going to publish many of the things I write. I'm working on a book I hope will be out in from eighteen months to two years." It would not be a children's book but rather a novel set in Tennessee, called *Wild Flowers,* she told *Country Style.* "It concerns music, in a way, but not much. It's about the lifestyles of people in the mountains. My book is about a girl, and it's kinda got some humor in it." The magazine asked if she would project herself in her writing. "Yeah, quite a bit," she said. "It's got lots of me in it. And lots of people I knew and grew up with. It also concerns my relatives. It's got a lot of truth in it."

Last summer, when Chet Flippo suggested Dolly should write her life story she said, "I'm already doin' that. I'm gonna call the whole thing *Blossom,* 'cause I used to be called Blossom when I was little, which I think will be a great movie and the whole thing—you know, to blossom into this and blossom into somethin' else." A few months later, she told Bob Allen, "I intend to go back up where I was born and raised. I don't get over in the holler where I was raised much, because it's a long, hard road back up into the mountains there. But I'm thinkin' of renting a camper and gettin' as far up the mountain as I can, soon, and then just parkin' it to write songs and work on my books. . . . But there's so many things undone. I want to be a better singer, a better writer, and I want to have more and more songs recorded by other people. I want to be a great entertainer. There will come a time when I won't want to be a star anymore—when I won't want to be on the road. I'll just want to be a writer—a book writer, a poet, a children's story writer. But I've got to know how big I could have been . . . I get enjoyment out of seein' how far I can go—just seein' how far a positive attitude can take me. I'm just curious to see. And I ain't nowhere *near* where I'm gonna be. You'll see!"

Earlier in '77, I had asked if she'd considered writing a straight autobiography. "Yeah, I will," she said. "And it'll be a good one, too. Because if I ever do it, like the secretive things—I don't know if I can do it while I'm livin'. I mean, I could do it while I'm *livin'*," she laughed, "but I just mean I don't know that I could ever put it out until later because of so many different thoughts and experiences and feelings, just things. I'm gonna make mine into a movie. I don't think I could ever make the whole thing into a movie, but my life is really like a play." She laughed mysteriously, with a faraway look in her eyes. "It's funny," she added. "There's so many things just in itself would make good movies, or good stories. Just certain things, like mine and Carl's marriage, would make a terrific movie or play. Just the fact of total separation would make a situation comedy thing. The way we are and stuff, and then my early childhood days, and then my life now." A serious look came over her face, and then just as quickly disappeared, followed by girlish laughter. "Life excites me."

The night before the Huntsville concert, RCA had taken writers for the trade magazines to Atlanta to see and meet their hottest star. Walter Campbell of *Record World* was in the audience at the sold-out house. "Dolly included songs from her upcoming album, *Heartbreaker*, along with her more familiar past songs which the audience instantly recognized, including 'Jolene' and 'Tennessee Mountain Home,' " Campbell wrote. "Part of Dolly's charm, and care in not forgetting from where she came, is her constant reference to her childhood in East Tennessee when she talks to the crowd. It is hard not to like someone so friendly and unpretentious . . . Dolly Parton's prominence in music, whether country or pop, is the result of her own creative, open mind and her commitment to that creativity. As a singer, songwriter, musician and personality, she now seems to be able to offer something for nearly everyone. From the audience response in Atlanta, certainly no one walked away disappointed."

The nearly 5,000 people who showed up the following night in Huntsville seemed happy to be there, too. Dolly, who was in spectacular voice that night, gave them a stunning version of "Heartbreaker," one that would rival the recorded version in musicianship and feel, and best it for sheer poignancy, the cry in Dolly's voice bringing out the song's real anguish. She also delivered a strong version of an otherwise lightweight song, "Love Is Like a

Butterfly," before introducing her band. Four of the early members of Gypsy Fever were still with her: Gregg Perry on keyboards, Joe McGuffee on steel guitar, Anita Ball and Richard Dennison on background vocals. "And my name is Dottie Parsons," Dolly said to the crowd's delight. "I want to do a song for you now that's also kinda special to me," she went on. "You know, a lot of the songs that I write are sad, and some of 'em are just plumb pitiful, and I think this might be one of them." The crowd laughed again. But no one was laughing when she finished her song, "Me and Little Andy," and a collective tear could be heard to fall underneath the audience's overwhelming applause.

"With You Gone," off the new LP, dragged a bit, and "I Will Always Love You," which followed that, had been performed better in the past. The highlight of "It's all Wrong But It's All Right" came when, after Dolly sang, "Could I use you for awhile?" a man who could bear it no longer cried out, "*Yeah!*" Dolly missed maybe half a beat. "He sounds *serious,* don't he?" she cracked, and struggled to regain her composure. "That's what I get for singin' this stupid song," she said with a laugh in her throat, and the crowd applauded. From there she went into a loose, nightclub version of "Here You Come Again," and the audience clapped along. With only a moment's pause, she slid into "Two Doors Down," before leaving the stage. The crowd rose to its feet. She returned to lead them in clapping to an even more rock-oriented version than her second on record. Then after saying Huntsville had been the last show of the tour and she was anxious to get back to Nashville, she was gone.

The overall quality of the concert had been quite high. Gypsy Fever (which was never actually referred to by name) had worked itself into a very tight musical unit, and Dolly had come off as the pro she is, generating magic that could be seen and felt by everyone in the house. But the glossy sheen that was apparent as early as Waco and strongly in evidence by Louisville was by now an all-out plastic coating. The only real moments of give and take between Dolly and the audience had occurred by accident. Missing were the spontaneous stories that had made her earlier concerts such authentically electrifying events, possessed of a magic of a totally different kind, a magic that came from an intimate evening with a most gifted young woman, giddy in the celebration of life. Although I saw only the last thirty minutes of a concert Dolly had given several days earlier in Birmingham, the earlier concert appeared to be far more static than the Huntsville show. Dressed in her current conservative California cut and topped off by a subdued platinum wig, Dolly did not much look like the woman I remembered. Viewed from the back of the hall, the little figure on stage, dancing and swaying back and forth with a hand-mike, looked rather like a human marionette, twitching and jumping to invisible strings. It was a sight that saddened me not a little. For a moment, the thought popped into my mind that this was not Dolly at all, but merely someone doing an acerbic impersonation, and that soon she would stop, and the real Dolly would come out and take her place. But even from the back of the hall, I knew the voice was only Dolly's, and when she hit a high note in "It's All Wrong But It's All Right" that went through me, I bit my knuckles white.

Don Roth was with me. For a long while, we didn't discuss the show at all. Finally I found the nerve to ask him if he had felt the same as I. "I thought it was enormously plastic," he said. "But you've got to understand that I watched her bust ass trying to *get* it plastic like that. It takes a lot of work to make a show seem that natural, for the same reason that Willie Nelson would never rehearse his guys, and whatever happens on stage just happens. The exact opposite goes into the Dolly thing, where every move, every breath, every smile has been taught. So, yes, it's *very* plastic. I agree. But so are most of the big shows around. Not all of them, but most of them, are very rehearsed, very thought out, especially if you're aiming for Vegas, which is exactly what I think she's aiming for."

A few days later, when thousands of country fans crowded into Nashville again for Fan Fair, Dolly was still out of town. If her fan club set up a booth, it went undetected by the majority of people who filed through. And when Dolly's name was mentioned at the Music City News Popularity Awards presentation, the fan audience responded with polite applause. A man from Iowa in town for his first Fan Fair visit summed up a lot of people's feeling when he told the *Tennessean*, "The only thing is, Dolly Parton isn't here." Her heart wasn't in Nashville, either, the program directors at some country stations across the country felt. Tex Lively, of KPIK in Colorado Springs, was reported in *Country Style* to have said he would not play any more Dolly Parton music "as long as it's the stuff like the last stuff. All of us feel she deserted the country folks."

Overall, though, the controversy over Dolly's career expansion has simmered down some in Nashville. Some people feel the concern over Dolly's management is still there, others say you don't hear Dolly's name mentioned much, inferring that Nashville has turned its back on Dolly because it feels she's done the same to it. "Well, you find mixed, very mixed emotions over this," says Clarence Selman. "There's still a phenomenal degree of bitterness, particularly on the part of the people who think she deserted her country fans. I don't feel that way. I think she just wanted to grow as an artist, but you'd be surprised at the number of people who don't share my feeling." Brenda Lee agrees. "I would say in some areas, yeah, there's still a lot of resentment. But I feel like Dolly has chosen the path that she wants to take, and I think she's done it with a lot of care. I don't think it was a decision that she just popped right up with overnight. It just depends on what you want out of life. And Dolly wanted more. And I think that she is smart enough to use her intellect as a sieve and shake through the people that love her and let the rest go. Because you can be hurt awfully bad, sometimes. Especially when you're out there. And it really is different out on the West Coast. It really is much faster. You can get caught up in all of that. And then you can get left behind, too. If I were talkin' about me, I'd say the same thing. If I got caught up in it, I'd hope I was ready to get left behind. Because it's a fact of life. It's something that's gonna happen."

Jimmy C. Newman says he doesn't hear much negative talk about Dolly anymore. "Now that she's successful," he says with a grin. "When one is not successful, then we can really jump on them more. But Dolly has a lot going for her. She's not necessarily a country music star anymore. She's accepted by everybody. Consequently, I think this helps our business, because she's a big star from country music, which always comes back." "Naw, I don't think anybody's down on Dolly," Marty Robbins says. "Everbody who complains, 'Let's keep country country,'—well, what the hell is country? I don't know what country is. I've never figured it out, myself. Once you pass Roy Acuff and Bill Monroe, you've passed country. There are so many different categories of music. How are you gonna put Ernest Tubb in country? That's not country. That's Saturday Night Jukebox Texas Barroom music. That's Ernest Tubb-type music. I do Marty Robbins-type music. Dolly Parton does what she thinks is her style of music, whether it's country, or whether it isn't."

"I think they were resentful in the beginning, but I don't think they are now," says Bob Bray of Celebrity Management. "There's a tremendous change taking place in Nashville right now. There's an exodus of people going to the West Coast, especially female artists who have seen the success of Olivia Newton-John and Dolly. I'm talking about people like Crystal Gayle. Kenny Rogers, who was already based on the West Coast but had his record success in Nashville, realizes he has to maintain that management association on the West Coast. Gatlin is managed out of New York, and yet his record success, again, is here. Dottie West is another female artist managed on the West Coast. I think all this has shaken up Nashville, in that they see now that artists want more than to be in the charts. There's more to a career than just having hit records, because there has to be something to sustain a career after the records begin to fall off. Everybody has peaks and valleys. I hope Nashville is waking up. It's just coincidental that Dolly was one of the first."

If Katz-Gallin has plans to ease Dolly totally out of country little by little, probably the last bastion would be the Grand Ole Opry. It's a subject Opry manager Hal Durham doesn't particularly like to talk about. These days, an Opry member is required to achieve twenty credits a year; a credit is given for every performance, with a member able to collect several per weekend, since a credit is awarded for a Friday night performance as well as for each of the two Saturday shows. Thus, a performer would not have to work the Opry twenty weeks a year to achieve his credits, making it easier for him to fulfill his road obligations and his Opry obligations, too. When Dolly was with Porter, she played the Opry every time Porter did, which amounted to "fifteen to twenty weeks per year," according to Durham. "But she hasn't been on as much since she left the Porter show," he says. "She formed her band, and she worked quite a bit for us when she was putting the band together. She was here for a number of weeks, and worked some extra shows that we did in the house when the park season was beginning, and she filled in for us on several occasions. But she has worked the Opry less since she's become more oriented toward the West Coast than when she was working exclusively out of Nashville. For example, here it is May, and Dolly's only been in three or four weekends, and then not for some time," he added. I asked Durham to check specifically how many appearances Dolly had made on the Opry in '78. The answer, as of May 31, was none. "Well, it goes in spurts for some of the acts," Durham explained. "I don't think it means anything except she hasn't been here in town." I asked him to check to see if she had made all of her credits in '77. "I'm sure she didn't do twenty shows," he said. "But my recollection is we didn't consider it a problem. She did a sufficient number of appearances. Dolly missed a good many appearances not only here, but other places, because of illness, and those same factors apply here as they do anyplace else. If we needed to bend our policy, we would for such people as Tammy Wynette, Dolly, Roy Acuff and Ernest Tubb," Durham said.

I asked how a performer might leave the Opry. "Most of the time they leave when they decide they don't want to make their appearances, or if they feel like their career interests are going in a different direction," he answered. "I think some people believe that if they want to be more of a pop artist than a country artist, the Opry handicaps them and they don't want the connection with the Opry anymore. Some people move to a different part of the country and turn in a different direction. There are different reasons." Would a performer ever be asked to leave the Opry for not making his performances? "I would say if a member doesn't make his required performances after a certain number of years, and circumstances were such that we felt he could have made them if he had elected to, yes," Durham said. About Dolly specifically, however, Durham added, "She does stay in touch with us, and I think still has a very warm feeling for the Opry, as we do her." As for the reaction of other Opry members to Dolly's new direction, Durham said, "I suppose there'd be a divergence of opinion on that. I read a review recently where the writer said Dolly had departed from her country music fans, that she was no longer a country music artist, and he was sad about it and didn't like her show. My own opinion is that Dolly is honest when she says that she's not trying to leave country music but simply trying to expand what she has to offer, to reach into other areas with what she is. It's an interesting debate," he said. "I guess it's like beauty being in the eye of the beholder. Country must be in the ear of the listener.

"I sure do admire Dolly," he continued. "And she really excites the Opry audience. I don't know whether she'd agree or not, but I think she just sort of fits the Opry, the Opry people. And this goes back years and years. It's not just some recent change in her. When she came on with Porter, I think, from the first, the audience reacted to Dolly. She's vivacious on stage, and I can't think of any of her performances that weren't exciting. I particularly remember the first night she worked it with her Family Band. It was touching to see her introduce members of her family as members of the band and talk about what she was going to do with the Family Band concept." Durham smiled a little wistfully. "I hope Dolly can always be a member of the Opry." Dolly, of course, insists she always will be. Last year, a reporter for a British paper asked her if she'd take her new pop and rock show there. "I would, and be proud of it," Dolly told him. "But I would be real careful not to offend my fans. I would probably not do 'My Love' because they wouldn't be familiar with that."

The health problems Durham mentioned continued to plague Dolly in the summer of '78. This time, pneumonia forced her to cancel several bookings in Texas and the Midwest. Friends saw her back in Nashville, driving around. When she was up to performing, however, she did twenty concerts from June 'til September with Eddie Rabbitt. Elektra Records got so excited over their boy opening for Dolly that they "minted" a "20 Dolly Bill" with a crude drawing of Dolly and Eddie replacing the portrait of Andrew Jackson in the center and the itinerary printed on the back. The purpose in having Andrew Gold open for Dolly on the May tour was to have him work the crowd into near frenzy by the time she came out on stage. However, the result was something less than that. The Huntsville crowd acted hostile toward Gold, shouting he played too loud. With Rabbitt, Dolly reportedly had the opposite problem. Quickly building a reputation as an exciting entertainer, Rabbitt worked the crowds up so they didn't want him to leave. Dolly quickly put together an excellent country and gospel show, leaving the rock stuff to Rabbitt.

"Dolly's been teasing me," Rabbitt said in July. "She said, 'I'll have to start opening for you pretty soon.' We made them go back and change their show around, to work up another show, new songs, different timings, medleys and things. But we get along real good. Our bands are good friends. She's got us doin' duets at the end of of her show. The night we got the idea, she said, 'Let's do two or three songs out there. I think it'd be great.' I said, 'Yeah,' and we had five minutes to work up 'Let It Be Me.' I didn't even know the words to it. We tried it unknown that very night. We told the band, 'Grab the key of D and every chance you get, go to G.' I'm learning a lot being with her. If nothing more, I'm learning what a great person is all about." One of the songs Rabbitt sang was "Could You Love a Poor Boy, Dolly?" a song he wrote with Dolly in mind years ago.

Their tour climaxed with an exhilarating sold-out concert at New York's Palladium on August 22, with Dolly turning in one of the most thrilling performances of her career and setting New York City on its ear. The day before, 5,000 people jammed the plaza at City Hall to hear Dolly's free lunchtime concert and watch Mayor Ed Koch present her with a key to the city and get a kiss in return. Afterwards, Dolly answered questions from the crowd—twice as many people as had gathered there earlier in the month to greet President Carter. Everyone, it seemed, wanted to meet Dolly, and a good many did at a party thrown in her honor at Studio 54, the city's hottest disco, following her Palladium show.

Certainly Dolly's new album, released just a few weeks before, would fit right in there.

RCA went all out to promote *Heartbreaker.* In Los Angeles, they erected a custom-built billboard on Sunset Strip which flashed "Dolly" in neon lights over the album cover design. Satin shorts with "Dolly" and "Heartbreaker" printed across the leg were used as radio station and record store giveaways, and major retail outlets were provided video footage of Dolly performing the title song. Radio time was bought for the album and single on pop adult, country and top 40 stations, with red vinyl copies of the single going out for promotion. On top of that, the record company printed "Here Comes Platinum Dolly Again" on the front of all their album order forms.

From the cover right on through the last cut on the second side, *Heartbreaker* is a brand-new Dolly, a Dolly so different from her "Jolene" days that she is liable to cause mass apoplexy among the hard-core country fans who refused to follow her down the *Here You Come Again* route. It's always been hard to classify Dolly's music, even on her early albums, and it's difficult to attach labels here, but the majority of tunes on *Heartbreaker* fall into two categories: easy-listening and disco! Not the soft hint of disco that appeared on *Here You Come Again,* but get down, get it on disco, the kind that has Dolly sassing, "I'm undone, so come and do me!"

The cover offers several clues. It's a montage of Dollies in what appear to be three fantasy situations. She wears the same outfit in each—a pink, ruffled dance hall girl dress and backless silver heels (there are two pairs of shoes, however), and her short Beverly Hills wig. In the first pose, she's got her dress and her leg hiked up gang-moll style to reveal the top of her thigh, and she looks askance at herself in the next pose, a surreal scene of Dolly jumping through (or *breaking* through, get it?) a mural, a flower/bridge scene off the wall of an Italian restaurant, perhaps. And in the third pose, she's off in the clouds somewhere. All that is preparation for the inside photo, a full-figure, hands-on-hips pose in which Dolly shoots to kill—but only from the eyes.

Just as Dolly plays out her fantasies on the cover of the album, and just as Katz-Gallin asks her to try on an array of visual images, producer Gary Klein, in the two albums he's done with her, has Dolly slipping on one musical wardrobe after another. *Heartbreaker* has Dolly acting out an aural dream and making all her musical fantasies come true. On a couple of the tunes, she's cast as Barbra Streisand (with whom Klein worked), particularly on "We're Through Forever ('Til Tomorrow)," a breathy, string-smothered M-O-R song Dolly sings with Richard Dennison. (Three other members of Gypsy Fever appear on the album, too, unlike on *Here You Come Again*). But from the pleasant, pastel, easy-listening tunes, Dolly rocks on out, disco-style, particularly on "Sure Thing" (which sounds as if she wrote it twenty minutes after seeing *Saturday Night Fever*), "With You Gone," and "I Wanna Fall in Love," all Parton originals.

It's strange hearing all this coming from Dolly's little-girl voice, but all the upbeat tunes are undeniably infectious and feel-good, from the funky horns on "Sure Thing" and "I Wanna Fall in Love" to the Latin rhythms and congas on "With You Gone," the latter tune also featuring Joe McGuffee on steel guitar in one of the strangest (and yet delightful) musical hybrids yet. Despite several simple, Dolly Parton-type tunes ("The Man" is essentially a country lyric—Dolly loves her father, as "the man" is revealed to be in a surprise ending, one of her devices from the country days—it's just set to an electronic beat), *Heartbreaker*, which credits Dolly "with" Klein as the producer, is in some ways far slicker than *Here You Come Again* ever dared to be. Never mind that the laid-back Dr. John (Mac Rebennack) drops in to play piano on a couple of tunes, Jim Keltner (a session drummer closely identified with Leon Russell for several years) adds special effects, and Jeff Baxter (one of the Doobie Brothers and a former member of Steely Dan) puts down a few licks on the guitar synthesizer. Mostly it sounds so slick because of the virtual philharmonic Klein laid in after Dolly went home, and one suspects the music would have been much more effective with just the basic rhythm tracks.

Dolly is new to the pop idiom, of course, and she may not yet be able to bring to it the depth she brought to a good many of her country tunes. That's particularly pointed up in her recording of the title tune, David Wolfert and Carole Bayer Sager's wonderful "Heartbreaker," which is so solid and well-crafted that it makes a good deal of the other songs on the album look rather like fluff. But there's every reason to think Dolly will be writing songs like this one before long, and singing them just as well as she does "Heartbreaker," the one tune on the album Dolly seems to really believe—or makes *us* believe—in her emotional, yet dignified delivery. "Sure Thing," although it's an absolute gas, isn't *really* the musical form it pretends to be, and Dolly doesn't sound entirely comfortable with some of her new style yet. But all all these songs are still representative of Dolly, and who cares if some of the songs are shuck and jive? They're not supposed to be "Jolene" and "Coat of Many Colors." What they're supposed to be is celebration of the fact that Dolly is feeling free enough to experiment with all sorts of musical forms. Some of them are ultimately faddish and trendy. But they are also fun and enjoyable listening. *Heartbreaker* is sure to live up to its title with some people in Nashville, but the irony of it all is that just about the time Dolly recorded it in California, Porter Wagoner was hunched over the control board in Fireside Studio, working on his newest musical love—none other than disco! Sometimes it seems like the more things change, the more they stay the same.

When someone in Nashville labeled Dolly "the Iron Butterfly," they meant it both as a compliment and as a cut. On the positive side, beneath her frilly soft exterior lies a core of steel, enabling her to push on and triumph over the most oppressive of circumstances, and still retain all of her feminine traits. And yet some people feel she is "ruthless—with soft wings," as one Nashvillian put it. In her book *Singers and Sweethearts,* Joan Dew quotes Fred Foster as saying, "Nothing stands in Dolly's way when she sets her mind to do something. She was very upset, very emotional, about leaving Monument, but she left nonetheless. I knew she was torn between loyalty to me and wanting to take an opportunity she felt she needed, so there was no way I could become angry with her. All I felt was a bitter disappointment, but of course time heals even that. Dolly has a way of leaving you with a good feeling even when you hate it that she's left. Instead of running roughshod over you, she sort of steps around you, if you know what I mean. And that in itself is a talent."

A study of Dolly's life reveals that despite her protest that she knows nothing about the women's movement, liberation is the word that best sums up what Dolly has been seeking from the day she was born. With an active imagination, Dolly, the child, was able to transcend her desolate surroundings and circumstances, and before long, that imagination and unyielding faith provided a way to spare her the bleak future that seemed so certain to be hers as a woman of the mountains. Freedom from poverty and isolation was only the first hurdle, however, with the long battle ahead for creative expression in many ways more difficult than escape from the mountains had ever been. Now, for the first time in her life, Dolly Parton is in control of her own destiny. However the story of Dolly Parton ends up, whether she will be remembered as an entertainer without peer, as a writer, a business woman or as a servant of God, whatever she will have done by the time she's ". . . old and settin' in a rockin' chair, crippled up with arthritis, can't go nowhere, can't pick, can't sing, my voice gone . . ." but still reading her fan mail, it will have been her choice. And chances are when it's all over, the Iron Butterfly's magnificent wings will be somewhat battered but still firmly attached.

Backstage in Huntsville, a reporter asked Dolly what she'd be doing if she weren't a rich and famous singer. Dolly hesitated not a moment. "I'd be wantin' to be," she said. "I'll never reach the peak," she told another journalist several years ago. "When I've reached a certain goal, I'll set another one. I have other things I want to be number one at, not all in music."

Sometimes the peaks are rocky and craggy, though, and footing on the climb is not always as secure as it may feel. "Oh, there'll be lots of mountains that I'll climb, and there ain't none so tall that I'd be afraid to start up it," Dolly told me. "I may not make it all the way on every mountain I climb, but that don't mean I ain't gonna be tryin'." And what if she doesn't make it up the mountain? I asked. "I'll get on another one," she said. "I'll try somethin' a little less treacherous. But I don't know that that's true. I'd probably keep tryin' to climb it over and over, until I either fell off and broke my neck, or just got to the top and looked back down on how far I'd come. I've never seen a mountain that I didn't think I could climb."

Discography

SINGLES

GOLDBAND
"Puppy Love/"Girl Left Alone" (*See* Albums, Goldband, below.)

MERCURY
"It's Sure Gonna Hurt" / "The Love You Gave"

ALBUMS
(Many numbers on some of the following albums were also released as singles.)

ALSHIRE
Dolly Parton Sings S-5351 (n.d.) (Formerly released as *Dolly Parton Sings Country Oldies* SF 29400.)

MONUMENT (all solo)
Hello, I'm Dolly MLP 8085 July 1967
As Long as I Love, SLP 18136 April 1970

(The two albums were later released as a double set, *Hello I'm Dolly/As Long as I Love* BZ 33876 Selected cuts from each were released as *The World of Dolly* KZG 31913, August 1972, re-released as *In the Beginning* MG 7623 Spring, 1978.

RCA (all solo)
Just Because I'm a Woman LSP 3349 April 1968
In the Good Old Days (When Times were Bad) LSP 4099 February 1969
My Blue Ridge Mountain Boy LSP 4188 September 1969
The Fairest of Them All LSP 4288 February 1970
A Real Live Dolly LSP 4387 July 1970
The Best of Dolly Parton LSP 4449 November 1970
The Golden Streets of Glory LSP 4398 February 1971
Joshua LSP 4507 April 1971
Coat of Many Colors LSP 4603 October 1971
Touch Your Woman LSP 4686 March 1972

My Favorite Songwriter: Porter Wagoner LSP 4752 September 1972
My Tennessee Mountain Home APL-10033 March 1973
Bubbling Over APL1-0286 September 1973
Jolene APL1-0473 February 1974
Love is Like A Butterfly APL1-0712 September 1974
The Bargain Store APL1-0950 February 1975
The Best of Dolly Parton APL1-1117 1975
Dolly APL1-1221 September 1975
All I Can Do APL1-1665 July 1976
New Harvest. . . First Gathering APL1-2188 February 1977
Here You Come Again APL1-2544 October 1977
Heartbreaker AFL1-2797 July 1978

PICKWICK/CAMDEN (Re-releases of RCA recordings.)
Just the Way I Am CAS-2583 1972
Mine ACL-0307 1973
I Wish I Felt This Way at Home ACL-7002 1975
Just Because I'm a Woman ACL-7017

GOLDBAND
Dolly Parton and Friends at Goldband LP7770 (Includes re-releases of "Puppy Love" and "Girl Left Alone," in addition to early efforts by other now famous artists.)

RCA (all duets with Porter Wagoner)
Just Between You and Me LSP 3926
Just the Two of Us LSP 4039
Always, Always LSP 4186
Porter Wayne and Dolly Rebecca LSP 4305
Once More LSP 4388
Two of a Kind LSP 4490
The Best of Porter Wagoner and Dolly Parton LSP 4556 July 1971
The Right Combination/Burning the Midnight Oil LSP 4628
Together Always LSP 4761
We Found It LSP 4841
Love and Music APL1-0248
Porter 'N' Dolly APL1-0646 August 1974
Say Forever You'll Be Mine APL1-1116 August 1975

RCA (collections)
Great Moments at the Grand Ole Opry CPL2-1904 (A two-record set on which Dolly Sings "Coat of Many Colors" and tells how she made her first appearance on the Opry as a child.) September 1976

GUEST APPEARANCES (on Other Artists' Records)
The Best of Chet Atkins and Friends RCA APL1-1985 (Dolly and Chet sing and play "Do I Ever Cross Your Mind," a Parton original which Dolly has yet to record on a solo album.) October 1976

Luxury Liner X (Emmylou Harris) Warner Bros. K-3115 (Dolly provides supporting vocal on "When I Stop Dreaming".)
Simple Dreams (Linda Ronstadt) Asylum 104 (Dolly provides supporting vocal on "I Never Will Marry", also released as a single.)

Singles: "Light of the Stable" Reprise RPS-1379 (An Emmylou Harris Christmas record on which Linda Ronstadt and Dolly provide harmony.)